CLIFFORD
GOLDSTEIN

Like a Fire in My Bones

*One of the church's most provocative authors
shares his enduring passion for drawing others
to a deeper knowledge of God.*

Pacific Press® Publishing Association
Nampa, Idaho
Oshawa, Ontario, Canada

Edited by B. Russell Holt
Cover and inside design by Michelle C. Petz

Copyright © 1998 by
Pacific Press® Publishing Association
Printed in the United States of America
All Rights Reserved

Goldstein, Clifford.
    Like a fire in my bones / Clifford Goldstein.
        p.   cm.
    ISBN 0-8163-1580-9 (alk. paper)
    1. Seventh-day Adventists—Doctrines.   2. Goldstein, Clifford. I. Title.
    BX6154.G633   1998
    286.7'32—dc21
                                                                                                        9746831
                                                                                                        CIP

98 99 00 01 02 • 5 4 3 2 1

Table of Contents

INTRODUCTION

It's not often that a book, especially one of my own, takes fourteen years to produce. Yet this one, *Like a Fire in My Bones,* did just that. Considering that I'm now at the not-so-tender age of forty-two, this book covers, literally, a third of my life. For some people, the fractions may be larger or smaller, but given the "fourscore and ten" years allotted to us all (with some margin of error), we're still talking about a long time for a book, no matter the age of the reader.

I come up with that figure, 14 years, because the earliest article in this compilation is dated 1983; the latest, 1997. Though I've written some before and some after those dates, these were the beginning and endtimes that seal off, chronologically at least, the pieces included in this compilation.

There are about sixty articles in *Like a Fire in My Bones,* covering everything from the attempt to blow up the Dome of the Rock in Jerusalem to what happens when our name appears in the investigative judgment. My goal, as I was deciding on which pieces to use, was to pick what I believe are the best, the most interesting, and those that could do the most good for my readers.

Many selections came from *Liberty* and from *Shabbat Shalom,* though other SDA publications, such as the *Adventist Review* and *Signs of the Times,* are included as well. Some are written specifically for SDAs, others specifically *not* for them. Either way, my desire has always been, and still always is, to feed the souls of those who read what I write, to draw them closer to a knowledge of God and of the truth that exists in His Son, Jesus Christ. Some articles are more direct than others in that goal; some not direct at all. But a knowledge of Christ is always the final end of where I want everything to go, because that's the only end which, really, leads to a new beginning.

As I consider how I've changed, grown in grace (I hope) over these long years, which cover almost my whole sojourn in Adventism (I joined the church in 1980), I can feel only a little, well, amusement at best, embarrassment at worst, as I look at some of the earliest works. Amazing how time gives us a new perspective on things, even on things that we once thought were unmovable. And yet, however much here and there I might now wish that I had phrased such and such a little differently or had been a little less dogmatic, a little more tempered in my fiery denunciations, for the most part, I would change very little of what you see produced in these pages (the ones I really cringed at aren't included), for the foundation of truth doesn't change. What changes are our weak, vacillating attempts to comprehend it.

These articles, for better or worse, reveal not only my attempt to understand truth but to spread that understanding to others as well. And for that purpose this book has been compiled. Only as we stand on the sea of glass will I know how successful, through God's mercy and grace, my endeavor has been.

Clifford Goldstein
Silver Spring, Maryland 1998

BLOOD AND JUDGMENT

The nine articles in this first section—covering eight years—deal with various ways of looking at Christ, both as our sacrifice and as our High Priest in the heavenly sanctuary. Most are written from an Adventist perspective, appearing in either the *Review* or *Ministry*.

Adventists might find "May Your Name Be Sealed," first published in 1989, of particular interest, because it explains the Jewish understanding of the heavenly sanctuary and the ministry of the archangel Michael, who defends God's people before the Father against the accusations of Satan. In short, this article shows our sanctuary message from Jewish sources that, in some cases, precede Adventism by hundreds of years.

"Who Shall Atone for Us?," written for *Shabbat Shalom*, provides insight into the Jewish understanding of the gospel. It's amazing to see, from a Jewish perspective, the concept of substitutionary atonement taught, in many ways, just as SDAs have understood it.

"Blood and Judgment," published in *Ministry*, tells of my own personal struggle with the gospel and the sanctuary. Published in 1996, this article attempts to help Adventists understand that, far from negating each other, or even being in tension with each other, the investigative judgment and the gospel are in perfect harmony. I tackle this same question, from another perspective, in "No Condemnation," which appeared in the *Review*. Meanwhile, in "Good News About the Judgment," I take the great truth of the gospel and the judgment and present it to the non-Adventist world through the vehicle of *Signs of the Times*.

These articles, with one exception (the last one), appear in chronological order, if for no other reason than showing how, over time, my own understanding of these crucial topics has grown.

CHAPTER ONE

Justified and Sanctified: God's Goal for Us

What is the proper balance between what God has done *for* us, justification, and what He is doing *in* us, sanctification—and why must we understand both?

The question of justification and sanctification raises the old issue of faith and works. Abel offered to God the "firstlings of his flock" (Gen. 4:4), an offer, made in faith, that God accepted; Cain offered "the fruit of the ground" (verse 3), an offering of works, that God rejected. Later, though, God declared, "I desired mercy, and not sacrifice; and the knowledge of God more than burnt offerings" (Hos. 6:6).

Paul said, "For if Abraham were justified by works, he hath whereof to glory; but not before God" (Rom. 4:2); yet James asked, "Was not Abraham our father justified by works, when he had offered Isaac his son upon the altar?" (James 2:21).

Faith and Works

Disputes over faith and works split Christendom in the 1500s, and the issue challenges Adventism today. Even Ellen White wrote at one time that "the merits of fallen man in his good works can never procure eternal life for him";[1] yet at another time she stated: "There are many in the Christian world who claim that all that is necessary to salvation is to have faith; works are nothing, faith is the only essential. But God's Word tells us that faith without works is dead, being alone."[2]

These positions don't contradict each other. Instead, the question is how we balance them.

Indeed, some lean so heavily on justification that it alone becomes redemption; others lean so heavily on sanctification that it alone becomes redemption. Rather, both justification and sanctification constitute redemption. Redemption is no more justification alone than baptism is immersion alone; redemption is no more *just* sanctification than baptism is *just* coming up out of the water. As immersing and rising compose the two parts of baptism, so justification and sanctification compose the two parts of redemption. One without the other is incomplete; together, though, they make a perfect whole.

Christ gives both justification and sanctification. "For without me," Jesus said, "ye can do nothing" (John 15:5). Of ourselves we can no more have faith, "the gift of God" (Eph. 2:8), than we can have works, which come also from God (see Phil. 2:12).

The Lord created Adam in "the image of God" (Gen. 1:27). After Adam sinned, his children, instead of also being created in the image of God, were created in the image of Adam, now a fallen sinner. "And Adam lived an hundred and thirty years, and begat a son in *his own likeness*, after *his* image" (Gen. 5:3). All humanity, created in the image of Adam, is under the curse of sin. "But the scripture hath concluded all under sin" (Gal. 3:22). All our righteousness and good works even those done by Christians under the prompting of the Holy Spirit, can no more make us acceptable to God than all the scrubbings, perfumes, and manicures can make a pig kosher.

The only good works and righteousness that save us are the perfect works and righteousness of Jesus, which He wrought for us, independent of us, yet which He offers to us in place of our own filthy garments. " I will clothe thee," Jesus says, "with change of raiment" (Zech. 3:4).

Jesus, by His perfect life and death, is qualified to supply us with an experience in righteousness. After He finished His work on the earth as a sacrificial lamb, He entered heaven as a high priest, ministering the merits of His death in our behalf. "For we have not an high priest which cannot be touched with the feeling of our infirmities; but was in all points tempted like as we are, yet without sin" (Heb. 4:15). And because Jesus didn't assume the "nature of angels" (Heb. 2:16) in His incarnation, but instead came in the "likeness of sinful flesh" (Rom. 8:3), the flesh that we are encumbered with, He proved that we, too, through the power of God, can resist sin. "Not even by a thought did He yield to temptation," wrote EllenWhite.[3] "So it may be with us."

Righteousness Is a Gift

Justification and sanctification, though inseparable, are not identical. Justification entails the legal declaration of forgiveness. It is the gift of a perfectly righteous, sinless, and holy character—a character that we sinners by our nature could never possess. We might reflect that character "perfectly," but we can never equal it.

God, though, accepts only a perfect righteousness, not even a perfect reflection of it, and because none of us have that perfect righteousness, Jesus came to the earth, worked it out for us, and offers it freely.

Imagine a school where you received only one of two grades, pass or fail. The only way to pass is to have a score of 100 percent. Ninety-nine percent will get you the same failing grade as only 9 percent. Some might have 70 percent or even 90 percent, but legally they are still in the same class as those with only 5 percent.

Except for Jesus, who has a perfect score, all humanity has a failing grade. The thief on the cross who might have had only a 30 percent, or a saint upon the earth after probation closes who might have a 94 percent—both will get to heaven by the same exact thing: the perfect righteousness, the 100 percent, of Jesus Christ given to them. Anything else is as insufficient as trying to master French by studying physics.

Beginning a New Life

But the good news of salvation, of redemption, does not end with this legal declaration of forgiveness anymore than baptism ends with immersion. We must come up out of the water "in newness of life" (Rom. 6:4), after first going under. Redemption begins, not ends, with forgiveness, just as baptism begins, not ends, with immersion.

Without sanctification, without Christ working in our lives to root out inherited and cultivated evil, we cannot presume justification. Salvation is not like the law of the Medes and Persians: Salvation *can* be revoked, just as faith can be lost.

In Matthew 7 Jesus contrasts two individuals. One hears His words and "doeth them" (verse 24); the other hears His words but "doeth them not" (verse 26). The obedient one, who does what Jesus commands, who has works—he stays faithful unto the end. His faith is perfected by works. The disobedient one, who doesn't do what Jesus commands, who doesn't have works—he falls away. His faith, without works, is dead.

And the good news about works is that, like justification, they also come from God. We procure sanctification as we procure justification—by unconditional surrender to God. Sanctification, too, can come only as we surrender ourselves to God, choose to die to self, and serve God daily. "Genuine sanctification . . . is nothing less than a daily dying to self and daily conformity to the will of God."[4] Then God can work in us "both to will and to do of his good pleasure" (Phil. 2:13).

Character development, obedience, and good works come only as we choose to allow God to work in us, to purge the dross and to mold us after the divine similitude. And the only way He can make these changes is if we submit, just as we did when we were born again. "As ye have therefore received Christ Jesus the Lord, so walk ye in him" (Col. 2:6).

In Ephesians 2 Paul gives a powerful example of the relationship between faith and works. "For by grace are ye saved through faith; and that not of yourselves: it is the gift of God: not of works, lest any man should boast" (verses 8, 9). Paul clearly states that salvation comes by faith, not works.

In verse 10 he writes that "we are his workmanship, created in Christ Jesus *unto good works,* which God hath before ordained that we should walk in them." Paul stresses salvation by faith, not works, yet in the next breath he says that we were created for good works, works that God hath "before ordained" that we should do.

No Contradiction

No contradiction exists. Though created for good works, we don't receive salvation by them. The only works that save us are the works of Jesus in our behalf. Nevertheless, we were created in Jesus to do good works, because works are an intricate part of the redemption process.

Our salvation didn't end at Calvary, because redemption does not end with forgiveness. The gospel is not just pardon, which is its foundation, but it is also restoration, which is its pinnacle. Justification is the first step toward God's ultimate goal for us: the reflection of Christ in us! "My little children, of whom I travail in birth again until Christ be formed in you" (Gal. 4:19).

The issues in the great controversy between Christ and Satan go beyond this earth, beyond the salvation of man. Though sin is confined to earth, it is a universal, cosmic issue. At Calvary, more than a mob witnessed the Cross. The universe was watching.

And though the complete penalty for sin was paid at the Cross, though God poured out His love in a way that made all the universe marvel, not all the questions about sin, rebellion, and the law of God were answered, even there. God was going to give the onlooking universe more—and He has been using humanity to give it!

"That through the *church* the manifold wisdom of God might now be made known to the principalities and powers in the heavenly places" (Eph. 3:10, RSV). And how is this wisdom made known to the principalities and powers in heavenly places? Jesus said, "Herein is my Father glorified, that ye bear much fruit" (John 15:8). God is glorified by the character He develops in us.

The first angel's message is "Fear God, and give glory to him" (Rev. 14:7). And we give glory to God by allowing Him to sanctify us so that we can bear much fruit. "The very image of God is to be reproduced in humanity," wrote Ellen G. White. "The honor of God, the honor of Christ, is involved in the perfection of the character of His people,"[5] which is why God's faithful remnant are those who "keep the commandments of God" (Rev. 12:17; 19:10). This obedience of God's law is not what saves the remnant—but is what the remnant render because they are already saved!

A false balance between faith and works, either one way or the other, will leave us wanting.

Finding the Balance

An emphasis on justification at the expense of sanctification can deceive a person into the false gospel that obedience, character development, and personal victory over sin are mere appendages to the gospel. John makes it plain: "Little children, let no man deceive you: he that *doeth* righteousness is righteous, even as he is righteous. He that committeth sin is of the devil" (1 John 3:7, 8).

An overemphasis on sanctification at the expense of justification can deceive a person into believing that his acceptance with God depends on his performance and that his good works guarantee him a place in heaven. Ellen White has stressed: "There is not a point that needs to be dwelt upon more earnestly, repeated more frequently, or established more firmly in the minds of all than the impossibility of fallen man meriting anything by his own best good works."[6] As Adventists, we bask in a blaze of gospel light unknown to previous generations. Yet we must present that light in a balanced manner, with proper emphasis on both aspects of redemption. Indeed, though a false balance is abominable to God, "a just weight is his delight" (Prov. 11:1).

---

[1] *Faith and Works*, 20.
[2] *Ibid.*, 47 .
[3] *The Desire of Ages*, 123.
[4] *Life Sketches*, 237.
[5] *The Desire of Ages*, 671.
[6] *Faith and Works*, 16.

All Scripture quotations are taken from the King James Version. This article originally appeared in the *Adventist Review*, October 20, 1988.

CHAPTER TWO

May Your Name Be Sealed

Since 1844 we have been living in the antitypical day of atonement. Christ, our high priest in the heavenly tabernacle, has been representing His people before the judgment bar of God. In the presence of an onlooking universe, God's true followers will have their *sins* blotted out of the books of heaven, a precursor to their entrance into the eternal kingdom, while Christ's false followers will have their *names* removed, a precursor to their eternal destruction.

This judgment scene is depicted in Daniel 7, with the coming of the Son of man to the Ancient of Days. "The judgment was set, and the books were opened" (Dan. 7:10). It is found again in Malachi, when the Lord, coming to His temple, proclaims: "I will come near to you in judgment" (Mal. 3:5). The judgment message is heralded in Revelation 14:7: "Fear God, and give glory to him; for the hour of his judgment is come." The date of this judgment is revealed in Daniel 8:14: "Unto two thousand and three hundred days; then shall the sanctuary be cleansed."

Writes Ellen White: "At the time appointed for the judgment—the close of the 2300 days, in 1844—began the work of investigation and blotting out of sins. All who have ever taken upon themselves the name of Christ must pass its searching scrutiny. Both the living and the dead are to be judged 'out of those things which were written in the books, according to their works.'"[1]

Though the doctrine of a pre-Advent (or "investigative") judgment is uniquely Adventist, the essence of that judgment has been understood by the Jews for centuries. Indeed, by seeing what the Jews believe about the Day of Atonement, we can find insights into our own understanding of the judgment.

Jewish Precedents

For the Jews, the cleansing of the sanctuary on the Day of Atonement, Yom Kippur, is the great judgment day. It is when every case is sealed for life or for death. This theme permeates Jewish understanding of the holy day, which is why it is such a solemn festival. Rabbi Yechiel Eckstein describes the Day of Atonement as "our final opportunity to plead for a merciful judgment." No wonder that many Jews who may never enter a synagogue during the whole year will be reciting prayers and fasting in the synagogue on this holy day.

The eleventh-century Jewish liturgy of the *Unetanneh Tokef* describes an early Jewish understanding of the Day of Atonement: "God, seated on the throne to judge the world . . . openeth the books of records; it is read, every man's signature (or name) is found therein. The great trumpet is sounded. . . . Angels shudder, saying: This is the day of judgment. . . . As a shepherd mustereth his flock, causing them to pass under his rod, so doth God cause every living creature to pass before Him to fix the limit of every creature's life and to foreordain its destiny. . . . On the Day of Atonement it is sealed who shall live and who shall die."

During the Day of Atonement today, Jews greet each other with a Hebrew saying that means "May you be sealed in the book of life for good."

In the *Prayer Book for the Day of Atonement*, the following words are prayed: "Remember us unto life, O king . . . and inscribe us in the book of life." They even ask the Lord to "silence the accuser [Satan]." They refer to the "advocate" and ask that "in consequence of his pleading, declare, I am pardoned." They ask the Lord to "justify us in the judgment" as well as "blot out the transgressions of thy people [Israel] that have been saved." They pray, "He, the Ancient of Days, sits as Judge. . . . In the book of life, blessing, peace, and good sustenance may we be remembered and sealed by thee."

These prayers, however, aren't just for the living. According to the *Jewish Encyclopedia*, "even the souls of the dead are included in the community of those pardoned on the Day of Atonement."

Drawing Out the Parallels

Though the Adventist understanding of the pre-Advent judgment does not *exactly* duplicate the Jewish understanding of Yom Kippur, parallels exist. In *Tokef*, we find the same elements prevalent in Daniel 7 describing the pre-Advent judgment. Both talk about God or, as Daniel calls Him, "the Ancient of days" (cf. Dan. 7:22). Both mention a throne: "His throne was like the fiery flame" (cf. verse 9). Both talk about books being opened (cf. verse 10), both deal with judgment ("and the judgment was set" [cf. verse 10]).

Also, just as the Jews understood the Day of Atonement as a time when every case is decided for life or for death, so do Adventists understand the pre-Advent judgment. Describing the results of that judgment, Ellen White wrote: "Every case has been decided for life or death."[2]

Like the Jews prayed, Adventists see the judgment as a time when people are sealed: "When Jesus leaves the sanctuary, then they who are holy and righteous will be holy and righteous still; for all their sins will then be blotted out, and they will be sealed with the seal of the living God."[3]

The Jews prayed that God will "blot out the transgressions of the people [Israel] that have been saved" during the Day of Atonement. So we, likewise, understand the pre-Advent judgment to be a time when God blots out the sins of His people, spiritual Israel, who also have been saved: "Then by virtue of the atoning blood of Christ, the sins of all the truly penitent will be blotted from the books of heaven."[4]

The Jews saw the Day of Atonement as involving the dead. Adventist also see the dead involved in the pre-Advent judgment: "While Jesus had been ministering in the sanctuary, the judgment had been going on for the righteous dead."[5]

The Jews saw the accuser, Satan, as part of the judgment scenario. We know that Satan is involved and that he stands as the accuser. In the words of Ellen G. White: "While Jesus is pleading for the subjects of His grace, Satan accuses them before God as transgressors."[6]

The Jews believed in an advocate who pleads in their behalf. Adventists, fortunately, also know Jesus as their advocate in the heavenly sanctuary. "Jesus will appear as their advocate, to plead in their behalf before God."[7] He "does not excuse their sins, but shows their penitence and faith, and, claiming for them forgiveness, He lifts His wounded hands before the Father and the holy angels, saying: I know them by name. I have graven them on the palms of my hands."[8]

A Heavenly Sanctuary

Actually, centuries before the Millerites, the Jews believed in a sanctuary in heaven too. The Talmud and other ancient Jewish writings that go back, in some cases, to the first centuries A.D. talk about the *heavenly and earthly temples*. The Jerusalem Talmud states, for example, that the "earthly Holy of Holies is just under the heavenly Holy of holies."[9] Indeed the Jews believed not only in a sanctuary in heaven but in a ministration there in behalf of God's people. They believed that a high priest ministered in this heavenly temple, and they believed that his name was—Michael! Says the *Jewish Encyclopedia*: "The rabbis speak of Michael (Metatron) as the captain of the heavenly host, as the high priest that offers sacrifice in the upper temple."

They also saw Michael as defending them against the accusations of the devil. Says one ancient rabbinical work: "Michael and Samael [Satan] both stand before the Divine Presence: Satan accuses, while Michael points out Israel's virtues."[10]

Important Contrasts

Obviously, Adventists do not see Michael's ministration in heaven exactly as the Jews do anymore than Adventists understand the Day of Atonement as the Jews do. Adventists know that the sacrifice has been offered once and for all, at Calvary. They know, too, that when "Samael" accuses God's people before the "Divine Presence," Michael defends them, not by pointing out Israel's virtues but by pointing out His own virtues in Israel's behalf.

Nevertheless, it is exciting to see these parallels between the Adventist and Jewish understanding of the issues, especially when we realize that the Jews held these beliefs centuries before Adventists appeared.

Most Important Parallel

Perhaps the most important parallel between Jewish and Adventist understanding of the Day of Atonement, the judgment, and the heavenly sanctuary has to do with the attitude of the Jews in regard to Yom Kippur, the day when Michael pleads in the heavenly temple. For the Jews, the Day of Atonement is the "final opportunity to repent of sin." For them, repentance is fundamental to the Day of Atonement drama. The Hebrew word for repentance comes from *teshuvah*, which means "returning to one's self." According to Jewish tradition, four conditions are necessary for true *teshuvah*: regret for past sins, forsaking of sin now, confession to God, and resolving not to sin again. These themes climax each year on Yom Kippur.

What about the church today? What lesson can we learn? "We are now living in the great day of atonement. In the typical service, while the high priest was making the atonement for Israel, all were required to afflict their souls by repentance of sin and humiliation before the Lord, lest they be cut off from among the people. In like manner, all who would have their names retained in the book of life should now, in the few remaining days of their probation, afflict their souls before God by sorrow for sin and true repentance."[11]

As we enter the final hours of the true Yom Kippur, we should be seeking for *teshuvah*. And then, thanks to the righteousness of Michael in our behalf, we can be assured that our names, too, will be "sealed in the book of life for good."

---

[1] *The Great Controversy*, 486.
[2] *Early Writings*, 280.
[3] *Ibid.*, 48.
[4] *Patriarchs and Prophets*, 357.
[5] *Early Writings*, 280.
[6] *The Great Controversy*, 484.
[7] *Ibid.*, 482.
[8] *Ibid.*, 484.
[9] Mishanah 5, 93.
[10] Midrash Rabbah on Exodus, chap. 18, sec. 5.
[11] *The Great Controversy*, 489, 490.

All Scripture quotations in this article are taken from the King James Version. This article originally appeared in the *Adventist Review*, May 18, 1989.

CHAPTER THREE

Who Shall Atone for Us?

While the command from Sinai against making and worshiping graven images still rang in their ears, the children of Israel nevertheless made and worshiped a golden calf. "These be thy gods, O Israel," they proclaimed, "which brought thee up out of the land of Egypt" (Exod. 32:4).

After Moses had destroyed the idol by grinding it into powder and strewing it upon water and punished the major offenders by having them slain with the sword, he interceded in behalf of Israel before God.

"Yet now, if thou wilt forgive their sin—; and if not, blot me, I pray thee, out of thy book which thou hast written" (verse 32). A literal rendition of the verse is "And now, if you will *bear* their sin—and if not, blot me out. . . ."

Moses literally asked God to "bear" the sin of Israel. He wanted God to forgive Israel by taking upon Himself their sins! This verse is one of many that conveys the concept of vicarious atonement, the idea of a substitute, even God Himself, bearing another's sin in order to bring forgiveness or atonement. This idea is seen in the word *nasa*, translated in verse 32 as "forgive."

Nasa, used hundreds of times in Scripture, has the basic meaning of "to bear," "to carry," "to lift up," and these renditions are how it is most commonly translated. The Bible tells of the ransacking of the "house of the Lord" by the Babylonians who "*carried* the brass of them [various items made of this metal] to Babylon" (2 Kings 25:13). Describing the construction of the table of shewbread in the Holy Place of the sanctuary, the Bible says, "And he made the staves of shittim wood, and overlaid them with gold, to *bear* the table" (Exod. 37:15). In praise to God, the psalmist says, "*Lift up* your hands in the sanctuary" (Ps. 134:2). In each verse the root for "carried," "bear," and "lifted up" is *nasa*.

Nasa deals also with the bearing of sin and guilt. One Levitical law said, "And if a soul sin, and hear the voice of swearing, and is a witness, whether he hath seen or known of it; if he do not utter it, then he shall *bear* his iniquity" (Lev. 5:1). After the death of Nadab and Abihu, the sons of Aaron who had sinned, Moses said to Aaron's other sons, "Wherefore have ye not eaten the sin offering in the holy place, seeing it is most holy, and God hath given it you to *bear* the iniquity of the congregation, to make atonement for them before the Lord?" (Lev. 10:17).

Nasa, commonly used for bearing sin, is used also for forgiving and pardoning sin. When Moses returned to Mount Sinai after the incident with the golden calf, the Lord passed before him and proclaimed, "The Lord, the Lord God, merciful and gracious, longsuffering, and abundant in goodness and truth, keeping mercy for thousands, *forgiving* iniquity and transgression and sin" (Exod. 34:6, 7). In Psalm 32, David says, "Blessed is he whose transgression is *forgiven*. . . . I said, I will confess my transgressions unto the Lord; and thou *forgavest* the iniquity of my sin" (verses 1-5). Job, sitting amid the rubble and ruin of his life, exclaimed, "And why dost thou not *pardon* my transgression, and take away mine iniquity? for now shall I sleep in the dust" (Job 7:21). In these verses, as well as in more than a dozen others, *nasa* is the triliteral root that is translated as "forgive" or "pardon."

The meaning conveyed in these verses is that the sinner appropriates forgiveness when someone else (even God) "bears" or "carries" his sin.

In Leviticus 10 the sons of Aaron were supposed to eat the flesh of the sacrifice in the Holy Place. By doing so, they would "bear the iniquity of the congregation" and thus "make atonement for them." This verse shows a link between someone—in this case the sons of Aaron serving as priests—who is to bear or carry the sins of others and atonement. Apparently, the bearing of sin, linked to forgiveness, is linked also to atonement.

The common word for atonement, *kaphar*, which means "to cover," "to appease," "to make atonement," is translated a few times the same as *nasa*: "forgive" or "pardon." If a slain man was found in the Promised Land, the Bible says that after the elders of the nearest city sacrificed a heifer, they were to wash their hands over the heifer and say "*Forgive*, O Lord, . . . thy people Israel, whom thou hast redeemed, and lay not innocent blood unto thy people of Israel's charge. And the blood shall be *forgiven* them" (Deut. 21:8, margin). Jeremiah, angry over the attitude of the people, said to the Lord, "Yet, Lord, thou knowest all their counsel against me to slay me: *forgive* not their iniquity" (Jer. 18:23). *Kaphar*, its basic meaning being "to atone," is here translated "forgive," just like *nasa*. Again, more links between atonement and the bearing of sin.

Another link between bearing sin and atonement is demonstrated in the sanctuary service of ancient Israel, which was used to deal with the sin problem. In Jewish thought, sin is not seen as a necessity but as the fruit of man's will. Man sins because he chooses to, so he is answerable for his wrongdoings. "As sin therefore is seen as rebellion against God," writes Rabbi David Rosen, "the consequence should be extremely severe."[1]

The consequence the law demands: death. The Bible teaches that a way of escape was made through the expiatory sacrifices of the animals in the temple service. "The sin offering was accordingly seen not only as purification for the individual," writes Rabbi Rosen, "but above all as a means of obtaining God's forgiveness."[2]

The ancient Israelite saw in the blood of the slain animal a way to obtain forgiveness and place his soul in a different relationship with God. "For this reason," says the *Jewish Encyclopedia*, "the blood, which to the ancients was the life power or soul, forms the essential part of the sacrificial atonement (see Lev. 27:11). This is the interpretation given by all the Jewish commentators, ancient and modern, on the passage."[3]

Says the Talmud: "Surely atonement can be made only with the blood, as it [Leviticus 17:11] says, *For it is the blood that maketh atonement*" (Zebahim 6a).

The animal, then, instead of the sinner, paid the penalty of sin, which is death. If the sinner had to *bear* his own iniquity, he would die. "Neither must the children of Israel henceforth come nigh the tabernacle of the congregation, lest they *bear [nasa]* sin, and die," (Num. 18:22). God, however, provided a substitutionary system so they would not have to bear their sins and face the penalty. Instead, they would bring an animal—a goat, a lamb, a bullock—to the sanctuary, where they would confess their sin on the animal, which then died in their stead. This confession would transfer their sin to the animal, whose shed blood was ministered in the sanctuary by the priest. When the sacrifice was finished, the priest had made "atonement *[kaphar]* for him as concerning his sin, and it shall be forgiven him" (Lev. 4:26).

This concept was vividly demonstrated on the Day of Atonement, when instead of a daily, individual atonement, Israel faced national salvation. "And Aaron shall lay both his hands upon the head of the live goat, and confess over him all the iniquities of the children of Israel, . . . and the goat shall *bear [nasa]* upon him all their iniquities" (Lev. 16:21, 22).

Here, instead of Israel bearing their sin, the goat did. This idea is key to atonement and forgiveness: Someone or something else bears, or carries, sin so the sinner does not have to. Thus the guilty sinner does not face the penalty.

"In every sacrifice," says the *Jewish Encyclopedia*, "there is the idea of substitution; the victim takes the place of the human sinner. The laying on of hands upon the victim's head is an ordinary rite by which the substitution and the transfer of sin are affected."[4]

Nasa, therefore, can refer to both forgiveness and bearing guilt. It simply depends on how it is used. If the sinner bears (*nasa*) sin, he pays the penalty; if a substitution is found to bear (*nasa*) sin, the sinner is forgiven.

This system of animal sacrifice for atonement worked well until the destruction of the temple in 70 C.E., when the Jews found themselves without a sacrificial center. "Woe unto us!" cried Joshua ben Hananiah, no doubt expressing the despair of his generation. "What shall atone for us?"[5]

Over the centuries, various theologies developed to deal with atonement and forgiveness of sin without blood. Prayer, suffering, fasting, charity, and good works have all been seen as a means of a bloodless atonement. For the Jews, repentance has become what has been called "the Jewish doctrine of salvation." The Talmud says that "the sinner who repents is on a (spiritual) level the completely righteous (who have never sinned) cannot reach" (Berachot, 43b).

Nevertheless, the idea of an atoning sacrifice, with a substitute to bear sin, has not been lost. It still hovers, woven in the warp and woof of the Jews, as it should, because substitutionary atonement, with blood, formed the basis of Judaism: "For it is the blood," says Leviticus 17:11, "that maketh an atonement for the soul."

For centuries one practice has been to swing a rooster or hen over one's head on or before the Day of Atonement while solemnly pronouncing the animal to be a vicarious sacrifice to be killed on the sinner's stead. (The bird was usually given to the poor.) Fish and plants as well have been used in this ritual. Today, after the restoration of the Jews in their ancestral homeland, and with Jerusalem in Jewish hands, many Jews are hoping to rebuild the temple and reinstate the animal sacrifices. Indeed, one yeshiva in Jerusalem is already training priests to minister in the new temple, where animals could again be used to bear the sins of the Jewish people.

By whatever means the Jews seek atonement, the Bible teaches that in order for us to be forgiven, our sins must be borne, or carried, by a substitute.

"Mine eyes are ever toward the Lord; for he shall pluck my feet out of the net. Turn thee unto me, and have mercy upon me; for I am desolate and afflicted. The troubles of my heart are enlarged: O bring thou me out of my distresses. Look upon mine affliction and my pain; and forgive [nasa] all my sins" (Ps. 25:15-18).

---

[1] Rabbi David Rosen, "Salvation and Redemption in Traditional Jewish Theology," *Face to Face* (Spring 1988), 5.

[2] *Ibid.*

[3] *The Jewish Encyclopedia* (New York: Funk and Wagnalls, 1902), II:276.

[4] *Ibid.*, 286.

[5] Quoted in *The Jewish Encyclopedia*, 278.

All Scripture quotations are taken from the King James Version. This article originally appeared in *Shabbat Shalom*, October-December 1989.

CHAPTER FOUR

Investigating the Investigative Judgment

No aspect of Seventh-day Adventism has faced more scrutiny, misrepresentation, and criticism than the pre-Advent judgment. While other Adventist doctrines such as the seventh-day Sabbath and conditional immortality are accepted by some Christians, the pre-Advent investigative judgment, "being uniquely our own, has laid us open as a church to more opprobrium, ridicule, and scorn from other Christians than any other doctrine we hold."[1]

Various evangelicals such as Donald Barnhouse,[2] Walter Martin,[3] and Anthony A. Hoekema,[4] and most recently, David Neff[5] have published articles or books attacking our belief that prior to the Second Coming, God convenes a judgment of those who have professed to serve Christ, those whose names are written in heaven (Dan. 12:1; Luke 10:20; Rev. 3:5). Though each writer has approached the issue from different perspectives, all conclude that the investigative judgment nullifies, or at least frustrates, the gospel. The doctrine, they claim, subtly teaches salvation by faith and works and thus robs the faithful of their security in Christ.

If these charges are correct, our critics are justified in rejecting the investigative judgment. Adventists ought to as well.

Is, however, the investigative judgment really antigospel? Must its adherents lack assurance in salvation? And finally, because Christians are saved by faith, what's the purpose of judgment anyway?

Faith and Works

In essence, the issue of the investigative judgment deals with the age-old tension between faith and works. Paul wrote: "For we maintain that a man is justified by faith apart from observing the law" (Rom. 3:28); yet John saw that in the end time, the saints would "obey God's commandments and remain faithful to Jesus" (Rev. 14:12).

These statements, of course, don't contradict each other. Instead, the question is

21

balance, and the place that reveals that balance is the earthly sanctuary service, the heart of the Adventist doctrine of the pre-Advent judgment.

The Bible says: "For we also have had the gospel preached to us, just as they did; but the message they heard was of no value to them, because those who heard did not combine it with faith" (Heb. 4:2).

The gospel was preached to ancient Israel through the sanctuary service, a pictorial representation of the entire plan of salvation. The sanctuary, in shadows, revealed atonement, mediation, confession, cleansing, the law, the judgment, justification, everything!

The first lesson taught was the sacrifice of the animal, symbolic of Christ's death. The entire sanctuary service, thus the whole plan of salvation, rests upon the substitutionary sacrifice of Jesus (1 Pet. 1:18,19; Rev. 13:8; Isa. 53).

Imagine a school that gave two grades only, pass or fail. In order to pass, the student must have a 100 percent average. A 95 percent earns the same failing grade as 20 percent. The student must have a perfect score on every exam; otherwise, he fails. If he makes one mistake, even answers one question wrong, he comes up short. If on one test he gets 95 percent but on ten others 100 percent, he fails because his grade would still average below 100 percent, enough to flunk him with those who average 30 percent. Either way, 99.7 percent or 30 percent, he fails.

The same with redemption. All have sinned, and therefore none ever achieve the perfect 100 percent needed for salvation (Rom. 3:23). Even if we were to become perfect, never sinning again, because of past sin we could not produce the righteousness needed for salvation. No matter how hard we try, how sanctified we become, unless we have a 100 percent score *credited to us*, outside of us, we are lost.

Jesus, because of His perfect sinless life and His death on our behalf, offers us His passing 100 percent grade (Rom. 5:17-19). His righteousness, which He wrought for us, independent of us, He freely offers us in place of our own failing grades. No matter who we are or what we've done, because of what Jesus accomplished for us on the cross, we can stand as accepted in the Father as He was, because He freely will credit to us, as undeserving as we are, Christ's 100 percent grade (Rom. 5:8).

This vicarious atonement was powerfully symbolized by the animal sacrifices (which always includes the first apartment ministry) in the earthly sanctuary service.

The Second Apartment

Unfortunately, many Christians want to end the gospel with the sacrifice and the first apartment, yet that is not where the sanctuary service ends. What about the second apartment ministry, when the sanctuary itself is cleansed of sin? Does not the Most Holy Place—on which the Day of Atonement, the great day of judgment, occurred—have lessons to teach Christians today?

Of course. Just as the altar of burnt offerings and the Holy Place symbolized Christ's death and mediation in our behalf, the Most Holy Place symbolizes Christ's work in the judgment in our behalf as well. Only by rejecting the teaching of the *entire* sanctuary can one avoid the lessons of the second apartment.

Yet in the Most Holy Place is where Adventists run into trouble, because here is where we believe that the pre-Advent judgment is taught, the doctrine that supposedly nullifies the gospel. When balanced out, however, with what precedes the second apartment ministry—i.e., the death of the sacrificial animal—the investigative judgment, instead of nullifying the good news, enhances it.

How? Because when our name comes up in judgment (see Rom. 14:10; Dan. 12:1; Rev. 21:27; Matt. 10:32, 33; Luke 12:8, 9), Christ's perfect righteousness—His 100 percent—covers us! That's the most important purpose of His death. What good would forensic justification do for us if, in the judgment, when we need it the most, it would no longer be valid?

Every morning and evening the priest offered a special sacrifice, a burnt offering that symbolized the continual availability of Christ's righteousness. Called the daily (the *tamid* in Hebrew) or the regular "continual burnt offering" (Exod. 29:42, KJV), this sacrifice assured the penitent Israelite of the constant accessibility of forgiveness. If he was sick, away from Jerusalem, or for some reason couldn't get to the sanctuary, he could still reach out by faith to the promise symbolized by these sacrifices, which burned on the altar twenty-four hours a day, every day—even on the Day of Atonement.

This point is crucial. During the solemn ceremony of Yom Kippur, this morning and evening sacrifice burned on the altar (Num. 29:7-11). In type, Christ's merits, symbolized by the slain animal, covered the sinner all through the typical Day of Atonement; in the antitype, Christ's merits cover His followers throughout the real day of atonement, the day of judgment, which is now. Thus, instead of nullifying the good news, the investigative judgment, when balanced with the Cross, lifts the gospel to its apogee!

The Judas in All of Us

Christians, those who profess to serve Christ, do face a judgment of their works (2 Cor. 5:9, 10; Rom. 14:10, 12). These works, however, are not what makes God decide to accept or reject them; rather, the works prove whether or not they have truly accepted or rejected Him. When a name appears in the pre-Advent judgment, God merely finalizes the choice that the person has already made.

Consider Judas. "Then Satan entered Judas, called Iscariot, one of the Twelve. And Judas went to the chief priests and the officers of the temple guard and discussed with them how he might betray Jesus" (Luke 22:3, 4).

Who forsook whom? Did Jesus desert Judas? No, Judas forsook Jesus, and his ruin is a dramatic example of what causes names to be rejected during the investigative judgment (Rev. 3:5; Matt. 10:32, 33; Luke 12:8, 9).

"Then Satan entered Judas, called Iscariot, one of the Twelve" (Luke 22:3). Why Judas? After all, he had an experience with Jesus. He had been stirred by the miracles of the Saviour. He saw the lame, the blind, the sick brought to Christ's feet and healed by a word or a touch. He saw Him raise the dead, cast out demons, and multiply the fish and the loaves. "He recognized the teaching of Christ as superior to all that he had ever heard," wrote Ellen White. "He loved the Great Teacher, and desired to be changed in character and life, and he hoped to experience this through connecting himself with Jesus."[6]

What, then, happened?

"He had fostered the evil spirit of avarice until it had become the ruling motive of his life. *The love of mammon overbalanced his love for Christ.* Through becoming the slave of one vice he gave himself to Satan, to be driven to any lengths in sin."[7]

Judas indulged in only one sin, and it brought his ruin, not because Jesus couldn't forgive it but because Judas didn't accept that forgiveness. Refusing to repent, he chose that sin, literally, over Jesus—an example of what happens to all who, though written in the book of life, are eventually blotted out of it (Rev. 3:5).

Satan knows the gospel. He knows "that there is not condemnation for those who are in Christ Jesus" (Rom. 8:1). He knows that a "man is not justified by the works of the law, but by the faith of Jesus Christ" (Gal. 2:16, KJV). Satan realizes, too, that nothing he can do will nullify, reverse, or void God's love for us and that "neither height nor depth, nor anything else in all creation, will be able to separate us from the love of God that is in Christ Jesus our Lord" (Rom. 8:39). Because Satan understands all these things, he knows that Jesus will never forsake us. Therefore, he tries to get us to forsake Jesus instead, and the only way he can do this is to lead us in sin and then keep us in it, because we will ultimately choose that sin over Jesus—just as Judas did.

For this reason, the battle with sin is central to the fight of faith (Gal. 5:21). We must resolutely wage war against sin, or it will overcome our commitment to Christ. Sin is deadly, not because it can't be pardoned. It can be. God longs to pardon our sin. The Cross proves that. Sin is deadly because, while it won't push God away from us, it will push us away from God.

Connected with Christ, though, Christians have the victory: "No temptation has seized you except what is common to man. And God is faithful; he will not let you be tempted beyond what you can bear. But when you are tempted, he will also provide a way out so that you can stand up under it" (1 Cor. 10:13).

This side of the Second Coming we will always have a sinful nature. We will always have to struggle with the clamors of our own fallen flesh. We will always be aware of the evil that dwells within us. But we don't ever have to yield to sin! Yielding, for a converted Christian, is a conscious choice. How could it be anything else? If God promises power not to sin, yet we do it anyway, it is only because we have decided not to avail ourselves of that power. We have chosen the *act of sin* instead. This decision of choosing our own sinful desires over Christ is basically what Judas did.

We sin only because we choose not to claim victory in Christ (1 John 2:9; Jude 24; Rom. 6:1, 2). The Lord can and does pardon sins when we confess them. But if we deliberately sin and keep sinning, sooner or later, like Judas, we can become so hardened in them that we will make the same decision to reject Jesus, whether we realize it or not.

Indeed, a Christian doesn't have to hang himself from a tree, have the rope break, and then have dogs eat him in order to have his name blotted out of the book of life. Instead, he can go to church, tithe, pray, even do some good works, and yet be blotted out of the book of life.

The investigative judgment is not when God finally decides to accept or reject us. All those written in heaven have already been accepted by God (Eph. 1:6). Instead, the judgment merely finalizes our choice to keep or reject Him. Here is where *our* decisions, as made manifest by our works, are sealed—one way or another.

Works do not save us, cannot save us, are not meant to save us (Gal. 2:21). But that does not mean they have nothing to do with salvation (Rom. 2:13). On the contrary, they are the proof, the evidence, the indication that we have been born again. "Show me your faith without your deeds," said James, "and I will show you my faith by what I do" (James 2:18).

Redemption is a package deal. If we have claimed forgiveness, we must claim victory as well, and those victories testify in the day of judgment that we have truly been redeemed. If we are converted, our works will prove it, and we have nothing to fear in judgment.

The Assurance of Salvation

Nevertheless, some insist that the pre-Advent judgment robs them of assurance. How much assurance do they want? If by absolute assurance they mean they cannot be lost no matter what they do once they have accepted Jesus, do they not subscribe to the once-saved-always-saved doctrine? If, however, when Christians daily surrender their lives to Jesus, claiming His promises of victory when tempted, claiming His promises of forgiveness when they fall, and always trusting in the merits of Christ imputed to them as their only hope of salvation, they will have all the salvation they need.

"Therefore, there is now no condemnation for those who are in Christ Jesus" (Rom. 8:1).

This verdict is only for those who "are in Christ Jesus" Who are they? It says: ". . . those who are in Christ Jesus" (verse 1). Walking in the Spirit is not what redeems you; it is the evidence that you are redeemed.

Some ask, How will I know if I have enough works to be saved? You don't, never have, and never will, which is why we need Jesus covering us with His righteousness when our names come up. All we can do is lean on Him, plead His merits in our behalf, and trust in Him as a righteous, compassionate Father who will judge us according to His infinite wisdom and mercy.

Cosmic Consequences

Perhaps the most important aspect of the investigative judgment, one often ignored by critics, is its purpose. Antagonists unfairly depict the doctrine as God scrutinizing the books in order to decide who is saved or lost. "The Lord knows those who are his" (2 Tim. 2:19). An omniscient God doesn't need the investigative judgment; the onlooking universe, however, does.

Sin is not just an earthly concern. Rebellion began in another part of creation, with the fall of Satan (see Isa. 14:12; Ezek. 28:11-16; Rev. 2:7-9). The principles involved in the controversy between Christ and Satan, though focused in the salvation of man, extend far beyond it (see Eph. 3:10). The book of Job is a microcosm of this great controversy: The first scene in heaven starts out with conflict, tension, and a contest between God and Satan in heaven, one that is viewed by the angels (Job 1:6; 2:1), even though the struggle is ultimately battled out on earth.[8]

God could have eradicated Satan at the moment he rebelled. Instead, at infinite cost to Himself, God is dealing with sin and rebellion in a just and open manner that will forever answer the charges made against Him. One way that He has chosen to help answer these charges is through the investigative judgment.

Even a cursory look at the earthly sanctuary service teaches that the plan of salvation didn't end at the sacrifice; it began there, with the sacrifice at the foundation upon which all the rituals rested. The end did not come until the final disposing of sin on the Day of Atonement, when all the sins accumulated in the camp were placed on the head of the live goat, which was then sent into the wilderness (see Lev. 16).

The same is true with Christ's earthly and heavenly ministry, which the entire Jewish sanctuary shadowed (see Heb. 7–10). Though Christ shouted "It is finished!" at Calvary; the Bible depicts Him ministering in the heavenly sanctuary (Heb. 7:25; 8:1; 9:11; 12:24-26). Why, almost two thousand years after Calvary, are we still here, mired in a pit of sin, suffering, and death? Christ must be doing something in heaven that He didn't do at Calvary, not in terms of securing our salvation—which He accomplished for us *in toto* there—but in terms of answering all the questions of the onlooking universe.

In Daniel 7:9, 10, a depiction of the pre-Advent judgment graphically unfolds before a vast heavenly throng: "Thousands upon thousands attended him; ten thousand times ten thousand stood before him. The court was seated, and the books were opened" (verse 10).

Why this judgment? Why the open books? For an omniscient, all-powerful God who knows the beginning from the end? Rather, it must be for those "thousands upon thousands" surrounding Him, who don't have the knowledge and omniscience of God Himself. Before these heavenly intelligences, the Lord is convening a judgment to show them just what sinners will be allowed to live in their presence for eternity.

"But before the great controversy will end," writes Adventist scholar A.V. Wallenkampf, "it must become evident to all heavenly intelligences on what basis some people will experience annihilation while others will be privileged to live in the presence of God throughout eternity. This will be made clear during the investigative judgment. The purpose of the judgment is not, as our challengers erroneously assume, to determine 'whether a person shall be saved or not,' as Hoekma put it."[9]

Apparently, too, these heavenly intelligences are satisfied because, after the judgment is over, they shout, "Yes, Lord God Almighty, true and just are your judgments" (Rev. 16:7).

False Balances

It's tempting for non-Adventists to twist a teaching like the investigative judgment. Actually, Adventists are the worst offenders. Many focus upon the law of the second apartment but entirely overlook the mercy seat there, at the expense of the cross. For them, the investigative judgment has become the legalistic, perfectionistic, and anti-gospel doctrine that it has been labeled. So much emphasis can be placed on the judgment-by-works aspect of salvation that people do lose their assurance in Christ. The focus becomes primarily on what *we* do, on *our* attainments, *our* good deeds, *our* victories, not on Jesus and what He has done, or is doing, for us.

In response, some go to the other extreme, ending the gospel at the Cross and the first apartment, with little or no emphasis on the role of the judgment or works. Such an imbalanced presentation leads people into the erroneous belief that we can never lose our justification (1 Cor. 9:27) or that our obedience has nothing whatsoever to do with our redemption (Matt. 5:27-30).

Instead, a balanced presentation of the plan of salvation, as revealed in the sanctuary service, presents the basic consonance between justification by faith and judgment by works. A balanced presentation protects Christians from accepting a cheap grace that can delude a person into false security (see Matt. 7:21-23) or from falling into a legalistic salvation-by-works trap (Rom. 11:6). A balanced understanding of the entire sanctuary, from the altar of burnt offerings to the Most Holy Place, reveals why we are still here in sin centuries after Jesus shouted "It is finished!" on the cross. And finally, a balanced presentation helps the Christian focus his attention, not on his own works, but on the present activity of Christ in his behalf.

Revelation 14 depicts an angel, near the end of time, having "the eternal gospel" (verse 6). What is his message? "Fear God and give him glory, because *the hour of his judgment has come*" (verse 7). For this angel, the "eternal gospel" includes the judgment. Small wonder, because when properly taught, the judgment, far from negation of the gospel, climaxes it!

---

[1]A. V. Wallenkampf, "Challengers to the Doctrine of the Sanctuary," in Frank B. Holbrook, ed., *Doctrine of the Sanctuary* (Washington, D.C.: General Conference of Seventh-day Adventists, 1989), 198.

[2]Donald Barnhouse, "Are Seventh-day Adventists Christians?" *Eternity*, 7 (September 1956), 44.

[3]Walter Martin, *The Truth About Seventh-day Adventism* (Grand Rapids: Zondervan Pub. House, 1960).

[4]Anthony A. Hoekema, *The Four Major Cults* (Grand Rapids: Eerdmans Pub. Co., 1963).

[5]David Neff, "A Sanctuary Movement," *Christianity Today*, Feb. 5, 1990, 20.

[6]Ellen G. White, *The Desire of Ages* (Nampa, Idaho: Pacific Press® Pub. Assn., 1940), 717.

[7]*Ibid.*, 716. (Italics supplied.)

[8]Clifford Goldstein, *How Dare You Judge Us, God!* (Nampa, Idaho: Pacific Press® Pub. Assn., 1991).
[9]Wallenkampf, 214.

Unless otherwise noted, all Scripture quotations are taken from the New International Version. This article originally appeared in *Ministry*, February 1992.

CHAPTER FIVE

Good News About the Judgment

Days after she drowned her two sons in a lake, then looked America in the eyes and lied about it, Susan Smith confessed.

Now she's in the custody of the strong arms of the law.

But what about the innumerable others who have gotten away with acts as heinous as hers? What about the rapists, the murderers, and the molesters who have never been caught, who have never seen the inside of jail—who have never answered for their evil?

Don't be fooled. Justice will be done for them too.

We All Face Judgment

We might hide our secrets from the law and even from friends and family—but no words, no matter how hushed; no actions, no matter how surreptitious; and no thoughts, no matter how fleeting, can escape the God of heaven. And He has promised to judge the world.

> God will bring every deed into judgment, including every hidden thing, whether it is good or evil (Eccles. 12:14).

> For we will all stand before God's judgment seat. . . . So then, each of us will give an account of himself to God (Rom. 14:10, 12).

> Those who oppose the Lord will be shattered. He will thunder against them from heaven; the Lord will judge the ends of the earth (1 Sam. 2:10).

Even Christians face judgment:

> It is time for judgment to begin with the family of God; and if it begins with us, what will the outcome be for those who do not obey the gospel of God? (1 Pet. 4:17).

Doubt whatever you want, but don't doubt that you will one day answer to your

Maker for sins and deeds that you thought were long ago lost and forgotten.

That's a scary prospect—and it ought to be.

Christians, however, enter the judgment with one crucial difference: On that day Jesus Christ, in all His holiness, perfection, and righteousness, stands in their place—in the place of each Christian. Unlike others, who must meet their Maker alone with all their deeds laid out accusingly before them, Christians have a Substitute—One whose righteousness and perfection is credited to them. It's the only way they can be accounted worthy of eternal life.

"There is now no condemnation for those who are in Christ Jesus, who do not live according to the sinful nature but according to the Spirit" (Rom. 8:1, margin). The reason there is "no condemnation" isn't because these people haven't sinned— they have. Instead, there's no condemnation because someone who hasn't sinned has taken their place: Jesus Christ. Acquittal comes not because *they* are worthy but because Jesus, their Redeemer, *is*.

This concept, called "substitutionary atonement," was taught by the Jewish temple service in the Old Testament. In Old Testament times, whoever wanted forgiveness for sin would bring in an animal, usually a sheep or a goat, to the temple. That animal was killed there, and its blood became the means of atonement: "For the life of a creature is in the blood, and I have given it to you to make atonement for yourselves on the altar; it is the blood that makes atonement for one's life" (Lev. 17:11).

In Hebrew, the word for atonement can mean "to cover." It's related to the word used to say that Moses' parents "covered" (with tar and pitch) the little ark they floated in the Nile to hide the infant Moses from Pharaoh's troops.

What covers, or atones, for Christians isn't tar and pitch but the perfect righteousness of Jesus Christ. The process of getting this covering is called "justification by faith," and it's the core of biblical salvation.

Prophecies in Blood

Each Old Testament animal sacrifice was, in actuality, a miniprophecy of Jesus' death on the cross. While most other prophecies were written on parchment by prophets, these prophecies were written in the blood of beasts. People could easily forget words scratched on a scroll or uttered by a prophet, but they wouldn't forget the face of a lamb as its blood spilled at their feet because of their sins. Nor would their memories retain the rebuke of a prophet as long as they would feel the warm blood spurting on their hands, blood that pointed to Christ's sacrifice on the cross.

> For you know that it was not with perishable things such as silver or gold that you were redeemed from the empty way of life handed down to you from your forefathers, but with the precious blood of Christ, a lamb without blemish or defect (1 Pet. 1:18, 19).

More than five hundred years before Jesus, Isaiah described the work of atonement that He would accomplish at the Cross:

He was pierced for our transgressions, he was crushed for our iniquities; the punishment that brought us peace was upon him, and by his wounds we are healed. . . .The Lord has laid on him the iniquity of us all (Isa. 53:5, 6).

The great news for those who accept Jesus as their Saviour is that at that moment, He becomes their substitute, the means by which they are "justified" or "set right" with God. In the sight of the One whom they must meet on judgment day, *Christ's* holiness, *Christ's* righteousness, becomes *their* holiness, *their* righteousness.

In fact, Jesus is interceding for Christians right now as well—just as the priest in the earthly sanctuary service interceded for the sinner: "For Christ did not enter a man-made sanctuary that was only a copy of the true one; he entered heaven itself, *not to appear for us in God's presence"* (Heb. 9:24, emphasis supplied).

Even now, those who have surrendered their lives in obedience to Christ, choosing to live only for Him and resting their hope of salvation on His merits, are accepted by God as if they had never sinned—just as Jesus never sinned. And on judgment day, this acceptance is affirmed for eternity.

Thousands of years ago, King David—who had committed crimes, not just sins—understood the wonderful provision that God made for repentant sinners: "Blessed is he whose transgressions are forgiven, whose sins are covered. Blessed is the man whose sin the Lord does not count against him" (Ps. 32:1, 2).

Fortunately for David, his sins—including murder, adultery, and lying—were atoned for by Jesus Christ, his Saviour and Substitute. In the judgment, God will not see David's evil deeds. Instead, when He looks at David's "account," He'll see Jesus' righteousness and perfection—the only means by which David can be taken into God's eternal kingdom.

Unveiling the Great Judgment

Daniel 7, which begins with a sweeping description of the great world powers from ancient Babylon right through the coming of Jesus Christ, unveils the great judgment that ushers in the end of the age. In verse 8, this chapter pictures a "little-horn" symbol of a religiopolitical power that will persecute God's people in the last days. Then it moves on to describe a judgment in heaven:

As I looked, thrones were set in place, and the Ancient of Days took his seat . . . . A river of fire was flowing, coming out from before him. Thousands upon thousands attended him; ten thousand times ten thousand stood before him. The court was seated, and the books were opened (Dan. 7:9, 10).

In another depiction of the same scene, Daniel writes that the little horn persecuted God's people "until the Ancient of Days came and *pronounced judgment in favor of the saints of the Most High*, and the time came when they possessed the kingdom" (verse 22, emphasis supplied).

Verdict is given in favor of the saints only because they have Jesus as their substitute. It can't come any other way. "All have sinned and fall short of the glory of God" (Rom. 3:23), so sinners can only be vindicated in judgment if they're covered by the blood of Jesus Christ.

The Bible says that Christians can have "confidence on the day of judgment" (1 John 4:17), not because of anything they have done but because of what Jesus has done for them.

But if Jesus stands as the Christians' substitute in judgment, couldn't they just continue to transgress God's law? Couldn't they reason, *Since Jesus covers my sins, I can do whatever I want and ask for forgiveness afterward. If David's adultery—and even the murder he committed—can be atoned for, can't anything I want to do be atoned for as well?*

The fact that Christ stands as the Christians' substitute on the day of judgment brings them the comforting assurance of salvation. But it doesn't mean that Christians aren't responsible for their acts or that they won't face a judgment of their works.

All will be judged by their works. The difference for Christians is that their works show, not whether they are good enough or holy enough in and of themselves to be saved (which they are not), but whether or not they have a true faith relationship with Jesus, who alone is worthy to be saved. It is the validity of this relationship that one's works reveal: "Faith by itself, if it is not accompanied by action, is dead. . . . *I will show you my faith by what I do*" (James 2:17, 18, emphasis supplied).

God is not mocked. Those who think that "faith" in Jesus allows them to sin with impunity show by those very sins that they don't have the faith that leads to salvation. Faith works, or it isn't faith at all.

Paul Stresses Obedience

The apostle Paul taught the concept of Jesus as our substitute more clearly than any other Bible writer. But while he insisted that salvation comes only through faith in Jesus and not by the works of the law, he also stressed that obedience and holy living were an inseparable part of the process. Repeatedly, he followed his expositions of the great truth of righteousness by faith with admonitions for obedience.

In his article "Judgment," in the *Dictionary of Paul and His Letters*, S. H. Travis directly challenges the idea that a judgment based on works contradicts Paul's concept of righteousness by faith. "Paul's focus on relationship to Christ," he wrote, "is not in conflict with his affirmation of judgment according to works. For he understands people's deeds as evidence of their character, showing whether their relationship to God is fundamentally one of faith or unbelief. . . . At the final judgment, the evidence of their deeds will confirm the reality of this relationship."*

At the cross, God proved His justice: He saw to it that the penalty for sin was paid. Instead of sinners paying that penalty themselves, however, Jesus paid it for them. By His death, He met the demands of the law—which had to be satisfied in order for God's justice to be done.

Of course, in meeting the demands of justice in this way, God proved His mercy as well. Through the death of Jesus, pardon could be given to sinners who accept Him as their Saviour. "God demonstrates his own love for us in this: While we were still sinners, Christ died for us" (Rom. 5:8).

Rather than leaving us to die in our sins, Christ died *for* us. His death provided the means whereby we all can have forgiveness for our sins.

On judgment day, anyone standing alone will receive the verdict of condemnation and death. No one has the righteousness and holiness needed for acceptance with God: "We have already made the charge that Jews and Gentiles alike are all under sin. As it is written: 'There is no one righteous, not even one' " (Rom. 3:9, 10).

But thanks to the mercy manifested through Christ's substitutionary death, no one needs to stand alone on the judgment day. Each of us—no matter who we are or what we've done—can have Jesus as our substitute.

Each of us.

Even Susan Smith.

---

*Gerald Hawthorne and Ralph Martin, eds., *Dictionary of Paul and His Letters* (Downers Grove, Ill.: InterVarsity Press, 1993), 517.

Scriptural passages are from the New International Version. This article originally appeared in *Signs of the Times*®, July 1995.

CHAPTER SIX

Blood and Judgment

Like good Protestants, Adventists claim that they believe in justification by faith. They say that salvation is by grace alone and that works cannot save them. They believe that they are saved by Christ's substitutionary death, "the only means of atonement."[1]

Yet ask what happens in the investigative judgment, and suddenly the soteriology of many members becomes more works orientated. It's no longer grace alone. The line between judgment by works and justification by faith becomes blurred, until Christ's death as "the only means of atonement" isn't quite what they believe. The substitution isn't quite complete enough.

Despite all the assertions, claims, and publications to the contrary, because of their misunderstanding of the investigative judgment, many Adventists are trapped in a salvation-by-faith-and-works model of atonement.

It has taken me fourteen years to realize how prevalent this problem is.

Experience of Justification

Part of the reason for my myopia about legalism in Adventism was that I had never struggled with it myself. Not only did I understand it intellectually and biblically; I experienced it as well. I had been walking through a field, praying and feeling the presence of God in a remarkable manner. Suddenly it was as if the heavens opened and a flash of God's glory burned across the sky. I dropped to my knees and cringed, because for the first time since I had accepted Christ, I saw just how wretched I was in contrast to a holy God. The overwhelming thought that consumed me was *Oh, Lord, how can You accept me?* Instantly an image of the Cross flashed through my head.

I understood justification by faith. I knew all the texts in Romans. I could give Bible studies on it. Yet that day I *experienced* the great biblical truth that my only hope of salvation was rooted in what Christ did outside of me, for me, and in place of me, 2,000 years ago at Calvary. I experienced the truth that no matter how sanctified and obedient I became, works—even the ones done through Christ in me—could no more justify me before God than the blood of pigs could wash away my sins. For me, justification by faith was no longer just a theological doctrine; it had become the foundation of my whole walk with Christ.

Wrong Assumptions

The problem, however, was that because this understanding had become so axiomatic to my Christian experience—I assumed it was for everyone else as well. When, therefore, I preached and wrote about victory, sanctification, and biblical perfection (all of which I still believe), I assumed that everyone began with the same premise I did about justification by faith. No matter how hard I preached obedience and holy living, I thought that those listening already understood that Christ's imputed righteousness—not obedience and holy living—was the only basis of salvation. I never dreamed that I was hammering more nails into their legalistic coffins.

My first inkling that my assumption was wrong was with what I did to my poor wife soon after we were married. So afraid that she might get caught up in the perfidious "new theology," I harped on the biblical truths of victory in Christ, overcoming sin, and character perfection. I never set these truths upon the foundation of justification by faith, simply because I thought she knew that basic teaching. Eventually, thinking that her salvation was based on what happened *in* her, rather than *for* her, she became discouraged, as would anyone who was looking inside themselves and what happens there for salvation.

I was concerned. We studied together Romans 3–5 and the great truth of righteousness by faith. Since then, though my wife still strives for character perfection, as all true Christians do, she places her hope of salvation in Christ's death for her, as all true Christians must.

Blood and Law

Though what my wife went through opened my eyes, something recently helped me to see the problem clearer. One pastor visiting an Adventist woman in a hospital told her that I was coming to town to preach. Her face turned red, and she gasped and uttered, "Goldstein scares me—he's trying to revive the doctrine of the investigative judgment within Adventism!"

When the pastor told me, my first thought was *What was this person's understanding of the investigative judgment that would cause her to have such a response?* Suddenly everything that I had been hearing over the years coalesced, and I then realized that the root cause of Adventist legalism was a misunderstanding of the pre-Advent judgment.

Adventists see the cleansing of the sanctuary in Daniel 8:14 as the antitypical fulfillment of the Levitical Day of Atonement, and rightly so. Yet what is atonement? Is it not God's act of saving a human being? Is it not God's work in our behalf? "But God commendeth his love toward us, in that, while we were yet sinners, Christ died for us" (Rom. 5:8). Is that not atonement? How is atonement achieved? It happens only one way: through blood. "For the life of the flesh is in the blood: and I have given it to you upon the altar to make an atonement for your souls: for it is the blood that maketh an atonement for the soul" (Lev. 17:11).

Thus any day dedicated totally to atonement—God's work for us—must be very good news. How is it, then, that we have turned the antitypical day of atonement into bad news?

Because Adventists believe in the obedience of the Ten Commandments, and because of the Levitical Day of Atonement centered upon the room in which the Ten Commandments were kept, the tendency has been to emphasize the law more than the blood. Yet in the type, everything happened with blood, not law. The mercy seat, that covered the law, was never lifted or removed on the Day of Atonement. According to Leviticus 16, the only thing that happened to the mercy seat on the Day of Atonement was that blood was sprinkled upon it (see verses 14, 15). The mercy seat always covered the law. The law, then, never comes into view, because it is the Day of *Atonement*, and only blood—not the law—atones.

The key element on the Day of Atonement was blood.

Blood, by the law, atoned for sin, and every drop symbolized the only blood that truly makes atonement: the blood of Christ. "Forasmuch as ye know that ye were not redeemed with corruptible things, such as silver and gold, from your vain conversation received by tradition from your fathers; but with the precious blood of Christ, as of a lamb without blemish and without spot (1 Pet. 1:18, 19). Blood, a symbol of the righteousness of Christ, is what gets the sinner through judgment.

Blood and Judgment

Just as blood was the only thing that got the penitent in Israel through the earthly Day of Atonement, it is blood, Christ's blood, that gets the penitent through the heavenly Day of Atonement. In His daily ministry, Christ as intercessor presents His own perfect life in place of the repentant sinner's imperfect one; in the yearly, He does the same thing. Whenever the name of one of His followers appears for judgment, Christ pleads His blood, His righteousness, in their stead. It can't be anything else, because nothing else—not even works done by Christ in us—is good enough.

"The pre-Advent judgment," wrote Norman Gulley, "is Christ-centered and not man-centered. It is not so much what individuals have or have not done per se that is decisive. Rather it is what Christ has done for them when He was judged in their place at the cross (John 12:31)."[2]

Ellen White understood this forensic aspect of the investigative judgment. "When in the typical service the high priest left the holy on the Day of Atonement," she wrote, "He went in before God to present the blood of the sin offering in behalf of all Israel who truly repented of their sins. So Christ had only completed one part of His work as our intercessor, to enter upon another portion of the work, and He still *pleaded His blood* before the Father in behalf of sinners."[3]

In the judgment, when names of God's people come up, Satan accuses them before the Father. He "points to the record of their lives, to the defects of character, the unlikeness to Christ . . . [and] to all the sins that he has tempted them to commit." What happens in response? "Jesus does not excuse their sins, but shows their penitence and faith, and, claiming for them forgiveness, He lifts His wounded hands before the Father and the holy angels, saying: I know them by name. I have graven them on the palms of My hands."[4] It doesn't matter if this happens when we are alive or dead: If we are converted Christians, we are covered by Christ's blood.

What about Ellen White's statement regarding how every thought, word, and deed will be investigated? For example, this one: "Sin may be concealed, denied, covered up from father, mother, wife, children, associates. . . . The darkness of the darkest night, the secrecy of all deceptive arts, is not sufficient to veil one thought from the knowledge of the Eternal."[5]

The Bible, of course, teaches the same thing: "For God shall bring every work into judgment, with every secret thing, whether it be good, or whether it be evil" (Eccles. 12:14).

Who among us—even the most Christlike and sanctified Sabbathkeeper—could stand when every thought and secret thing is presented before God for judgment? Not one. That's why we need a substitute in the judgment. Second, which secret things, which thoughts, which evil deeds, can't be pardoned by the blood of Christ? None. For the repenting and confessing Christian, who leans totally upon the merits of Christ, everything is covered by Him who "lifts His wounded hands before the Father." That's the essence of the good news!

Judgment by Works

Of course, the wonderful, liberating news of Christ as our substitute in the pre-Advent judgment *never* implies release from obedience to the law. Forensic righteousness merely frees us from the bondage and futility of trying to be saved by the law.

No matter how adamant they were about justification by faith, the New Testament writers were just as adamant about obedience and a religious life. "Little children," wrote John, "let no man deceive you: he that doeth righteousness is righteous, even as he is righteous" (1 John 3:7). "And they that are Christ's have crucified the flesh with the affections and lusts. If we live in the Spirit, let us also walk in the Spirit" (Gal. 5:24, 25). "Do we then make void the law through faith? God forbid; yea, we establish the law" (Rom. 3:31).

Those under the delusion that righteousness by faith doesn't require strict obedience to God's commands will one day find themselves crushed by these words:

"I never knew you: depart from me, ye that work iniquity [lawlessness]" (Matt.7:23).

Christ, our substitute in the judgment, doesn't negate a judgment by works either. On the contrary, works show that we have a saving faith. "Even so faith, if it hath not works, is dead, being alone. Yea, a man may say, Thou hast faith, and I have works: shew me thy faith without thy works, and I will shew thee my faith by my works" (James 2:17,18).

Travis observes correctly: "Paul's focus on relationship to Christ is not in conflict with his affirmation of judgment according to works. For he understands people's deeds as evidence of their character, showing whether their relationship to God is fundamentally one of faith or of unbelief. . . . At the final judgment, the evidence of their deeds will confirm the reality of this relationship."[6]

Assurance and Judgment

How unfortunate that for more than a century the investigative judgment has been twisted and even used as a disciplinary tool! As a result, instead of teaching the pre-Advent judgment as the climactic application of Calvary in our behalf, many Adventists have put the judgment in tension with, and even opposition to, the cross. When salvation should have been rooted in what Christ has done for us, the investigative judgment has been so taught that we have focused attention upon ourselves and how well we perform, a hopeless prospect for even the holiest and most sanctified Seventh-day Adventist Christian.

No wonder so many Adventists don't have assurance of salvation. Far from negating the gospel, however, the pre-Advent judgment—*when taught in relationship to the Cross*—affirms that our salvation comes only from faith in what Christ has done for us, and nothing else. Too bad many Adventists have missed this crucial aspect of the plan of salvation.

---

[1] *Seventh-day Adventists Believe . . . A Biblical Exposition of 27 Fundamental Doctrines* (Silver Spring, Md.: Ministerial Association, General Conference of Seventh-day Adventists, 1988), 106.

[2] Norman Gulley, "Daniel's Pre-Advent Judgment in Its Biblical Context," *Journal of the Adventist Theological Society*, Autumn 1991, 59.

[3] Ellen G. White, *The Great Controversy* (Nampa, Idaho: Pacific Press® Pub. Assn., 1911), 429. (Italics supplied.)

[4] *Ibid.*, 484.

[5] *Ibid.*, 486.

[6] S. H. Travis, "Judgment," in Gerald Hawthorne and Ralph Martin, eds., *Dictionary of Paul and His Letters* (Downers Grove, Ill.: InterVarsity Press, 1993), 517.

This article originally appeared in *Ministry*, February 1996.

CHAPTER SEVEN

No Condemnation

My wife, raised in the Adventist Church, once described how she had been taught the investigative (or pre-Advent) judgment.

"Well," she began, her words tinged with sarcasm, "they tell you that the judgment is going on in heaven right now and that you never know when your name comes up, but if you're not perfect when it does—then you're blotted out of the book of life forever. But you don't know that this has happened, and thus you're still trying to be perfect, although it's already too late. Your probation is closed—and you're eternally lost."

However accurately depicting what many Adventists believe, that concept perverts not only the doctrine of the judgment but the Cross as well. No wonder many Adventists struggle for assurance or have joined other churches or have rejected Christ entirely. With beliefs like that, who could blame them? As a church we have reaped—and will continue to reap—a bitter harvest until we teach the judgment in light of the gospel.

To begin, the key verse for understanding the pre-Advent judgment isn't in Daniel, Leviticus, or Revelation, but Romans. "There is therefore now no condemnation to them which are in Christ Jesus, who walk not after the flesh, but after the Spirit" (Rom. 8:1). In one sense, the verse itself alludes to judgment (after all, how could there be even the question of condemnation if there wasn't some kind of reckoning?), but it also gives the outcome, and that is—no condemnation.

Why this acquittal, especially when "all have sinned, and come short of the glory of God" (Rom. 3:23), when "there is none that doeth good, no, not one" (verse 12), and when "all we like sheep have gone astray; we have turned every one to his own way" (Isa. 53:6)? You might need faith to believe in the Resurrection, the Second Coming, and the Trinity, but not our inherent sinfulness and evil. Our depravity is

39

the most empirically verifiable of all Christian teachings.

This acquittal is even harder to understand when compared with human courts, where the verdict of "no condemnation" comes (ideally) only if the accused is innocent. In the cosmic drama, however, our guilt or innocence isn't in question: We have committed everything that we've been accused of. We can be sure, too, that if "the very hairs of [our] heads are all numbered" (Matt.10:30), our sins are as well.

Why, then, "no condemnation" for those who unquestionably deserve condemnation? Because the condemnation of our sins has already fallen on Jesus Christ. We are acquitted, not because we're innocent, worthy, or perfect but because Jesus Christ is—and the judgment against our sin was poured out upon Him at Calvary. Jesus was condemned so that we—in the judgment—won't be.

"Now is the judgment of this world," Jesus said, just prior to His death. "Now shall the prince of this world be cast out" (John 12:31). The world as a whole was judged at the cross, and the verdict was—guilty. Yet the penalty was poured out at the cross as well, on Christ, which is why, when His true followers face judgment as individuals, there is no condemnation."

Paul wrote, "For he hath made him to be sin for us, who knew no sin; that we might be made the righteousness of God in him" (2 Cor. 5:21). God poured out His righteous wrath against sin and because Christ "became sin for us." God's wrath was poured out on Him so that we never have to suffer the wrath we deserve.

"Christ hath redeemed us from the curse of the law, being made a curse for us: for it is written, Cursed is every one that hangeth on a tree" (Gal. 3:13). The law brings a curse because it points to sin, and because all have sinned, all are under the curse. The good news is that at the cross Christ became that "curse for us" so we don't have to face the penalty that the curse would otherwise bring.

One doesn't have to be a Seventh-day Adventist, with an understanding of what happened in 1844, to believe in a future judgment. "God shall bring every work into judgment, with every secret thing, whether it be good, or whether it be evil" (Eccles.12:14). For "the Lord shall judge his people" (Heb. 10:30). The difference is that truly repentant Christians (unlike those who must meet their Maker alone, with every past act laid out accusingly before them) have a substitute, Jesus Christ, who—having already paid the penalty for their sins—stands in their place when their names appear in judgment.

Ellen White depicts what happens in the investigative judgment: "While Jesus is pleading for the subjects of His grace, Satan accuses them before God as transgressors. . . . He points to the record of their lives, to the defects of character, the unlikeness to Christ which has dishonored their Redeemer, to all the sins that he has tempted them to commit, and because of these he claims them as his subjects.

"Jesus does not excuse their sins, but shows their penitence and faith, and, claiming for them forgiveness, He lifts His wounded hands before the Father and the holy angels, saying: I know them by name. I have graven them on the palms of My hands."[1]

No matter how many good works we do, no matter how sanctified our character, no matter how obedient to law—we're still not good enough to stand before God alone in judgment. Isaiah wrote that all our righteousness is "as filthy rags" (Isa. 64:6). No wonder that in order to get through the judgment, we must have someone standing in our stead who has never transgressed, who has never broken the law, and who has spotless garments. We do—Jesus Christ, upon whom the condemnation of our sins was poured out 2,000 years ago. Because of Christ alone there is "no condemnation" for us, both now and in the judgment.

This crucial aspect, that of Christ as our substitute, is not usually explained in teachings about the pre-Advent judgment. Yet you can no more understand that judgment without the Cross than you can understand the earthly Day of Atonement without the sacrifice of the animal. During the typical Day of Atonement, to go into the Most Holy Place without blood would lead to physical death; during the antitypical one, to teach the judgment without blood, Christ's blood, leads only to spiritual death.

Perhaps for many Seventh-day Adventists the biggest cause of perplexity and discouragement regarding the judgment has been selected Ellen White quotes regarding the character of the final generation, those who are alive when the judgment ends.

First, no matter who these people are or how purified they have become, even by the power of the Holy Spirit, each one has still broken God's law. They are all sinners, and thus none of them have any righteousness, in and of themselves, to be able to stand successfully in the judgment. Their good works—even those done under the unction and power of the Holy Spirit—can't save them. To teach anything else is to teach that everyone is saved by grace except the final generation, which gets there by works.

"God has only one criterion for salvation," wrote Beatrice S. Neall, "faith in the merits of a crucified Savior. Justification alone is our title to heaven. For God to change the requirements on the last generation would be unjust."[2]

What saves those living at the end of time is what saves all of Christ's true followers in every generation: Jesus lifting His wounded hands before the Father and saying, "I have graven them on the palms of my hands." Christ, as his or her substitute alone, is the only hope of everyone, including the final generation.

But what about a statement like this? "Those who are living upon the earth when the intercession of Christ shall cease in the sanctuary above are to stand in the sight of a holy God without a mediator. Their robes must be spotless, their characters must be purified from sin by the blood of the sprinkling."[3] Doesn't that contradict the idea that it's Christ alone as their substitute who gets them through the judgment?

No! Look at the time element in that quote. Christ's intercession has ceased. This means that the names of these people have already come up in judgment. Jesus, having been judged in their stead at the cross, has already stood in their place and pleaded His blood in their behalf. By this time their sins have been blotted out in the same way that the sins of every generation are blotted out—Christ standing before the Father and presenting His perfect righteousness in place of their "filthy rags." We mustn't confuse the means of salvation (Christ as our substitute) with the result (Christ in us). Whatever the character of the final generation is, whatever standard of obedience and biblical perfection they reach, what saves them in the judgment is what saves the thief on the cross (or anyone else, for that matter), and that is Jesus Christ as their perfect substitute.

Some, of course, want to use this good news as an excuse for sin, which perverts the gospel just as much as, if not more than, teaching the judgment without the Cross does. Every sin we commit—even those we repent of—leaves an opening through which Satan can enter and deceive us. The more we sin, the more we fall, and the more opportunities the enemy has to turn us away from Christ. Satan knows that the only way he can destroy us is to lure us into sin and leave us there, for by doing so he will surely sever us from a saving relationship with Christ. Sin hardens us and desensitizes us to good and evil, right and wrong, and sooner or later Satan can use our sin to turn us away from Christ, whether we ever realize it or not. Satan succeeded so well with Judas—who was so deceived by his sin that he thought he was helping Christ by betraying Him—that he is using the same tactic on each of us as well.

Part of the good news, however, is not only pardon but also power. The key is a daily total surrender of self to Christ, claiming His promises of strength when tempted, His promises of forgiveness when betrayed, the whole time leaning only upon the merits of Christ, who 2,000 years ago faced the condemnation of our sins so that we—sinful, fallen transgressors—don't have to face that condemnation in the judgment.

Here is the essential truth, both of the gospel and the judgment. For the sake of untold thousands, maybe millions, among us, the judgment must never be taught without the Cross at its foundation. To learn one without the other is to pervert both.

Sadly, as my wife's words showed, it's a lesson we haven't learned yet.

---

[1] *The Great Controversy*, 484.
[2] Beatrice S. Neall, "Sealed Saints and the Tribulation," in *Symposium on Revelation—Book I*, ed. Frank Holbrook (Silver Spring, Md.: Biblical Research Institute, 1992), 267.
[3] *The Great Controversy*, 425.

This article originally appeared in the *Adventist Review*, August 1996.

CHAPTER EIGHT

Dressed for Success

Some say that the world will end in fire, others in ice. Both are wrong. It will end in light.

Jesus compared His second advent to lightning that is visible across the whole sky (Matt. 24:27), and Paul wrote that Jesus, at His return, will destroy the antichrist power "with the brightness of his coming" (2 Thess. 2:8, KJV).

Of course, the return of Jesus brings about not only the end of the antichrist but also the end of the world. So, for many people, His return will not be good news, since it brings their destruction (see, e.g., Rev. 19:11-21). For others, though, it will be the beginning of an eternity of bliss in an existence where sin, suffering, and death no longer reign (see Rev. 21, 22).

What makes the difference? Who, at the end of the world, will rejoice in Christ's coming, and who will be destroyed? Considering the momentous issues, these are two questions for which we ought to have answers. Fortunately, in the parable of the wedding feast, Jesus gave the answers.

A Wedding Banquet

"The kingdom of heaven," Jesus began, "is like a king who prepared a wedding banquet for his son. He sent his servants to those who had been invited to the banquet to tell them to come, but they refused to come" (Matt. 22:2, 3, NIV).

In this prophetic parable, Jesus pictured a wedding banquet. It was a king who was hosting the banquet; an invitation to share the joyful occasion with him, then, was no small honor. The servants who carried the invitations represented anyone God used—clergy or laity—to bring others to a saving relationship with Jesus Christ. Since God Himself initiated the gospel, the imagery is fitting: The call to salvation isn't a cheap gimmick to get people to join a religion; it's an appeal from the Lord

Himself, an invitation to be among those whom He will redeem for Himself at the end of the world.

Unfortunately, those who were invited didn't heed the invitation. When they didn't come, the king tried again: "Then he sent some more servants and said, 'Tell those who have been invited that I have prepared my dinner: My oxen and fattened cattle have been butchered, and everything is ready. Come to the wedding banquet' " (verse 4).

What incredible patience and love God has! This parable shows that He—knowing the horror, the terror, the eternal consequences that await those who refuse to come—is determined to call as many as possible. He even tries to entice us with the future glories (represented by the dinner) we can enjoy if only we will heed the call.

However, Jesus said, even with the second round of servants, those on the guest list still "paid no attention" to the call. Some were too busy with their farms and businesses. Others responded more violently to the king's invitation; they seized his "servants, mistreated them and killed them" (verse 6). The king ends these people's role in the story by bringing them to justice (see verse 7).

Both Good and Bad

But there's still a wedding to celebrate, a feast to be enjoyed—and to have a feast, a proper celebration, one needs guests. So the king sent servants out once again to find people to celebrate with him.

"Go to the street corners and invite to the banquet anyone you find."
So the servants went out into the streets and gathered all the people they could find, both good and bad, and the wedding hall was filled with guests (verses 9, 10).

With these words, Jesus portrayed the spreading of the gospel into all the world. He apparently anticipated that many would respond, because His parable pictured the wedding furnished with guests. But Jesus then said something unusual. He said that both "good and bad" came to the feast. What did He mean by that?

The history of the church—from its earliest days right up to today—shows that not all those who profess Christ, who claim to be Christians, exemplify His life and teachings. The Crusades, the Inquisition, the shooting of abortion doctors—all done by those who have responded to the invitation—prove the truth of Christ's words. History testifies that both "good and bad" have come to the wedding feast.

Jesus then said:
When the king came in to see the guests, he noticed a man there who was not wearing wedding clothes. "Friend," he asked, "how did you get here without wedding clothes?" The man was speechless.
Then the king told the attendants, "Tie him hand and foot, and throw him outside, into the darkness, where there will be weeping and gnashing of teeth. For many are invited, but few are chosen" (verses 11-14).

What Jesus represented here is the final judgment of His church—those who have, for better or worse, come to the wedding feast. Though much debate exists over the nature of this judgment, one thing seems clear: Prior to Christ's second advent, there will be a judgment involving those who have professed to follow the Lord.

The New Testament indicates that all who profess Christ will face a final judgment session. The author of the book of Hebrews wrote: "The Lord will judge his people" (Heb. 10:30, NIV). Peter wrote, "It is time for judgment to begin with the family of God; and if it begins with us, what will the outcome be for those who do not obey the gospel of God?"(1 Pet. 4:17, NIV). And the apostle Paul, writing specifically to Christians, said, "We will all stand before God's judgment seat" (Rom. 14:10, NIV).

The prophet Daniel helps us place the time of this judgment. He described a scene he saw, in vision, unfolding in heaven. Thousands upon thousands of beings stood before God, he said, and "The court was seated, and the books were opened" (Dan. 7:10, NIV). Daniel mentioned the judgment three times—and interestingly enough, after each mention, he wrote next of the ushering in of God's kingdom, which happens at the end of the world (or Christ's second coming, in other words).

Whatever the details, then, prior to Christ's return, there is a judgment that results in the establishment of God's kingdom.

Proper Attire

The most crucial aspect of this judgment—for those who profess to serve Christ, anyway—has to do with the wedding clothes Jesus spoke of in His parable. Those who have them remain at the wedding; those clad in something else are cast where there is "weeping and gnashing of teeth," a phrase Jesus used to describe the final punishment of the wicked. The old expression "Clothes make the man" holds more truth than anyone would have supposed—at least when it comes to wedding clothes and the final judgment!

What are these clothes that literally make a difference for eternity? In the Bible, the righteousness of Jesus Christ is often represented as a garment given to those who follow Him, not just in name but in deed too. "I counsel you to buy from me . . . white clothes to wear, so you can cover your shameful nakedness," Scripture records Jesus as saying (Rev. 3:18, NIV). And it says that the church is to put on "fine linen, bright and clean," "without stain or wrinkle or any other blemish." This fine linen, it adds, "stands for the righteous acts of the saints" (Rev. 19:8; Eph. 5:27, NIV).

Some debate whether this righteousness is that which is *credited* to Christians because of their faith in Christ or that which is actually *exhibited* in their lives and characters as a result of their faith in Christ. Actually, it must be both. Christians must have the perfect righteousness of Christ credited to them—a righteousness that comes through faith, "apart from works" (Rom. 4:6, NIV). But that faith relationship that Christians have with Christ will inevitably result in their lives actually reflecting His righteousness as well. So when someone's life doesn't reflect Christ's righteousness, that fact reveals that that person doesn't have the relationship with Christ necessary to being credited with His righteousness.

As one scholar put it, one doesn't need to have the wedding garment of personal righteousness *to be invited to* the party—both the good and the bad were invited. But one has to have the garment of personal righteousness *to stay at* the party.

In other words, through this parable Jesus was teaching that He will accept us as we are, no matter how dirty and defiled our clothes. But He was also saying that we must allow Him to give us a change of clothes, one that results in a changed life. Though not explicit in the parable, it was the king who supplied the wedding clothes. Only the Lord can supply the righteousness He requires. We must be willing to accept what's offered. If we're not, on Judgment Day, our works will reveal the falsity of our faith, and we will be cast out.

We are living in the last days just prior to the Second Coming, the time when the King comes to see His guests. And what this parable has to say to us is clear. Salvation isn't a matter of just showing up at the party. A mere profession of faith isn't good enough. Warming pews, singing hymns, and throwing a few dollars into the collection plate isn't the essence of following Jesus. When Jesus returns, He expects to have a people prepared to meet Him, a people covered by righteousness that is not only credited to them but that also is reflected in their lives and characters.

In this prophetic parable, in other words, Jesus explains that in order to meet Him at the end of the world, we must have a righteousness that, in and of ourselves, we can never acquire, a righteousness that comes only by faith. This faith, which clings to what Jesus accomplished at His first coming, prepares us for the time when—in a blaze of light—He will reclaim us when He returns.

This article originally appeared in *Signs of the Times,*® September 1996.

CHAPTER NINE

The Full and Final Display

Why are we still here? It's been 2,000 years since Christ "died for us" (Rom. 5:8), "redeemed us from the curse of the law" (Gal. 3:13), and cried, "It is finished!"

The answer is that the great controversy involves more than humanity's redemption accomplished at Calvary or the reconciliation of humanity to God or even the Cross itself. The issues regarding sin, rebellion, and God's law include the entire intelligent universe, which has a stake in the resolution of the conflict. Only by grasping this cosmic perspective can we explain the continuance of evil long after Christ's victory in our behalf.

Abraham on Moriah

One hint of the universe's interest in the plan of salvation appears in the aborted sacrifice on Mount Moriah. After the command to offer Isaac as a burnt offering, Abraham binds him on the altar; as he lifts the knife to slay the boy, an "angel of the Lord" cries out, "Lay not thine hand upon the lad, neither do thou any thing unto him: *for now I know that thou fearest God*" (Gen. 22:12).

The angel testified that he learned something new about Abraham: Abraham feared God. Had the angel reason to doubt? Abraham had lied to Pharaoh about the identity of his wife, and he took Hagar to produce a child rather than believe God's promise that Sarah would be "a mother of nations; [that] kings of people shall be of her" (Gen.17:16). Now, after Abraham placed his son upon the altar and lifted the knife, any doubts that the angel might have harbored about Abraham's faith vanished.

"The sacrifice required of Abraham was not alone for his own good," wrote Ellen White, "nor solely for the benefit of succeeding generations; but it was also for the instruction of the sinless intelligences of heaven and of other worlds. The field of the controversy between Christ and Satan—the field on which the plan of redemption is wrought out—is the lesson book of the universe. . . . Heavenly beings were witnesses of the scene as the faith of Abraham and the submission of Isaac were tested. . . . All heaven beheld with wonder and admiration Abraham's unfaltering obedience."[1]

The angel's declaration "For now I know that thou fearest God" reveals the cosmic interest in what happens on the earth, "the lesson book of the universe." This idea appears in Job too. Satan twice accused the patriarch before the onlooking "sons of God" (Job 1:6; 2:1), so these cosmic beings must have witnessed the drama on earth. Paul reinforced this reality of the universe's interest in what happens here when he wrote, "We are made a spectacle unto the world, and *to angels*, and to men" (1 Cor. 4:9).

Jesus on the Cross

Why is the onlooking universe interested in what happens here, and what role did the Cross play in answering their question?

"The plan of redemption," wrote Ellen White, "had a yet broader and deeper purpose than the salvation of man. It was not for this alone that Christ came to the earth; it was not merely that the inhabitants of this little world might regard the law of God as it should be regarded; but it was to vindicate the character of God before the universe."[2]

Satan disparaged God's character, raising questions about His government, law, and justice. Christ came to "vindicate the character of God before the universe."

Did the universe, then, have all questions about the character of God resolved by the life and death of Jesus? Heavenly beings saw their beloved Commander beaten, scourged, mocked, and spat upon. They saw the One whom they praised in His celestial glory, condemned by His own creation. They witnessed the greatest example of selfless love ever manifested in the history of eternity. Nevertheless, not all the universe's questions about good and evil, right and wrong, law and justice, were yet answered. "His intent was that now, through the church, the manifold wisdom of God should be made known *to the rulers and authorities in the heavenly realms*" (Eph. 3:10, NIV).

After describing Christ's death and explaining how Satan was exposed as a murderer and had "uprooted himself from the sympathies of the heavenly beings," Ellen wrote that nevertheless, "Satan was not then destroyed. The angels *did not even then understand all that was involved in the great controversy.* The principles at stake were to be more fully revealed. And for the sake of man, Satan's existence must be continued. Man as well as angels must see the contrast between the Prince of light and the prince of darkness."[3]

This idea doesn't diminish the reality that the full and complete penalty was paid for sin by Jesus in our behalf at the cross. Nor does it compromise the promise that every sinner, no matter what his or her sin, can be accepted and fully pardoned by what Jesus accomplished on the cross. And it certainly does not weaken the incomprehensible love manifested at Calvary. Instead, it proves that the whole universe awaits the final disposal of all issues regarding the great controversy.

Of course, the sovereignty of the King of the universe does not depend upon human fidelity. "What then? If some did not believe, their unbelief will not nullify the faithfulness of God, will it? May it never be! Rather, let God be found true, though every man be found a liar" (Rom. 3:3, 4, NASB). In His infinite wisdom and foresight, the Lord has chosen to use fallen humanity as part of His plan to resolve the great controversy in an open and fair manner that will forever answer Satan's charges. Yet His vindication does not have to depend upon us. Rather, the Lord knew what He would be able to do in His people, and He will accomplish His purposes in them (see Phil. 1:6). If, however, within the limits the Lord has set for Himself in dealing with sin, He could not have used humanity, then He would have found another way to satisfy the question raised before the onlooking universe.

The Manifold Wisdom of God

Nevertheless, the Lord has chosen to use His church to help resolve the great controversy. But how?

"Let your light so shine before men, that they may see your good works, and glorify your Father which is in heaven" (Matt. 5:16). "Herein is my Father glorified," He said, "that ye bear much fruit" (John 15:8). "And [he] said unto me, Thou art my servant, O Israel, in whom I will be glorified" (Isa. 49:3).

These verses prove that God is glorified by the loyal works and the character development of His people.

"Sing, O ye heavens: for the Lord hath done it: shout, ye lower parts of the earth: break forth into singing, ye mountains, O forest, and every tree therein: for the Lord hath redeemed Jacob, and glorified Himself in Israel" (Isa. 44:23; see also Isa. 61:3; Ezek. 36:22; Isa. 60:21).

"The honor of God," Ellen White writes, "the honor of Christ, is *involved* in the perfection of the character of His people."[4]

Notice the verb she used: "involved." The character of God's people is not the only factor dealing with the honor of God. Though the Cross by far forms the focus and center of the gospel, the plan of salvation itself involves questions that extend beyond merely getting us off the planet. The real concern deals with the character of God Himself. Is He fair and just, and does He deserve the worship, loyalty, and adoration of His creation? The Lord wants to use His people—who have a born-again experience that connects them to their only source of power (see John 15:5; Phil. 2:12; Col. 1:27)—to help answer these questions.

"It becomes every child of God," writes Ellen White, "to vindicate His [God's] character."[5] We can vindicate Him, however, only because of the cross. Vindication comes only as we surrender ourselves daily to the provisions of salvation made available to us by the merits of what Jesus accomplished for us at Calvary. No human glory is involved.

This concept is inseparably tied to the three angels' messages: "And I saw another angel fly in the midst of heaven, having the *everlasting gospel* . . . , saying with a loud voice, Fear God, and *give glory to him*; for the hour of his judgment is come" (Rev. 14:6, 7). They start out with "the everlasting gospel," which has its foundation in the Cross. Then we are to give "glory to God," and we can do that only by a conversion experience that results in obedience, which is why the third angel's message says, "Here is the patience of the saints: here are they that keep the commandments of God, and the faith of Jesus" (Rev. 14:12). Only by faith in Jesus can God's people remain loyal in keeping His commandments and thus glorify God before men and angels.

The Hour of His Judgment

The first angel's cry that "the hour of His judgment is come" (Rev. 14:7) means not just that God is judging but that He Himself is being judged: the hour of *His* judgment is come (perhaps one reason why we are told to give Him glory).

In Psalm 51 David's plea for mercy, cleansing, and the blotting out of his sins is interpreted with a parenthetical section: "For I acknowledge my transgressions: and my sin is ever before me. Against thee, thee only, have I sinned, and done this evil in thy sight" (verses 3, 4). Without that section the verses read: "Have mercy upon me, O God, according to thy lovingkindness: unto the multitude of thy tender mercies blot out my transgressions. Wash me thoroughly from mine iniquity, and cleanse me from my sin. . . . *That thou mightest be justified when thou speakest, and be clear when thou judgest.*"

Paul quotes from this psalm: "God forbid: yea, let God be true, but every man a liar; as it is written, That thou mightest be justified in thy sayings, and mightest overcome when thou art judged" (Rom. 3:4). Today's English Version reads: "You must be shown to be right when you speak; you must win your case when *you are being tried.*"

Though the immediate context of Psalm 51 was David's repentance after his fling with Bathsheba, the mention of the blotting out of sins and the idea of God "*being tried*" evokes the idea of the *pre-Advent judgment*, when God allows Himself to be "tried" by how He judges us. The pre-Advent judgment scene of Daniel 7, when the "judgment was set, and the books were opened" (verse 10), occurs before "thousand thousands . . . and ten thousand times ten thousand" heavenly beings, who witness the judgment in heaven.

The cry that "the hour of his judgment is come" in Revelation 14:7 is heard prior to the close of probation, because it is immediately followed by the warning against the mark of the beast and a call to keep God's commandments. However, in Revelation 15, after the "temple of the tabernacle of the testimony in heaven was opened [which is the second apartment of the heavenly sanctuary, where judgment occurs] . . . seven angels came out of the temple, having the seven plagues" (verses 5, 6). By this time judgment must have already ended and probation closed. Now the angels, having left the heavenly edifice, release these horrible scourges upon unrepentant humanity. Having witnessed the judgment scene itself, they are convinced of God's justice and mercy, which is why they cry out, "Thou art righteous, O Lord, which art, and wast, and shalt be, *because thou has judged thus*" (Rev. 16:5). No wonder the Bible says, "But the Lord of hosts shall be exalted in judgment" (Isa. 5:16).

All through Revelation this cosmic perspective appears. Heavenly beings are seen worshiping God before His throne. "Holy, holy, holy," the four beasts cry, "Lord God Almighty, which was, and is, and is to come" (Rev. 4:8). Using imagery from the judgment of Daniel 7, John writes of angels around the throne of God: "And the number of them was ten thousand times ten thousand, and thousands of thousands; saying with a loud voice, Worthy is the Lamb that was slain to receive power, and riches, and wisdom, and strength, and honor, and glory and blessing" (Rev. 5:11, 12).

Only with the cosmic perspective does the investigative judgment even make sense. The Lord doesn't need the judgment to know "them that are his" (2 Tim. 2:19) any more than He needed Mount Moriah to know the depth of Abraham's faith. Heavenly intelligences, though, are not omniscient, and they didn't know Abraham's heart any more than they know all the issues in the great controversy. The investigative judgment, by revealing more, is part of God's overall plan to deal with sin and rebellion in a fair and just way that will answer their questions forever.

For this reason, the sanctuary in heaven is real—not because God needs it for Himself but because the heavenly intelligences need it to witness how God deals with sin and the process by which He saves sinners. Through the sanctuary God allows the onlooking universe to clearly see another step in resolving the great controversy.

"In the judgment of the universe," writes Ellen White, "God will stand clear of blame for the existence or continuance of evil."[6]

The Full and Final Display

This cosmic perspective helps make sense of the antitypical day of atonement as well. In the earthly type the sanctuary was cleansed, symbolic of the pre-Advent judgment, when the heavenly sanctuary is cleansed as well (see Dan. 8:14). In the earthly system, however, not just the sanctuary was cleansed—the people were too!

"This shall be a statute for ever unto you: that in the seventh month, on the tenth day of the month, ye shall afflict your souls, . . . for on that day shall the priest make an atonement for you, to *cleanse you*, that you may be *clean* from *all your sins* before the Lord" (Lev. 16:29, 30).

The sanctuary structure itself was cleansed "from the iniquities of the children of Israel," while the people themselves were to be "clean from *all* your sins before the Lord." Thus, this once-a-year ritual produced a clean sanctuary and a clean people together: "He shall make an atonement for the holy sanctuary, and he shall make an atonement for the tabernacle of the congregation, and for the altar, and he shall make an atonement for the priests, and for all the people of the congregation" (verse 33).

Besides the Cross, the Lord is using two factors to help clarify issues in the great controversy: the character development of His people and the investigative judgment. On the Day of Atonement both these elements climax. God will have a clean people on earth who, because they have allowed God to cleanse them from their sin, bring honor and glory to Him; simultaneously, in heaven, when the sanctuary *is cleansed of sin* during the judgment, God is glorified too. *The Day of Atonement is the only time when both these elements happen at once in a grand and glorious climax before the onlooking universe!*

Besides the cleansing that occurred in the sanctuary itself, symbolic of the heavenly judgment, the earthly *Yom Kippur* was an example in miniature of what God is going to have *en masse*: a faithful people who glorify Him before the onlooking universe. If one person can glorify God by his or her character development ("Herein is my Father glorified, that ye bear much fruit" [John 15:8]), how much more a whole generation? What God did to the people themselves in ancient Israel in type on a small scale symbolized what God wants to do *to His modern* people in reality on a grand scale. This demonstration of the love of God climaxes the plan of salvation, when *the issues are resolved* enough in the minds of the unfallen universe so that God can *justly pour out devastating plagues* upon the planet and at the same time resurrect and translate untold masses into the presence of sinless beings.

"The church," wrote Ellen White, "is the repository of the riches of the grace of Christ; and through the church will eventually be made manifest, 'even to the principalities and powers in heavenly places,' the final and full display of the love of God."[7]

Final Generation

Unfortunately, the idea of a final, faithful generation is usually taught in the context of soteriology and perfectionism, not eschatology. Whatever character the final generation form, however strictly they "keep the commandments of God" and exercise the "faith in Jesus" (Rev. 14:12), they are saved only by what saved the thief on the cross: the righteousness that Jesus wrought for them, in place of them, outside of them, 2,000 years ago at Calvary. Anything else is salvation by works. God is not trying to perfect a generation holy enough to earn their way to heaven; rather, He seeks those who by beholding Him will reflect His character and remain loyal in a manner that will honor and glorify Him before the onlooking universe.

Obedience to the law, or even character perfection, can never blot out sin. Only

Christ's substitutionary righteousness can. Obedience comes when we love God and want to glorify Him before the onlooking universe. "For this is the love of God, that we keep his commandments" (1 John 5:3).

The Big Picture

Only against the backdrop of this cosmic panorama does Adventism work. The Cross and the reconciliation it brought make better sense only in the context of God displaying both justice and mercy before the onlooking universe. Christ's high priestly ministry in a literal sanctuary, including the pre-Advent judgment, becomes more meaningful when understood as another step in ending the great controversy in an open and fair manner before heavenly intelligences. The emphasis on a loyal remnant and faithful generation—studied in the context of the universe's questions about God's law, justice, and mercy—far from conflicting with the truth of justification by faith, take that truth to its grand conclusion.

Perhaps the most important aspect of the cosmic dimension, from a human perspective, is motive. How much better to strive for holiness, not as fire insurance but out of love for God and a desire to glorify Him before humanity and angels.

We may then expect that the final generation will be composed of those who are so moved by Christ's sacrifice that they determine to obey Him, no matter the costs so that "the name of our Lord Jesus Christ may be glorified in [them]" (2 Thess. 1:12).

---

[1] Ellen G. White, *Patriarchs and Prophets* (Washington, D.C.: Review and Herald Pub. Assn., 1958), 154, 155.

[2] *Ibid.*, 68.

[3] ———, *The Desire of Ages*, (Nampa, Idaho: Pacific Press® Pub. Assn., 1940), 761.

[4] *Ibid.*, 671.

[5] ———, *Testimonies for the Church* (Nampa, Idaho: Pacific Press® Pub. Assn., 1911), 5:317.

[6] ———, *The Desire of Ages*, 58.

[7] ———, *The Acts of the Apostles* (Nampa, Idaho: Pacific Press® Pub. Assn., 1911), 9.

Unless otherwise noted, all Scripture quotations are taken from the King James Version, and all emphasis in quotations is supplied by the author. This article originally appeared in *Ministry*, October 1994.

The Constantine Connection

The following thirteen articles cover a favorite SDA topic: prophecy. In reading these articles, one can see how the world has changed in the past ten years, and— surprise of surprises!—how it has changed in a direction that fits our understanding of last-day events.

"Communists, Catholics, and Adventists," published in the *Adventist Review* in 1990, talked about my surprise one morning to open the newspaper and see "Mikhail Gorbachev, leader of the world's number one Communist nation," talking face to face in the Vatican with Pope John Paul II, and the possible prophetic implications of that amazing meeting.

"Iraq in Prophecy," published in the *Adventist Review* during the Gulf War frenzy, touched the often sticky issue about the nation of Israel, even the Middle East as a whole, in Bible prophecy. Few articles ever got me more hate mail, both from SDAs and non-SDAs, who didn't appreciate my spin on the war as it related to prophecy (and my position that it *didn't* relate to prophecy)."

Another *Adventist Review* article, "The Catholic-Protestant Connection," recounts my adventure on the Washington mall during one of these hyped-up Washington for Jesus rallies and how fascinating it was to watch, right before my eyes, Protestants and Catholics put aside their differences in order to unite for common political goals. Along that same line, the article "Truth Matters," published years later in *Liberty*, takes that same theme, showing how readily Protestants are compromising doctrine in order to ally themselves with Roman Catholics, all in order to achieve a political unity. Few articles published in *Liberty* have ever drawn such a response as this one, including a fifty-page letter by a zealous Roman Catholic attempting to convince me that his church was the only true one (don't worry, the letter isn't in this compilation).

CHAPTER TEN

Antichrist

Ever since the apostle John wrote that "antichrist shall come" (1 John 2:18), Christians have speculated about its identity. The early church thought it was the Romans. The medievals feared that antichrist was the Hussites, the Wycliffites, the Ottoman Turks, or the Jews. Luther and the Protestant Reformers named papal Rome as antichrist. Spanish Jesuit Francisco Ribera rid papal Rome of the stigma by identifying antichrist as a still unknown end-time personage or power, a scenario bought by today's evangelical world. Current speculators about antichrist encompass Henry Kissinger, secular humanism, Communism, the Trilateral Commission, the Illuminati, Ronald Reagan, the European Common Market, and even a computer in Belgium.

Though history shows that God's people have suffered from outside oppressors— such as Egyptians, Babylonians, Greeks, and Romans—some believe that the antichrist will rise from within Christendom itself!

And with good reason. Indeed, the word *antichrist* may mean not only "against Christ" but "in the place of Christ." Thus the apostle Paul warns that antichrist "opposeth and exalteth himself above all that is called God, or that is worshipped; so that he as God sitteth in the temple of God, shewing himself that he is God" (2 Thess. 2:4). This power does not openly defy God; instead, antichrist purports to speak for God and take His prerogatives.

While Christians disagree over the identity of antichrist, all agree that ancient Israel was the true church of the Old Testament. Yet read what Jesus said of it: "Wherefore ye be witnesses unto yourselves, that ye are the children of them which killed the prophets. . . . I send unto you prophets, and wise men, and scribes; and some of them ye shall kill and crucify; and some of them shall ye scourge in your synagogues, and persecute them from city to city: that upon you may come all the righteous blood shed upon the earth, from the blood of righteous Abel unto the blood of Zacharias son of Barachias whom ye slew between the temple and the altar. . . . O Jerusalem, Jerusalem, thou that killest the prophets . . ." (Matt. 23:31-37).

Israel's history proves the truth of Jesus' words. Many of the prophets "were stoned," . . . were sawn asunder, . . . were slain with the sword" (Heb. 11:37)—by the Israelites themselves! Jesus warned that their treachery would continue—and it did. They killed Him too.

These crimes were not committed by sun-worshiping Babylonians, child-sacrificing Moabites, or heathen idolaters—but God's own people!

And what of the Christian church as it carried the gospel into the world? After a few centuries the church and paganism, like an innocent youth and a prostitute, united. For more than a thousand years the great truths of salvation were repressed by the ones commissioned to preach them. Meanwhile those who adhered to the Bible were accused of heresy, blasphemy, and sedition; they were hunted, branded, exiled, and slain—all in the name of Jesus.

Daniel, writing about this antichrist power almost a thousand years before it existed, warned that it would make "war with the saints" (Dan. 7:21). John the revelator in the first century repeated the same warning about the same power: "And it was given unto him to make war with the saints, and to overcome them" (Rev. 13:7).

This persecuting power was not the Ottoman Turks from the south, Attila the Hun from the east, or the Vikings from the north—*it was the church!*

Today Christians assume that antichrist will arise outside the stained-glass windows of their sanctuaries, but historically the danger has arisen from the pew and pulpit within. Those commissioned to spread the gospel will once again be the very ones who in the name of God suppress it.

Jesus warned that "It is not everyone who keeps saying to me 'Lord, Lord' who will enter the kingdom of Heaven, but the man who actually does my Heavenly Father's will. In 'that day' many will say to me, 'Lord, Lord, didn't we preach in your name, didn't we cast out devils in your name, and do many great things in your name?' Then I shall tell them plainly, 'I have never known you. Go away from me, you have worked on the side of evil!' " (Matt. 7:21-23, Phillips).*

This warning was not addressed to secular humanists, Communists, Henry Kissinger, or the Trilateral Commission; they do not cast out demons in Christ's name. Christians do. And Jesus says that many of them are not with Him. "He that is not with me," He adds, "is against me" (12:30).

Of course, not all Christians will align with antichrist, just as all Jews did not kill Christ. Is there a litmus test to tell who'll be on whose side?

God describes His remnant and their characteristics as they will be seen at the height of antichrist's reign: "And the dragon [Satan] was wroth with the woman [the church], and went to make war with the remnant of her seed [the last-day faithful], which keep the commandments of God, and have the testimony of Jesus" (Rev.12:17).

Again, "the Revelation of Jesus Christ" (1:1) reveals the last-day faithful in direct contrast to those who receive the antichrist's mark (14:9-11): "Here is the patience [or endurance] of the saints: here are they that keep the commandments of God, and the faith of Jesus" (verse 12).

The marks of the antichrist's followers are plain:

They will persecute the followers of Christ.

They will disobey the commandments of God.

They will lack the testimony of Jesus (called in Rev. 19:10 "the spirit of prophecy").

They will not endure.

They will not have faith.

If these marks characterize you, beware! Heed the adage, "We have met the enemy—and he is us."

---

*From J. B. Phillips: *The New Testament in Modern English*, Revised Edition, © J. B. Phillips 1958, 1960, 1972. Used by permission of Macmillan Publishing Co., Inc.

Unless otherwise noted, Scripture quotations are taken from the King James Version. This article originally appeared in *Liberty*, May/June 1985.

CHAPTER ELEVEN

The Constantine Connection

Constantine reigned more than fifteen hundred years ago in a culture and era much different from ours. Yet parallels exist between what happened under Constantine and what is happening today as the Christian Right brings church and state together in America. Indeed, the steps seem so similar that one might see where the union of church and state would lead America, by reviewing where it has led Rome.

Historians agree that Constantine was a shrewd, calculating politician, one who understood the signs of the times and acted accordingly. "He was distinguished by that genuine political wisdom," wrote historian Philip Schaff, "which, putting itself at the head of the age, clearly saw that idolatry had outlived itself in the Roman Empire, and that Christianity alone could breathe new vigor into it."[1] Constantine united himself to the church because he needed it politically. "Therefore, that I may enjoy a happy life and reign, I will . . . join myself to the cause of the Christians," he said, "who are growing daily, while the heathen are diminishing."[2] The church, meanwhile, used the state to further its own ends.

"There was another line along which Constantine pursued the task of bringing Church and State together," wrote historian Andrew Alflodi. "He called Christians in ever-increasing numbers to the higher administrative posts of the empire."[3] Of course, not everyone he placed was a devout Christian. (Constantine—by having his wife, son, and brother-in-law murdered—left some doubts about his own Christian experience.) Though he preferred Christians, he would accept loyal pagans for government jobs.

According to Eusebius, non-Christian soldiers in Constantine's army were paraded to a field where, "uplifting their hands toward heaven," they had to recite a prayer asking God to bless them and the nation.

Schaff wrote that many of Constantine's "laws and regulations breathed of the spirit of Christian justice and humanity."[4] He even passed a series of "pro-family" decrees that helped stop infanticide (a common practice when parents had babies they didn't want or felt they couldn't care for). He also made laws that attempted to bring morality into the empire.

Constantine believed that he had a divine mandate to rule the nation. He believed that he was called to save his people from "the deadly pestilence of utter corruption" and thus save the empire from the wrath of God. He erected Christian symbols on government property. He gave the churches government funds and even made the world's first Sunday law. Constantine, no doubt, wanted a Christian empire. He got it; Christianity became the dominant power in the state.

Today the American government is increasingly aligning itself for political reasons "to the cause of the Christians." Polls indicate that a full 40 percent of American adults claim to be "born again." Add more than fifty million Roman Catholics to these largely evangelical Christians, give them a common cause, and Christians could become the dominant political force in America, a possibility the government sees. How else could one explain the prominence of James Robison and W. A. Criswell at the 1984 Republican convention? Why did Ronald Reagan, before the 1984 election, say that "politics and religion are necessarily related"? Why did Vice President George Bush—once an opponent of the fundamentalists—tell the first meeting of the Liberty Federation that "America is in crying need of the moral vision . . . this new organization will bring to America"?[5] Why are so many politicians espousing Judeo-Christian ethics and morality? Because, as Michael Carrington, of Christian Voice, explains, candidates "understand the ultimate ethic—getting elected."[6]

Meanwhile, just as in Constantine's day, the church is using the state to achieve its own ends. Says Gary Jarmin, of Christian Voice: "The Republican Party is a tool"[7] (though one wonders just who's using whom).

And just as in Constantine's day, Christians are being brought into the government in increasing numbers. The New Right is aggressively getting its people elected or appointed on local, state, and federal levels of the government. Perhaps the trend toward Christianizing the state was best epitomized by White House associate liaison director Carolyn Sundseth, who told White House staffers to "get saved or get out." But not every politician the New Right supports must be a devout believer. Loyal pagans will do, for now.

The New Right also wants morality back in America, and they have an agenda of "pro-family" legislation to bring it about. And, like Constantine, they would mandate prayer by law. The New Right believes that it has been called of God to save the state from corruption and from the wrath of God. The members want more government funds for religious functions and Christian symbols on government property; and one doesn't need great imagination to see the New Right pushing for a national Sunday law to help end America's decadence.

Yes, Christians may go too far, just as Constantine did. In attempting to remove secular humanist philosophy from public schools, they might make Christian philosophy dominant instead. Or because they view church-state separation as hostile to religion, they might seek to trash the entire concept. "I believe this notion of the separation of church and state," said prominent Baptist W. A. Criswell, "is the figment of some infidel's imagination."[8] Even Marion G. (Pat) Robertson, who's waiting for a nod from God before running for president, describes church-state separation as a "totalitarian concept."

Where will it all lead? Where did it all lead ancient Rome? Constantine at first promised "that liberty is to be denied to no one, . . . but that to each one freedom is to be given to devote his mind to that religion which he may think himself adapted."[9] Yet as one historian noted, "To affirm Christianity was to deny paganism."[10]

Eventually Constantine closed pagan temples, stopped pagan sacrifices, forbade divination, astrology, and magic. He began a systematic campaign to eradicate paganism, even though he had promised that everyone would be allowed to worship according to his own choice.

And it didn't stop with pagans. Constantine persecuted unorthodox Christians as well. In an imperial edict against Christian heretics, he warned: "All ye who devise and support heresies by means of your private assemblies, with what a tissue of falsehood and vanity, with what destructive and venomous errors, your doctrines are inseparably interwoven. . . . All your counsels are opposed to the truth, but familiar with deeds of baseness." "We give warning by this present statute that none of you henceforth presume to assemble yourselves together."[11] As the power of the church grew, those who didn't follow the official "line" were rooted out. His policy was continued by succeeding leaders; soon anyone dissenting from the "orthodox" faith was destroyed at the instigation of the church.

"The Falwells and the Robertsons may settle for a watered-down state-endorsed religion for the time being," warns church-state expert Dr. Stan Hastey. "But in the long haul, what they seek is a state dominated by the orthodox. And they will decide what is orthodox."[12]

By uniting his rule with the church, Constantine set in motion a repressive church-state regime that persecuted dissenters. America, by moving in the same direction, is in danger of creating a similar monster.

It has been said that those who forget history are doomed to repeat it. We have just been reminded of a little history.

---

[1] Philip Schaff, *History of the Christian Church* (Grand Rapids: Wm. B. Erdmans Co., 1902), 3:13.
[2] *Ibid.*, 20.
[3] Andrew Alflodi, *The Conversion of Constantine and Pagan Rome* (London: Oxford University Press, 1948), 49.

[4]Schaff, 16.

[5]"Bush, in undeclared candidacy, courts new Falwell Organization," Religious News Service, January 27, 1986, 1.

[6]Joseph Conn, "From Prayer to Power," *Church and State*, February 1986, 6.

[7]Sidney Blumenthal, "The Righteous Empire," *The New Republic*, October 22, 1984, 19.

[8]Jim Buie, "Praise the Lord and Pass the Ammunition," *Church and State*, October 1984, 6.

[9]Eusebius, "Church History," Book X, chapter v, in *Nicene and Post-Nicene Fathers*, second series, 1:379.

[10]Herman Doerries, *Constantine the Great* (New York: Harper and Row, 1972).

[11]Eusebius, "The Life of the Blessed Emperor Constantine," book III, chapters lxiv, lxv, in *Nicene and Post-Nicene Fathers*, 1:539.

[12]"Feminists and religious thinkers discuss 'threat' from the right," Religious News Service, January 14, 1986, 4.

This article originally appeared in *Liberty*, September/October 1986.

CHAPTER TWELVE

Iraq in Prophecy?

With Iraq's invasion of Kuwait, the Middle East has again seized the attention of the world.Prophecy students are scouring verses of Holy Writ in an attempt to find, hidden in the writing of the prophets, tomorrow's headlines.

Though for the most part Seventh-day Adventists have not been absorbed with the Middle East, in recent years many church members have accepted a theology that applies prophecies of Daniel and Revelation, as well as statements of Ellen White, to *current* events in the Middle East, such as the Iran-Iraq war, or most recently, the confrontation between the U.S. and Iraq over Kuwait. Are the events in the Middle East part of the present truth message that God has entrusted to Seventh-day Adventists? And what are the dangers to the church if this Middle East—centered interpretation is wrong?

Theology, Not Geography

No question, Bible stories that have dealt with salvation have focused almost entirely on the Middle East. But why? Was the land itself—the rocks, the trees, the hills, somehow, in and of itself, holy? Or was this emphasis placed on the Middle East simply because of who lived there?

"Now the Lord had said unto Abram, Get thee out of thy country, and from thy kindred, and from thy father's house, unto a land that I will shew thee. And I will make of thee a great nation" (Gen. 12:1, 2).

This great nation, of course, was ancient Israel, the Jews, who sat in the center of the civilized world. Travelers, merchants, wayfarers from Africa, Asia, and Europe would readily come in contact with this unique people who worshiped the Lord as God. With the Jews placed at the apex of civilization, the surrounding nations could learn about the true God, the Creator of heaven and earth.

The Middle East's importance, therefore, came not because of any mystical quality in the dirt but because God had centered His salvation activity for the world in Palestine by placing His ancient people there. Had for some reason the Lord sent them northward into Europe, then the Bible might have been filled with such names as Bonn, Paris, and London; not Jericho, Damascus, and Jerusalem!

The issue isn't geography, but theology. The Middle East was important because Israel was important, and Israel was important only because of its special relationship with the Lord. Israel alone—in a covenant with God—is what made the Middle East *at that time* the focus of the Bible.

Holy Land?

If the birth of Israel thousands of years ago in the Middle East made the area significant, then wouldn't its rebirth do the same there today too?

It depends. If the covenant promises made to ancient Israel are applicable to modern Israel, then yes, Israel's presence would again make the Middle East prophetically important. This view—that the covenant relationship to ancient Israel was unconditional and that it applies to the Jews as a corporate body even now—is dogma for many evangelists, which explains their obsession with the modern Hebrew union.

Adventists as a whole don't accept this understanding of the covenant. Repeatedly the promises in Scripture made to ancient Israel were conditional. "It shall come to pass, *if* thou shalt harken unto the voice of the Lord . . ." reads promise after promise. Israel as a political entity didn't obey the voice of God, and therefore the promises made to it *as a nation* were eventually invalidated. Instead, the promises went to the New Testament church, composed of Jews and Gentiles from all over the world. "You are a chosen people," Peter wrote to believers in various countries, "a royal priesthood, a holy nation, a people belonging to God, that you may declare the praises of him who called you out of darkness into his wonderful light" (1 Pet. 2:9, NIV).

Adventists believe that "if you are Christ's, then you are Abraham's seed, and heirs according to the promise" (Gal. 3:29, NKJV). Few among us believe that modern Israel enjoys the same covenant promises made to their ancestors. Instead, the remnant church—with the gospel, the sanctuary, the law, the health message—has taken the place of ancient Israel. Also, how many hundreds, if not thousands, of times has Ellen White referred to us as Israel or spiritual Israel?

What, then, is the significance of the return of the Jews to Palestine? It's important to them, of course—and after what the Jews have suffered, they certainly have the right to safe and secure borders. But does their presence make the Middle East holy or the center of biblical prophecy? If a large number of Jews makes a place sacred, then for years the holiest place on earth must have been Brooklyn!

The Middle East was significant *only* because God's people were there. Where are they now? In more than one hundred and eighty nations all over the world.

Therefore, why would the Bible now direct us toward the Middle East, when it is no longer the center of God's salvation activity for the world? The answer, of course, is that is doesn't. Nothing in Ellen White's writings ever points to the Middle East as the focus of last-day events.

Some, however, teach that they do. One proponent quotes Ellen White's statements that when the prophesies of Daniel and Revelation are understood as they should be, a great revival will happen among God's people. He then asserts that because all the prophecies of Daniel have been fulfilled, in order for Ellen White's statements to make sense Daniel has to be reinterpreted and its prophecies placed in the future.

This reasoning is false on two major points. To start, all the prophecies of Daniel have clearly *not* been fulfilled: "And in the days of these kings shall the God of heaven set up a kingdom, which shall never be destroyed" (Dan. 2:44). "And at that time shall Michael stand up, the great prince which standeth for the children of thy people: and there shall be a time of trouble, such as never was" (Dan. 2:1).Which of these events have already happened? (See also Dan. 7:27).

Also, Ellen White's statements about Daniel and Revelation don't automatically mean that the books need a future fulfillment. If, for example, Adventists understood 1844 and the investigative judgment the way they should, the way that the pioneers came to understand them, that alone could bring revival.

Faith Undermined

Actually, Ellen White warns against those who apply past prophecies to the future: "Some will take the truth applicable to their time, and place it in the future. *Events in the train of prophecy that had their fulfillment away in the past are made future, and thus by these theories the faith of some is undermined.*" She then describes in even more detail exactly what is being promoted within Adventism now: "From the light that the Lord has been pleased to give me, you are in danger of doing the same work, presenting before others truths which have had their place and done their specific work for the time, in the history of the faith of the people of God. You recognize these facts in Bible history as true, *but apply them to the future.* They have their force still in their proper place, in the chain of events that have made us a people what we are today." How accurately she describes those today who, while paying lip service to the historical Adventist interpretation of, for instance, Daniel 8, nevertheless place it in the future. The activities of the ram, the goat, and the little horn of that chapter— so crucial to Adventist interpretation—have now become Ayatollah Khomeini's Iran or Iraq or the United States involved in a Middle East conflict. The subtle, long-range effect of this type of interpretation can only, as Ellen White warned, undermine faith.

It's no coincidence that Daniel 8, unquestionably depicting "the chain of events that have made us as a people what we are today," is one chapter that has been subjected to much reinterpretation. Keeping in mind Ellen White's statement: "After this period of time, reaching from 1842 to 1844, there can be no definite tracing of *the* prophetic time," if we place all of Daniel 8 in the future, then we must place the 2300 days, the center of the chapter, in the future as well, with a date other than 1844 for the cleansing of the sanctuary, in verse 14. Also, because the 70-week prophecy of Daniel 9, which points to Jesus, is inextricably linked to the 2,300 days of Daniel 8, then it, too, must be given future dates as well. When many Adventists are not firmly rooted in our historical interpretation of these crucial prophecies to begin with, it's easy to see how these theories can destroy our message.

In recent years Adventists have suffered from a dearth of study and preaching on prophecy. As a result, many members feel a vacuum, a need. Someone then appears, quoting Ellen White, preaching orthodox Adventism (at least in certain areas), even doing a good work (such as printing and distributing Spirit of Prophecy books), and sincere saints, impressed by the apparent faithfulness of the ministry, let down their guards and get snagged in false theology. Satan will do anything to deceive us, and if he can have those who, while appearing to be faithful Adventists, introduce speculative theories that can subtly undermine the message—he will do it!

Of course, the situation in the Middle East is dangerous, and it could bring about an economic collapse that sets the stage for final events. But to take the precious prophecies that have given our church a distinct message and turn them into Saddam Hussein's battle plans is a perversion of historical Adventist interpretation, a misuse of Ellen White, and a subtle attempt at sabotaging the truth on which our church is founded.

This article originally appeared in the *Adventist Review*, October 4, 1990.

CHAPTER THIRTEEN

The Third Jerusalem Temple

World War III. It could start with the Red Army plunging into Western Europe, over oil in the Persian Gulf, from a superpower clash in a South American jungle, or by accident.

But over a mount in Jerusalem?

Snug in the corner of the Old Walled City is the Temple Mount. Once the home of the first and second temple, the Mount for centuries has been the site of the Dome of the Rock and the Al-Aks Mosque, which, outside Mecca and Medina, are Islam's holiest shrines. The Muslims control the Mount, and they have threatened a jihad, a holy war, against Israel—"an act that could easily trigger a worldwide war"[1]— if their control is jeopardized or the shrines damaged.

In March 1983, dozens of Jews were arrested for trying to blow up the Dome of the Rock. In January 1984, Israeli security thwarted an assault on the Mount, recovering grenades, mines, and antitank rockets. Months later, more Jewish extremists were arrested by the Israelis for assault, for car bombing, for killing four people at an Islamic college, and other charges, including a plot to blow up the Dome of the Rock. One of the arrested men, a pilot, wanted to steal an F-16 and blast the mosques off the Mount.

"If the attempted explosions had succeeded," the Muslim Supreme Council warned, "all Arab countries would have immediately launched a holy war against Israel."[2]

Which is what some of the extremists want. If they obliterate the mosques, they believe that the Muslims would wage such a vicious jihad that "the Messiah would come to save his people from destruction."[3]

Not sharing this messianic expectation, the Israeli government has faithfully protected Muslim sovereignty over the Mount. "If the shrines were destroyed," said one Israeli official, "we'd be the first to rebuild them."

When Israeli troops liberated East Jerusalem in 1967, General Moshe Dayan promised that there would be no interference with Muslim control of the Mount, a promise every Israeli administration has kept. When an Israeli flag was found blowing in the breeze above a police building on the Mount in August 1984, the Muslims protested, tensions rose, and the Israelis removed it the next day.[4] Most Israelis are not religious, have no compulsion to rebuild the temple, and scant, if any, messianic expectation—so few want a war because of a hill, no matter how holy.

And the hill is holy. On it sits the Dome of the Rock, built by the Umayyad caliph of Damascus between A.D. 688 and 691 to protect a rock. The rock, about half the size of a tennis court, is what Muslims believe God used to create the world. Below it is the "Well of Souls," where spirits await judgment, and "some say that they can be heard, if you listen carefully."[5] On the rock Mohammed is said to have ascended to heaven. Islamic tradition teaches that his footprint is embedded there, along with the handprint of the angel Gabriel, who kept the boulder earthbound as it tried to follow Mohammed heavenward.

Mohammed's alleged ascension site is also believed to be Mount Moriah, where the Jews went to temple. Here Abraham brought Isaac as a sacrifice, and here sat Solomon's temple—perhaps the world's first prefabricated building: the stones were cut and shaped elsewhere, carted to the Mount, and fitted there. Leveled by the Babylonians in the sixth century B.C., the temple was rebuilt after the captivity ended. Rebuilt by Herod centuries later, the temple was destroyed by the Romans in A.D. 70.

Since then, pious Jews have beseeched God four times a week to "renew our days as they once were"—a plea to restore the temple. Medieval philosopher Maimonides wrote that every generation was obliged to rebuild the temple—but only if the site were retaken, if a leader descended from David appeared, and if the enemies of the Jews were destroyed. These requisites led rabbinical scholars to conclude that the temple could not be rebuilt until the Messiah arrives. With the birth of Israel in 1948, some rabbis believed that the long-awaited "messianic era" had begun, and talk started about a new temple.

"We should not forget," said Rabbi Sholom Chaim Harcohen Aviner, "that the supreme purpose of the ingathering of the exiles and the establishment of our state is the building of the temple."[6]

While most Israelis would disagree with Aviner, others are learning the temple rituals and studying the manufacture of priestly garments. In Jerusalem, Yeshiva Ateret Hacohaninm trains young Jews for the priesthood in a fifteen-year course that includes animal sacrifices. Because the only place to sacrifice is at the temple, and because the only place the temple can be erected is on the Mount, where the Dome of the Rock is, another Jewish-Muslim conflict could explode.

And Christians might detonate it.

When the Jews seeking to destroy the Dome Mosque were arrested by Israeli police in March 1983, their $50,000 legal expenses were paid by evangelicals from Texas. The group arrested in the January 1984 assault possessed, besides mines and rockets, Christian Bibles, and police believe that their shekels, too, were initially fundamentalist dollars.

"It's an abomination sitting on the Mount," says evangelical Doug Krieger, talking about the Dome of the Rock. "King David owns the place, not the Arabs."

Though David's dead, Kreiger wants it for the king's kin, the Jews. As the executive director of the Jerusalem Temple Foundation, "a small group theologically committed to the rebuilding of the temple," Kreiger, along with millionaire Terry Reisenhoover, the chairman of the foundation, is raising millions of dollars for the third temple. Foundation money supports Yeshiva Ateret Hacohanim, paid the lawyers of those arrested in the 1983 assault, and lobbies the Israeli government to rebuild the temple.

Why?

About two thousand five hundred years ago the prophet Daniel, using prophetic symbolism, wrote about a 490-year period that began from "the commandment to restore and to build Jerusalem"[7] (destroyed by Babylon in 586 B.C.). This specific commandment to rebuild the city was issued by Artaxerxes in 457 B.C.; the end of the 490 years came in A.D. 33. Popular evangelical theology separates the last seven years of the time span from the first 483, inserts more than nineteen hundred years between them, and places those last seven years at an indefinite future date. According to Daniel, during this seven-year period, "the sacrifice and the oblation"[8] will cease. Because only at the Jerusalem temple can "the sacrifice and the oblation" be offered, millions of evangelicals believe that the temple, along with its services and animal sacrifices, must be reinstated before Jesus returns.

"There will apparently be a Temple rebuilt shortly before or at this time," writes the best-selling seer of end-time events, Hal Lindsey, "because sacrifices and offering will be resumed. Jews wishing to return to this type of observance of Mosaic law could do so only in a Temple rebuilt on its ancient site."[9]

If the temple is built it will be despite the Waqf, the Muslim political-religious trust that administers the area. Despite Israeli largess in giving them the Mount, the Waqf is eliminating any evidence linking the site to Judiasm or any pre-Islamic period. Ancient walls, including one from the second temple, have been bulldozed or buried; trees have been planted over historical sites and the land recontoured to make them unrecognizable; and buildings have been placed over historical artifacts.[10] Non-Muslims are allowed on the Mount for only a few hours on specific days and only in part of the area. The Waqf allows no one except Muslims to pray there.

"The church was founded on the Mount, Pentecost was on the court," complains Kreiger, "and we can't even pray there."

He might not be allowed to pray on the Mount, but according to Jewish law—

which has declared all Jews "unclean" until the Messiah comes—Jews are not even allowed up there. On the Mount was the Holy of Holies, the most sacred room of the temple. Only the high priest, after much preparation, was allowed in this room, and then only for a special service on the Day of Atonement. Violation meant death. Because no one is sure of the exact location of the Holy of Holies, Jewish law has banned the faithful from the area, lest some accidentally step on the sacred spot. The ban extends into the heavens, which is why Jews are forbidden to fly over the temple site. Though many Orthodox adhere to the law, most Israelis, orthodox and secular, ignore it.

Every year, Jews petition the Israeli government for the right to pray on the Mount, and every year they are denied. In 1983, however, the High Court ruled that Jews have the right to pray there but left the matter with the government, which refuses to agitate the Waqf. Former Ashkenazic chief rabbi of Israel Shlomo Goren had even designated a part of the Mount where Jews can enter. Rabbi Meyer Kahane, of New York, founder of the militant Jewish Defense League and newly elected member of the Knesset, has vowed to lead Jews in prayer on the Mount and has called for removal of the mosques.[11]

Some Jews want the mosques removed so that a temple can be built. Others, like Kahane, view the Muslim presence itself as an insult, a dagger in the heart of Judaism. And still others want to hasten the advent of the Messiah. Their sentiment is embodied in the popular Israeli song: "All the world is against us. Never mind—we shall overcome."

"If you follow this line of thinking," says Ariel Simon, a professor at Israel's Bar-Ilan University, "which has intensified since the Holocaust, and you combine it with a messianic approach, then your foremost religious obligation is to bring about the days of the Messiah as soon as possible."[12]

Pitching in to hasten the advent (or return) of the Messiah are the evangelicals. Though they have a major disagreement with the Jews over the identity of the Messiah, they nevertheless feed the 3,000-year-old messianic passion of the Jews.

"We told the chief rabbis that they have made a synagogue of the Wailing Wall," said Crier, "when they really belong on the Mount."

Executing scripture that he understands to describe a third temple, Kreiger asked the rabbis, "How will the glory of the Lord return to the Temple if you just have the Wall?"

These Christians and Jewish fundamentalists agree that the temple should be built, but Muslims don't—and it's their Dome of the Rock that sits over the heart of the ancient temple. And that's why many evangelicals believe the mosque must go—even if by divine intervention.

"Perhaps through an earthquake or some similar disaster which may demolish the Dome of the Rock, Israel will again have access to this location," writes evangelical Salem Kirban.[13]

If the mosques were destroyed, either by divine or human agencies, who would rebuild the temple?

Stories about a temple already built in the United States, ready to box and ship when the site is prepared, were reported in the Christian press as far back as 1967.[14]

When asked about rumors that the evangelicals were building one, Kreiger answered, "I can't say."

Is it true that the evangelicals built it in Texas?

"I can't say," Kreiger said again, "except that there have been things which have already started. More has been done in the last three years than has happened in the last 2,000."

Did they have all the material?

"I can't say, except that we already have the gold in abundance."

If they are constructing one, is the idea, once the Dome is gone, to ship it over— prefabricated, like Solomon's?

"I can't say," he repeated, "except that if the site were cleared, there would be a temple there immediately."

There might also be World War III.

---

[1]Grace Hales, "Shrine Under Siege," *The Link*, August/September 1984, 9.

[2]*Ibid.*, 12.

[3]Barbara and Michael Ledeen, "The Temple Mount Plot," *The New Republic*, June 18, 1984, 23.

[4]"Israel Removes Its Flag From Area of Islamic Shrine," Religious News Service, August 3, 1984.

[5]Alstar Dunan, *The Noble Sanctuary* (London: Longham Group Limited, 1972), 34.

[6]Halsell, 6.

[7]Daniel 9:25.

[8]Verse 27.

[9]Hal Lindsey, *The Rapture* (New York: Bantam Books, 1983), 3, 4.

[10]Ledeen, 21.

[11]Steve Rodan, "Many Israelis Alarmed by Election of Rabbi Kahane," Religious News Service, July 3, 1984, 7.

[12]Edward Greenstein, "Jeopardizing Jewish Morals," *Baltimore Jewish Times*, September 7, 1984, 63.

[13]Salem Kirban, "Questions Frequently Asked Me on Prophecy" (Salem Kirban, Inc., 1972), 7.

[14]"Israel: Things to Come," *Christianity Today*, December 22, 1967, 35.

This article originally appeared in the *Adventist Review*, October 4, 1990.

CHAPTER FOURTEEN

ISRAEL: Is This Where Armageddon Will Begin?

Each year Bible colleges graduate believers by the hundreds armed with the fundamentals of futurism—the belief that Armageddon will center around the Jews and Israel. Oral Roberts, Kenneth Copeland, Jim Bakker, Jimmy Swaggart, and thousands of other preachers expect Armageddon to occur in Palestine. Evangelical Christian magazines daily print articles that center on the prophetic role of Jews and Israel in the last days. "We must note the fact," writes one futurist, "that the entire universe, all the stars, the sun, and the moon are subordinated by God to Israel's calling. That is how important Israel is in God's eye!"

These beliefs are not confined to Sunday School. Jerry Falwell has brought futurist convictions into debates about defense, foreign policy, and arms control. Presidential aspirant Pat Robertson, a futurist enthusiast, predicted in 1982 that a war in Lebanon would lead to the destruction of Russia as a world power. President Reagan's statements about Armageddon and the Middle East hint that he, too, has been influenced by futurist theology.

What is the origin of futurism? Is it biblical? And with the growing political strength of evangelical Christianity in the United States, what effects could this have on the country?

Futurism originated after the Reformation. Martin Luther, at first wanting to *reform* the papacy, eventually damned it as the antichrist. "You must be armed with Scripture," he wrote, "so that you can not only call the pope the antichrist but also to know how to prove it so clearly that you could die with this conviction and stand against the devil in death."

The label stuck, and soon Protestants of every hue and shape were fingering Rome as "the seat of the true and real antichrist." Wanting to reverse the bad publicity, Francisco Ribera, a Spanish Jesuit, published a commentary in 1590 that argued that the antichrist referred not to Rome but to an individual who would arise just before the second coming of Jesus. This antichrist, Ribera said, would reign in Palestine, and along with the Jews (restored in the land), would rebuild the temple.

The public-relations campaign worked so well that by the nineteenth century many Protestant pulpits were preaching versions of futurism, especially in the British Isles, where futurism became incorporated into a more complex theology called dispensationalism. In the twentieth century the *Scofield Reference Bible*—the most widely circulated commentary Bible in history—has promoted futurism to millions through its elaborate system of footnotes. Some futurist aficionados revere these notes almost as highly as Scripture itself.

In recent years, the undisputed high priest of futurist prophecy has been Hal Lindsey whose book *The Late Great Planet Earth* has gone through more than forty printings, been translated into thirty-one languages, and sold an astronomical 18 million copies!

"Before the Jews were a nation," writes Lindsay, "nothing was relevant. Now when that occurred, there began to be a countdown of all kinds of prophetic signs falling into place."

"The clearest sign of Christ's return," according to Leon J. Wood in *The Bible and Future Events*, "is the modern state of Israel."

This futurist obsession with modern Israel stems from the promises God made thousands of years ago to ancient Israel. "Thou art an holy people unto the Lord thy God, and the Lord hath chosen thee to be a peculiar people unto himself, above all the nations that are upon the earth" (Deut. 14:2). God promised the Hebrews material prosperity. "Blessed shalt thou be in the city, and blessed shalt thou be in the field. Blessed shall be the fruit of thy body, and the fruit of thy ground, and the fruit of thy cattle, the increase of thy kind, and the flocks of thy sheep. Blessed shall be thy basket and thy store" (Deut. 28:3-5). He even promised military victories: "The Lord shall cause thine enemies that rise up against thee to be smitten before thy face" (verse 7).

God promised ancient Israel these blessings, and many more, because He wanted the Jews to evangelize the world. The Gentiles, by seeing Israel's great prosperity, would say: "We will go with you: for we have heard that God is with you" (Zech. 8:23). Gentiles would flock to Jerusalem and be converted to the God of the Jews. The temple would "be called an house of prayer for all people" (Isa. 56:7), and "all the nations" would "call Jerusalem the throne of the Lord" (Jer. 3:17).

Yet futurists overlook the fact that God gave Israel these promises on the condition of obedience. "It shall come to pass, if thou shalt hearken diligently unto the voice of thy God, to observe and to do all his commandments . . . the Lord thy God will set thee on high above all the nations of the earth" (Deut. 28:1).

Along with these promises came a warning: "It shall come to pass, if thou will not hearken unto the voice of the Lord thy God, to observe to do all his commandments," then "cursed shalt thou be in the city," "cursed shalt thou be in the field," "cursed shall be the fruit of thy body." Instead of victory, "the Lord shall cause thee to be smitten before thine enemies: thou . . . shalt be removed into all the kingdoms of the earth" (verses 15, 16, 18, 25).

The conditional nature of the blessing is best stated in Jeremiah 18:9, 10. "If at any time I declare concerning a nation or a kingdom that I will build and plant it, and if it does evil in my sight, not listening to my voice, then I will repent of the good which I had intended to do to it" (RSV).

As the Bible shows, Israel *as a nation* refused to listen to the voice of the Lord. Gentiles did flock to Jerusalem, but to burn the city, not to worship there. Every calamity the Lord warned about happened, until Israel was, indeed, "removed into all the kingdoms of the earth" (Deut. 28:25).

In the parable of the landowner who planted a vineyard, Jesus illustrated Israel's failure. When the owner sent his servants to receive the fruit of the vineyard, the tenants killed them one by one. Finally, he sent his son—and they killed him too. The owner destroyed the tenants and gave the vineyard to others. Jesus, using the vineyard to symbolize the land of Israel and the tenants to symbolize the nation's unfaithfulness, told the leaders, "The kingdom of God shall be taken from you, and given to a nation bringing forth the fruits thereof" (Matt. 21:43).

Despite the conditional nature of the promise, in spite of Israel's failure to meet the conditions and in spite of Christ's declaration that the kingdom would be taken from Israel because of their failure, futurists insist that the Old Testament promises to the Jews have remained valid for almost 2,000 years. And they apply these promises to the modern state of Israel even though it is a secular country that has made no agreement with God to abide by the conditions outlined in the Bible.

"For the last thirty-seven years," wrote futurist Wim Malgo in 1985 about the Jewish state in Palestine, "we have witnessed the progressive fulfillment of God's promise to the nation of Israel." J. Dwight Pentecost writes that the promises "made by God with Israel in regard to their relation to the land must be seen to be an unconditional covenant."

Directly linked to this mistaken insistence that God's promises to Israel are unconditional is a related error—the failure of futurism to recognize the New Testament teaching that the church has taken the place of ancient Israel this side of the Cross. In the parable of the vineyard, Jesus said that the kingdom of God would be taken from Israel and given to a nation bringing forth fruits. The gospel hasn't gone to just a single nation; it has spread all over the world. Believers worldwide compose the "nation bringing forth fruits."

Writing to Christians scattered in churches throughout the Middle East, Peter addressed them with the titles of Israel: "Ye are a chosen generation, a royal priesthood, an holy nation" (1 Pet. 2:9). Paul, writing to Gentile believers in Ephesus, reminded them that at one time there were "aliens from the commonwealth of promise" but were now "fellow citizens with the saints, and of the household of God"(Eph. 2:12, 19).

The gospel promises don't *exclude* the Jew; he becomes part of the spiritual Israel (the church) through faith in Jesus, the same as everyone else. "If ye be Christ's, then are ye Abraham's seed, and heirs according to the promise" (Gal. 3:29). In Romans 11, Paul uses the symbol of the olive tree to represent Israel. The Jews are the original church, "the natural branch," while the Gentiles are the "wild" olive branches. Because of unbelief and disobedience, the natural branches, the Jews, were "broken off," while the wild branches, the Gentiles, were "grafted in among them." Yet Paul warned the Gentiles that if they were disobedient, they could also be cut off. Paul explained that if the Gentile branch, which "is wild by nature," could be grafted in, "how much more shall these, which be the natural branches, be grafted into their own olive tree," *if* (notice the condition Paul expresses) they "abide not still in unbelief" (verses 23, 24).

Hundreds of Old Testament promises that the Lord made to ancient Israel remain unfulfilled because Israel remained unfaithful to the conditions. Futurism, rejecting the idea of conditions, applies these promises to modern Israel. The outcome is a variety of improbable scenarios for the end of the world. By applying to modern Israel the promises of military victory made to ancient Israel, futurists believe that Russia will be defeated in a war against the Jews.

The book of Revelation is filled with imagery from the Old Testament and its setting in ancient Palestine. Just as Paul and Peter applied the titles of literal Israel to spiritual Israel, Revelation applies the ancient Palestinian images from the Old Testament spiritually too. For example, Revelation talks about God's people coming out of "Babylon." Yet Babylon—a clear false religious and political system that was the enemy of God's people in ancient Israel's time—hasn't been a nation for over two thousand years and, according to Isaiah, would never be restored. John in the Revelation couldn't have been referring, therefore, to the literal nation of Babylon. Instead, he was using the Old Testament literal image to teach a New Testament spiritual truth: God's people must leave the teaching of false religion, i.e., spiritual Babylon. Futurism, refusing to see the spiritual interpretations of these images, applies them literally, which explains its obsession with the Middle East.

To reject futurism, however, doesn't necessarily mean to reject Israel. Millions who see no prophetic significance in the Jewish state nevertheless support Israel's right for a safe and secure homeland. And their support comes without all the theological trappings of futurism, which include, for some, another holocaust. "Millions of devout Jews," says Jerry Falwell, "will again be slaughtered." With supporters like that, who needs the PLO? Jews may well worry.

But Jews aren't the only ones worrying. Others are concerned about how this popular theology might affect government policy. President Reagan's statements about Armageddon before the 1984 election had people questioning "whether the President's apparent belief in a particular biblical scenario for the end of the world means that he might consider nuclear war a divine instrument" (*Time*, Nov. 5, 1984). Others, too, wonder whether the president's description of Russia as an "evil empire" came from futurist theology, which describes Russia as . . . well, an evil empire. Some believe it to be more than a coincidence that many staunch opponents of a nuclear freeze or arms reduction are futurist evangelicals, whose scenarios of the last days always include nuclear war. Hal Lindsay, whose books on Bible prophecy speculate that nuclear war between America and Russia will occur before the Second Coming, once gave a talk to Pentagon strategists about that very subject: nuclear war between America and Russia.

Rejecting Lindsay and the futurist scenario for the Second Coming, however, doesn't mean rejecting the Second Coming. Jesus was clear—He will return, and prior to that return will be "great tribulation, such as was not since the beginning of the world" (Matt. 24:21). This time of trouble could conceivably include war in the Middle East. But if so, it will not be because modern Israel has prophetic significance today.

Jesus also gave another specific prophecy about the Second Coming. He warned that before His return false teachings would abound—teachings that could, He warned, "deceive the very elect" (verse 24).

Futurism doesn't explain this prophetic warning. It fulfills it!

This article originally appeared in *Signs of the Times,*® June 1987.

CHAPTER FIFTEEN

The Religious Right and the Destruction of Israel

"I am very thankful for the Christian friends we have," said Menachem Begin, Israeli prime minister from 1977 to 1983."The friendship between Christians and the Jewish people is a new phenomenon of our time. It is indeed the beginning of the redemption of Israel."

Most Jews, though not as hyperbolic as Begin in their evaluation of Christian support for Israel, are nevertheless thankful. But what must be understood is that these Christians expect no peace for Jerusalem; instead, they are awaiting the soon destruction of millions of Jews in Palestine.

Futurism, the theology of Israel's staunchest Christian friends, teaches that anti-Semitism will reach a climactic frenzy worse than the Holocaust. "And in that period of time particularly," writes John Walvoord, a leading futurist scholar, "the whole world will be gripped by a hatred for the Jews that will be inspired by Satan himself."[1]

Dr. Jack Van Impe writes of an era that is "going to be the greatest of anti-Semitism in world history. In fact, it will be the devil's last attempt to liquidate, obliterate, and blot out the Jew."[2]

"As terrible as Jewish harassment has been in the past," warns author Hal Lindsey about the future, "anti-Semitism will reach its most feverish pitch."[3]

"The Crusades, which tried to recapture the holy places in Palestine from the Muslims, exterminated many Jews in Europe," writes futurist scholar Charles Ryrie. "Even the English and the French, as late as the thirteenth century, wiped out entire Jewish communities in their countries. And while Columbus was discovering America, Jews were being expelled from nearly all of Western Europe. Hitler added to this awful record by exterminating more than 6 million Jews. But the worst bloodbath in Jewish history is yet to come."[4]

"The sad condition of being scattered to the ends of the earth," writes Walvoord

77

about the Jews, "has persisted until the twentieth century, and with it has come untold sufferings of the people of Israel, climaxing in the terrible scourge of Hitler, who murdered some 6 million of the people of Israel. But, according to the prophets, the end is not yet and ahead of Israel is a terrible time of suffering before the day of restoration."[5]

Antichrist's Final Solution

The personage behind this slaughter of the Jews is the antichrist. Speculation abounds concerning his identity. In 1970 Hal Lindsay saw French newspaper editor Jean-Jacques Servan-Schreiber as a potential candidate. Everyone from Guru Maharishi and Sun Myung Moon to Henry Kissinger and Ronald Reagan has come under suspicion. Jimmy Swaggart thinks "he will probably be a Syrian Jew."

And as if one antichrist weren't enough, some have predicted that there will be two. "The Bible indicated that there will actually be *two* antichrists. One will be a European who will rule the political and religious world from Rome. The other antichrist will be a Jew posing as a religious prophet."[6]

No matter who the antichrist is or how many there are, futurists agree on one thing: He wants to destroy the Jews.

"The antichrist is on the verge of realizing his great desire," writes Jimmy Swaggart, envisioning last day events, "the desire of all evil men, past and present—the final solution: total annihilation, every Jew dead."[7]

Most Jews at best want Israel living in peace with the Arabs; at worst, at least within safe, secure borders. Israelis gave away more than half the country to try to secure peace. Yet for Begin's Christian friends, peace is not part of the prophetic picture, at least not until Jesus sets up His earthly kingdom.

"You and I know," says Jerry Falwell, who was given the coveted Jabotinsky award by Begin, "that there's not going to be any real peace in the Middle East until one day the Lord Jesus Christ sits on the throne of David in Jerusalem."[8]

Presidential aspirant Pat Robertson agrees: "There's not going to be any peace until God's peace, what we call the Peace of Jerusalem, which the Prince of Peace brings to the troubled region."[9]

Prior to the coming of the Prince of Peace, Israel is to face massive war. "The armies of all nations will be gathered in the area of Israel, especially around Jerusalem," writes Lindsey. "Think of it: at least 200 million soldiers from the Orient, with millions more from the forces of the West headed by the antichrist of the Revived Roman Empire."[10]

Walvoord writes of "the descent of the tremendous army of 200 million men upon the land of Israel to participate in the final world conflict."[11]

Warns Jimmy Swaggart, "With his [the antichrist's] millions of men recruited from Russia and China, plus the Revived Roman Empire, he will come down to cover the nation of Israel like a cloud of locusts."[12]

"Jerusalem will see nothing but war," Lindsey writes in his book *There's a New World Coming*. "One Gentile army after another will invade the city of Jerusalem and march up and down its streets."

Israel's Bloodbath and Conversion

The titles of futurist pamphlets, tracts, or chapters of Religious Right books about Israel include "A Bloodbath for Israel," "Why Russia Invades Israel," "World War III and Israel's Final Holocaust," "The Suffering of Israel," "Holocaust From the East," "Israel in the Tribulation," and "Russia Invades Israel—When?"

During these coming wars, Jews are going to be slaughtered en masse. "Heartrending as it may be to contemplate, the people of Israel who are returning to their ancient land are placing themselves within the vortex of this future whirlwind which will destroy the majority of those living in Palestine."[13]

Hal Lindsey writes of "multiplied millions of soldiers slaughtering each other in and around Israel."[14]

How many Jews are expected to die?

"Some theologians," says D. H. Wilmington, of Liberty Baptist College, ". . . feel that on the basis of reading Zechariah 13 . . . two-thirds of the Jews will be slaughtered."

"At this time," writes evangelist J. O. Grooms, "two-thirds of the people in Israel will be killed."[15]

The Bible Knowledge Commentary says, "At that time two-thirds of the Jewish nation will be struck down and perish."[16]

This coming carnage is supposed to take only a few years. "Only one-third of the Jews will survive this brief three-and-one-half-year period," explains theologian Richard W. DeHaan in his *Israel and the Nations in Prophecy*.[17]

Says Swaggart, "Two-thirds of Israel will die," during this tribulation period.

The *Liberty Bible Commentary*, says, "Two-thirds of Israel's population will die as the result of the wrath vented against them by the antichrist."[18]

Based on Israel's present population of 4 million, 2.7 million Jews will be killed. Some fundamentalist theologians believe that the toll will be far higher. The figure, they say, will include not just Israelis but all the world's Jews, perhaps gathered in Israel. Author Grace Halsell, in her book *Prophecy and Politics*, quotes a futurist on what he expects to be the fate of the Jews: "There are about 13.5 million Jews in the world today. So God is telling us that 9 million Jews will be killed in this battle—more than all the Jews killed by the Nazis."[19]

The Bible does speak of last-day catastrophes. The prophet Daniel (Daniel 12:1) warns of a "time of trouble, such as never was," and religious Jews have believed in a period of "Messianic woes" to precede the Messiah's advent. The book of Revelation also is filled with dire warnings of doom to precede the Messiah's return. The futurists place the Jews and Israel at the apex of these events, making the return of the Jews to

Palestine a crucial factor for the Second Coming.

"The clearest sign of Christ's return is the modern state of Israel," says futurist Leon J. Wood.

"Before the Jews were a nation," says Hal Lindsey, "nothing was relevant."

"We must note the fact that in the entire universe," writes Wim Malgo, "all the stars, the sun, and the moon are subordinated by God to Israel's calling. That's how important Israel is in God's eye."[20]

And Israel is to be the center of Armageddon. "In the center of the stage is the little nation of Israel," writes Walvoord, "insignificant in number among the billions of the world's population yet the fuse for the final world conflict which is ahead."[21]

Though the whole world is involved in the final conflict, the Jews, says Walvoord, are to have it the worst: "Though the judgments will obviously fall on all races and people, it seems that Israel is to be the special object of satanic hatred."[22]

This unparalleled persecution of the Jews, however, is not without a good cause. "The great tribulation," writes Richard DeHaan, "will be the means of Israel's conversion, and this will precede the glorious second coming of the Lord Jesus to the earth."[23]

Most futurists agree that this mass destruction of the Jews will cause the survivors, believed to number only 144,000, to accept Jesus. "The final persecution of the Jews," explains Walvoord, "will awaken Israel's understanding to what has taken place. . . . This clear fulfillment of prophecy will lead to the startling realization that the first coming of the Messiah is past and His second coming is near. In the horror of the last three and a half years of great tribulation, these new believers will cling to the hope of Christ's second coming."[24]

"Israel's future will climax," says Swaggart, "with Jesus Christ being accepted as their Messiah, and with them spreading His gospel throughout the world."

"The final reason for the Tribulation," explains Falwell, "will be to purge Israel. As gold is purified through the heat of the fire, so the nation of Israel will come through the Tribulation fit for the Master's use."[25]

"There will be," says Lindsey, "144,000 Jewish Billy Grahams turned loose at once!"

Eschatological Expectations

Most Jews seem ignorant of the Religious Right's scenario for their future. Gerald S. Strober, a New York Jewish leader with close ties to Falwell, says: "Jerry Falwell's support for Israel is the most significant manifestation yet of evangelical concern for Israel's security in that it brings together *positive theological elements* and considerable political muscle" (italics supplied).

One wonders what positive theological elements Strober was thinking of: the new wave of anti-Semitism, the Russian invasion of Israel, the mass destruction of the Jews, or perhaps the accepting of Jesus by the survivors?

Nathan Perlmutter, of the Anti-Defamation League, once wrote: "For ourselves, however, no matter Pat Robertson's, Bailey Smith's, Jerry Falwell's friendship for Israel is rooted in the New Testament; we've an open mind. If the Messiah comes, on that very day we'll consider our options. Meanwhile, let's praise the Lord and pass the ammunition."[28]

Perlmutter is missing the point. During the Holocaust, many "Christians" didn't help Jews because the Christians believed that the Holocaust was the Jews' punishment for rejecting Jesus. They expected the Jews to be persecuted and killed. Their theology encouraged them to do nothing.

Today, millions of Christians follow another similarly distorted eschatology, one that teaches, expects, and predicts mass destruction of the Jews. Should persecution come, how much support should the Jews expect from those whose greatest hope—the second coming of Jesus—is predicated upon another Holocaust?

Jimmy Swaggart envisions the scenario: "The antichrist will amass his armies . . .The hated Jews will now be put to death . . . he can take out his venom and hatred upon those who brought the Messiah into this world—the Jews. . . . It will be a time of such horror that it beggars description.

"The antichrist will fling his armies against all Israel, but especially against Jerusalem. It will be door-to-door fighting, house-to-house confrontation, and the city will be leveled. The Jews will have their backs to the wall. The Bible says that half of the city will fall. It speaks of women being ravished and raped. . . .This is what Adolf Eichmann, Adolf Hitler, and Himmler could not bring to pass."[27]

Jerry Falwell agrees. "Millions of devout Jews will again be slaughtered."

"When you have true love for a people," says Jimmy Swaggart of the Jews, "then it comes as a real shock when they don't reciprocate."

"I am going to be their [the Jews'] friend whether they want me or not."[28]

With friends like these, who needs the PLO?

For Swaggart, Falwell, and millions of other "friends," rivers of Jewish blood must again flow. Then Israel will be "redeemed."

Probably not what Begin had in mind.

---

[1]John Walvoord, *The Return of the Lord* (Grand Rapids: Zondervan Pub. House, 1955), 124.

[2]Jack Van Impe, *America, Israel, Russia* (Jack Van Impe Ministries, 1984), 23.

[3]Hal Lindsey, *There's a New World Coming* (New York: Bantam Books, 1984), 156.

[4]Charles Rorie, *The Living End* (Old Tappan, N.J.: Fleming Revell Co., 1973), 78.

[5]John Walvoord, *Israel in Prophecy* (Grand Rapids: Zondervan, 1962), 107.

[6]Lindsey, 87.

[7]Jimmy Swaggart, *The Battle of Armageddon* (Baton Rouge: Jimmy Swaggart Ministries, 1982), 26.

[8]Quoted in Dinesh D. Sousa, "Is This the Year the World Ends?" Washington *Post*, January 4, 1987.

[9]*Ibid.*

[10]Lindsey, 194.

[11]John Walvoord, *The Nations in Prophecy* (Grand Rapids: Zondervan Pub. House, 1967), 141.

[12]Swaggart, 24.

[13]Walvoord, *Israel in Prophecy*, 113.

[14]Lindsey, 215.

[15]J. O. Grooms, *Russia Invades Israel—When?* (Lynchburg, Va.: 1983).

[16]J. Walvood and R. Zuck, eds., *The Bible Knowledge Commentary* (Wheaton, Ill.: Victor Brooks, 1985), 1569.

[17]Richard W. DeHaan, *Israel and the Nations in Prophecy* (Grand Rapids: Zondervan Pub. House, 1968), 84.

[18]Jerry Falwell, ex. ed., *Liberty Bible Commentary* (New York: Thomas Nelson Publisher, 1983), 2689.

[19]Grace Halsell, *Prophecy and Politics* (Westport, Conn.: Lawrence Hill and Co., 1986), 26.

[20]Wim Malgo, "News From Israel" (West Columbia, S.C.: Midnight Cry Ministry, 1986),5.

[21]John F. Walvoord and John E. Walvoord, *Armageddon* (Grand Rapids: Zondervan Pub. House, 1974), 23

[22]Wavloord, *Israel in Prophecy,* 111.

[23]DeHaan.

[24]Walvoord and Walvoord, *Armageddon*, 118.

[25]Jerry Falwell, "Nuclear War and the Second Coming of Jesus" (Lynchburg, Va.: Old-Time Gospel Hour, 1983), 14.

[26]Nathan Perlmutter, *The Real Anti-Semitism in America* (New York: Arbor House Pub. Co., 1982), 172.

[27]Swaggart, 23-27.

[28]Quoted in "Falwell Attempts to Mend Interfaith Fences," Washington *Post,* April 4, 1985.

This article originally appeared in *Liberty*, November/December 1987.

CHAPTER SIXTEEN

The Catholic-Protestant Connection

Amassed on the Mall, between the round dome of the Capitol building and the sleek obelisk of the Washington Monument, 125,000 charismatic Christians pray for the political and spiritual healing of America. Amid the waving arms and fluttering tongues, I wander, a sack filled with copies of *The Great Controversy* slung over my shoulder. No sooner do I hand out one book than someone else reaches for me.

Above me, on a bright stage festooned with various national flags and a red, white, and blue "Washington for Jesus '88" sign, Christian leaders from around the world gather on this rainy April day to sing, preach, and admonish America to return to "the godly values that made this nation great."

Of course, Christians preaching a political gospel have been making pilgrimages to Washington for decades. The heavy concentration of Catholic speakers, however, including a Jesuit from the Vatican and a video appearance from Mother Teresa, adds an interesting dimension to Washington for Jesus '88. Roman Catholics and other conservative Protestants, once bitter enemies, are finding common ground for fellowship and unity. Meanwhile, surrounded by praises, prayers, and songs of tongue-speaking Protestants and Catholics who want to see America return to "the law of God," I distribute copies of *The Great Controversy* as fast as I can pull them out.

And although I don't know how closely those on the stage are adhering to a predetermined script, there's one scenario they follow to a tee. I carry copies of it in my sack. Indeed, the drama being performed before my eyes was written out 100 years earlier in the book in my hands!

"Catholicism," wrote Ellen White, "is gaining ground upon every side."[1] The large Catholic presence at Washington for Jesus '88 is one example of those gains. Former Jesuit Peter De Rosa in his best-selling *Vicars of Christ* wrote: "Papal prestige today is very high. In this century, pontiffs have achieved world renown. Historic events and instant communication have contributed to make them 'Spokesmen of Religion.' "[2]

Though the Catholic Church still has its critics, even avowed enemies, overt hostility against the papacy has evaporated. Dwindling are the days when even devout Catholics such as Dante consigned some people to the deepest circles of "the sad halls of hell." Gone is the vehement antipapal rhetoric of Martin Luther, who wrote: "You must be armed with Scripture so that you cannot only call the pope the antichrist but also know how to prove it so clearly that you could die with this conviction and stand against the devil in death." "In the U.S. over the past two centuries," said New York Archbishop John Cardinal O'Connor, "Catholics have felt like second-class citizens. Now we come more and more to recognize not only our rightful role as citizens but our responsibility as church leaders to contribute to the body politic."[3]

Astonishing Prediction

For many years Roman Catholics in America did feel like second-class citizens, or worse. Anti-Catholicism was as much a part of Pilgrim doctrine as was the Trinity and Sunday keeping, and many of the colonies excluded Catholics. In the following centuries as Catholics poured out of ships onto the American shore, Protestants poured out sermons, pamphlets, and books warning against this "loathsome mass."

In this environment Ellen White wrote *The Great Controversy*. Her criticisms, therefore, of the "papists" and the "Romanists" were not necessarily prophetic but simply common fare for the time. Where she becomes prophetic, however, was when amid all this American anti-Catholicism she wrote: "The Protestants of the United States will . . . reach over the abyss to clasp hands with the Roman power."[4]

The Protestant attitude toward the Roman Catholic Church has, indeed, flip-flopped. In 1951, when Harry Truman wanted to send General Mark Clark as ambassador to the Vatican, American Protestants shrieked, and Truman backed down. When Ronald Reagan in 1984 named William Wilson as ambassador to the Vatican, the Protestants mostly yawned. When John F. Kennedy ran for the presidency in 1960, his ties to Rome almost cost him the race; in 1984, when Geraldine Ferraro ran as Walter Mondale's vice-presidential candidate, Americans were more concerned about her husband's alleged links to organized crime than they were about hers to the Vatican.

Perhaps the greatest symbol of the Protestant metamorphosis was the warm reception they gave John Paul II on his American tours. In previous centuries, had the pope come to America, a mob might have lynched him; on John Paul's trips, the only mobs he faced were those who welcomed him. "No other man in the world today," said Billy Graham during the pope's first visit, "could attract as much attention on moral and spiritual subjects as John Paul II. . . . The pope has reached millions of Protestants."[5]

If a century ago Ellen White could write that the papacy "is now regarded by

Protestants with far greater favor than in former years,"[6] what would she say today about the Protestants falling over each other to praise John Paul during his American visits? What would she say about Anglican Archbishop Runcie's call for unification between the churches, with the pope as the spiritual leader, the "universal primate" over the united body? The June 14, 1982, *Time* magazine reported that during the pope's triumphal visit to the British Isles, Scottish Protestant leader John McIntyre said that John Paul's visit "would give Scots an entirely new opinion of 'the character and nature of the papal office.' " In recent years clergyman and writer Richard John Neuhaus has stressed that the Roman Catholic Church is in a unique position to help rebuild the moral character of America. Neuhaus's religion: Lutheran.

Over the years, panels of Catholic and Protestant theologians have been ironing out theological differences, including justification by faith, the doctrine that launched the Reformation. A panel of Catholics and Lutherans that had met in Milwaukee, Wisconsin, in the 1980s reached an essential agreement on justification and said that the "remaining points of difference about this doctrine were no longer a reason to keep their churches apart." Indeed, many Catholics are fine Christians, and the Protestants see no reason why they can't unite.

As the religious barriers crumble, Catholics and Protestants are finding that they have common political goals, such as the prolife cause, prayer in school, and tuition tax credits—and they are uniting to promote their agenda. "The Roman Catholic bishops," writes Professor John Swomley, "are working in an informal alliance with fundamentalist Protestants not only on the abortion issue but to get government support of private church schools."[7]

"When the leading churches of the United States," Ellen White wrote, "uniting upon such points of doctrine as are held by them in common, shall influence the state to enforce their decrees and to sustain their institutions, then Protestant America will have formed an image of the Roman hierarchy."[8]

Catholics and Protestants are finding other points in common besides the desire to use the state to support their institutions. On October 15, 1986, a delegation of conservative Southern Protestants from the Lord's Day Alliance, "the only national organization whose sole purpose is the maintenance and cultivation of the first day of the week as a time of rest," went to Rome. They presented Pope John Paul II with a plaque of appreciation, which read: "The Lord's Day Alliance of the United States expresses appreciation to His Holiness Pope John Paul II, for his outstanding service in preserving the Lord's Day throughout the world."[9]

Times have changed. "American Catholicism today enjoys an unprecedented opportunity to play a major role in the shaping of American policy," said an October 19, 1986, Washington *Post* editorial. "American Catholicism has made enormous strides in recent years. It is finally in a position to play a major role in a society that desperately needs the kind of intellectual and spiritual leadership it can provide."

In 1888 Ellen White wrote that Protestants are "opening the door for the papacy to regain in Protestant America the supremacy which she has lost in the Old World."[10]

In 1984 the conservative Catholic weekly *The Wanderer* published an article about the ascendancy of Catholic power in America. "The Rubicon has been crossed," said the author. "The consequence of this, I think, will be nothing less than the beginning of the Catholic era in American history."[11]

The Catholic era in American history? At Washington for Jesus '88 I see it dawning. The pages of *The Great Controversy* are acted out before me, as if Ellen White wrote the screenplay and these men and women are merely following their lines. I realize, too, that instead of being just a spectator, I am part of this drama myself, for the script calls for the spreading of the three angels' messages to these people as well.

I empty my sack of the last copy of *The Great Controversy*, and as I carry it in my hand, a heavy middle-aged woman stops, looks at the book, and asks, "Are you giving that book away?"

I hand it to her and say, "Pray as you read it."

"Oh, I will," she responds, thrilled. "A while back some man came to my door, wanting to sell me the book. I wanted to buy it but didn't have the money. And now I meet you, giving it away? I know God wants me to read it."

I look around. In the background the Capitol sits like the dome of St. Peter's; on stage, priests and ministers kneel side by side, praying for revival in America; in the crowd, more than one hundred thousand Protestants and Catholics fellowship together; and next to me, a woman eagerly takes *The Great Controversy*, saying that God wants her to read it. Everyone is playing his or her part, perfectly.

"I know that He does too," I answer, playing mine.

---

[1] *The Great Controversy*, 566.
[2] Peter De Rosa, *Vicars of Christ* (New York: Crown Pub., Inc., 1988), 38.
[3] Quoted in the Washington *Post*, October 19, 1986.
[4] *The Great Controversy*, 588.
[5] Quoted in Clifford Goldstein, *Hands Across the Gulf* (Nampa, Idaho: Pacific Press Pub. Assn., 1987), 5.
[6] *The Great Controversy*, 563.
[7] John Swomley, *Religious Liberty and the Secular State* (Buffalo: Prometheus Books, 1987), 124.
[8] *The Great Controversy*, 445.
[9] *Sunday*, October/December 1986.
[10] *The Great Controversy*, 573.
[11] *The Wanderer*, November 15, 1984.

This article originally appeared in the *Adventist Review*, June 7, 1990.

CHAPTER SEVENTEEN

Communists, Catholics, and Adventists

A few weeks ago I did something that I never do on Sabbath: I sneaked a look at the morning paper. What I saw was Mikhail Gorbachev, leader of the world's number one Communist nation, meeting with Pope John Paul II, spiritual father to more than 850 million Roman Catholics. And though this tête-à-tête was, by any standards, extraordinary, it should put fire in the blood of Seventh-day Adventists, for we alone can understand its real significance.

Vatican, Not Israel

As Adventists we are almost the only Christians left who adhere to the historicist view of prophecy, the view that places the Catholic Church, not Israel and the Jews, at the forefront of last-day events. Indeed, we understand that the Vatican, along with the United States, is to be a major player in enforcing the mark of the beast.

Yet for years the one question that always dogged me was How would the Roman Catholic Church ever gain the political power needed to fulfill its end-time role? While Protestantism—especially in America—once a bulwark against Catholicism, has clearly reached "across the gulf" and grasped the hand of the papacy in a direct and dramatic fulfillment of prophecy, Communism seemed to be an implacable foe. How would the papacy be able to regain extensive political power while it faced the guns, tanks, barbed wire, and militaristic atheism of the Communist world?

With the sudden whirlwind of events in Eastern Europe, however, culminating most recently in the Kremlin-Vatican visit, the walls are crumbling, the barbed wire is being cut, the guns are being turned away, and the open antagonism to religion is becoming a relic of the past. Gorbachev invites the pope to Russia, announces the legalization of the once-outlawed Ukranian Catholic Church, and even wants to exchange diplomatic missions. These moves, according to an article in the New York

Times, show that the Soviet Union "must reckon with the Vatican as a moral and political force." Before long the two most powerful military forces in the world, the United States and Russia, will both have diplomatic relations with the papacy!

Though Ellen White was clearly writing in another context than this one, her words "Catholicism is gaining ground upon every side" have captured, if not the details of the event, the general trends behind them.

Significance for Adventists

The change in the East-West relations has significance to Adventists in regard not only to the papacy but to the United States as well. As long as the United States and Russia remained open enemies, it seemed impossible for America to be in a position to force the world into worshiping the beast. Now suddenly America and Russia seem to be "beating their swords into ploughshares." Many Communists are now saying to America, to one degree or another, we want your form of government, your economic system, your technology, and your help. If the current trends continue, the stage is fast being set for America, along with the papacy, to exert the type of worldwide influence needed in order for them to fulfill their prophetic roles.

Great changes will still need to take place before the second coming of Jesus. Yet the recent extraordinary events in Communism prove that unbelievable changes can happen at a pace faster than anyone could have imagined. If last year someone would have told me that within a year there would be a Solidarity government in Poland, that the Berlin Wall would be null and void, that the Communists would be losing power in Czechoslovakia, Hungary, East Germany, and Bulgaria, and that the Soviets would be encouraging these reforms—I would have thought that I had backslidden, left the church, and was smoking pot! Ellen White's statement that "the final movements will be rapid ones" has taken on, for me at least, a new significance.

Need for Caution

Of course, we still don't know exactly what will happen. Gorbachev could be sent packing to Siberia, and the East-West rivalry could degenerate to the way it was before, even worse. Nevertheless, *if* the current trends continue, especially at the present pace, we will witness a radical restructuring of the world order in a direction that seems to be setting the stage for the final events in Bible prophecy.

John Paul called his meeting with Gorbachev "a sign of the times that have slowly matured, a sign that is rich in promise." He's right. The meeting is, indeed, a sign of the times—but probably not the sign that he thinks it is. And he's right, too, that the sign is rich in promise—the promise of our Lord's soon return.

This article originally appeared in the *Adventist Review*, January 18, 1990.

CHAPTER EIGHTEEN

Who Leads the New World Order?

When Saddam Hussein invaded Kuwait, George Bush began expounding upon the "new world order" he wanted to create. On October 30, 1990, he declared that the United Nations can "help bring about a new day . . . a new world order." On November 17, in Prague, he said that the Gulf crisis offered a historic opportunity to forge "for all nations a new world order." In his State of the Union address a year ago, he mentioned the "long-held promise of a new order." In Georgia last February addressing families of troops in Saudi Arabia, the president said that there is "no place for lawless aggression in the Persian Gulf and in this new world order we seek to create."

Thus the new world order was born. The phrase itself, though achieving popularity during the Gulf crisis, was coined long before August 2, 1990, when Saddam made Kuwait Iraq's nineteenth province. On the back of every dollar bill, below the Masonic symbols of the pyramid and the all-seeing eye, is the Latin phrase *Novus Ordo Seclorum*, which can be translated "New World Order."

The phrase has become the verbal lingo of the 1990s, yet few here or abroad can explain what it means. For George Bush the new world order involves some fuzzy notion of "collective security" under the umbrella of the United Nations and a world court. For Mikhail Gorbachev, the new world order is a type of democratic Soviet Union linked to the European Federation.

Only one leader, Pope John Paul II, seems to perceive clearly what the new world order should be. And, according to Malachi Martin's recent hardcover *The Keys of This Blood*, the pope not only has a calculated blueprint for the new world order, but is determined that he—not George Bush, Mikhail Gorbachev, or anyone else—should lead it.

The gist of *The Keys of This Blood* is that Pope John Paul II is in a three-way competition to head a new world order. The cover jacket reads: "The struggle for world dominion between Pope John Paul II, Mikhail Gorbachev, and the capitalist West." Since the book's publication in 1990, the competitors have been narrowed by a third, as Gorbachev no longer leads the former Soviet Union, much less the world. Western capitalism appears the more enduring (though not invincible) foe. Whatever the obstacles, John Paul is determined, Martin wrote, to "endow his pontificate with an international profile and, as pope, move around among world leaders and nations, vindicating a position for himself as a special leader among leaders, because in that competition he plans to emerge the victor."[1]

Of course, John Paul is only the latest in a centuries-long line of popes seeking political dominion. What differs now is that—as Communism disintegrates, as the West continues its moral slide, as international finance rocks with instability—this pope could, under the right circumstances, lead his own version of the new world order, a modern application of Augustine's *City of God* theology, in which the church would play the major role in shaping all aspects of society.

By early 1990 John Paul had visited more than 90 nations and given 1,559 speeches in 32 languages. He has been seen or heard in the flesh or on audio-video circuits by 3.5 billion people. He has been hosted at the White House, praised by numerous Protestant leaders, fraternized with dozens of world figures, formalized diplomatic relations with the United States and the Soviet Union, and was addressed by Mikhail Gorbachev as the "world's highest moral authority." Most important, John Paul II has been credited, more than any other man, with the collapse of Communism in Eastern Europe, the harbinger of the new world order he wants to head.

"Over a period of 10 years," wrote Martin in *The Keys of This Blood*, "among 92 nations across the length and breadth of five continents, he [the pope] established himself as a world leader, as one free from all disfiguring partisanship; as someone endowed with an all-embracing mind; and as the possessor of an international profile of perhaps the highest personal definition achieved by any one individual in recorded history. He became, on those terms, an acknowledged and accepted world leader."[2]

Neither East Nor West

Despite his impressive record as a world statesman, John Paul II is still far from wielding the political clout of some of his predecessors, such as Pope Gregory VII, who kept German Emperor Henry IV waiting barefoot outside the pontiff's castle for three snowy days before letting him inside. Or Innocent III, a monarchial pope who promoted crusades and wielded unrivaled political hegemony. John Paul's inability, for instance, to stop the Gulf War, which he decried ("No, never again war, which destroys the lives of innocent people"), highlights his limitations.

Clearly, no matter how defunct the Communists or decadent the capitalists, they still have all the guns. Joseph Stalin's question "How many divisions does the pope have?" is still pertinent today.

Nevertheless, Martin asserts that John Paul has been seeking to involve the papacy in international politics to a degree unmatched over the past two decades. "It was the first distinguishing mark of John Paul's career," Martin wrote, "that he had thrown off the straitjacket of papal inactivity in major world affairs."[3] He stressed that John Paul wanted to "take up and effectively exercise once more the international role that had been central to the tradition of Rome, and to the very mandate Catholics maintain was conferred by Christ upon Peter and upon each of his successors."[4]

The pope, obviously, has a spiritual vision for the new world order. Unlike other leaders fuzzily conjecturing about the new world order, John Paul, Martin writes, is "adamant on one capital point: No system will ensure and guarantee the rights and freedoms of individuals" unless they are "rooted in the teaching of Christ, as proposed by Christ's church. . . . This is the backbone principle of the new world order envisaged by the pope."[5]

The pope believes that neither oppressive Marxism, with its godless ideology, nor materialistic capitalism, with its financial inequities, is an acceptable system. For John Paul, it was "unthinkable that the Marxist East and the capitalist West should continue to determine the international scheme of things."[6] In his first social encyclical since Communism's demise in Eastern Europe (called his "new world order" encyclical), *Centesimus Annus*, the pope expressed reservations about capitalism as a viable alternative to Communism. "The historical experience of the West," the pope wrote, "shows that even if the Marxist analysis and its foundations of alienation are false, nevertheless alienation—and the loss of the authentic meaning of life—is a reality in Western societies too. This [alienation] happens in consumerism, when people are ensnared in a web of false and superficial gratification rather than being helped to experience their personhood in an authentic and concrete way."

Instead, the pope envisions a new world order "centered and dependent upon Christ,"[7] which means, Martin wrote, "the acceptance and implementation of Christ's revelation announced by the papacy and the Roman Catholic Church."[8]

Recent events could make his version of the new world order a reality, at least in Europe. The pope himself has said that "a united Europe is no longer a dream. . . . This is the most auspicious moment to gather up the stones of the walls [that were] torn down and to construct together a common European home."

No doubt, either, whom John Paul wants to lead it.

The Blood of These Keys

The pope, by virtue of his position as "claimant Vicar of Christ," says Martin, believes that he should be the ultimate arbiter of truth in the new world order. "In all phases of education," wrote Martin, "in all aspects of moral behavior, and in all questions about the ultimate truths undergirding the life and death of every human being, the man claims for his papal persona the right, the privilege, the duty, and the due authority to stand as judge."[9] The pope sees himself not as one world leader among many but as the one who, by virtue of his exalted position, should be the preeminent authority. "That authority," wrote Martin, "that strength, is symbolized in the Keys of Peter, washed in the human blood of the God-Man, Jesus Christ. John Paul is and will be the sole possessor of the Keys of this blood on that day."[10]

Martin never mentions the papacy's bloodstained record as authority in the old order, one supposedly based on the Keys of Peter. History bears grim witness that most of the blood on those Petrine keys didn't belong to Christ, but to Reformers such as Huss and Jerome, whom the popes burned at the stake, or the Jews, who were driven into ghettos and persecuted, or the humble Waldensians, who were butchered en masse.

Though Pope John Paul, with a clarity and forthrightness unlike any of his predecessors, has spoken out in favor of religious freedom (see his speech for the celebration of the "World Day of Peace," January 1991), history has shown that *any* religious system—Protestant, Catholic, Muslim—fancying itself as mankind's moral and spiritual guardian has persecuted dissenters.

Both John Paul in *Centesimus Annus* and Malachi Martin in *The Keys of This Blood* refer to the gospel as the context for their church's political aspirations, yet they quote no deeds or words of Jesus as their example for a political imperative, because Jesus left none. Jesus never involved His ministry in politics, but dealt with spiritual issues alone. Jesus sought to solve His nation's woes not with legislative decrees, but with the call to repentance. "The kingdom of God," He said, is "within you" (Luke 17:21), not in the halls of political power.

The Catholic Church has taken the unbiblical position of being not only a reconstituted church, but a state as well, with nuncios, ambassadors, diplomatic intrigues, even its own currency. Many prominent Catholics see the danger of mixing the kingdom of heaven with the kingdom of earth. During the debate over the appointment of an ambassador to the Vatican in the mid-1980s, for example, New Right fundraiser Richard Vigeurie, a Catholic, warned: "It is a mistake for the administration to afford diplomatic recognition to any church. As a Catholic, I have the greatest respect and love for the pope, but the state he leads is not of this world, and the United States should not act as if it is."

America's Founding Fathers, including such "infidels" as Thomas Jefferson, had a vision of this gospel principle separating the kingdom of God from earthly ones. Understanding the dangers of legislated religion, Jefferson railed against those "fallible and uninspired men" who assume "domination over the faith of others, setting up their own opinions and modes of thinking as the only true [i.e., truth] and infallible" and then endeavor "to impose them on others."[11]

In *Centesimus Annus*, John Paul claimed that "the church's method is always that of respect for freedom," but he immediately added that "freedom attains its full development only by accepting the truth." He's right: Those who didn't accept Rome's old world order found that their freedom couldn't attain "its full development" while they languished and died in dungeons or at the stake.

The Moral Imperative

Unlike Bush's vision of a new world order, John Paul not only has an agenda but enough moral stature to promote, if not enforce, it. And Martin says people are listening. "The only thing John Paul has not found in his papal travels," wrote Martin, "is any disagreement with him about the need for a binding ethic that must obligate the society of nations. Christian believers and cryptobelievers, nonreligious believers and positive atheists—even those who have a diehard antireligious attitude and policy—are all prepared to go that far with the pontiff."[12] Though Martin exaggerates (as apologists tend to do), no doubt many people do see the need for a binding ethic.

In *Centesimus Annus*, John Paul wrote: "The world is ever more aware that solving serious national and international problems is not just a matter of economic production or of juridical or social organization, but also calls for specific ethical and religious values."

Fair enough. Yet, if John Paul—or George Bush or any future leader—ever does amass the power not only to define but enforce his own specific "religious values," what will be the result? Scripture and history leave little doubt: People will wish that the new world order had remained nothing more than George Bush's nebulous political logo or just a Latin phrase on the back of dollar bills.

---

[1] Malachi Martin, *The Keys of This Blood* (New York: Simon and Schuster, 1990), 480.
[2] *Ibid.*, 641.
[3] *Ibid.*, 23.
[4] *Ibid.*, 22.
[5] *Ibid.*, 19.
[6] *Ibid.*, 21.
[7] *Ibid.*, 374.
[8] *Ibid.*, 74.
[9] *Ibid.*, 34.
[10] *Ibid.*, 639.
[11] Virginia Statute of Religious Liberty, January 16, 1786.
[12] *Ibid.*, 160.

This article originally appeared in *Liberty*, January/February 1992.

CHAPTER NINETEEN

The New World Order

As the old world order collapses, many people would like to define and lead the new one, such as George Bush. Though various other contenders exist, one man is quietly and effectively positioning himself to be that leader: Pope John Paul II.

At first glance he does not seem like a valid contender. Indeed, for most of the twentieth century the popes remained in a sorry position politically. Caught between the overwhelming ideologies of the Marxist East and the capitalist West, the Vatican hovered on the sidelines, a minor player in the hardball geopolitics of the superpowers. Stalin best expressed the relative impotency of Rome amid the *real-politik* of the nation-states when he asked, "How many divisions does the pope have?"

Now, however, as Communism has gone belly-up and humanity moves toward some version of the much-heralded new world order, the games nations play have been altered. Foremost among these changes has been the introduction of a new player in the millennial endgame of geopolitical jockeying: John Paul II. And nowhere is the sudden rise of the papacy as a powerful political factor more graphically explained than in Malachi Martin's recently published hardcover, *The Keys of This Blood*.

From the earliest pages, Malachi Martin, a former Jesuit, states that John Paul II is hurling the papacy into the arena of international politics as it has not experienced for centuries. "It was the first distinguishing mark of John Paul's career," writes Martin, "that he had thrown off the straitjacket of papal inactivity in major world affairs." John Paul "had served notice that he intended to take up and effectively exercise once more the international role that had been central to the traditions of Rome, and to the very mandate Catholics maintain was conferred by Christ upon Peter and upon each of his successors." According to Martin, the pope sees himself not as one world leader among many but as the one who, by virtue of his position, should be the preeminent authority in the day that the new world order is established. "That authority," writes Martin, "that strength, is symbolized in the keys of Peter, washed in the human blood of the God-Man, Jesus Christ. John Paul is and will be the sole possessor of the keys of this blood on that day."

Though John Paul does not have that divine authority, it is sometimes hard to tell. He has been an honored guest at the White House, has had Protestant leaders swoon over him, has hobnobbed with world leaders, has been called the "holy father" by George Bush, has formalized diplomatic ties with the United States and the Soviet Union, was addressed by Soviet leader Mikhail Gorbachev as "the world's highest moral authority," and has been credited, more than any other person, with the collapse of Communism in Eastern Europe, an event seen as a harbinger of the new world order. Even Peter did not have that kind of pull.

Unparalleled Authority

The essence of John Paul's view of the new world order, says Martin, is this: Neither oppressive Marxism with its godless ideology nor materialistic capitalism with its financial inequities is an acceptable system, and neither should remain. Instead, the pope envisions a new world order "centered and dependent upon Christ." According to Martin, this dependence on Christ means the "acceptance and implementation of the message of Christ's revelation announced by the papacy and the Roman Catholic Church."

Of course, popes have been making similar announcements for centuries. Now, though, with the collapse of Communism, with the instability in international finance, with the moral decline of the West, the world—linked by massive communication facilities—is heading in a direction that could grant such an internationally revered figure as John Paul II unparalleled political authority. Ultimately, according to the book of Revelation, something like that will happen as a massive union of church and state (much like what John Paul envisions) overwhelms the world.

Martin states that this pope intends to break away from "*the two hundred years* of inactivity [that] had been imposed upon the papacy by the major secular powers of the world." Two hundred years ago takes us back to the 1790s. Seventh-day Adventists have placed the end of "time and times and the dividing of time" of the little horn (Dan. 7:25) in the 1790s, particularly 1798, when the pope was captured by the French general Berthier. We have seen that event as the infliction of the "deadly wound" that eventually would be healed: "And I saw one of his heads as it were wounded to death; and his deadly wound was healed" (Rev. 13:3).

Without knowing it, Martin is telling us that the papacy's wound is healing. "Over a period of ten years, and among ninety-two nations across the length and breadth of five continents, he [the pope] established himself as a world leader, as one free from all disfiguring partisanship; as someone endowed with an all-embracing mind . . . ; and as the possessor of an international profile of perhaps the highest personal definition achieved by any one individual in recorded history. He became, on those terms, an acknowledged and accepted world leader."

In *The Keys of This Blood*, Martin sees the pope as being in a geopolitical struggle with opposing forces for political supremacy. Martin paints everything in apocalyptic terms: "Only one power," he says, "can ultimately be the victor in the millennium endgame," and John Paul is expending all the energy of his papal office to be that victor. In this context Martin's talk of a "one world government" and "globalists" does not seem too far-fetched, especially when the book of Revelation depicts the universal political power that Rome (along with some help from Protestant America) will exert in the last days. This pope, says Martin, is determined to regain for the papacy "the international role that had been central to the tradition of Rome, and to the very mandate Catholics maintain was conferred by Christ upon Peter and upon each of his successors."

Ellen White and the Papacy

More than one hundred years ago, in another book that dealt with the papacy's "international role," Ellen White warned that the "Roman Church is far-reaching in her plans and modes of operation. She is employing every device to extend her influence and increase her power in preparation for a fierce and determined conflict to regain control of the world."

Her words that "it is a part of her [Rome's] policy to assume the character which will best accomplish her purpose" take on an interesting dimension in contrast to what Martin writes: "John Paul had a certain invaluable immunity from the suspicious and prying eye. That white robe and skullcap, the fisherman's ring on his index finger, the panoply of papal liturgy, the appanage of pontifical life, all mean that the rank and file of world leaders, as well as most observers and commentators, would see him almost exclusively as a religious leader."

"She [the papacy] has clothed herself in Christlike garments," Ellen White warned. Says Martin: "John Paul's rockbound certitude—deriving from his Catholic faith and from his personal endowment as the sole vicar of God among men—is that any human effort that is not ultimately based on the moral and religious teaching of Christ must fail."

"Rome is aiming to reestablish her power, to recover her lost supremacy," said Ellen White. "She is silently growing into power. Her doctrines are exerting their influence in legislative halls, in churches, and in the hearts of men. . . . Stealthily and unsuspectedly she is strengthening her forces to further her own ends." Martin writes that John Paul planned "to endow his papacy with an international profile and, as pope, move around among world leaders and nations, vindicating a position for himself as a special leader among leaders, because in that competition he plans to emerge the victor."

What gives *The Keys of This Blood* extra punch is that the author is not an overenthusiastic Seventh-day Adventist frantically trying to interpret present-day events into our specialized prophetic scenario. Malachi Martin is a devout Catholic (he dedicated this book to the "Immaculate Heart"), a former Jesuit who loves his church and is concerned about its future. His devout Catholicism, of course, gives the book a slant and prejudice in favor of the pope and the Roman Church. And whether or not all his details can be corroborated (in 698 pages he gives no footnotes) is irrelevant to its basic message.

What's important is that the gist of this book—written by someone who is probably not acquainted with Adventists' understanding of prophecy—is that Pope John Paul II is involved in an international struggle to gain the political supremacy that he believes his office entitles him to, and so far, as an international figure of gargantuan proportions, he has been meeting with unparalleled success.

Of course, not everyone will fit into John Paul's vision of the new world order. Certain people have "a deeply rooted opposition amounting to a nourished enmity for all that John Paul represents as churchman and as a geopolitician." Though some of these groups have shown a willingness "to accept some form of merger with the various tides advancing on their positions," others will "remain lodged in relative isolation in their historical crevasses, *holding on to their traditions.*" Martin mentions Seventh-day Adventists as one such group.

For these people, Martin writes that "any satisfactory relief of their pathos must await near-future historical events of a worldwide magnitude." He does not explain what these "events of a worldwide magnitude" will be or how those "holding on to their traditions" will fit in. Scripture, however, describes what happens in the last-day union of church and state: "And he had power to give life unto the image of the beast, that the image of the beast should both speak and cause that as many as would not worship the image of the beast should be killed" (Rev. 13:15).

Scripture teaches that no human new world order will succeed. Not George Bush's. Not the papacy's. Only God's.

"And the seventh angel sounded; and there were great voices in heaven, saying, The kingdoms of this world are become the kingdoms of our Lord, and of his Christ; and he shall reign for ever and ever" (Rev. 11:15).

This article originally appeared in the *Adventist Review*, August 1, 1991.

CHAPTER TWENTY

Superpower: America in Prophecy

Once the sand of Desert Storm settled, the United States came out on top of not only Iraq but the world. Whereas just a few years ago pundits were bemoaning America's decline, they now regard the United States as the world's premier political and military heavyweight.

Time called America "the world's sole remaining superpower."[1] Charles Krauthammer, writing in the *New Republic,* said that "there is no prospect in the immediate future of any power to rival the United States."[2] And Yassir Arafat, responding to America's new status, called Washington, D.C., "the New Rome."[3]

The New Rome! Why? Because old Rome was the unrivaled superpower of its age, and America is now in that position.

Arafat's symbol, of course, immediately evokes the Adventist interpretation of Revelation 13, in which America—the lamblike beast with two horns (verse 11)—appears about the time the papacy received its temporary wound, the 1,260-year period ending in the eighteenth century.[4] Though this beast starts out with gentle, lamblike qualities, reflecting the peaceful characteristic of religious freedom in America, it soon speaks "as a dragon," exercising "all the power of the first beast before him" (verses 11, 12) and even giving power to the "image of the beast" (verse 15). Who is that "first beast before him?" Rome! And America is now . . . the new Rome?

These commentators unknowingly said for the first time in history, the United States is set to fulfill its prophetic role.

False Alarm

What's exciting is that just a few years ago alarmists were decrying America's demise. "Johnny can't read," "Johnny can't write," "Johnny can't fight" were the warnings. Japanese and German students were smarter, better educated, and better trained than American kids, and thus the nation was declining. Capturing the sentiment of economists, historians, and political scientists who were warning of America's decline, author Paul Kennedy in the *Atlantic Monthly* repeated the quip "Rome fell, Babylon fell, Scarsdale's turn will come."[5] John McLaughlin, in the *National Review*, asked, "Is America going to the dogs?"[6]

Now in the aftermath of the Gulf War, talk of America's demise has proved premature. The United States has been losing its economic edge, no doubt, but that didn't stop it from leading the coalition against Saddam Hussein. Marks and yen, in and of themselves, don't automatically translate into geopolitical power. America, despite its economic woes, has assumed a leadership role of not only the West but of almost all the world.

When, for example, a Marxist-led coalition overthrew the government in Ethiopia, whom did both sides ask to mediate? America. When Boris Yeltsin, the first freely elected Russian leader in a thousand years, took office, where was the first place he visited? America. When the Baltic states began their breakaway from the Soviet Union, from whose constitution were their leaders quoting? America's. When Kuwait was invaded, whose military led its liberation? America's. To which nation has Gorbachev looked to save his country? America. No wonder a National Public Radio correspondent called George Bush the "president of the world."

This trend began even before the Gulf War, which didn't make the United States the new world leader; it simply revealed that, after the collapse of Communism, America already was.

Thus, writes Krauthammer, we now have "a highly unusual world structure with a single power, the United States, at the apex of the international system."[7]

America of the Pioneers

The United States' unrivaled superpower status "at the apex of the international system" fits perfectly into the Adventist scenario of the last days. By identifying the lamblike beast of Revelation 13:11 as the United States, our pioneers basically predicted that at some point America would have to become the world's dominant political and military power. Otherwise, how could it enforce "the mark of the beast" upon the world? What's especially remarkable is that their interpretation was initially made when America was hardly a world power, much less a *dominant* one.

In 1851 J. N. Andrews wrote the first Adventist article identifying Protestant America as the beast power.[8] In the 1884 edition of *The Great Controversy*, Ellen White named America as the beast as well. "The image to the beast," she wrote, "represents another religious body clothed with similar power. The formation of this image is the work of that beast whose peaceful rise and mild professions render it so striking a symbol of the United States."[9]

If this interpretation, in which America would enforce the mark of the beast upon the world, seemed implausible even three years ago, how did it appear in the mid-1800s, when the big powers were still the Old World ones—Prussia, Austria-Hungary, and England? In 1851 America had a peacetime military of about twenty thousand men, about one-tenth the combatants of Waterloo alone. In 1814 (less than forty years before Andrews wrote his article), the British burned Washington, D.C.; in 1876 General Custer's seventh U.S. Calvary Regiment was wiped out by Sitting Bull's braves. Thus, twenty-five years *after* Andrews' prediction, only eight years *before* Ellen White's, America was still fighting Indians. *And this was the nation that was going to force the world to make an image to the beast?*

Not until World War I did the United States become an international force to be reckoned with. Nevertheless, even in 1933, when Hitler became führer, the United States had only the sixteenth-largest army in the world—smaller than those of Spain, Turkey, and even Poland. After World War II America enjoyed unrivaled supremacy, but not for long, because the Soviet Union soon challenged it everywhere, including space. In the 1950s Americans panicked because the Russians were orbiting satellites over their heads while, as Tom Wolfe wrote in *The Right Stuff,* American "rockets always blew up."[10]

Once the Soviet Union did become a superpower on par with the United States, it was hard to see how America could ever fulfill its prophetic role. If because of Soviet military might the United States couldn't kick the Communists out of Poland, how could it ever enforce a particular brand of religion upon the world?

Now, of course, everything has changed. The Communists are on the run in Moscow, not to mention Poland. Despite the victory of the reformers, the Soviet Union is in a political, military, and economic meltdown, which makes it dependent upon the West, especially the United States. As a result, America is in a more powerful position to exert geopolitical influence everywhere.

"America," wrote correspondent Jim Hoagland in the Washington *Post,* "would now determine all major global events."[11]

"If this new world order means anything," writes Krauthammer, "it is an assertion of American interests and values in the world."[12]

Speaking Like a Dragon

America certainly has good values worth asserting, lamblike qualities such as democracy and religious freedom. Unfortunately, according to prophecy, the nation will speak like a dragon, and instead of asserting these positive values, it will enforce an apostate religious system, "an image to the beast," upon the world.

Of course, great changes still need to happen before this nation fulfills its prophetic destiny. America's precarious financial situation cannot be ignored either. Nevertheless, America's ascension as the new, unrivaled superpower fits a major piece of the prophetic puzzle squarely into place. It is an unmistakable sign of the Second Coming.

But before Christ returns, those who "keep the commandments of God and the faith of Jesus" (Rev. 14:12) need to prepare for "a time of trouble, such as never was since there was a nation even to that same time" (Dan. 12:1). And because Scripture predicts this nation will "cause that as many as would not worship the image of the beast. . . be killed" (Rev. 13:15), God's people need to prepare for religious persecution as well.

America is not called "the new *Rome*" for nothing.

---

[1] *Time*, July 29, 1991, 13.

[2] Charles Krauthammer, "The Lonely Superpower," *New Republic*, July 29, 1991, 23.

[3] *Newsweek*, August 12, 1991, 33.

[4] For more details, see *The Great Controversy*, 433-450.

[5] Paul Kennedy, "The (Relative) Decline of America," *Atlantic Monthly*, August 1987, 33.

[6] John McLaughlin, "Is America Going to the Dogs?" *National Review*, July 31, 1987, 22.

[7] Krauthammer, 23.

[8] J. N. Andrews, "Thoughts on Revelation XIII and XIV," *Second Advent Review and Sabbath Herald*, May 19, 1851.

[9] Ellen White, *The Spirit of Prophecy*, 4:278.

[10] Tom Wolfe, *The Right Stuff* (N.Y.: Bantam Books, 1984), 201.

[11] Jim Hoagland, "Of Heroes . . . ," Washington *Post*, August 29, 1991.

[12] Krauthammer, 26.

This article originally appeared in the *Adventist Review*, December 5, 1991.

CHAPTER TWENTY-ONE

Satan's Consummate Deception

We believe that prior to the second coming of Christ the controversy about allegiance to God will divide the world into two camps: those who keep Saturday, the true Sabbath, and those who observe Sunday, the false Sabbath. But if this is so, how will the billions who live in lands where Sunday has no religious significance be drawn into the controversy? While it is not difficult to envision a national Sunday law in the United States or other Western nations, what about Muslim, Hindu, and Buddhist countries, where Sunday is about as holy to the people as the Aztec God Quetzalcoatl is to High-Church Anglicans in Canterbury? How will the flag-burning fanatics in Iran who march their children across mine fields for the glory of Allah or the Orthodox Jews in Jerusalem who stone cars that drive through their districts on the *Shabbat* or billions of other non-Christians ever be persuaded to keep Sunday holy?

We don't know. Though the Bible and the Spirit of Prophecy teach that these issues will be worldwide and that each individual will understand the issues clearly enough to make a rational choice between allegiance to God's law and allegiance to man's, how all nations will be caught up in the final events has not been revealed. All this article can do, then, is show one *possible* way that all those on the earth might be deceived.

In the last days of Jesus' earthly ministry He warned about false christs. "Then if any man shall say unto you, Lo, here is Christ, or there; believe it not. For there shall arise false Christs, and false prophets, and shall shew great signs and wonders; insomuch that, if it were possible, they shall deceive the very elect" (Matt. 24:23, 24).

Ellen White, in *The Great Controversy*, describes how Satan himself will come as one of these false christs. "As the crowning act in the great drama of deception, Satan himself will personate Christ. . . . In different parts of the earth, Satan will manifest himself among men as a majestic being of dazzling brightness, resembling the description of the Son of God given by John in the Revelation (Rev. 1:13-15). The glory that surrounds him is unsurpassed by anything that mortal eyes have yet beheld" (p. 624).

Though this deception could dupe Christians, what about the Muslims in the Sahara Desert, the Jews in Galilee, or the Buddhists in the Himalayas? How could Satan's "crowning act" affect them?

The answer lies in the eschatology of these other faiths. Christians are not the only ones expecting a Saviour. The Jews are still awaiting the Messiah's first appearing. Buddhists, Hindus, and Muslims also anticipate the arrival of a supernatural personage. "In all three religions [Islam, Hinduism, and Buddhism]," writes Jack Gratus in his book *The False Messiahs,* "there are variations on the belief in a future saviour who will arise after a period of universal upheaval to bring peace and happiness to the world." And it is this universal hope of an end-time divine deliverer that could open the rest of the world to Satan's consummate deception.

Messianic Woes

"All the prophets prophesied," says the Talmud, "only for messianic times." The great Jewish philosopher Moses ben Maimonides (1135–1204) taught that the coming of the Messiah was basic to Judaism. In the twelfth of his thirteen Articles of Faith, he stated: "I firmly believe in the coming of the Messiah; and although He may tarry, I daily hope for His coming." Despite great confusion about the Messiah's advent, many believed, and still do, that He would appear during a time of great trouble, called the "Messianic Woes," when He would rescue His people and usher in a millennium of peace. "Only the cataclysmic intervention of a divinely endowed being," wrote Abba Hillel Silver in his classic *History of Messianic Speculation in Israel,* "at the moment of the nation's deepest degradation, could destroy the wicked powers which oppressed it, restore the people, cleansed by suffering, to its ancient glory, and rebuild the broken harmonies of the world."

The Advent hope, coupled with the jumbled theories concerning it, opened the Jews to a stream of messianic shams. Simeon Bar Kokba declared, "I am the Messiah!" and led a revolt against the Romans in A.D. 231 that left hundreds of thousands of Jews dead. In the fifth century, pseudomessiah Moses of Crete promised to lead the Jews dry-shod across the sea into Jerusalem. On the Day of Redemption many of the Jews, expecting the water to part, jumped into the sea and drowned.

Serene of Syria, Obayah Abu-Isa ben Ishak, David Alroy, Solomon Molcho, Abraham Abulafia, Isaac Luria, Shabbetai Zebi, Jacob Frank, and others all made messianic declarations—and through the centuries thousands of Jews have believed them, often with disastrous results.

Even today a feverish messianism pulses among some Orthodox Jews. A few years ago zealots in Israel tried to blow up the Dome of the Rock in Jerusalem. Their motive, according to the *New Republic*, was to so enrage the Arabs that they would wage such a vicious jihad against Israel that "the Messiah would come to save his people from destruction."

The Muslim Mahdi

Not only do Muslims believe in a divine "Restorer of the Faith" but many associate him with the returned Jesus. The Koran makes reference to the Christ's second coming (IV, 159). Known in Islamic tradition as the Mahdi, the twelfth in a line of Imams, the "Rightly Guided One" will usher in a thousand years of peace and justice after ending the reign of "antichrist." According to one Islamic tradition, the antichrist will devastate the whole world, leaving only Mecca and Medina in security, as these holy cities will be guarded by angelic legions. Christ at last will descend to earth and in a great battle will destroy the "man-devil."

Though all orthodox Muslims believe in the return of a divine "Restorer," they disagree on the exact nature of the return, a situation that has bred a procession of bogus Mahdis. Among them was Mohammed Ahmad, the Mahdi of Sudan, who revolted against the Egyptian administration in 1881 and after several spectacular victories established a theocratic state that lasted until 1898, when the British conquered it. Mirza Ghulam Ahmad, claiming to be the Mahdi, gained a following in the 1800s. Ali Mohammed of Shiraz declared: "I am, I am the promised one. . . . I am the one whose name you have for a thousand years invoked, at whose mention you have risen, whose advent you have longed to witness." He was shot by a firing squad. His sect exists today, known as the Baha'i.

Hindu and Buddhist Expectations

According to Hindu belief, the god Vishnu incarnates himself whenever evil prevails. The most important incarnation, however, will be in the form of Kalki, who will appear in the clouds with a flaming sword in his hand, riding on a white steed. He will destroy all evildoers in an apocalyptic battle that will initiate a thousand-year reign of peace on the earth.

"So similar is this expectation to the Christian messianic hope," wrote Wilson Wallis in *Messiah: Christian and Pagan*, "that some years ago the Reverend John Newton of Lahore took advantage of this prediction and wrote a tract showing that the true deliverer and king of righteousness had already come in the person of Jesus Christ. So striking seemed the fulfillment from a Hindu standpoint, that some hundreds in the city of Rapore were led to a faith in Christ as avatar [incarnation] of Vishnu."

In the 1830s one shaman claimed that he was the incarnation of a Hindu god and led a rebellion against the British, who shot him dead. In northern India a Hindu beggar claimed that he was Kalki come to liberate the masses and initiate a thousand years of peace. After he was jailed his movement fizzled, as have dozens of other Hindu messianic movements.

According to some Buddhist sects, a long procession of bodhisattvas as incarnations of Buddha has appeared on the earth to bestow knowledge upon humankind. In some sects a future saviour, the last Buddha, called Maitreya, "Son of Love," is expected to appear from heaven and bring great spiritual blessings. Though there is little incentive in Buddhism for any would-be messiahs, in Japan in 1910 a journalist appeared on the streets of Tokyo and claimed to be the Messiah-Buddha, asserting that he was the "consummation of all the prophecies since the beginning of the world." He and his small movement eventually faded away.

This Same Jesus

Ever since Jesus said, "Behold, I come quickly," Christians have been anticipating His return. Though the Bible, especially the New Testament, teems with Advent texts, Christians disagree on when He will come, where He will come, how He will come, and what He will do when He does come.

This Advent hope—coupled with the confusion over particulars—has nurtured countless false christs. In 1534 radical Anabaptist John of Leiden declared himself a messianic king and took over the city of Münster in Westphalia. James Nayler, a seventeenth-century Quaker leader in England, had a large following who believed he was the messiah. In Russia messianic movements started under several false messiahs, including the notorious Skoptsy sect of the 1700s, whose leader demanded that his male followers be castrated. In China a self-proclaimed messiah, Hun Hsiu-Ch'üan, initiated a rebellion that took 20 million lives between 1850 and 1864. In America William E. Riker claimed he was the Holy Spirit and in the 1940s founded Holy City, California—his New Jerusalem.

Even today, false christs abound. Sun Myung Moon's messianic claims have received much publicity. Jesus Christ Lightning Amen, a middle-aged recluse reported to be living somewhere in an Arizona desert, gets less publicity but nonetheless believes he is the messiah.

The Consummate Deception

The world's great religions have at least two important similarities that could become factors in Satan's grand deception: All expect a divine personage to usher in an era of peace, and all have discord within their own faith about the nature of his coming.

In *The Great Controversy* Ellen White describes the chaos prior to the Second Coming. She quotes Revelation 12:12: "Woe to the inhabitants of the earth and of the sea! for the devil is come down unto you, having great wrath, because he knoweth that he hath but a short time." She places this verse in the last days: "Fearful are these scenes," she writes, "which call forth this exclamation from the heavenly voice. The wrath of Satan increases as his time grows short, and his work of deceit and destruction will reach its culmination in the time of trouble."

Historically, messianic fervor among the different faiths climaxed during crisis times because the people saw a divine deliverer as their only hope. Imagine, then, the messianic expectation of Hindus, Jews, Muslims, and Christians as they face "a time of trouble, such as never was since there was a nation even to that same time" (Dan. 12:1), especially since most expect the messiah to come during a time of trouble.

Then, in the midst of this great turmoil, Satan will appear in different parts of the earth in unsurpassed glory. He comes—a majestic being of dazzling brightness—to the Islamic world in the way Mahdi is expected, and Muslims bow down on their prayer carpets before the "Rightly Guided One," who will usher in the thousand years of peace. In glory unsurpassed by anything that mortal eyes have yet beheld, he arrives among the Hindus, who see him as Kalki, the final and climactic incarnation of Vishnu. The Jews rejoice; their long-awaited *Machaich* has finally arrived, not as a humble servant but as they have been expecting, a powerful king who will end the "Messianic Woes." The Buddhists see Maitreya, come to bestow blessings upon humankind. Meanwhile, Christians shout, "Christ has come! Christ has come!" All these groups—already confused about the nature of the Advent—have been duped in the past by charlatans with much less deceptive power than the devil. If people today believe that a Sun Myung Moon is the returned Christ, what will happen when Satan himself in unsurpassed glory makes the claim?

Also, if a divine personage—a false Jesus, Kalki, or Maitreya, it doesn't matter which—appeared on the earth, it wouldn't take long for millions of Communists to realize just how unreal "socialist realism" is.

Satan, impersonating Christ, speaks deep truths, heals the sick, and performs other miracles. In the Hindu world he quotes from the Vedas, before Muslims he quotes from the Koran, and before Christians "he presents some of the same gracious, heavenly truths which the Saviour uttered." Then, because the world is suffering in a terrible time of trouble, he tells the non-Christians that to help end the woes they all should have a common day, Sunday, to worship God. In this "strong, almost overmastering delusion," he makes the same appeal to the Christian world, claiming "to have changed the Sabbath to Sunday."

And the billions of the world—desperate for the wars, the earthquakes, the famines, the pestilence, and the violence to stop—obey the words of their long-awaited saviour and pay homage to the false Sabbath, thus receiving the mark of the beast.

Peace

Perhaps it is no coincidence that the world's great religions all expect a divine personage to usher in an era of peace. Satan will orchestrate his paramount subterfuge by fulfilling mankind's expectations. He is preparing the world for it now. A few years ago the New Age movement spent hundreds of thousands of dollars advertising in the world's foremost newspapers that the Messiah of the Jews, the Mahdi of the Muslims, the Christ of the Christians, the Maitreya of Buddhists, and the Krishna of the Hindus were all names for one individual and that he would bring peace to the world. In October of 1986 the pope brought together 150 religious leaders from a dozen faiths—everyone from the Archbishop of Canterbury to the Dali Lama—to pray for world peace.

Yet peace hasn't come, and won't. As the earth descends into the time of trouble, billions will plead for Maitreya, Kalki, the Messiah, or Jesus to come. And as Satan executes his grandest lie, he just might appear to each religion as the peace bringer for whom they have long been waiting.

This article originally appeared in *Ministry*, August 1987.

CHAPTER TWENTY-TWO

Truth Matters

A few years ago I attended my first Roman Catholic wedding. The bride, dressed in flowing white, placed a bouquet of roses at the foot of a statue of Mary and then knelt down before it. Later, the priest gave the couple a framed picture of Jesus that, he said, brought happiness to the homes in which it hung on a wall.

While I didn't doubt the piety or the sincerity of either the bride or the priest during what was in many ways a moving and beautiful ceremony—as I left, these convictions seared into my mind: *Thank God for Martin Luther. Thank God for the Protestant Reformation. Thank God for those who died so that we could have biblical Christianity instead of, well, whatever one calls kneeling before a statue and the belief that a picture on a wall would bring happiness to a home.*

I thought of that wedding after reading again the document *Evangelicals and Catholics Together: The Christian Mission in the Third Millennium* (*ECT*), signed last year by influential American Evangelicals and Catholics, in which they attempted to affirm the unity "in Christ" of the two communions so that the faithful could contend together "against all that oppose Christ and His cause."

After the initial brouhaha over the document, some signers backtracked (two Southern Baptists were pressured into deleting their names), and clarifying statements were made. The most comprehensive apologetic was *Evangelicals and Catholics Together: Toward a Common Mission* (Word Publishers, 1995), edited by Charles Colson and Richard John Neuhaus, two signers of *ECT*. Composed of six essays, three by Roman Catholic signers and three by Protestant ones, the 227 pages explained the rationale, motives, and intent of those behind one of the most remarkable statements in centuries of Protestant and Catholic relations.

Though much could be said about each essay, I'm going to comment on Chuck Colson's lead piece, "The Common Cultural Task: The Culture War From a Protestant

Perspective." Chuck Colson is a best-selling Evangelical writer, the winner of the Templeton Prize for Progress in Religion, and the founder and chair of Prison Fellowship Ministries. I have read Colson for years, and, despite disagreement with some of his stands, I've always admired his courage, intelligence, and Christian commitment.

Nevertheless, Colson began by quoting the late Francis Schaffer: "Truth demands confrontation; loving confrontation, but confrontation nevertheless."

Truth does, indeed, demand confrontation—that's why I'm confronting Colson's essay.

Truth demands it.

In his piece, Colson eloquently develops a theme he has addressed before: the damage of relativism upon modern society. He bemoans the loss of first principles, the loss of absolutes, even the loss of the concept of truth itself. "For the first consequence of postmodernism," he wrote, "is the loss of belief in the existence of truth itself. And without a belief in truth, any culture descends into decay and disorder."

With that Colson helps establish a premise of the entire piece: We in the West are in moral decline because we no longer believe in absolutes. Though not as clear-cut as he makes it (after all, Tomas de Torquemada believed in absolutes; so did John C. Salvi), the argument is crucial and correct. The loss of absolutes can lead only to moral anarchy. In fact, it already has.

Colson throws down the gauntlet. We're in a culture war on which hangs the fate of our civilization. Early on he divides the sheep from the goats in this battle: "No longer can Americans agree on foundational moral and intellectual assumptions or even a common methodology or a common language for discussing these issues. On one side of these and other significant issues are those who appeal to objective criteria, such as biblical teaching, principles of natural law, or traditional custom. On the other side are those who, having rejected every appeal beyond mere self-interest, rely solely upon subjective criteria: *How do you feel about it?* or *Everybody has to have a choice.*"

His argument has flaws. Since when, for instance, have "natural laws" and "traditional custom" become "objective criteria" for truth? In his *Politics*, Aristotle argued from natural law for slavery, and the ancient Phoenicians had a "traditional custom" of human sacrifice. Nevertheless, Colson correctly depicts the ideological, cultural, and social confrontation between those who believe that truth exists and those who don't. It's the absolutists versus the relativists, and Colson puts conservative Protestants and conservative Roman Catholics on one side (the absolutists) and liberal Christians, postmodernists, deconstructionists, radical poststructuralists, and humanists on the other (the relativists). These are the battle lines.

Unfortunately, life's never that simple, and neither are Colson's arguments in defense of *Evangelicals and Catholics Together* based on this premise. In fact, despite repeated assertions—both in *ECT* and in his essay on how Catholics and Evangelicals weren't "willing to compromise their profession of faith"—the mere fact that he signed the document, and his spirited defense of it, are compromises themselves.

Quoting Michael Novak, Colson wrote, "Truth matters." However, from what he has written, and from the positions he has taken, what Colson really meant is, "Only some truth does."

The fatal flaw in his argument is that by focusing only on the contest between those who believe in truth and those who don't, his position downplays the contest among the truths themselves. Many basic crucial "truths" held by Roman Catholics and Evangelicals clash fundamentally. Colson admits that the differences are "many and significant," though they must not be (in his thinking) that many and that significant because he later phrases the differences as merely "the distinctives of their respective traditions," as if all that divided the two "traditions" were nothing but tradition (in another source he called it "petty quarreling"), or in the words of *ECT*, "needless and loveless conflicts."

Sorry, but basic Protestant belief isn't just tradition. It's truth based on the Word of God, and the issues that separate biblical Christianity from Roman Catholicism aren't "petty" or "needless" but instead are fundamental truths, truths that Colson contended for fervently in one part of his essay ("The message of the Church," he wrote, "is that there is truth, whether people like it or not—intellectual, moral, and spiritual truth"), then turned into nothing but "the distinctives of their respective traditions" in another.

One example in which his statement "Truth matters" should really be "Only some truth does" is Colson's admonishing Evangelicals to confront culture with God's Word and the power of the gospel: "To do so, we must recenter ourselves on the key doctrines of historical Christianity. This means reappropriating our heritage *in the Reformation* as well as our heritage as Christians, which goes back even earlier, through the early Church to the times of the apostles" (italics supplied).

In the same essay calling for Evangelicals to reclaim their "heritage in the Reformation" Colson calls for Catholics and Protestants to "join together in a defense of truth of our shared faith"! Maybe I'm missing something here, but a reclaiming of the Reformation heritage—considering that the Reformation was based on much outright rejection of Roman Catholic teaching, doctrine, and authority—would necessitate separation from Rome, not unity with it.

Apologists for this Catholic-Evangelical rapproachment like to stress that Luther, at least in the beginning, never meant to separate from Rome. But the Reformation was more than Luther, just as Christianity is more than Paul, and separation from Rome eventually became the focal point of the whole movement, especially when Protestants convinced themselves, from avid Bible study, that the Roman Church was the antichrist itself.

"The prophecies concerning the antichrist," wrote historian LeRoy Edwin Froom, "soon became the center of controversy, as the Reformers pointed the incriminating finger of prophecy, saying, Thou art the Man of Sin! Rome was declared to be the Babylon of the Apocalypse, and the papal pontiffs, in their succession, the predicted Man of Sin. Separation from the Church of Rome and its pontifical head therefore came to be regarded as a sacred, bounden duty. Christians were urged to obey the command, 'Come out of her, my people.' To them, this separation was separation not from Christ and His church but from antichrist. This was the basic principle upon which the Reformers prosecuted their work from the beginning."

In light of Colson's call for Evangelicals to reclaim their Reformation heritage, some quotes by leading Reformers should help them better understand what that heritage is.

"Yea, what fellowship hath Christ with antichrist? Therefore it is not lawful to bear the yoke with papists. 'Come forth from among them, and separate yourselves from them, saith the Lord' " (English Reformer and martyr Nicholas Ridley [1550-1555]).

"Not because they do any injustice to the Papacy, for I know that in it works the might and power of the Devil, that is of the antichrist" (Swiss Reformer Ulrich Zwingli [1484-1531]).

"The great antichrist of Europe is the king of faces, the prince of hypocrisy, the man of sin, the father of errors, and the master of lies, the Romish pope" (English Reformer John Bale [1495-1563]).

"Daniel and Paul had predicted that the antichrist would sit in the temple of God. The head of that cursed and abominable kingdom, in the Western church, we affirm to be the pope" (Swiss Reformer John Calvin [1509-1564]).

Two excerpts, meanwhile, from one of Luther's writings should help debunk the growing myth that Luther remained a loyal, if somewhat disgruntled, son of the Roman Catholic Church: "The pope is not and cannot be the head of the Christian church and cannot be God's or Christ's vicar. Instead he is the head of the accursed church of all the worst scoundrels on earth, a vicar of the devil, an enemy of God, an adversary of Christ, a destroyer of Christ's churches; an arch church-thief and church robber of the keys of all the good of both the church and the temporal lords; a murderer of kings and inciter of bloodshed; a brothel-keeper over all brothel-keepers and all vermin, even that which can't be named; an anti-Christ, a man of sin."

In the same work, this loyal, faithful Roman Catholic elaborated: "O Loyal God, I am far, far too insignificant to deride the pope. For over six hundred years now he has undoubtedly derided the world, and has laughed up his sleeve at its corruption in body and soul, goods and honor. He does not stop and cannot stop, as St. Peter calls him in 2 Peter 2[:14], 'insatiable for sin.' No man can believe what an abomination the papacy is. A Christian does not have to be of low intelligence, either, to recognize it. God himself must deride him in the hellish fire, and as our Lord Jesus Christ, St. Paul says in 2 Thessalonians 2[:8], 'will slay him with the breath of his mouth at his glorious coming.' "

Luther titled that work, *Against the Roman Papacy as an Institution of the Devil.*

For this reason, when Colson wrote "In short, Luther opposed only what he deemed to be corruption in the medieval church," he was engaging in politically correct historical revisionism so popular now among Evangelicals and Catholics eager to unite (notice, he wrote that Luther rebelled against "what *he deemed* to be corruption"; Colson is so politically correct that he can't even come out and directly name it for what it was). Whatever corruptions might have incited Luther's revolt, it quickly became a theological, *Bible-based* conviction that the Roman system wasn't merely God's bride (a biblical term for the church) in need of purification but that it was, in fact, "the whore of Babylon," the antichrist power itself.

Thus Colson's call to reclaim our Reformation heritage in a document in which he calls for unity with a system the Reformation unanimously denounced as the antichrist, proves that his real position isn't "Truth matters" but "Only some truth does."

Another point where truth is sadly victimized, both in Colson's essay and *ECT*, is through the argument that Roman Catholics and Evangelicals share enough common truths to be "one in Christ."

Colson wrote: "What we emphasize is that *Evangelicals and Catholics* affirm many of the same truths. The deity of Christ, His death on the cross for our sins, His resurrection from the dead, His second coming, the infallibility of Scripture—these truths, affirmed in *Evangelicals and Catholics Together*, provide a solid foundation for all Christians. Those who can affirm these truths have something in common of monumental significance."

Of course, those who hold these truths do, indeed, have something more in common with each other than they would, say, with Mormons in Utah, animists in Borneo, and Santerias in south Florida. But what suddenly, after almost five hundred years, makes these broad truths the foundation for unity? Catholics and Protestants held to these same basic truths all during the bitter centuries since the Reformation. Their common belief in "the deity of Christ, His death on the cross for our sins, His resurrection from the dead, His second coming, the infallibility of Scripture"—wasn't deemed enough to stop them from murdering each other over their religious (and political) differences during the Thirty Years' War. The Roman councils that condemned thousands of Protestants to death could have, without any hesitation, affirmed these same positions. Meanwhile, Rome's adherence to these truths didn't stop the Reformers from unanimously naming it the antichrist. And yet now, suddenly, these beliefs are touted as the basis for "unity in Christ"!

What makes the claim even more absurd is that a fundamental disagreement over one of these truths, Christ's "death on the cross for our sins," started the Reformation. Despite the semantic gymnastics between Catholics and other Protestants over justification by faith, that fundamental problem has not been resolved. In fact, indulgences (just one example of how far apart the two "traditions" are)—

blatantly contradictory to the gospel (and the issue that first incited Luther's rebellions)—are still practiced in the Roman Catholic Church. Here's a quote taken from a Roman Catholic newspaper regarding a Vatican decree on the issue: "The decree issued by the Apostolic Penitentiary Office in response to the queries received from diocesan bishops says indulgences they grant via the airwaves are as valid as those the pope grants the same way.

"In order to be eligible for the indulgence, a Catholic must also go to Confession, repent, receive Communion, and pray for the intentions of the pope.

"Plenary indulgences, *which do away with all the punishment due for a sin*, are granted by the pope through apostolic blessings and three times a year can be granted on his behalf by local bishops" (italics supplied).

That's better (perhaps) than Tetzel hawking indulgences outside of Wittenberg in order to help pay for the building of St. Peter's in Rome, but it's not, in any biblical or Pauline sense, "justification by faith," and every gospel-oriented Protestant knows it. The question is Would Chuck Colson look Fr. Richard Johnson Neuhaus in the face and tell him so? That all depends on whether "Truth matters" or if "Only some truth does."

Another professed point of unity between Catholics and Evangelicals is their common belief in "the infallibility of Scripture." Colson can't really believe those words unless Neuhaus has convinced him that Tobit, Judith, Maccabees, Ecclesiasticus, and Baruch are infallible, sacred writ, like Exodus and Romans. Roman Catholics added these books to the Canon—books that Evangelicals regard as apocryphal—in order to help prove doctrines like purgatory and auricular confession, which Evangelicals recognize as unbiblical. And yet Colson states that Catholics and Evangelicals are unified in their belief in "the infallibility of Scripture," when they don't even agree on what constitutes Scripture and when the Catholic version includes books that Protestants reject as uninspired.

Perhaps the most far-reaching compromise, the one with the most practical and tangible implications, is the idea that Catholics and Evangelicals should, Colson wrote, "work together in the common task of evangelizing the unbelieving world." That's an incredible statement, especially considering that Evangelicals have for years considered Roman Catholics a ripe field for evangelism. What Colson is saying, essentially (and what *ECT* says openly), is that Evangelicals don't need to preach the gospel to Roman Catholics; in fact, rather than "sheep stealing" (as *ECT* put it), they should cooperate in preaching the "gospel" to unbelievers.

The question is, "unbelievers" in what? If Colson is satisfied in evangelizing the world with a lowest-common-denominator Christianity, then his position's valid. If, on the other hand, he wants to spread the gospel according to Luther and Paul (as opposed to the canons of the Council of Trent), then—however politically incorrect I might sound—the "unbelieving world" must include Roman Catholics as well.

Recently Protestant author and pastor John McArthur, before a live audience, discussed the issue of sheep-stealing raised in *Evangelicals and Catholics Together*, which promoted the idea that because Catholics and Evangelicals are all Christians, they don't need to evangelize each other. McArthur called it a "frightening statement," saying that the church he pastored was full with former Roman Catholics who, he said, often gave testimonies like this: "I was in the Catholic Church, I went to the Catholic church, I grew up in that whole system, I never knew Christ. I never knew God. . . . The church was a surrogate Christ, the church has all the authority. I sucked my life from the church, from the system, but as far as the knowledge of Christ, or the reality of the forgiveness of sin, or the power of the Holy Spirit in my life, I absolutely didn't have any idea about that." McArthur stressed that many of these former Catholics, after reading *ECT*, came to him in tears, saying, "If someone hadn't given the gospel to me, I would have never come to know the Lord Jesus Christ."

I wonder what Colson's response to those people would be?

Colson's in this conundrum because he's trying—however sincerely—to defend a false premise, and that's the *ECT* document itself. If you start with false premises and inherent fallacies, you will usually add more fallacies while defending your initial ones.

ECT, despite its religious language (and despite its fervent denials), is essentially a political statement. Or if that seems too strong an assertion—*ECT* at least arose out of a political need. The document stresses that Catholics and Evangelicals have a shared faith and that using that shared faith as a base, they should unite to pursue "the right ordering of civil society." *In other words, because we share a common faith ("All who accept Christ as Lord and Saviour are brothers and sisters in Christ"), because we are already united religiously ("There is but one church of Christ"), why not use this commonality to unite politically?*

That's a bogus position. The order is reversed. They already *have* political unity. *ECT* admitted that their common opposition to abortion was the catalyst for this newfound discovery of each other as brothers and sisters. The problem isn't politics (that's what's uniting them)—it's their radically different faiths. Religion has divided, and still does divide, Catholics and Evangelicals, and *ECT* attempts to get these religious differences out of the way—either by downplaying them or stressing all the points the two "traditions" have in common—so they can continue to pursue their common political agenda.

Unfortunately, their religious differences strike to the heart and soul not only of Scripture itself but of its greatest truth: the gospel. Evangelicals and Roman Catholics are preaching different gospels, and despite superficial commonalities, at the core they are radically different religions. Colson's conundrum comes from not recognizing this fact.

Politics, it has been said, is the art of compromise. That might work well for those hammering out policy issues in smoke-filled rooms, but it's a disaster for religion.

Yet that's exactly what the Evangelicals have done with *ECT* is about politics (and it spends a lot more time on political and moral issues than on theological ones), and it's black-and-white proof of just how much politics corrupts religion. Is it a coincidence that one of the most politically active Evangelicals in America, Pat Robertson, signed his name on *ECT*? Of course not. It's par for the course.

Because of their desire for political unity, these Evangelicals have put their names on a statement that calls upon them to refrain from preaching justification by faith, as taught by Luther and Paul, to Roman Catholics—and then in the same breath denies that there is any compromise! How gullible those people must think we are!

How ironic, too, that Colson's essay—bemoaning the loss of truth and absolutes—epitomizes that very loss of truth and absolutes. Colson's stance exemplifies the thing he rails against. Postmodernist relativism has permeated even more than we realize: It has reached the Evangelical churches. Colson's essay proves it.

"We have to demonstrate," Colson wrote, "that there is *a* truth before we can proclaim *the* truth."

Fair enough. But before proclaiming *the* truth, Colson needs to distinguish it from *untruth*.

How can he do that? I have a suggestion, at least for starters.

Attend a Catholic wedding.

This article originally appeared in *Liberty,* September/October 1996.

WHY I FIND RELIGIOUS TOLERATION INTOLERABLE

This section, with articles mostly from *Liberty*, is the most controversial of all, because it deals with the delicate subject of politics and religion, including some New Right bashing for which I have been castigated, criticized, and condemned to hell (even by fellow Adventists) ever since I started writing for *Liberty* in the mid-1980s.

Nevertheless, I hold firm to my position that the Christian Right, whatever good things they might espouse, represent a dangerous threat to religious freedom and could become the force that makes America speak "as a dragon."

In "Assault on Separation," I talk about the radical change of attitude in American Protestantism regarding separation of church and state and how today many Christians—those who have benefited most from separation—have now turned against it, an interesting trend in the light of last-day events.

The article "In Pursuit of the Millennium" deals with the curious paradox of Christian Right theology and politics: the relentless pursuit of political power by those whose theology teaches that Christians will be a persecuted minority in the last days before Christ returns.

The earliest piece in this chapter, "Who's Afraid of a Judeo-Christian America?" published in *Ministry* in 1986, recounts my first experience at a New Right meeting where participants expressed their determination to make America a "Judeo-Christian nation." I confronted a speaker (a U.S. Congressman) and said, "When you say Judeo-Christian, don't you really mean Christian? And when you say Christian, don't you really mean Protestant? And when you say Protestant, don't you really mean Fundamentalist?" His answer was that he meant, by Judeo-Christian, a nation based on the Ten Commandments and then he specifically said that the first *three* commandments dealt with man's relationship to God, the last seven with man's relationship to man. Please! When these people can't even get the Ten Commandments right, who wants them enforcing these commandments on America?

Also included in this section is the curiously titled work, "Why I Find Religious Toleration Intolerable" (for which I won my first journalism award). Why would an editor of a religious freedom magazine find religious toleration intolerable? Read the article and find out.

CHAPTER TWENTY-THREE

The Cross and the Constitution

Of course, religion and politics mixed often produce a volatile brew, which is why the American Constitution separates them. The recent onslaught of conservative Christians into the political mainstream, though less visible than in the 1980s, now threatens that separation because of their overt hostility to the traditional wall between church and state. No risk would exist, however, if politically active Christians would adhere to a principle of religious liberty best expressed by the central event of their faith: the Cross of Jesus Christ.

Here the Son of God Himself—nails in His hands, nails in His feet, thorns mashed in His brow—was hung beaten and bloody between heaven and earth because He gave humans the free choice to serve Him. Had He not allowed this freedom, man would not have broken God's law, suffered the consequences of transgression ("for the wages of sin is death," Rom. 6:23), and Jesus Christ would not have been crucified. In essence, Jesus died because He granted mankind religious liberty.

The Lord deemed religious freedom so sacred, so fundamental to the principles of His divine government that, instead of depriving man of freedom, He paid the penalty for the abuse of it. Rather than force us not to sin, He became "sin for us" (2 Cor. 5:21); rather than curse us with chains on our minds, He became a "curse for us" (Gal. 3:13); and rather than make us live without free choice, He "died for us" (Rom. 5:8). Jesus chose suffering, humiliation, and death rather than deprive man of free will. The Cross reveals religious freedom in manifestly divine terms.

At Creation, God weaved into the infinite web of Adam's brain the ability to choose right and wrong, to obey or disobey. Had He not patterned free choice within Adam's mind, God would have had no need to warn him against eating produce from the tree of the knowledge of good and evil. Also, as Jesus created the first couple, He coiled deep within their loins those who would one day abuse their

119

freedom to the point of beating, spitting on, and finally nailing their Creator to a cross!

This moral freedom is not confined to earth, or merely to man, but reigns as a moral principle of creation. Otherwise, how could Lucifer have rebelled against God, unless he were given, as was Adam, not only the capacity to choose wrong but the freedom to act upon that choice?

Thus says the Lord God: "You were the seal of perfection, full of wisdom and perfect in beauty. You were in Eden, the garden of God; every precious stone was your covering. . . . You were the anointed cherub that covers. . . . You were perfect in all your ways from the day you were created, till iniquity was found in you" (Ezek. 28:12-15, paraphrased).

The Bible records those iniquities: "For you have said . . . I will exalt my throne above the stars of God: I will sit also upon the mount of the congregation: I will ascend above the heights of the clouds; I will be like the Most High" (Isaiah 14:13, 14, paraphrased). Perfection, therefore, must include the ability to choose wrong, because though originally "perfect in all . . . [his] ways," Lucifer eventually became boastful, self-exalting, and jealous, all leading to his downfall.

God could have blotted out Lucifer (described in Revelation 12:9 as the dragon) and the other angels who abused their freedom or created them unable to make wrong choices. Instead, war broke out in heaven: "Michael (Jesus) and his angels fought against the dragon; and the dragon fought and his angels, and prevailed not; neither was their place found any more in heaven" (Revelation 12:7, 8). Lucifer's fall brought man's fall, which ultimately brought Christ to the cross. Again, Jesus could have spared Himself the agony of Calvary had He forced Lucifer, the angels, mankind, and all His creation to obey Him, but this He refused to do.

No wonder that while upon the earth, Jesus never forced anyone to follow Him. Better than any He knew the fearful cost of sin and disobedience, yet He allowed men to disobey, to reject, and finally to kill Him, even though by so doing they would bring ruin upon themselves, their families, their nation.

A rich young ruler asked Jesus what he needed to be saved. When Jesus answered, the ruler walked away. Jesus knew the consequences of that decision, and though He loved the man, *because* He loved him, He didn't force the issue. Never did Jesus defy free will. He pled, He wept, He admonished, but never coerced.

Jesus never taught that everyone will be saved or that all faiths are different paths to the Father. "I am the way, the truth, and the life" (John 14:6); "no one cometh to the Father but by me." He warned those in His time about hell, judgment, and the wages of sin, just as He warns us today. Nevertheless, now, as then, He grants all freedom to make their own choice of how, or even if, they will serve Him.

How ironic, too, because if anyone had the right to force obedience, it was Christ. As God, the Creator of the universe (Colossians 1:16), the great *I Am*, He made Lucifer, the angels, mankind, giving them form, substance, intelligence. All that they, or we, are or ever could be comes only from Jesus, in whom "we live, and move, and have our being" (Acts 17:28). He deserves our worship, praise, and obedience, yet if He Himself won't force it, even at the cost of the cross—how dare anyone else?

The Founding Fathers of America understood this principle of free will. Thomas Jefferson wrote that God, though "being Lord both of body and mind, yet chose not to propagate it [religion] by coercions on either, as was in His Almighty power to do." In other words, even though God has the power to force us to obey, He doesn't, and all attempts at coercion are "a departure from the plan of the Holy Author of our religion."[1]

James Madison wrote that "whilst we assert for ourselves a freedom to embrace, to profess and to observe the religion which we believe to be of divine origin, we cannot deny an equal freedom to those whose minds have not yet yielded to the evidence that has convicted us. If this freedom be abused, it is an offense against God, not against man. To God, therefore, not to man, must an account be rendered."[2]

Because of these sentiments, the Founding Fathers wrote the First Amendment of the Constitution: "Congress shall make no law respecting an establishment of religion, or prohibiting the free exercise thereof." These simple sixteen words express the principle of religious liberty embodied by the life, and especially the death, of Jesus Christ. How? Because they *restrict* the government from throwing its power behind any religion, thus protecting citizens from the coercion that sectarian legislation brings.

The First Amendment says that the government shall make "no law respecting an establishment of religion." This clause restricts the government from promoting, funding, or forming any religion. The second clause is a restriction also, not allowing the government to prohibit the free exercise of religion. The clauses are linked because once religion becomes established by law, it can hinder the free exercise of others. "Put differently," writes Christian philosopher Richard John Neuhaus, "free exercise of religions requires the nonestablishment of religion."[3]

When a religion is established, it becomes the legal, official faith, and laws will reflect that faith, laws that can—and inevitably do—conflict with the belief and practices of other persuasions. If, however, government is not allowed to pass laws regarding religion, it will never be able to persecute or discriminate against on the basis of religion, thus reflecting the principles of freedom that Christ embodied. Far from being "neutral" toward religion, the religious references in the Bill of Rights reflect Christianity at its purest.

In 1785, Patrick Henry introduced a bill in Virginia that would levy a general tax "for the support and maintenance of several Ministers and Teachers of the Gospel who are of *different persuasions and Denominations*." In response James Madison, the author of the First Amendment, penned his famous *Memorial and Remonstrance*, in which he called Henry's bill "a dangerous abuse of power" that threatened the nation's most basic freedoms. He warned that fifteen centuries of "ecclesiastical establishments" have given birth to superstition, bigotry, and persecution, and this bill could do the same in America. So alarmed was Madison at this "first experiment on our liberties" that he compared it to the Inquisition! "Distant as it may be in its present form from the Inquisition, it differs from it only in degree."

All this against poor Henry's little bill that wanted only some taxes for "different persuasions and Denominations"?

Yes, because Madison understood the essence of Christ's principles of religious freedom, and he knew that to protect those principles the government must be kept from hindering or promoting religion. "There is not a shadow of a right," he wrote, "for the general government to intermeddle with religion." In a recent book, evangelical pastor and New Right activist Joel Hunter displayed rare sensitivity and awareness on this issue: "Institutional expression is not without force. As has been mentioned, the power of government and its various institutions is force. . . . And all activities carried on by governmental institutions can't help but convey the force linked with governmental institutions. To believe otherwise is amazingly naive."[4] And force, as Jesus taught, lived, and died for, is not what God wants, needs, or advocates.

Unfortunately, many Christians have manifested insensitivity, if not hostility, to the establishment of the First Amendment. In 1798, Presbyterian elders complained to George Washington that the Constitution lacked any explicit recognition of "the only true God and Jesus Christ, whom he hath sent."[5] Over the years, well-meaning Christians have tried to pass legislation that would promote religion, especially theirs, either by pushing laws that would allow government-sponsored prayer in school or by seeking constitutional amendments that would declare America a Christian nation under "the Lordship of Jesus Christ."

In the past century, the courts have had to stop attempts to promote devotional Bible readings in public schools (*Abington School District v. Schempp,* 1961), legislated prayer in public schools (*Engel v. Vitale,* 1962; *Wallace v. Jaffree,* 1985), and endless attempts to divert tax dollars for private, religious education. In 1985, conservative columnist William Rusher advocated a constitutional amendment that would "acknowledge . . . the existence of a Supreme Being."[6]

However innocuous these issues might seem, all represent violations of the principle that governmental authority is not to promote any religious activity. Those opposed to this legislated support are branded anti-God and antireligious, yet in most cases they are seeking to protect faith, not hinder it, when they advocate a strong separationist stance.

The problem many Christians have is that the phrase church-state *separation* doesn't sound good. It implies a void, a chasm, an alienation. Church-state *accommodation* sounds so much more benign. Yet the Founding Fathers knew *accommodation* wasn't worth the persecution, bloodshed, and suffering that is often caused.

No question, Christians *have* the right to be involved in government, to help enact laws, and to bring their values into society. Drugs, violent crime, and poverty rot America from within, and this country needs many of the values that conservative Christians offer. Nevertheless, as they seek to minister to America's ailing soul, Christians, in their zeal for their Lord Jesus Christ, must be careful not to crush out the principles of religious freedom for which He died.

---

[1]Thomas Jefferson, "A Bill for Establishing Religious Freedom."
[2]James Madison, "A Memorial and Remonstrance," 1785.
[3]Richard John Neuhaus, "Free exercise of religion—not establishment of religion—is the issue," quoted in *NFD Journal*, August 3, 1987, 3.
[4]Joel Hunter, *Prayer, Politics, and Power* (Wheaton, Ill.: Tyndale House Publishers, 1988), 37.
[5]Edwin S. Gaustad, *Faith of Our Fathers* (San Francisco: Harper and Row, 1987), 78.
[6]*Church and State*, October 1985, 3.

This article originally appeared in *Liberty*, September/October 1991.

CHAPTER TWENTY-FOUR

Jesus and the First Amendment

In recent years the First Amendment has come under increasing attack. Described as "hostile" to religious freedom, particularly Christian freedom, it is condemned as part of a "secular humanist conspiracy" to place America under the control of "atheists and Communists." The wall of separation between church and state, as embodied in the amendment, is damned as the "figment of some infidel's imagination," a "misleading metaphor," a "pile of stones here and a pile of stones there," and a "totalitarian concept." Presidential hopeful Pat Robertson even links the separation of church and state with the Soviet Union, not America.

Further, the authors of the First Amendment are accused of formulating their ideas on separation of church and state from the "anti-Christian" theology of the rationalist Enlightenment.

Actually, far from being anti-Christian or in any way hostile to religious freedom, the First Amendment's principles are found throughout the Bible and are basic to the teachings of Christ.

Biblical Concepts

The cross of Calvary is a divine revelation of the sanctity of freedom. Christ was crucified because He gave man religious liberty. Had God not created man with the capacity and freedom of choice, man would not have rebelled, and Christ would not have needed to die for that rebellion.

Yet so fundamental was the principle that men should serve God only by free will, not by force, that Jesus, man's Creator, stepped down from heaven, became a helpless infant, lived a life of grinding poverty in human flesh, toiled for more than thirty years among His creation, and finally suffered a degrading death, all because He gave man religious liberty.

Jefferson understood this principle, which was the reason he exalted liberty as one of the "unalienable rights" that the "Creator" endowed upon men. So unalienable was this liberty that God Himself refused to infringe upon it, choosing instead the way of the Cross rather than coercing man's will. And if God will not force obedience, how anti-Christian for politicians or church leaders, who (wrote Jefferson) "being themselves but fallible and uninspired men," to assume "domination over the faith of others, setting up their own opinions and modes of thinking as only true and infallible" and then "endeavoring to impose them on others."

Though Jesus Christ promised freedom from sin, He didn't force freedom upon anyone. Though He, better than anyone, knew the fearful consequences of disobedience, He never forced obedience. Coercion was just another form of the bondage He came to free men from. "God who gave us life," wrote Jefferson, "gave us liberty." And God didn't give men that liberty, only later to trample upon it Himself or to allow a civil institution to trample upon it instead: "We maintain therefore that in matters of religion," wrote James Madison, "no man's right is abridged by the institution of civil society and . . . religion is wholly exempt from its cognizance."

For three and a half years Jesus ministered to mankind, seeking by a revelation of God's love to lead men to a voluntary submission to God. He unraveled the gnarled bones of cripples, raised to life those reeking in death, opened unlit eyes to light and silent ears to sound, and filled deflated souls with words of hope and cheer. His whole life was dedicated to one purpose: He lived to bless others. Yet He was "despised and rejected of men." He was attacked verbally, physically, mentally. He was stoned and cursed. His own creation attacked Him, rejected His teaching, twisted His words, and by doing so led their nation to ruin.

Yet He never compelled, never defiled, the sanctity of free will, never intruded upon the conscience of those who, needing Him most, scorned Him the hardest. Once a rich young ruler, after asking Jesus what he must do to have eternal life, turned away at the answer. Though Jesus loved the young man and knew the tragedy of the mistake, He did not threaten him with temporal punishment; forced worship was contrary to His principles of freedom. Jefferson correctly wrote that all attempts to influence religious belief by temporal punishments were "a departure from the plan of the Holy Author of our religion."

When Peter sought to use the sword to defend the truth, Jesus said: "Put up again thy sword into his place: for all they that take the sword [i.e., in religious matters] shall perish with the sword" (Matthew 26:52). Civil laws, not spiritual laws, need the power of the sword, and by denying Peter the sword, Jesus forbade the church to use the state to make laws that interfere in matters that belong between man and God alone. "To God alone, therefore, not man," wrote Madison, "must an account of it [religion] be rendered."

Jesus never taught that people can go to heaven any way they choose. "I am the way, the truth, and the life," He said. "No man cometh unto the Father, but by me"

(John 14:6). But He never appointed civil government as the divine agent to lead sinners and lost souls to Him (that's the work of the Holy Spirit). He respected what Saint Augustine would later describe as "the liberty of self-ruin." Forced obedience, such as compelling someone to be baptized, will no more enhance his stature with God than will sprinkling holy water on a baby chimpanzee make it religious.

"If ye love me," Jesus said, "keep my commandments" (John 14:15). Love that comes from an intelligent appreciation of God's character is the basis for all true worship. "He that hath seen me hath seen the Father" (verse 9). For years, through miracles, stories, parables, deeds, and ultimately His death, Jesus sought to teach people about God and His love. Worship from any motive other than love is as profitless as state-enforced prayer. Jesus knew the centrality of love, which was why He said that one of the greatest commandments was to "love the Lord thy God with all thy heart, and with all thy soul, and with all thy mind" (Matthew 22:37).

The Lesson of Job

The book of Job dramatically represents true worship as opposed to coercion. Satan wanted to turn Job from God, to change his religious beliefs, and even to get him to curse God. To "convert" Job, he destroyed his property, killed his children, and tortured him "with sore boils from the sole of his foot unto his crown" (Job 2:7). Eventually Job's wife cried out to him: "Dost thou still retain thine integrity? curse God, and die" (verse 9).

Satan's attack against Job exemplifies the state despotism that uses the sword to force people into religious conformity. "Never in civilization," wrote Theodore White, "since the earliest ziggurats and temples went up in the mud villages of prehistoric Mesopotamia, had there been any state that left each individual to find his way to God without the guidance of the state." And to help each spiritual quest, the state—like Satan—used torture, destroyed property, even murdered children, in order to change the religious view of its citizens. Every state-enforced religious law, no matter how benign, has the power of the government behind it, the power of the police and the courts, the power of jail, fines, torture—the power of Satan.

God, however, did not use force to keep Job on His side. He did not threaten Job with worse calamities—the dungeon, the rack—the stake—if he dared to swerve from obedience.

And Job stayed loyal anyway. "Though he slay me," he exclaimed, "yet will I trust in him"(Job 13:15). Why? Because Job had a relationship with the Lord, one born out of experiencing God's love; and upon this experience he built his faith and from that faith developed his unwavering trust. If his faith had come from anything else—such as a legislative decree—it would have crumbled as dust. State-enforced religion is a curse to the ones it enslaves and an abomination to the God whose principles of government are based on free choice. Madison well understood the principles of true worship, which was why he wrote that religion "can be directed only by reason and conviction, not by force or violence."

The Christian Amendment

For more than two hundred years these great principles of religious freedom have been inscribed in the U.S. Constitution: "Congress shall make no law respecting an establishment of religion, or prohibiting the free exercise thereof." Only Jesus expressed it better: "Render therefore unto Caesar the things which are Caesar's, and unto God the things which be God's" (Luke 20:25).

The First Amendment position—which is essentially that religion is between man and God, not man and the state, and that the state has no right to establish or prohibit religion—is firmly rooted in Christian theology. Far from being hostile to Christianity, or even neutral toward it, the First Amendment is Christian!

"Indeed, without searching very far," wrote William Lee Miller in *The First Liberty*, "one could claim that this broad river of history—let us call it dissenting protestantism—had more to do, over all, over time, pound for pound, head for head, with the shaping of the American tradition of religious liberty than did the rational Enlightenment.

"We owe separation of church and state today," wrote Jerry Combee in *National Review*, "at least as much to the influence of evangelical Christianity . . . as we do the so-called rationalistic Enlightenment of Madison and Jefferson. Indeed, the gulf between the Evangelicals and Enlightenment may not have been nearly as great as contemporary intellectual history claims." As far as religious liberty is concerned, no gulf existed: Madison and Jefferson were fundamentally evangelical in their theology of freedom.

For years, Baptists and Presbyterians in America argued amicably over whether Jefferson learned his lessons on freedom from Baptists or Presbyterians. One source quotes Mrs. Madison as saying, "I have a distinct remembrance of Mr. Jefferson speaking on the subject, and always declaring that it was a Baptist church from which these views were gathered." It doesn't matter whether Jefferson and Madison formulated their views from Helwys, Locke, Whitherspoon, Hume, Voltaire, or Jesus Himself. What matters is that their views on religious liberty are rooted in the character of God.

Christians who lead the assault against the First Amendment, thinking that they are fighting the rationalistic, atheistic philosophy of the Enlightenment, are really subverting the principles of freedom that Jesus Christ embodied. It's the theology of one generation, of those who established religious freedom—against the theology of another generation, of those who would undermine it. And the issue is theology. "God hath created the mind free." "A departure from the plan of the Holy Author of our religion." "To God, therefore, not man, must an account of it [religion] be rendered."

These are not the words of atheistic, hedonistic infidels worshiping the goddess of reason. These words reflect basic Christian theology about the nature of man and his relationship to God. Whether or not Madison and Jefferson knew it, they were simply reiterating, in more universal terms, what Roger Williams (a staunch Puritan biblicist) said in the previous century: "An enforced uniformity of religion throughout a nation or civil state confounds the civil and religious [and] denies the principles of Christianity and civility."

"A figment of some infidel's imagination"? "A totalitarian concept"? These words describe the philosophy behind the assault on the First Amendment, not the First Amendment itself.

This article originally appeared in *Liberty*, September/October 1987.

CHAPTER TWENTY-FIVE

Why I Find Religious Toleration Intolerable

You'd think that with a name like Goldstein, I'd be favorable to religious toleration. But I'm not, and my name has much to do with it.

My disdain for religious toleration began twelve years ago, when I was planning to move to Holland. My mother, upset, said caustically, "But how do the Dutch treat the Jews?"

"Don't worry," my grandmother interrupted, "the Dutch have been very tolerant of the Jews."

Tolerant? They were tolerant of Jews? How nice of them! I couldn't wait to move to Holland and be tolerated.

Toleration, of course, is better than intoleration, better than gas chambers, boycotts, and official government persecution. But if toleration is the absence of gas chambers and official persecution, then I didn't need to run off to Holland to be tolerated. I could be tolerated right here in the United States.

But is that what my freedom in the United States is: toleration? Are religious minorities in the United States being merely tolerated? Is toleration what religious liberty is all about?

A state's religious freedoms are usually determined by how the state views religion. If, for example, a state views religion as "the opium of the people" (Karl Marx), the state will be hostile toward religion. The result will be jail, exile, and trips to the Gulag for those who want to follow their faith. Whatever religious freedoms the state does allow will represent toleration.

Or if a state takes the view that "both the spiritual sword and the material sword are in the power of the church . . . , therefore the one sword should be under the other, and the temporal authority subject to the spiritual" (Boniface VIII), or that "the Church of Rome is one monarchy over all the kingdoms of the earth . . . , therefore the Church of Rome must have not spiritual power, but also supreme temporal power" (Leo XIII), the results will be the Inquisition, the stake, and the dungeon. Any deviation allowed will also be the result of toleration.

But if the state takes the view that "God hath created the mind free; that all attempts to influence it by temporal punishments or burthens [burdens], or by civil incapacitations, tend only to beget habits of hypocrisy and meanness, and are a departure from the plan of the Holy Author of our religion" (Thomas Jefferson); or that "religion, or the duty which we owe our Creator, and the manner of discharging it, can be directed only by reason and conviction, not by force or violence" (James Madison), then there are no Gulags, no Inquisitions, and no need for religious toleration.

Why? Because if the government believes that every man's faith must be founded on personal conviction, without coercion by others, the state will stay out of religious matters. When the state views religious freedom not as a privilege to be granted to its citizens but as a God-given inalienable right for every individual, faith is placed outside its jurisdiction. Religion is between God and man, not man and the state, and "there is not a shadow of right in the general government to intermeddle with religion" (James Madison). The government has no more right to "tolerate" your religious beliefs than the Miami Sanitation Department has the right to tolerate tap dancing in Bulgaria or skinny-dipping in Panmunjom.

Webster defines *toleration* as "the capacity for or practice of allowing or respecting the nature, beliefs, or behavior of others." Yet the idea of "allowing" someone inherently implies the right to forbid. If you are allowed by the city to walk on the grass, then the city also has the right to forbid it. If the state allows you the privilege of holding your beliefs, then it can also forbid you that privilege. But if faith is a personal relationship between man and God, then Caesar has no more right to tolerate your faith than your breathing.

In 1689, an era of great religious strife, John Locke published his monumental *Essay on Toleration*. His argument for toleration of deviant faiths asserted that no man is so complete in wisdom that he can dictate another man's faith. Each individual, Locke held, is a moral being responsible to God for his own faith; therefore any compulsion contrary to the will of the individual could bring no more than outward conformity. Locke's approach, though progressive, gave only a limited form of religious freedom—toleration for dissent in a state with an established church. (That same year, perhaps coincidentally, England passed the *Act of Toleration*, which permitted all citizens—except Jews, Catholics, and Unitarians—the right to worship as they pleased.)

America's founding fathers wanted something better than toleration for their new republic. James Madison was even uncomfortable with the term. In 1776, as a delegate to the Fifth Virginia Convention, Madison was appointed to a committee to prepare a declaration of rights. The committee, under the influence of George Mason, proposed that "religion, or the duty which we owe our Creator, and the manner of discharging it, can be directed only by reason and conviction, not by force or violence; and therefore, that all men should enjoy the fullest toleration in the exercise of religion, according to the dictates of conscience."

Madison, however, didn't want the term *toleration* included, and he proposed an alternative version: "That religion, or the duty we owe our Creator, and the manner of discharging it, being under the direction of reason and conviction only, not of violence or compulsion, all men are equally entitled to the full and free exercise of it according to the dictates of conscience."

In his *Autobiographical Notes* (1832), Madison explained: "This important and meritorious instrument was drawn up by George Mason, who had inadvertently adopted the word 'toleration' in the article on the subject. The change, suggested and accepted, substituted a phraseology which declared freedom of conscience to be a natural and absolute right."

When the state takes the views "that all men are created equal, that they are endowed by their Creator with certain unalienable rights," and among those "natural and absolute" rights is the "full and free exercise of it [religion] according to the dictates of conscience," the result is not toleration but religious liberty. Toleration is the counterfeit of intoleration, not its opposite. Intoleration assumes the right of the state to withhold the right of conscience; tolerance assumes the right of granting it. The rights of religious minorities in this country are just that: rights, not toleration.

In an address to the French National Assembly in 1790, a delegation of French Jews said: "America, to which politics will owe so many useful lessons, has rejected the word *toleration* from its code, as a term tending to compromise individual liberty and to sacrifice certain classes of men to other classes. To tolerate is, in fact, to suffer that which you could if you wish, prevent and prohibit."

Toleration is what allows Jews their few synagogues in Russia or Baptists their few churches in East Germany. Toleration is what gave Jews and Christians their third-class status as *dhimmis* in the Islamic world. Toleration is what allowed Jews living under the Papacy the right to go outside the ghetto during the day (but not at night). Toleration, in varying degrees, is what Christians have in China, what Jews have in Romania, and what non-Greek Orthodox sects have in Greece. But toleration is *not* what we have in America.

Of course, things can change. Professor Robert Alley, in "The Despotism of Toleration," warned that the "evidence is persuasive that whenever persons advocate some form of a Christian state or argue for the messianic role of the United States as God's chosen nation, there is a corollary, the introduction of toleration as a principle. And while the implementation may be benign in the beginning, the departure of Madison's principle of religious freedom as a natural right is replaced with the 'despotism' of toleration."

Toleration? *Intolerable!*

This article orginally appeared in *Liberty*, January/February 1987.

CHAPTER TWENTY-SIX

The Christian Right: Will it Bring Political Pentecost to America?

Across America, conservative Christians are flexing political muscle. By mobilizing volunteers, registering voters, lobbying, forming PACs, raising funds, publishing literature, purchasing television time, and supporting or even running candidates, the evangelical movement, once a 98-pound political weakling with sand kicked in its face, has become the undisputed heavyweight of American neo-conservatism.

Its goals, too, are nothing short of Olympian. Says New Right chieftain Paul Weyrich, "We want to govern America."

Pat Robertson, for one, is willing to cooperate. He seeks nothing less than the presidency—deferring his official candidacy until September 1987, however, enables him to continue his ministry and public exposure on his 700 Club.

These ambitions don't hint at a surreptitious conspiracy to overthrow the republic, or of a coup d' état with jets strafing Capitol Hill. Instead, the New Right wants to elect leaders who will pass laws that reflect the values of the "moral majority" of Americans.

What could be more democratic? Whether one agrees or disagrees with the New Right, evangelicals are exercising the prerogatives of a free society. Their desire to turn pacifist conservatives into political militants is for the most part legal, effective, and constitutional.

But is all this Christian? Is the evangelical explosion into politics a political pentecost, an outpouring of God's Holy Spirit upon a people divinely ordained to heal America's moral wounds? And though the New Right claim the Bible as their guide, does it sanction their activity, or are they reading their marching orders wrong?

However one might feel toward Jerry Falwell, Paul Weyrich, or Pat Robertson, even a secular humanist should be able to see that America is turning into a moral outhouse. Pornography—either in literature, television, movies, or video—is a multibillion dollar business. The children of those who watched *Mayberry RFD, Leave It to Beaver,* and *I Love Lucy* are now entertained with the sex, violence, and drugs of *Dynasty, Dallas,* and *Miami Vice.* As Mr. Robertson said in his Constitution Hall speech: "Instead of absolutes, our youth have been given situational ethics and the life-centered curriculum. Instead of a clear knowledge of right and wrong, they have been told 'if it feels good do it.' Instead of self-restraint they are often taught self-gratification and hedonism." More than four thousand fetuses are aborted daily in this country, one in every four—in some states, one in every three. In 1984, U.S. Customs officials seized 14 tons of cocaine, a small percentage of what flows in the bloodstream of an estimated 4 million Americans. Crime is rampant, whether committed by E. F. Hutton (2,000 counts of wire and mail fraud) or James Huberty (the 1984 McDonald's Restaurant massacre). Meanwhile divorce, AIDS, teenage suicides, alcoholism, and other corporate ills infest America like suppurating sores.

And so the New Right coalesced, a clot to heal America's moral wounds. They want to awake the electoral Laodiceans of conservative Christianity, convert them into a political juggernaut, and legislate America back to its Judeo-Christian senses.

Here's the fatal flaw: They've written state and local statutes, congressional bills, and proposed constitutional amendments, but to be effective, laws must be written in the heart (see Jer. 31:33)—the only place they work true reformation! Undoubtedly Christians have the right to help make civil laws, and God uses these laws to help keep order, but the New Right wants more than law and order. They want their Christian consensus at the heart of a new civil religion intended to bring morality back to America. Yet they can no more make America moral by passing laws than they can make a myna bird Jewish by putting a skullcap on its head and teaching it Hebrew. That's why no matter how much political clout the New Right amasses, no matter how many parties they take over or judges they appoint or laws they pass or conservatives they elect—even putting Pat Robertson in the White House—the New Right's plans for a moral America are doomed. They're attempting God's work with man's methods.

No one understood this principle better than Jesus, which was why He didn't join any political party or involve Himself with the government—not because He was indifferent to the problems but because He knew that the people's needs were spiritual, not political. Men need conversion, not civil legislation. For a true reformation, change must begin in the individual soul, not in courtrooms or legislatures. Men need a personal experience with God, an experience that no amount of law, court decision, or government decrees can provide.

Not that there weren't political ills for Jesus to rail against. The brutal Roman government under which Jesus lived exuded corruption, intolerance, and oppression. Political favors were bartered like fruit in a market. Bribery and nepotism were national passions. Even the office of the high priest, the most sacred post in Palestine, could be bought and sold like bogus gems. The gap between the rich and poor gaped wide.

Shoeless beggars with bleeding soles wandered the streets in search of food. Prostitution, religious bigotry, murder, robbery, polygamy, adultery, divorce, slavery, and a myriad of ills contaminated the nation.

Yet Jesus attempted no civil reform, nor did He rail against national enemies. He didn't form watchdog groups in Jerusalem to bark, growl, and bite when the government didn't pass a law or appoint an approved official. He didn't warn the leaders that unless they got in harmony with the Holy Scriptures and ended corruption, nepotism, and bribery, He was going to target them. He didn't put Himself or His disciples into the government to initiate change. He didn't form PACs to lobby the leaders and curry their favor or post moral report cards in the synagogues. And Jesus—who could have rained lightning upon the leaders—didn't display His miraculous powers before the Sanhedrin, or even Pilate or Herod, to coerce them into accepting His mission and plans for the nation. In fact, the only time He stood before the Sanhedrin and Pilate and Herod, He was in bonds.

Jesus lived in an era when the Sabbath had been encumbered with rabbinic regulations that wrapped the day in chains. Instead of enjoying Sabbath rest, the Jews had to toil through the tangles of laws, laws that forbade the wearing of false teeth, that regulated the distance one could travel, and that dealt with whether a person after bathing should dry his whole body at once or limb by limb. Jesus, Himself the Lord of the Sabbath, was accused of desecrating the day.

How did Jesus react to these regulations? Did He lobby the leaders to change the laws? Did He and His followers march on Jerusalem or promote Peter, James, or John for a post in government? Did He go directly to Herod or Pilate and petition for change, pointing out that a Sabbath reform law would greatly benefit the nation? No. Instead, Jesus lived, taught, and exalted the truth, giving the people then, as well as today, an example of the principles of the kingdom of God.

In ancient Israel, leaders had persuaded their followers that devotion of their property to the temple was more laudable than providing for their parents (see Mark 7:9-13). Once a son pronounced the word *corban* over his possessions, devoting them to the temple, he could retain use of them throughout his lifetime, but after his death they went to the priests. The parents, even if destitute, received nothing.

Jesus attacked the abuse, but He didn't form a profamily PAC, Citizens Against Corban, to lobby for a law against this national disgrace. He didn't threaten the leaders with loss of office if they didn't purge the sin from Israel. He used no coercion other than the Spirit of God and the power of the Word. Indeed, when He rebuked the spiritual leaders for this sin, He didn't use political threats or picket signs; instead, He quoted Scripture!

Perhaps the closest Jesus came to initiating a national reform was when He cleansed the temple of the sheep and cattle scalpers whose irreverent racket gave the sacred building all the dignity of a flea market. Yet again, when He shouted, "Take these things hence" (John 2:16), the money changers, merchants, and priests fled, not because they were afraid of Christ's political clout but because He spoke with the power and authority of God. It was a spiritual conflict, and Jesus employed spiritual, not political, pressure.

Jesus stayed out of politics, but He didn't ignore problems or refrain from condemning the corrupt leaders. "Woe unto you, scribes and Pharisees, hypocrites!" (Matt. 23:13), He proclaimed, accusing them of a host of spiritual and civil crimes. He called them the children of those who "killed the prophets" (verse 31) and predicted that they, too, would kill prophets (verse 34). Yet He never threatened them politically. He never said, "Truly, truly I say unto you, clean up or clear out."

So faithfully did Jesus adhere to the principle of separation of church and state that when a man asked, "Speak to my brother, that he divide the inheritance with me," Jesus refused. "Man," he answered, "who made me a judge or a divider over you?" (Luke 12:13, 14). Christ's mission was spiritual, not civil, advice: "Take heed, and beware of covetousness: for a man's life consisteth not in the abundance of the things which he possesseth" (verse 15).

Jesus showed sensitivity to religious freedom, too, a right God conferred on man at Creation. Never did He attempt to force people to follow Him, either by threats or legislation. "Behold, I stand at the door, and knock," He said; "if any man hear my voice, and open the door, I will come in to him" (Rev. 3:20). Jesus knocks at the door of men's conscience; He doesn't kick the door down with a warrant in His hands.

For a time in His ministry Jesus had a large and enthusiastic following. The people were also politically restless. They wanted Jesus in the Jerusalem "White House." But Jesus wouldn't accept the candidacy. "Jesus, knowing that they intended to come and make him king by force, withdrew again to a mountain by himself" (John 6:15, NIV).*

Why? Because Jesus knew that the kingdom of God was not to be established by governmental decree, court decision, or legislative bodies. "The kingdom of God is within you," He said (Luke 17:21), and the battle against evil is to be fought within each individual soul, not in Washington. Evil will be truly eradicated, not by trying to legislate it away but by the Spirit of God implanting Christ's name in humanity. "As many as received him, to them gave he power to become the sons of God, even to them that believe on his name: which were born, not of blood, nor of the will of the flesh, nor of the will of man, but of God" (John 1:12, 13). Here is the only power that can uplift mankind and thus cure America's ills. And the church, God's designated agency for reforming society, is to do this work through teaching and practicing the Word of God, not through lobbying the government.

The New Right says America's spiritual backslide began when the courts "took God out of the classroom." A common denominator for the drug abuse, teenage pregnancy, and pornography does exist, but it's not *Engel v. Vitale* (the Supreme Court decision that forbids government-sponsored prayer in school)—it's man's sinful nature. Says the Bible: "All have sinned, and come short of the glory of God" (Romans 3:23).

In 1984 Congress passed equal access legislation, a significant victory in which the New Right participated. This law allows students to hold Bible studies on school property before and after classes. Has the result been more Bible studies and less teenage drug abuse or pregnancy? Tom Minnery, a *Christianity Today* writer, wrote that "on the whole there apparently are no larger number of Bible study groups materializing in the nation's high schools.

"In fact, the biggest influence on teenagers as a societal group this year is not a wealth of Bible study opportunities but a pig lot of sordid, soft-porn movies. Titles such as *Porky's Revenge, Hardbodies,* and *Private Lessons* moved *Newsweek* to report recently that 'teenage audiences are grossing out on gross-outs.' "

Minnery warns, "Gospel values triumph ultimately when they are victorious in the heart of the lost, not when they advance in the courts and halls of Congress."

To fight sin with politics is as fruitless as stabbing at demons and as unbiblical as the evils they seek to correct.

Christians are to heal the sick, to comfort the needy and downtrodden, to spread the good news of salvation, and to let the character of God be revealed in their lives as a witness to the world. This was the work of Jesus, and this is to be the work of the church.

Now, however, a segment of the evangelicals are engaged in a new ministry, one that's alien from the commission Christ left His church. The prominence of pastors Jerry Falwell, James Robison, and W. A. Criswell in influencing sections of the 1984 Republican convention platform is one example of the New Right's growing political, if not spiritual, muscle. Their decisive influence in local Republican organizations is another. The Reagan administration's support of government-sponsored prayer in school is another. Appointments of hundreds of fundamentalists to government posts is another. And now we have a New Right candidate campaigning for the presidency! The conservative evangelical movement, once a ninety-eight-pound political weakling, has developed impressive biceps, triceps, laterals, and pectorals. It's now the heavyweight, and instead of having sand kicked in its face—it's doing the kicking!

And, sadly, the harder it kicks, the harder it gets to hear the gentle rebuke of Him who said, "Learn of me; for I am meek and lowly in heart."

*The text credited to NIV is from the *Holy Bible, New International Version.* Copyright© 1973, 1978, International Bible Society. Used by permission of Zondervan Bible Publishers. This article originally appeared in *Liberty,* November/December 1986.

CHAPTER TWENTY-SEVEN

Assault on Separation

In a blue-and-yellow shuttle bus heading to a Texas airport, I sat across from a young couple. Both were carrying Bibles, and both looked about as Southern Baptist as I do Jewish. I initiated a conversation, and when the woman said her husband was a lawyer, I mentioned I was editor of a magazine that dealt with church-state separation.

"Church-state separation?" he scowled. "Shouldn't I have the religious freedom to enforce my beliefs on others?"

"That's certainly a new angle," I answered, "but what about the religious freedoms of those who don't want your beliefs enforced on them?"

He scowled again, and the exchange ended.

A Symbolic Shift

That conversation symbolized an important change in conservative American Christianity, one that can have prophetic implications: conservative Protestants' new distrust of, if not unabashed hostility to, church-state separation.

Addressing 4,000 attendees in South Carolina, Pat Robertson derided church-state separation: "It's a lie of the left, and we're not going to take it anymore."[1]

A popular book among the New Christian Right—called *The Myth of Separation*, by David Barton—asks on the back cover: "Did you know that separation of church and state is a myth?"[2]

Attorney Jay Sekulow, a lawyer for Pat Robertson's American Center for Law and Justice, wrote: "Our purpose must be to spread the gospel on the new mission field that the Lord has opened—public high schools. Yes, the so-called 'wall of separation between church and state' has begun to crumble."[3]

And David Muralt, director of Citizens for Excellence in Education in Texas, says that separation of church and state is "a heathen idea. It's totally alien to the foundation of our country. We were a Christian society."[4]

Perhaps the most significant shift has occurred among America's largest Protestant denomination, the Southern Baptists. In recent years its leaders have deviated from the historic Baptist's position as firm adherents to church-state separation and adopted the New Right stance instead.

According to Baptist Bill Moyers, the leaders of the Southern Baptist Convention "have committed themselves to a partisan strategy of collusion between church and state, that also makes a mockery of the historic Baptist principles of religious liberty."[5]

The about-face is even more remarkable considering early Baptist history. Baptists faced terrible persecution in both the Old and New World, which explains their once-fervent advocacy of church-state separation. Virginia Baptists were the ones who pressured James Madison to include in the U.S. Constitution a Bill of Rights protecting religious freedom.

Why the Assault?

U.S. citizens, then, can thank Christians, specifically Baptists, for the inclusion of the First Amendment principles of separation of church and state in the U.S. Constitution. Why, then, are many Christians, even many Baptists, now leading the assault against it?

The Virginia Baptists in Madison's day wanted separation of church and state for one reason: As a minority, they were suffering persecution without it. They were jailed, fined, whipped, and beaten because of their refusal to adhere to the wishes of the established church in Virginia—the Anglican Church. As long as the established church and the state stayed united, the Anglican Church used the strong arm of the state to enforce—to one degree or another—its dogmas and decrees. The Baptists refused to accept this, thus finding themselves in conflict with the law.

In contrast to the Virginia Baptists, the Anglican Church clearly backed the collusion of church and state, arguing that Christianity was crucial to inculcating the values and morals needed to maintain a civil society. Thus they reasoned the state was obliged to sustain the established church. The Anglicans declared that the "hardships which such a regulation might impose upon individuals, or even bodies of men, ought not to be considered."[6]

This same attitude appears among many Christians today, especially those in the majority, such as New Right Christians and Southern Baptists. Like the established Virginia Anglicans, these groups are now firmly and safely entrenched in American society. They aren't, for example, like seventh-day Sabbathkeepers, whose numbers are relatively small and who don't have the electoral clout to influence legislation as the New Right increasingly has.

Present Barriers for Protection

The New Right doesn't want separation of church and state any more than the Anglicans in Virginia wanted it. Why? Because no matter how much electoral and political power the New Right gains, church-state separation forms a barrier against imposing religious dogma on the nation by law. Therefore, they want to dismantle the barrier because even with all the political and majoritarian clout possible, they can't breach the constitutional principle of separation embodied in the Bill of Rights.

"The very purpose of the Bill of Rights," wrote former U.S. Supreme Court justice Robert Jackson, "was to withdraw certain subjects from the vicissitudes of political controversy, to place them beyond the reach of majorities and officials and to establish them as legal principles to be applied by the courts. One's right to life, liberty, and property, to free speech, a free press, freedom of worship and assembly, and other fundamental rights may not be submitted to vote; they depend on the outcome of no elections."[7]

According to prophecy, however, those rights, at least the ones involving freedom of worship, will not remain "beyond the reach of majorities and officials." In *The Great Controversy* Ellen White states clearly that "even in free America, rulers and legislators, in order to secure public favor, will yield to the *popular demand* for a law enforcing Sunday observance. Liberty of conscience, which has cost so great a sacrifice, will no longer be respected" (page 592; italics supplied).

A "popular demand" for Sunday enforcement? This is the tyranny of the majority at its worst. Revelation 13, talking about the same impending persecution, says that "he had power to give life unto the image of the beast, that the image of the beast should both speak, and cause that as many as would not worship the image of the beast should be killed" (verse 15).

However, as long as church-state separation remains a bedrock principle of U.S. law, the religious persecution outlined in Revelation and Ellen G. White's writings can never materialize.

For this reason the New Right's hostility toward church-state separation could have prophetic implications. Some Americans have always opposed church-state separation, but they have usually been a radical fringe, not a movement, that according to a report in the August 14, 1994, Washington *Post*, has become the "most powerful organization" within the Republican Party.

Indeed, even with the wall of separation the New Right has been able to make impressive political gains, especially as seen in the 1994 elections. If the New Right has influenced so much now, what might it do once the wall dividing church and state crumbles?

We don't know exactly what will cause the fulfillment of prophecy. We know only that the principles of separation, which have given U.S. citizens freedoms most people throughout history have only dreamed about, will be replaced. What will come will be a system of "religious liberty" that, as the lawyer on the shuttle bus envisioned, allows those in power to impose their religious views upon others.

He was young enough, too, that he might just see his vision fulfilled.

[1]"Pat Robertson Calls Church-State Separation 'A Lie of the Left,' " *Church and State* 47, No. 1 (January 1994), 18.

[2]David Barton, *The Myth of Separation* (Aledo, Tex.: Wall Builder Press, 1989), back cover.

[3]Quoted in "Their Own Words" (Silver Spring, Md.: Americans United for the Separation of Church and State).

[4]Quoted in *The Journal of Church and State* 35, No. 4 (Autumn 1993), 935.

[5]In a foreword to William R. Estep, *Revolution Within the Revolution* (Grand Rapids, Mich.: Eerdmans, 1990), viii.

[6]Thomas E. Buckley, S. J., *Church and State in Revolutionary Virginia* (University Press of Virginia, 1977), 27.

[7]*West Virginia State Board of Education v. Barnette*, 1943.

This article originally appeared in the *Adventist Review*, January 1995.

CHAPTER TWENTY-EIGHT

In Pursuit of the Millennium

Though Jesus warned that the church would be persecuted in the last days, the New Religious Right's attempt to rule America is preparing the church to be persecutor, not persecuted.

"Christians are not going to take that [political impotency] any more," warned New Right leader Gary Jarmin. "They are going to resort to political takeover from the grass-roots up."[1]

"The tide is turning in our direction," said Tim LaHaye. "We're going to do it again and again, until we flood the country. . . . If every Bible-believing church in America would trust God to use them to raise up one person to run for public office in the next 10 years, . . . we would have more Christians in office than there are offices to hold."[2]

Christians, of course, have the right to be involved in politics, and their religion bids them improve society. But the New Right is not talking about clothing the naked, feeding the hungry, and visiting widows and orphans—social actions Jesus Himself sanctioned. Instead, they seek political dominance.

"We are going," declared Pat Robertson, "to take over."[3]

Doesn't quite sound like a people expecting to face the devil's wrath anytime soon. Indeed, this attitude epitomizes a blatant irony about the burgeoning political beast of American fundamentalism. For decades they have produced fiery sermons and sensational books about Armageddon, the rise of antichrist, and the great tribulation—all of which they believed imminent. Now, much of the speculation about the mysterious number 666, the mark of the beast, the seven last plagues, even the time of the second coming of Jesus has been replaced by pamphlets promoting political involvement, scorecards on candidates' voting records, and seminars on how to form political action committees. Many seem more interested in the identity of the next president, not the dreaded antichrist. They are digging in for the long haul on earth, not preparing for heaven with Jesus.

"With the quiet passing of the predicted Armageddons," wrote Harold Smith in *Christianity Today*, "and a new fascination with political clout, the church's eternal perspective has grown strangely dim."

Not only has the perspective dimmed, but it has been repudiated, if not in words, at least in deeds. The fundamentalist crusade to remake the world into its own image contradicts its theology. Most New Right Christians are premillennial dispensationalists. They believe that world history has been divided into special dispensations, or ages, of which we are not in the last. They expect war, famine, and crime to increase in this dispensation until the second coming of Jesus, who then establishes a 1,000-year reign of peace on earth. Almost all major fundamentalist seminaries—Bethel, Dallas, Liberty, Temple—adhere to the basic scenario, as do most TV superstars like Falwell, Robertson, and Swaggart. And all see the return of the Jews to Palestine as proof that the end is near. "The regathering of Jews to Israel is a clear sign, in both the Old and New Testament," writes Pat Robertson, "that our age is just about over."[4]

Some, like Falwell, believe that Christians will be raptured off the earth before the terrible time of trouble that precedes the Second Coming (hence the name pre-tribulationist); others, like Roberts, believe that Christians will be in the middle of the clash. Either way, all expect the world to be embroiled in a "time of trouble, such as never was" (Dan. 12:1), and many expect Christians at some point to be persecuted. When asked if he believed the church would suffer persecution, even Hal Lindsey—the undisputed guru of the pretribulationists credo—replied: "In my perception of prophecy and current events, it definitely will."

Pat Robertson, too, expects that Christians will be persecuted. Warning about the antichrist, a future demagogue who "will be like a combination of Adolf Hitler, Joseph Stalin, Genghis Khan, Mao Tse-tung, and other dictators who have butchered millions of people,"[5] Robertson has written that Christians will go "through a time of tribulation until Jesus comes back." He believes that "there has always been a struggle between the people of God and those who serve Satan. Throughout history there have been successive martyrdoms of Christians, and it is the height of arrogance to assume that only twentieth-century Christians in the United States will be spared any type of persecution. . . . There will be people during the tribulation who love Jesus, and will give their lives for Him."[7] He believes also that we are now living just prior to the second coming of Jesus, when "those who refuse to accept Christ will grow worse and worse in their wickedness, and that it will be increasingly difficult for the church and the world to coexist."[8]

How does Robertson reconcile the impending persecution of Christians in this country with his following appeal to the faithful? "Imagine what could happen in America's 175,000 precincts if just 10 evangelical Christian volunteers could be mobilized to assist in each one. The American political process would be revolutionized, and the future of the nation changed forever."[9] *Forever?* What about the antichrist, who sometime soon is supposed to persecute all those Christian volunteers?

Somehow his bid for the presidency—the most powerful slot in the most powerful nation in the world—doesn't synchronize with his belief that Christians will soon face persecution. Actually, the whole fundamentalist scenario, including the persecution of Christians, contradicts their desire to "take over" America.

The New Right counters arguments against Christians in politics. They are, they claim, seeking to better society. "We will work to better the world because the Bible tells us to, and we await Christ's return because the Scriptures say it will happen," wrote Ed Dobson and Ed Hinson, two faculty members at Liberty University. Defending Christians in politics, they wrote that "evangelical preachers are in the arena of politics to improve secular society." They claim it's their Christian duty to "make the world as good a place as [they] can, [and] to use Christianity as a force for positive change."

Certainly, Christians *are* to use their religion for "positive change." Though the New Testament warns of the wars, famines, and the increase of lawlessness that the New Right predicts—it says also that Christians should be involved in uplifting humanity from the suffering that the present wars, famine, and lawlessness have produced. Jesus spent His whole life serving others, and He admonished His followers to do likewise. Yet Jesus was talking about a ministry to the moral, physical, and spiritual needs of mankind, the New Right is talking politics—an approach that Jesus never sanctioned and one that contradicts the belief that Christians will be a small, persecuted lot in the last days.

Other fundamentalists see the incongruity. "This proud, rich, arrogant church now covets power," writes charismatic preacher David Wilkerson. "Not the power of God—but political power. It covets the White House, Congress, and the Supreme Court. . . . It sounds so pious, so spiritual, and vital. Like Israel, many of God's people are crying for an imperial pulpit—with a spiritual leader who will root out the entrenched powers of evil and legislate a new moral system. The pointed, accusing finger of thundering prophets and weeping watchmen is to be replaced by the refined pen of Christian congressmen enacting moral laws."

This church, Wilkerson warns, "is not going to be the vehicle of God's dominion on earth, but rather the object of His wrath and abhorrence.

"You can be sure God has a people for Himself in these final days, but they are a despised, holy and separated remnant."[10]

Wilkerson has a point. Whether or not one accepts the fundamentalist interpretation of the New Testament itself—it does teach that Christians will be persecuted in the last days. The book of Revelation warns of an apocalyptic power, symbolized as a beast (whom Christians identify as the antichrist), that will employ economic and physical pressure to force the world into compliance with his rule. Revelation warns that those who "keep the commandments of God, and have the testimony of Jesus Christ" (Rev. 12:17) will face persecution because they refuse to accept the religious and political reign of the "beast." Revelation 14:12 describes the same small group as those who "keep the commandments of God, and the faith of Jesus." Jesus himself warned his followers that "some of you shall they cause to be put to death. And ye shall be hated of all men for my name's sake" (Luke 21:16, 17), while Paul warned that "all that will live godly in Christ Jesus shall suffer persecution" (2 Tim. 3:12).

"Throughout the book of Revelation," writes Texas evangelist Stan McGehee, "we see true Christians suffering persecution, not taking over the world! Likewise, Paul tells us that it is Christ's rule that will put down rebellion and ungodliness (1 Cor. 15:24, 25). Alarmingly enough, the Bible speaks of man's established religious-political rule as that of antichrist!"[11]

McGehee, too, has a point. Though the New Right's thrust into politics contradicts *their* scenario for the last days, the political ascendancy of the church perfectly fits the scenario of those Christians who believe that the churches themselves will be the persecuting power warned about in the New Testament!

Seventh-day Adventists, for example, as far back as the 1880s, have warned that the churches in America would gain political power and that they would "influence the state to enforce their decrees,"[12] resulting in persecution of dissenters, depicted in the Bible as those who "keep the commandments of God, and have the testimony of Jesus Christ." This church-state alliance, and the tyranny that ensues, is, they believe, how the prophecies of Revelation warning of last-day persecution will be fulfilled. Many see the rise of the New Right as preparing the churches to become the beast—not face its wrath!

Inherent in fundamentalist theology are the seeds that could ultimately place them in that role. All fundamentalists of the New Right believe that Jesus will establish a 1,000-year reign of peace on the earth, the "millennial kingdom." Though some deny that they can usher in the millennial kingdom themselves, many want to at least help it along.

In their book *Designed for Destiny*, Jerry Combee and Cline Hall, of Liberty Baptist College, quote Ernest Lee Tuveson in *Redeemer Nation: The Idea of America's Millennial Role.* "Modern man is, it seems, faced by the final challenge of history." That is to "create the millennium, or go down into the lake of fire."

"Of course," Combee and Hall write, "creating the 'millennium' exceeds our human power alone,"[13] the idea being that though we alone can't create it, we can at least give the Lord a hand. Referring to the president as "the high priest and prophet of American civil religion," Combee and Hall imply that America could be God's tool for ushering in utopia: "But imagine the world freed from the threat of domination by the 'evil empire' Soviet Russia and other nations with similar goals.

"America and other nations could beat their swords into plowshares. . . .

"All the treasure and genius now harnessed for war could be marshalled for good. . . .

"No countries would face external obstacles to democracy. . . .

"Liberty and democracy would reign from pole to pole. . . .

"After all that, the question remains: Is it America's destiny to deliver the world from tyranny?"[14]

In 1986, Pat Robertson challenged George Bush and Jack Kemp for delegates at the Michigan Republican Party convention. After Robertson did well, he sent out a letter to supporters stating: "*The Christians have won.* . . . What a breakthrough for the kingdom."

A breakthrough for the kingdom? What kingdom? Perhaps the same one that Combee and Hall want their Christianized U.S.A. to help usher in.

"Can you believe what they are now preaching?" writes Wilkerson. "They are saying 'Jesus can't come until we subdue the earth. He can't come until we take dominion and bring Him back a world we have brought into submission.' "[15]

"Today a popular theory among certain evangelicals," writes McGehee, "is that Christians are to take over the world and present it to Christ when He returns. This view is in direct opposition to Biblical doctrine."[16]

These utopian visions contradict not only fundamentalist premillennialism, which teaches massive apocalyptic pandemonium, but contradicts what the New Testament itself says about conditions prior to the second coming of Jesus. "Then shall be great tribulation," Jesus said (Matt. 24:21), "such as was not since the beginning of the world to this time, no, nor ever shall be."

This isn't the first time the faithful have sought to establish the kingdom of God on earth. During His early ministry, Jesus had an enthusiastic following who wanted to set Him upon an earthly throne as a king who would save them from the Romans and usher in the long-expected era of peace. Today, some still want to usher in that kingdom, now using political action committees, voter registration drives, and congressional report cards. Yet Jesus no more needs them today than He did 2,000 years ago. The book of Daniel symbolizes the establishment of the kingdom of God as a stone "cut out without hands" (Dan. 2:34) that crushes all nations until they "became like the chaff of the summer threshing-floors; and the wind carried them away, that no place was found for them" (verse 35). Doesn't quite sound as if God needs Pat in the White House to help.

Nevertheless, the New Right isn't going to let Bible truth stand in their way. They see themselves as God-ordained vehicles to bring in a new world order, and many see America in that same role.

"There is yet time for America to claim the promise of its revolutionary destiny," writes Combee and Hall, extolling God's plans for America.

"To be the liberator of mankind and the leader of revolutionary progress in the world. . . .

"To be the launching pad for the evangelization of the world before the second coming of Jesus Christ."[17]

Falwell has the same vision for America but in a little different light: "Our government has the right to use its armaments to bring wrath upon those who would do evil by hurting other people. . . . If God is on our side, no matter how militarily superior the Soviet Union is, they could never touch us. God would miraculously protect America."[18]

Despite the Bible teaching that Christians are to be a persecuted minority in the last days, the New Right has embarked upon an unabashed quest for political control of the most powerful nation in the world. Despite the Bible teaching that the earth will be thrust into unprecedented turmoil, they entertain millennial visions of America's role in presenting to Jesus a world "brought into submission." Despite biblical warnings that a religious-political power will persecute those who "keep the commandments of God, and have the testimony of Jesus Christ," they are forming a religious-political power that could produce this very beast!

Indeed, despite the Bible truth that the millennium will be established only through the power of God, who erases the existing world order—the members of the New Right are placing themselves in a position in which their political might could be employed to help usher in the long-expected "kingdom." This, of course, could lead to the persecution of anyone seen as interfering with their millennial dreams and visions!

And they are working with the determination that comes from being certain that you are doing God's will. "You have to not set yourself against the hick fundamentalists," Jimmy Swaggart once told opponents. "You have set yourself against God."[19]

"Yea, the time cometh," Jesus warned, "that whosoever killeth you will think that he doeth God service" (John 16:2).

Preparing to face the sword? On the contrary. The New Right's preparing to wield it.

---

[1] *Newsday*, December 1, 1985.

[2] *Christianity Today*, December 13, 1985.

[3] *U.S. News and World Report*, September 24, 1979.

[4] Pat Robertson, *Pat Robertson Answers* (New York: Thomas Nelson, 1984).

[5] *Ibid.*, 155.

[6] *Ibid.*, 151.

[7] *Ibid.*, 156.

[8] *Ibid.*, 30.

[9] _____*America's Dates With Destiny* (New York: Thomas Nelson, 1986), 303.

[10] David Wilkerson, *The Laodicean Lie!* (Lindale, Tex.: World Challenge, Inc., n.d.).

[11]Stan McGehee, "*Political Christianity*" (Fort Worth, Tex.: Stan McGehee Evangelistic Association, n. d.).

[12]Ellen White, *The Great Controversy* (Nampa, Idaho: Pacific Press® Pub. Assn., 1888), 445.

[13]Jerry Combee and Cline Hall, *Designed for Destiny* (Wheaton, Ill.: Tyndale House, 1985), 113.

[14]*Ibid.*, 114.

[15]Wilkerson.

[16]McGehee.

[17]Combee and Hall.

[18]Quoted in Erling Jorstad, *The New Christian Right* (Lewiston, N.Y.: Edwin Mellen Press, 1987), 18.

[19]*Ibid.*, 167.

This article originally appeared in *Shabbat Shalom*, April-June 1988.

CHAPTER TWENTY-NINE

The Truth About Religious Liberty in the United States

What nation is openly hostile to Christianity? In what nation does the government systematically uproot the goals, standards, and rights of Christians? In what nation has religious liberty been in chains for years? In what country do Christians confront atheistic conspiracies against them and their children?

The United States of America.

That is, if you believe New Right rhetoric about religion in the United States. If you accept half of what they say, you'd think that America is as hostile to Christians as any Communist nation is.

For years Jerry Falwell, Tim LaHaye, and others have been talking about the "death of religious freedom" in America and the need to "regain our religious rights." In 1981 Pat Robertson, concerned about "open hostility against religion," formed his Freedom Council "to restore our religious freedom."

New Right allies in the Roman Catholic Church and in the U.S. Government agree. Cardinal John Krol has spoken out against "judicial hostility toward religion." Terry Eastland, director of public affairs at the Justice Department, has warned about government "hostility toward religion." United States Attorney General Ed Meese has said that the government's "principle of neutrality toward all religions has often been transformed by some into hostility toward anything religious." Secretary of Education William Bennett has spoken about the "assault of secularism on religion." Even President Reagan has lamented about those who "are intolerant of religion."

But is the government hostile to religion? Is there a need to "restore our religious freedom"? Or is the New Right's claim that the present church-state balance restricts Christian liberty really just an attempt to undermine the present system and replace it with one more accommodating to their point of view? Unquestionably, the New Right sees the "poor heathens" on the Supreme Court as prime enemies of religious freedom. They are, in the words of Pat Robertson, an "unelected despotic oligarchy" who have for "the past two decades tortured its [the First Amendment] clear-cut meaning." Even William Bennett bemoans the "utter chaos" of the Supreme Court's "four decades of misguided court decisions."

Among their misguided and hostile decisions: those dealing with school prayer, Bible reading, funding of religious institutions, and the Ten Commandments.

When in (1962) the Supreme Court banned state-sponsored prayer in public school, an outraged public flooded the Senate and the House with mail against the decision. Since then, numerous attempts have been made to amend the Constitution to allow this religious exercise in public school. Pat Robertson, before the Senate Judiciary Committee, favored a bill that would "restore prayer in school." Calling for a "reversal of the antireligious court rulings of the past 20 years," he asked the Senate to "curb this intrusion of the federal judiciary into the free exercise of religion." The bill failed.

In 1985, the Supreme Court (*Wallace v. Jaffree*) struck down an Alabama law allowing one minute for "meditation or voluntary prayer." Tim LaHaye called the *Jaffree* decision "an act of war against this nation's religious heritage," and there have been more cries for a constitutional amendment to restore prayer.

Yet no amendment is needed. Children can pray in school—all they want, when they want. No law bans them. Speaking before the Senate, Robertson said that if the president designated a day for thanksgiving to God, "no school children could thank God on the day if school were in session." This statement is false. They could thank God all day; and if they didn't disturb the class, they could even thank Him out loud. What Robertson really meant is that no school official is allowed to stand up before a class—filled, for example, with children from Catholic, Jewish, Mormon, Adventist, agnostic, atheist, Buddhist, Taoist, Muslim, existentialist, and secularist homes— and lead them in prayer.

The safest way to preserve religious freedom for all faiths is for the government to be neutral toward all faiths. The court in *Engel* said that it's simply not the job of the state "to compose official prayers for any group of the American people to recite as part of a religious program carried on by the government." In *Jaffree*, Justice Stevens wrote that an endorsement of even silent prayer is inconsistent with the government's stance of "complete neutrality toward religion." To advocate prayer or a time specifically for prayer is not neutrality toward religion—it is establishment of religion, which the Constitution forbids.

The High Court placed prayer outside of government jurisdiction—and considering that prayer is part of man's personal experience with God, how preposterous to place it within! It's the work of parents and churches, not public schools, to promote prayer and religion, and in America churches have the right to do so. "It is error alone," said Thomas Jefferson, "which needs the support of the government."

Far from being hostile to religion, *Engel* and *Jaffree* are among the best safeguards we have to keep our religion free from government intrusion, which is what state-sponsored prayer in public school is: intrusion.

Other decisions attacked as "anti-God" are *Schempp* and *Murray* (1963), which forbade Bible readings in the school as part of state-sponsored religious exercise. Said the Court: "They are religious exercises required by the states in violation of the command of the First Amendment that the government maintain strict neutrality, neither aiding nor opposing religion."

Billy Graham declared himself shocked at this assertion. Robert Cook, president of the National Association of Evangelicals in 1963, called the decision a "sad departure from the nation's heritage under God." Cardinal McIntyre of Los Angeles said that the decision could "only mean that our American heritage of philosophy, of religion, of freedom is being abandoned in imitation of Soviet philosophy." Cardinal Cushing of Boston deemed it "a great tragedy that the greatest book that was ever published cannot be read in the public school system."

Yet the Bible *can* be read in the public school system. The decision outlawed only state-sponsored devotional reading of the Bible in public school, not the Bible itself. The Court specifically said that the Bible could be "part of a secular program of education." The Court did not prohibit devotional readings by students, even on school grounds. It simply stopped school officials from using it in religious exercises.

Vituperation against these "disastrous anti-God decisions" continues. What's particularly surprising is the Catholic chorus among the vituperators. During the 1800s, when Bible reading was common in public schools, canon law forbade Catholics from reading or even possessing copies of Protestant Bibles, such as the King James Version, then widely used in public schools. Refusing to participate in worship services, Catholic children were punished, expelled—and in some cases beaten. In 1843, when a Philadelphia school board allowed Catholic children to refrain from Bible exercises or to use their own version, riots broke out, people were killed, and Catholic churches burned. In Maine a priest was tarred and feathered because he urged a parishioner to go to court when the local school board adopted a regulation requiring all children to read the King James Bible. In Boston a teacher beat an eleven-year-old Catholic boy named Tom Wall until he agreed to read the Ten Commandments from the King James Bible. When the teacher was taken to court, the judge dismissed all charges.

By prohibiting government intrusion into religion, *Abington v. Murray* lessened the chance of similar attacks on our religious freedom.

Imagine a Jewish child's humiliation if the teacher read to the class the verse in Revelation that talks about "the synagogue of Satan" (Rev. 2:9). How would a Catholic feel if 2 Thessalonians 2:3 were read, which refers to "that man of sin" (whom Reformation Protestants identified as the pope)? What of the atheist child who had to listen to the psalm that says "The fool hath said in his heart, there is no God" (Ps.

14:1)? Or the polytheistic Hindu child who heard the teacher read that "God is one" (Deut. 6:4)? These children, forced by law to attend school, would have to listen to religious indoctrination or face the humiliation of leaving the room. *Abington v. Murray* protects them against this intrusion of their liberties.

Other court decisions seen as an assault on religious freedom concern the use of federal funding in parochial schools. Though the Supreme Court has allowed use of federal funds for transporting children to parochial schools, the loan of textbooks to parochial schools, and federal grants for the construction of nonsectarian buildings on religious campuses, other decisions have forbidden Caesar to fund the things of God.

For example, in *Meek v. Pittinger* (1975), the Court ruled that the loan of educational equipment (except textbooks) to private schools violated the establishment clause. In *Committee for Public Education v. Nyquist* (1973), the Court ruled that the state grants for maintenance and repairs of parochial school buildings and partial tuition reimbursements or tax deductions were unconstitutional. In *Lemon v. Kurtzman* (1971), the Court ruled that reimbursing nonpublic schools for teachers' salaries, textbooks, and instructional materials was unconstitutional. In two recent cases (*Aguilar* and *Grand Rapids* [1985]), the High Court struck down laws that allowed publicly funded instruction in parochial schools.

Cardinal Krol said that rulings like these prove that the state is "becoming the instrument of the agnostic or atheist." Secretary of Education Bennett seeks to get tax money into religious schools. Even the Holy See has entered the fray. Its Charter of Family Rights, published in 1983, states: "Public authorities must ensure that public subsidies are so allocated that parents are truly free to exercise this right [religious education of their children] without incurring unjust burdens."

Yet the First Amendment reads that the government shall not make any law respecting the establishment of a religion. Wrote Justice Black: "The most effective way to establish any institution is to finance it; and this truth is reflected in the appeals by church groups for public funds to finance their religious schools."

When government funds a parochial school, in effect a Protestant is paying to promote Catholic or Jewish beliefs, or vice versa. How free is the Jew who pays taxes that are used to promote Roman Catholicism, which teaches that the priest can turn a piece of bread into the body of God, a belief that is blasphemous to the Jew? Or how free is the Catholic who pays taxes to support a Lutheran school, when Martin Luther called Pope Paul III "the scum of all the scoundrels in Rome"?

In some cases, such as *Lemon v. Kurtzman*, the Court denied aid because the government would have to monitor every dollar to ensure that none went to religious enterprises. Envisioning hordes of government inspectors prowling the halls of religious schools to make sure, for example, that tax dollars went to pay for tissue paper in the girls' powder room and not to pay for a statue of Our Lady of Fatima in the chapel, the Court rejected aid rather than allow such an entanglement between church and state.

Also, government regulations follow government funds. Church officials have removed the cross and other religious emblems from their walls in order to get state booty. They have been forced to dilute their curriculum's religious content, and in one instance they even agreed to remove their clerical collars in order to qualify for funds. The Supreme Court has ensured that they can keep their collars on.

In *Stone v. Graham* (1985), the Court—believing that the "Ten Commandments are undeniably a sacred text in the Jewish and Christian faiths"—ruled a law unconstitutional that placed a privately purchased copy of the Ten Commandments on the wall of every Kentucky classroom. Though the Court said that the commandments, along with the Bible, could be integrated into "an appropriate study of history, civilization, ethics, comparative religion, or the like," it was again accused of being antireligious. All it said was that the place for the Ten Commandments to be posted is not in a classroom with children who by law are forced to be there. These decisions are no more proof of hostility against religion than forbidding a pig to sleep in one's bed is proof that one hates pigs.

Pat Robertson's assertions that we need to "restore" religious liberty to America is absurd. Every weekend in this nation millions of citizens, without fear of government harassment, file into Baptist, Pentecostal, Mormon, Greek Orthodox, Scottish Presbyterian, Unification, Unitarian, Roman Catholic, and Methodist churches, and on and on—all sitting on millions of dollars worth of land the "hostile" government lets them own tax free!

Christians own and operate thousands of elementary and secondary schools, colleges, and seminaries across the country. They print millions of dollars worth of Bibles, tracts, books, and magazines every year—often from their own publishing houses and printing presses. They own television stations, radio stations, and hospitals. Not only are Christians free to believe anything and to raise millions of tax-free dollars to promote their beliefs, but the "hostile" government has even made laws to ensure that they are not discriminated against because of them.

In the history of Christianity, no government has given its citizens as much religious freedom as the American government has, and all that the Supreme Court decisions say to the country is: Pray, read your Bible, build your schools, follow your convictions—but don't ask the state to advance, promote, or pay for them!

This article originally appeared in *Liberty*, January/February 1988.

CHAPTER THIRTY

Honor the Emperor

Just finished viewing *The Clinton Chronicles*, an eighty-minute video "investigating the alleged criminal activities of Bill Clinton." The tape accused the president, among other things, of being a cocaine addict and murderer during his Arkansas governorship. It asserted that besides using his office to protect dope smugglers, Clinton ordered numerous people killed, including Jerry Parks, the head of a private Little Rock security firm that had worked for Clinton's 1992 presidential campaign. Though no one has been charged, *The Clinton Chronicles* featured the victim's son, Gary Parks, claiming that because his father had evidence of Clinton's adulterous affairs, the governor had had him shot.

"Bill Clinton had my father killed," Gary said on the tape, "to save his political career."

What's revealing about the video is not its scurrilous accusations. Even David Brock, the *American Spectator* journalist who made national news with the story that accused Clinton of using state troopers to facilitate extramarital affairs, has attacked the video as "character assassination." Certainly no FOB (Friend of Bill), Brock called *The Clinton Chronicles* "an admixture of fact, half-truths, innuendo, and outright falsehoods that does nothing to advance the public's knowledge of Clinton." No, what's revealing about the video is the gleeful readiness with which many Christians, like Jerry Falwell, have been promoting it. That readiness, ironically, says more about American right-wing Christianity than the video does about Bill Clinton.

Sunday Morning Smut

"I am appalled that a minister of the gospel would show disrespect for the president of the United States and call him a liar. I am appalled at the disrespect you would show to the leadership when you, as a minister, are told by the Bible you teach and preach, to respect and honor the king and obey the powers that be, because they are ordained of God."

Interestingly enough, this rebuke wasn't aimed at Jerry Falwell by another minister angered at Falwell's attacks on the president. Instead, it came *from* Falwell himself, directed at a fellow minister who had the audacity to criticize then-President Ronald Reagan in the 1980s.

Who said politics doesn't corrupt? Jerry Falwell has gone from preaching Christ to selling *The Clinton Chronicles* on his Sunday morning *Old-time Gospel Hour*. One has to wonder what the saints—who tuned in to hear the Word of God—thought about hearing Paula Jones' accusations that Clinton tried to get her to "perform oral sex." Not exactly an expository sermon on John 3:16. One irate mom even called a radio station in Jacksonville, Florida, and complained that Falwell's explicit descriptions of the Clinton's alleged sex act caused her nine-year-old to start asking questions that she didn't want to answer. The station yanked the show and threatened to cancel Falwell completely if he didn't stick to religion and get off politics. Good advice all the way around.

One could argue that preachers do have the right—even the obligation—to get involved in political issues, especially those with moral implications. One could even argue that they can use the church to do so. But when a preacher uses his Sunday morning electronic pulpit to sell (at a good profit, no doubt) two videos (there's another one called *Clinton's Circle of Power*) that make wild accusations against the president of the United States, accusations that the preacher himself admits he can't prove, then we have blatant evidence—unlike the unsubstantiated claims in *The Clinton Chronicles*—that the real corruption is in Lynchburg, not in Little Rock.

"It is not for Jerry Falwell," said a spokesperson for the ministry, "to say whether any of the charges [on the videos] are true or false, but they ought to be covered, and people can make decisions."

If it's not for the Reverend Falwell to say that the videos are true, then, considering their hair-raising accusations, why would Falwell—an ordained Baptist minister—sell them during his ministry air time? If he's hawking material that even he admits might be false, why should people believe anything else he says? It's hard enough selling people on the gospel itself, but when that's interspersed with something that its own promoter admits might be fiction, Christianity becomes like a script from *Raiders of the Lost Ark*, and Christ like Indiana Jones.

"These videos are giving Christianity a bad name," said prominent evangelist Tony Campolo. "We in the Christian community ought not to be spreading rumors if we can't prove they're true, we ought not to be denigrating people."

Campolo even offered to appear on *Old-Time Gospel Hour* to rebut the charges. Falwell refused Campolo (though he offered Clinton or someone from his staff a chance to refute them), and despite the long-delayed-and-somewhat-muted criticism coming from various Evangelicals, he still promotes *The Clinton Chronicles*, claiming to have sold tens of thousands of copies.

Falwell isn't the only Christian distributing *The Clinton Chronicles*. I ordered mine from Jeremiah Films, which sells it for $19.95 (the friendly voice on the end of the 800 number said that if you order 51-100, you get them for $10.95; more than 100, and it's yours for the rock-bottom price of $9.95). A promotional brochure says that Jeremiah Films "was founded in 1978 by Patrick Matrisciana, who saw the desperate need for professional, godly, informative, and educational filmmaking. Each film project is thoroughly researched and documented. A combination of biblical accuracy in conjunction with hard-hitting facts uncovering error and heresy have made Jeremiah Films a notable and powerful voice in today's Christian world."

One could wonder what accusing the president of the United States—without any firm evidence—of helping smuggle more than "$100 million a month of cocaine" into Arkansas has to do with "biblical accuracy." I don't remember *The Clinton Chronicles* ever talking about the Bible; instead, it dealt with Clinton's "criminal background," called him a "pathological liar," asserted that "he has no loyalty to his nation," and on and on. It accused him of crimes that would have made the burglaries, cover-ups, and obstruction of justice in Watergate seem like nothing more than Nixon pilfering a few rolls of toilet paper from *Air Force One*. The video then ends with a disclaimer: "If any additional harm comes to anyone connected to this film or their families, the people of America will hold Bill Clinton personally responsible." This is hardly "informative," or "professional," much less the "godly" journalism that Jeremiah Films claims for its products. It is, however, "educational," a show-and-tell about how Christianity is polluted when immersed in politics.

The Pitfalls of the Prince

The Christian promotion of *The Clinton Chronicles* symbolizes something more important than just a shaky video or even the virulent hatred that many professed Christians have for Clinton. Instead, it shows what politics is doing to those involved in the New Christian Right.

Clinton isn't the first president to incur the wrath of the righteous, of course. Thomas Jefferson was vilified unmercifully by those admonished by the Lord to be "merciful." But there's something ungodly, almost demonic, about the hatred toward Clinton among those told to "love your enemies." It's what one expects to find in politicians, not in Christians, not even in Christian politicians. Rather than making America Christian, the New Right's involvement in politics seems to be making it *un-Christian*. For the Republican Party to promote *The Clinton Chronicles* is one thing (though, to my knowledge, and to its credit, the Republican Party has stayed out of it), but for those who profess to follow Christ to do so proves how they themselves are being sullied by the system that they claim God has called them to purify.

Christian writer E. G. White wrote in the past century that "the union of the church with the state, be the degree ever so slight, while it may appear to bring the world nearer to the church, does in reality bring the church nearer to the world." Exactly. The New Right is gaining political power, but as a result, what's changing is not so much the nation but the church itself! The involvement in politics isn't lifting America up; it's dragging the church down.

"Whatever position adopted by the church," wrote historian-philosopher Jacques Ellul, "every time she becomes involved in politics, on every occasion the result has been unfaithfulness to herself and the abandonment of the truths of the gospel. . . . Every time the church has played the power game . . . she has been led to act treasonably, either toward revealed truth or incarnate love. . . . It would seem that politics . . . is the occasion of her greatest falls, her constant temptation, the pitfall the prince of the world incessantly prepares for her."

Though the New Christian Right often portrays its struggle as spiritual—Christ against Satan, light against darkness, truth against error—it's really engaged in a worldly battle, using worldly methods. Running stealth candidates, taking over party caucuses, forming political alliances, engaging in mudslinging, promoting scurrilous attacks on the president of the United States—all of which the New Right does—might all be part and parcel of the political process but it shouldn't be confused with Christianity, however much Christianity is the professed motive.

"Secular revolutions," wrote Ellul, "in reality do not essentially revolutionize the world at all. They use the methods of the world to change the world. They operate with the basic framework of sinful civilization. Thus utilizing what this world itself offers them, they become its slaves."

In his now-famous quote, Christian Coalition national director Ralph Reed said: "I do guerrilla warfare. I paint my face invisible and travel at night. You don't know it's over until you're in a body bag. You don't know until election night."

That might be good politics, but it has nothing to do with the gospel. In fact, it hurts the gospel immensely. When Reed—a professing Christian who heads a professedly Christian organization (the *Christian* Coalition)—mingles Christianity with his "guerrilla warfare," he might get his candidates elected, but he doesn't do much for Jesus.

In a *New Yorker* article on the growing political power of the New Right, Sidney Blumenthal wrote, "Across America, the flag and the cross are becoming one." How much good this union is for the flag might be debatable; what isn't debatable is how bad it is for the cross.

Honor the Emperor?

Though the latest, and in many ways the most blatant example, Falwell's promotion of *The Clinton Chronicles* isn't the only indicator of how politics is degrading the church. The back cover of a book of Christian poetry called *The Parched Soul of America* excerpts some verse inside: "A draft-dodging, drug-exhaling, sodomy-protecting, shady-dealing, tax-raising, child-exploiting, baby-killing, feminist-pandering, religion-robbing, border-betraying, gun-confiscating, military-reducing womanizer becomes Commander-in-Chief." The book then has the audacity to be dedicated to "Jesus of Nazareth, the Master Assembler of words and our Emancipator." Somehow I think it would have been better if Jesus were left out of it entirely.

How any professing Christian could not be opposed to, or even appalled at, some of the president's positions is beyond me. But the question isn't whether or not Christians should agree with the president's politics, or even speak against them, but whether they will let that opposition compromise their Christianity, as Falwell has clearly compromised his, amply proven by the hawking of *The Clinton Chronicles* during his Sunday morning ministry.

One could argue that we frown on the obsequious German church that kowtowed to the Nazis but laud the courage of Dietrich Bonhoeffer, who died because of his anti-Nazi stance. Bonhoeffer was, after all, involved in a plot to kill Hitler, something that makes Falwell's promotion of *The Clinton Chronicles* seem like nothing more dangerous than passing out *Bush/Quayle in '92* buttons. But America is no Nazi Germany, Clinton is no Hitler (though you'd never know it by the vitriolic attacks coming from Christians), and Falwell is certainly no Bonhoeffer.

In his rebuke of the minister who criticized Reagan, Falwell alluded to 1 Peter 2:17: "Honor all men. Love the brotherhood. Fear God. Honor the emperor" (RSV).*

"Honor the emperor"? An interesting admonition from a Christian writing at a time when Christians were being persecuted by the emperor. The Epistle in various places even encourages Christians to stay faithful amid those specific trials. "Beloved, do not be surprised at the fiery ordeal which comes upon you to prove you, as though something strange were happening to you. But rejoice in so far as you share Christ's sufferings, that you may also rejoice and be glad when his glory is revealed. If you are reproached for the name of Christ, you are blessed" (1 Pet. 4:12-14, RSV).

Though scholars disagree on the exact date of the letter, and thus the specific emperor behind the persecution, evidence points to none other than Nero, the incarnation of Roman evil himself. Nero makes Clinton—even if *The Clinton Chronicles* were true—look like a wet nurse. By the end of his reign Nero had killed his wife, mother, and stepbrother, and instigated persecution in the church. Historian Kenneth Latourette writes that under Nero, Christians "were wrapped in the hides of wild beasts and then torn to pieces. Others, fastened to crosses, were set on fire to illuminate a circus which Nero staged for the crowds in his own gardens. . . . Tradition, probably reliable, reports that both Peter and Paul suffered death in Rome under Nero."

Thus, if Peter could tell believers to "honor the emperor"—while no doubt being appalled at the emperor's moral character, much less his policies—the biblical principle would seem to admonish Christians to at least show respect for the office of the president, if not necessarily for the occupant. Unfortunately, as the promotion of

The Clinton Chronicles proves, political principles have swallowed up biblical ones.

Then there's Jesus Himself, who didn't exactly live under a liberal democracy. And Herod and Pilate weren't Gandhi and Disraeli, either. Yet in all the Gospels, only a tiny fraction of Christ's words were directed against the political leadership. Luke alone records him calling Herod "that fox" (in the sense of being sly or crafty), and that rebuke was spoken in the context of Christ being warned that Herod would kill Him unless He went away. Not exactly a political rally. Jesus certainly had plenty of political ills to rail against, and Herod and Pilate had morals that could have preoccupied Christ's ministry had He chosen to allow them to. Instead, as Jesus said, His kingdom was "not of this world," and He lived and ministered accordingly, a truth apparently lost on the Christian Right.

The issue here isn't Clinton; it's Christ and what things like promotion of *The Clinton Chronicles* does to His witness, which He entrusted to His church to present to the world. Falwell's airing of excerpts from the video probably raised good money, but how many souls were won to Christ that Sunday morning on the *Old-Time Gospel Hour*? Certainly some hurt, guilt-ridden, scared people listening really needed to hear "the old-time" gospel a lot more than what a former Arkansas police investigator had to say about Clinton, in the context of the dope-smuggling accusation—that "*probably* he took advantage of some of the coke."

The Cost of Success

Great leaders, it has been said, don't move the masses in a specific direction; instead, they see what direction the masses are already heading in and jump to the head. The New Right hasn't created the political movement that is propelling it to political stardom; rather, it has sensed where the people were going, and has taken the lead in getting them there.

You don't need a weatherman, Bob Dylan wrote, to see which way the wind's blowing, and it's clearly blowing down the same path as the New Christian Right. The movement is not a fad, like hula hoops, bell-bottoms, and punk rock. It has commandeered American political conservatism, has irrevocably changed the Republican Party, and will undoubtedly reshape American politics long into the new millennium. Not bad for a bunch of "Bible thumpers."

What the New Christian Right adherents need to ask themselves is no longer "How can our movement be successful?" but rather "What will success do to our Christianity?" Or more precisely—in light of *The Clinton Chronicles*—"For what is a man profited, if he shall gain the whole world, and lose his soul?" (Matt. 16:26).

*Bible texts credited to RSV are from the Revised Standard Version of the Bible, copyright 1946, 1952, 1971, by the Division of Christian Education of the National Council of the Churches of Christ in the U.S.A. Used by permission. This article originally appeared in *Liberty*, July/August 1995.

CHAPTER THIRTY-ONE

Joe Ficarra's Sabbath Quarry

"Tell me to stuff it—I'm a taxidermist," the sign on the wall says.

Joe Ficarra did stuff it, the head of a six-point buck. Now, in back of his shop on the corner of Pleasure House Road and Virginia Beach, he carefully digs out excess putty from behind its brown glass eyes with their light-purple pupils. "You have to set the eyes right," he says. "The eyes are the soul of the mount."

Ficarra learned taxidermy from a $9.95 correspondence course. The first animal he stuffed, a squirrel, "looked like a road accident," he says. Five years and hundreds of mounts later, a half dozen heads on the wall attest to his mastery of the art.

"This was a beautiful piece of work by the Creator," he says, pointing to the unfinished mount. "I now have a chance to breathe life back into it. It's my personal monument to His work. Plus it's a pleasant way to make a buck."

The sign in front of his shop doesn't say "Taxidermy" but "Ficarra's Jewelers." Afraid that he might offend customers opposed to hunting and fishing, he stuffs the beasts and birds discreetly. His only advertisement is in the yellow pages. There is probably no other jeweler-taxidermist in the country. When a jewelry customer enters the shop, Joe washes his hands, takes off his tool belt, and waits on him. "Most probably think that I'm in the back casting rings or something."

Ficarra, 40, has reddish-blond hair and a light mustache. He is built squat and sturdy, a hard man to knock down. On a gold chain around his neck hangs a brown tooth with the gold letter "F" inset. He wears two leather belts, one with taxidermy tools, the other with a black .380 Berretta. Jewelry stores have been robbed in the area. The gun is not an ornament. He knows how to use it.

Joe got his first BB gun at eight, and his first rifle at twelve, a .22 Winchester lever action, with which he demolished rats. The first day he was allowed to hunt in the woods, he returned to the cabin by noon with a buck. "Outside of my family," he says, "there's nothing that means more to me than hunting and fishing."

A country boy whose mother lived "in the suburbs of Maybrook, Virginia, a town that had two buildings," Joe isn't the type likely to get embroiled in a dispute over constitutional law. Yet by purposely getting himself charged with hunting on Sunday, in violation of a Virginia state statute, he has enmeshed himself in an establishment clause quagmire that could keep him battling for years.

"I'm not really interested in church-state issues," he admits, working on the deer's other eye. "I just don't want people telling me that I can't hunt on Sunday. To me, it's simply a matter of hunter's rights. You can go to a tractor pull on Sunday. You can shop at the mall. You can shoot skeet, go to a football game, even buy beer. But I'm stuck at home, watching wrestling on TV. It really sticks in my craw."

He answers the phone. "No, ma'am," he says after a minute. "I can't help you," and then hangs up. "You can't believe the calls I get. This woman wanted to know if there was fur on the back of her Persian rug, and if so, could I fix it, because it looks cracked." He shakes his head as he goes back to the mount. "One woman wanted me to stuff a black widow spider. The best calls are at night, when these drunks ask, 'Hey, how much is it to go to such and such?' I say, 'I think you want a *taxicab*, not a *taxidermist*.' One drunk called for a taxi, and I said, 'Wait twenty minutes and we'll be right there. Just wait for the cab.' I hope he's still there."

Joe's challenge to the Sunday law started during a poker game last winter with a half dozen hunting buddies and his lawyer and friend, Gary Byler. Someone talked about the unfairness of the Sunday hunting ban, and Gary was surprised that the law still existed. A registered lobbyist, Gary said he'd look into it. At their next poker game, a week later, Byler said there was no way this law was going to be changed legislatively.

"He told us that wealthy landowners didn't want city slickers on their property all weekend. There's a powerful resistance to Sunday hunting. One state senator said that he has had his seat threatened for even bringing up the idea of lifting the ban."

The other way, Gary said, was for someone to get arrested for Sunday hunting and then challenge the law in court. When Joe asked, "Who'd be stupid enough to do that?" everyone looked at him.

"At first I hesitated," he says. "I've got a clean record, no arrests. I worried how much it was going to cost. I was worried, too, about how this could hurt my taxidermy business. And then there was my family."

The next night, at dinner, when he told his son, Justin, that he might be breaking the law, the 9-year-old's eyes widened. Joe explained why and asked, "How would you feel in school if someone came up to you and said, 'Your dad was arrested'?" Justin said that he would simply explain. "That was all I wanted to hear."

His wife, Bess, was a little harder to convince. Could he go to jail? What would it cost? Would there be bail?

"I'm like most everyone—living from paycheck to paycheck," Joe says. "I couldn't put a lot of money in this or lose time from my work."

Gary Byler offered to forgo the retainer fee, so the only expenses would be court costs. Joe called a toll-free violation line to determine the penalty, and the game warden said the fine (up to $500) would be at the arresting officer's discretion, and the officer would decide whether Joe would be arrested, or even if his gun would be confiscated. *Virginian Pilot Ledger-Star* sports editor Bob Hutchinson, who heard of Joe's plan, called him, saying he would write a story about what Joe was doing. The publicity would help the case. Yet on the Saturday before the last Sunday of hunting season, he still hadn't made up his mind. Then Hutchinson called back to say that he had already written an article saying that Ficarra was thinking about filing suit.

"I felt kind of locked in," he says, taking a hammer to the side of the mount. "With the next day the last day of hunting season, it was either do or die. So I called up the wildlife office and told them what I was going to do, where I was going to do it, and when. The guy on the other end of the line told me, 'You're barking up the wrong tree, Bud. This doesn't work. I've seen this before."

On Sunday, February 9, Joe and his hunting buddy, David Byler (Gary's brother), pulled up in Joe's 1977 Ford Ranger at the appointed place, a quail field in the Virginia Beach borough of Pongo. Not wanting his quail hunting gun, an Italian-made double-barreled "over-and under" worth thousands of dollars, to be confiscated, he brought an old 16-gauge single-shot instead. "I paid $15 for it years ago," he says, "and I think I got took."

When game warden Craig Thomas appeared, Joe told him he wanted to get charged only with hunting on Sunday. "He could have had a real nasty attitude and said 'Why don't you just go ahead, buster, and see what I charge you with.'" Instead, Officer Thomas went down a checklist to see if Joe had a valid hunting license, was the proper distance from the road, and had legal ammunition for quail hunting. Then, after Joe loaded his gun with birdshot (you don't have to shoot a quail on Sunday to be fined, just having loaded the gun in a field is enough), Officer Thomas issued a citation: Virginia Summons G0003382, with a fine of $100 for "hunting wild bird on Sunday." Dave photographed the incident.

Joe Ficarra began stalking his biggest game.

A customer walks in the front door, and Joe comes out of the back room to meet him. He might not have advertised he's a taxidermist, but the stuffed beasts, fowl, and fish in the jewelry shop could give the secret away. A ten-foot blue marlin ornaments one wall. A hooded merganser sits on a block of wood in a jewelry case. A black bear head growls over another case, while a Canada goose, through brown glass eyes, watches. Near the front of the shop is a walleye, a largemouth bass, a raccoon, a perch, and long-nosed gar.

The customer, a scruffy-bearded, beer-gutted slab of "good old boy," buys a black baseball cap with a mallard drake emblem on the front. The hat says "Virginia Sportsman Association." Joe ordered the hats to raise money for his defense. He had twelve dozen hats made at $7 each, which he sells for $25. Only two remain.

"Once Hutchinson's article came out in the *Ledger-Star*," Joe says, "I got my fifteen minutes of fame." UPI, AP, the Washington *Post*, even *USA Today* picked up the story, including the local media. Garvey Winegar, of the Richmond *Times-Dispatch*, wrote that the "astringent message of John Calvin, who proclaimed anything he didn't personally care for as a sin, remains alive in Virginia. The Sunday law against hunting is a fine example."

People called from all over the commonwealth, even from other states, wanting to help. With Gary's legal help, Joe founded the nonprofit Virginia Sportsman Association for Sunday Hunting, Inc. A sign proclaiming its existence is fastened to the front of the left jewelry case, the one with the hooded merganser.

"I am fifteen years old," wrote one supporter, "and I haven't liked the Sunday huntin' law either. . . . If Joe Ficarro [sic] can read this, please let him."

"I love it," Joe cackles. "He probably thinks I'm some illiterate redneck."

Though not exactly a theologian, Joe understood a basic principle of religious freedom. "It should be up to the preachers to fill the pews on Sunday," he says, "not the state. Plus, being in the woods can be more of a religious experience than sitting in a pew counting the lice on the hat of the lady in front of you."

On April 25 Joe appeared before John B. Preston, judge in the Circuit Court of Virginia Beach, charged with violating statute 29.15211, which calls Sunday "a day of rest for all species of bird and wild animal life." The defense subpoenaed Virginia Game and Inland Fisheries director James Remington, who testified that "there is no biological basis for a general prohibition on Sunday hunting." Byler then argued that the law was established, not for biological reasons, but for religious purposes only, and therefore was unconstitutional.

Lower circuit court judges don't usually declare laws unconstitutional, and Judge Preston was no exception. Though apologetic (he even retired to his chambers for ten minutes before rendering the verdict); he found Joe guilty. Fined $100 and released on $250 bond, Joe would be back in court June 14 to appeal the decision.

Joe was used to bagging his game. This one wasn't going to get away so easily.

Down Independence Avenue, about six miles from Ficarra's Jewelers, sit two perpendicular rows of brick and wood offices. On the end office, the one closest to the street, a sign reads "Gary L. Byler, Attorney-at-Law." Upstairs, the receptionist's office is sleek, modern, op art on the wall. A red Coke can on her desk stands out from the blue and brown decor.

"The statute is religious," says Gary Byler, sitting in his office. "It prefers the Christian religion to others, and we're going to fight it on all fronts."

Fast-talking, kinetic, Byler is in his thirties, wears preppy glasses, and thrives on his work. He's enjoying the publicity too. "This story has been picked up by local and national news," he says. "I still get phone calls all the time from the media. Which is what we want."

On the back wall behind his desk are seven diplomas. He earned his B.A. from

Georgetown and his law degree from the University of Virginia. On the opposite wall are two photographs of him with President Reagan during the year (1982–1983) he worked at the White House, "the youngest guy there." A libertarian, he left the Office of Cabinet Affairs after only one year because, he said, "I have an aversion to using my talents for the government."

Byler was raised in Virginia Beach, in a house not far from his office. His father, a well-known developer, owns the building that Gary works in. "To be honest," he says proudly, "I wouldn't have started a practice here if it were not for the good name of my father."

Gary himself doesn't hunt. His idea of leisure is "taking a few beers, a radio, and sitting out in a boat, sunbathing." Nevertheless, he initiated the idea to challenge the Sunday hunting ban. "Sunday is the traditional Christian Sabbath," he says. "It's not coincidence that the ban happens to fall on that day. Let them make it on Wednesday to prove that it's not religious."

A few years earlier the Virginia Supreme Court struck down commercial Sunday laws because they were so haphazard, preferring one group over another. "Everything is legal on Sunday," he said, "except hunting." Even here, he explains, the law is not applied evenly, because raccoon hunters are allowed to hunt until 2:00 a.m. They claim that they can't get their dogs out of the woods by midnight. "The raccoon lobby," he says, "is strong."

Byler then pulls out the original statute that banned Sunday hunting in the Colonies. "The date is March 1642," he says. "It reads 'Be it also enacted, for the better observation of the Sabbath and for the restraint of diverse abuses committed in the colony by unlawful shooting on the Sabbath day as aforesaid, unless it shall be for the safety of his or their plantations or corn fields or for defense against Indians, he or they so offending shall forfeit . . . twenty pounds of tobacco.' "

Byler laughs. "Now we know why Jefferson wrote the Virginia Statute for Religious Liberty. The Sunday ban definitely has a religious origin, and this proves it. We are going to use this document in the appeals court tomorrow. We're going at it with all we've got."

On Thursday, June 14, a ceremony on the municipal grounds in Virginia Beach commemorates Flag Day.

On the bench, in the circuit court of appeals, courtroom 4, Judge Thomas Shadrick, gowned in his black robe, goes through the docket. Young, handsome, sunburned, the judge looks like the former college athlete he probably is. His short black hair is light, singed with gray along the temples. Three prisoners, one after another, dressed in orange jumpsuits are escorted in and out before him by armed police.

Joe sits with his wife while Gary scampers in and out (he has five other cases that day). Joe is dressed in blue jeans, a blue-and-white flannel shirt, and a bolo tie clasped with a piece of deer antler. "Redneck formal wear," he quips. He closed his shop, leaving a sign in the window: "Gone to court to fight for Sunday hunting." AP, UPI, and a few local journalists, including Bob Hutchinson, who first broke the story, sit on the wooden seats. A TV crew from local station WTKR waits outside.

At 11:02 a.m. the bailiff calls out, "The Commonwealth of Virginia versus Joe Ficarra." Joe, Gary, and a law clerk who helped with the case sit at a table on the judge's right; the prosecutor, Robert McDonald (a family friend of the Bylars, who once even worked in Gary's office) sits at the judge's left, with game warden Craig Thomas dressed in his green uniform.

Gary presents a copy of the original law to the judge, contending that it violates church-state separation because it was for the "better observation of the Sabbath."

"Was this the act your client was charged under?" the judge asks.

"No," Gary answers, explaining that though the religious language was removed, the religious intent remained in the statute. "The legislature has restricted the offending language, but not the offending law."

He quotes Virginia Game and Inland Fisheries director James Remington from the last trial, who said that there was "no biological basis for prohibiting Sunday hunting." Therefore, Gary says, the law is "an illegal establishment of religion."

He argues that the law violated the equal protection law also because it allowed for fishing and raccoon hunting, nothing else, and that it discriminated against those who have Sunday as their only day off, thus people like Ficarra are placed in the position where they must "choose between earning a living or pursuing a pastime." Furthermore, it placed an economic hardship on Joe Ficarra, because if people could hunt more, he would have more taxidermy business.

When Byler finishes, Robert McDonald stands before the bench, saying that what Ficarra did "violated sound public policy in the Commonwealth of Virginia since John Smith was courting Pocahantas."

He claims that there is no "precedent that a law restricting activity on Sunday has anything to do with religion." He asserts that the Sunday hunting ban gives people a day of rest from noise, reduces staff for the Game Commission, gives animals a day of rest, and is a day of rest for citizens of the community.

"Clearly," he asserts, "it has a rational basis."

He quotes a former Sunday law case that says that just because a closing law happens to coincide with a day of religious observance "doesn't create any type of presumption of a religious purpose."

He says that numerous laws "limited one's right to hunt: there are various seasons which are enacted, there are bag limits, and all kinds of other things which reduce and regulate the ability of citizens in the commonwealth" to hunt, therefore rejecting the argument that the law was specially discriminating against certain classes, or placed a special economic hardship on Ficarra.

He rejects Remington's statement as only "his opinion and not something that the commonwealth agitated."

In a sixty-second rebuttal, Gary pounces on the day of rest notion because people could "skeet-shoot and target-shoot, and the firing of a firearm is permitted" on

Sunday. He rejects the argument that Sunday hunting would demand more staff: "In fact, I would argue the opposite: if Sunday hunting were legal, they wouldn't need so many people in the field to arrest people like Joe Ficarra who do hunt on Sunday."

He attacks the notion that the Sunday ban just "happens to coincide" with the Christian Sabbath and again used the 1642 statute as proof.

Judge Shadrick, more accustomed to cases of car theft and check forgery than establishment clause issues, doesn't hesitate to render a verdict.

"I think quail are entitled to a day of rest," he says. "Guilty. A $100 fine."

Outside, on the court steps, Gary, Joe, and his wife, Bess, reporters, and a TV crew gather.

"My lawyer warned me," Joe says, "that this probably would happen. But we're not going to stop. We're talking about the little guys, the blue collar guys. There's no big money guys behind me. The big money can go fly to Arizona or wherever it's legal to hunt on Sunday."

"We're still going to fight," Gary says in response to a question. "Though we hope that the legislature will see the errors of their ways and change this law. But until they do, it is going to stay in the hopper or be struck down. We will effect our appeal in 30 days to the Virginia Court of Appeals. We will go all the way to the United States Supreme Court if we need to."

Until then, "all species of wild bird and wild animal life" in Virginia will have Sunday as "a day of rest" from the sport of hunting.

And so will Joe Ficarra, whether he wants it or not.

This article originally appeared in *Liberty*, January/February 1991.

CHAPTER THIRTY-TWO

Who's Afraid of a Judeo-Christian America?

If anyone should favor Judeo-Christian values, it's me—a Jewish Christian! Yet when the New Right talks about enforcing the "Judeo-Christian ethic," I worry. What about the millions of Americans who happen to be neither Jewish nor Christian? What about the Jews and Christians (not to mention Jewish Christians) whose concept of what comprises the Judeo-Christian ethic differs from those seeking to enforce it upon the nation?

I worry because the hundreds of Christian denominations in America disagree over everything imaginable. Christians don't agree on how Jesus came, when He came, why He came, what He did when He was here, where He went when He left, what He is doing now, and what He will do next. Christians argue over whether Jesus was God or a man and over the nature of His being a God-man. They disagree over texts in Daniel, Revelation, James, John, Deuteronomy, Malachi, and every other book in the Bible.

And it's not just Protestants versus Catholics. Baptists argue with Methodists, Episcopalians with Mormons, Jehovah's Witnesses with Lutherans, and Pentecostals with Adventists. Also, Catholics argue with Catholics, Baptists with Baptists, charismatics with charismatics—and they bicker with the Jews, who bicker among themselves! So in this milieu, whose definition of *Judeo-Christian* will become law? And what will happen to those who disagree?

In January 1986, I attended a Christian World Affairs Conference in Washington, D.C., sponsored by Faith-America. Hundreds of ministers, Christian educators, church leaders, and religious booksellers were there—Episcopalians, Presbyterians, Baptists, born-again Catholics, charismatic Methodists—a wide spectrum of American Christianity. The speakers included presidential aspirant Jack Kemp, Secretary of Education William Bennett, Secretary of the Army John Marsh, and others.

The conference gave participants an overview, from a conservative perspective, of the world's economic, political, and military situation. It dealt with the Strategic Defense Initiative (Star Wars), Sandinistas, the deficit, tax reform, the Soviet Union, terrorism, Ronald Reagan, oil, immigration policy, AIDS, education, abortion, and other issues. I shared the concerns about immorality, pornography, abortion, Communist aggression, and economics—and I appreciated these conservative Christian patriots' worries about the dangers America faces.

Yet I worried about the meeting itself! In the talks I attended a tone pervaded— an undercurrent of militancy, jingoism, and aggressiveness. Lack of sensitivity, if not hostility, to the concept of separation of church and state prevailed, as well as animosity toward the pluralism of American democracy. I worried about the amens that I heard from the audience when former congressman John Conlan, the host of the meetings, said that the Constitution of the United States doesn't even mention "separation of church and state." (At that point a man sitting next to me whispered, "The words 'separation of church and state' appear in the Russian constitution.")

What is a Judeo-Christian?

One speaker, William Dannemeyer (R-Calif.), talked about the conflict between Christians and secular humanism. He used the word that had been bandied about at the meetings: *Judeo-Christian*. I wondered exactly what he and the others meant by it, so I went to the microphone and asked.

"Congressman," I asked, "I share your concerns for America. But when you say Judeo-Christian, don't you really mean Christian? And when you say Christian, don't you really mean Protestant? And when you say Protestant, don't you really mean Fundamentalist?"

"I'll tell you what I mean by it," he replied. "The Ten Commandments." He mentioned "the first three," which he said deal with man's relationship to God and "the last seven," which deal with man's relationship to others.

I know the Ten Commandments. The first *four*—"Thou shalt have no other gods before me. Thou shalt not make unto thee any graven images. . . .Thou shalt not take the name of the Lord thy God in vain. . . . Remember the sabbath"—deal with man's relationship to God. The congressman was missing one.

Which Commandment?

Then it hit me: Dannemeyer was giving the Catholic version! Catechisms in Catholic secondary schools (and some Lutheran catechisms) drop the second commandment, which forbids idol worship and divide the tenth commandment into two. When I explained the discrepancy, Dannemeyer didn't seem to realize the difference. He said he knew only what he had been taught since childhood.

My point exactly! These well-meaning people want America to follow the Ten Commandments. But whose version? They want God back in school. But whose

God? And what about those Americans who have other gods before Jehovah or those whose gods are wood and stone? Some people keep their Sabbath on Saturday; others on Sunday. Some don't keep it at all. Some believe that the Ten Commandments were abolished at the cross. Christians can't even agree on something as fundamental as the Ten Commandments, yet they want to make them the law of the land! If the New Right brings Judeo-Christian morality back to America, whose interpretation will be enforced?

Violent Religion

Throughout the past 2,000 years, millions have suffered abuse, jail, torture, even death because their religious convictions differed from an officially sanctioned version of Christianity. But because the First Amendment forbids Congress to pass any law "respecting an establishment of religion," this nation has been spared much of the violence and turmoil that has rocked most of the rest of the world. Many assert that with the safeguards we have in this country, religious persecution could never occur. But now, charging that the Establishment Clause is hostile to religion, the New Right seeks to eliminate the best assurance we have that religious persecution will not spill across our "amber waves of grain."

How will Protestant parents feel when Susie comes home from public school fingering rosary beads? Or how will Catholics feel when little Johnny talks about Joseph Smith and the angel Moroni? Or how will Catholics and Mormons feel when Protestant textbooks in public schools declare rosary beads and Joseph Smith of the devil? Establish a civil religion in America—any kind, under any name—and those who disagree with its tenets will be ostracized, alienated, and persecuted.

After questioning Mr. Dannemeyer, I sensed a little of what could come to those who don't conform to the New Right's Judeo-Christian America. Now the audience realized that I was not one of them. I was a discordant note in their battle hymn for a new republic. It was as if I were a self-confessed child molester or the perfidious Norman Lear himself.

Later I talked with a Christian friend whom I hadn't seen in years. She was excited about the New Right's plans for America. I explained my concerns for religious freedom. I warned about the danger should one group's definition of Judeo-Christian morality become law and the difficulties it could cause for the Christians who don't agree.

"No problem, Cliff," she said, hoping to assuage my fears. "First, we Christians will take control of the government—and then we can fight it out among ourselves."

I worry.

This article originally appeared in *Ministry*, July 1986.

CHAPTER THIRTY-THREE

The Hialeah Animal Sacrifice Case

November 4, 1992; downtown Washington, D.C. Newspaper headlines visible at fifty feet declare Bill Clinton president-elect. Rushing past them, I jaunt along the wet, leafy sidewalks toward the United States Supreme Court, to cover a crucial free exercise trial—the *Hialeah* animal sacrifices of the Church of the Lukumi Babalu Aye.

Lukumi Babalu Aye is, definitely, not mainline Protestant. Its members, called Santeros, practice an ancient Afro-Caribbean faith known as Santeria. Santeros celebrate birth, death, and marriage with animal sacrifices. In their rituals they decapitate goats, chickens, doves, and turtles—often twenty animals at a time—usually in private homes. In one ceremony a priest slices the throat of a chicken, chops off its head, bites into the headless bird's breast, and rips the animal open with his teeth before stuffing the open chest with herbs, tobacco, and bits of dried fish—all in an attempt to please Babalu Aye, a Santeria god. The city of Hialeah wants the practice stopped.

Thinking that this case is not going to present the usual courtroom dialogue, I enter the side entrance off Maryland Avenue. Having cleared security, I pick up a press pass—a little orange card with my seat number, G-5. Because of the publicity associated with this case, the press section is filled, and G-5 puts me behind a massive pillar cloaked in a heavy red drape. I gape over the cowlick of a reporter to my left and glimpse the corner of a justice's robe. Straightening up, I stare at the pillar, notebook and pen in my lap. How am I supposed to cover this story?

Then it hits me: If cases are decided without the judges seeing all the parties involved, I should be able to cover this case seeing only a red drape and the dandruff of the obtrusive reporter.

One of the first voices I hear is Douglas Laycock's, arguing for the church of the

169

Lukumi Babalu Aye, which is petitioning the High Court to strike down four ordinances that ban animal sacrifices—rituals central to the church's faith.

"This is a case," Laycock declares, "about open discrimination of a minority religion." This discrimination is unconstitutional, and therefore the laws should be struck down as an infringement of the free exercise of the Santeros.

More than fifty thousand Santeros live in south Florida, where many fled from Castro's suppression of their religion. In 1987 the Santeria church, wanting to open a public place of worship, bought land in Hialeah, a Miami suburb. In anticipation of an animal-sacrificing church, complaints about paganism, and decapitated goats and chickens found in parks, under trees, and on courthouse steps, Hialeah passed four ordinances making animal sacrifices for religious purposes a first-degree misdemeanor punishable by a $500 fine and/or 60 days in jail. The Santeria church sued the city, claiming that the laws violated its free exercise rights. When the United States district court in south Florida upheld the laws, the Santeros appealed to the U.S. Supreme Court (whose acceptance of the case brought the litigants to the courtroom, and me to my seat behind the pillar).

As Laycock speaks, other voices interrupt. They belong to the Supreme Court justices, and when a woman speaks, I know it is Justice O'Connor.

Laycock proposes that the only way to prove animal sacrifices illegal is to show that Santeria is false, and that would constitute "a heresy trial."

A justice asks: Merely because one of the Santeros' gods tells them that something is right, is it then legally protected?

Laycock argues that because one can kill animals in Hialeah for any reason but religious sacrifice, the ordinances are not neutral but aimed at a specific religious practice. For that reason, he asserts, they are unconstitutional.

Laycock's point here deals with an issue of fundamental importance—not only in this case but for religious freedom in general. *Church of the Lukumi Babalu Aye v. City of Hialeah* is the first free exercise case to be heard by the U.S. Supreme Court since its 1990 *Smith* decision. In *Smith*, the Court (5-4) largely abandoned previous jurisprudence in dealing with the free exercise clause. For decades prior to *Smith*, the Court usually placed a "strict scrutiny" on any governmental action that restricted the free exercise of religious practices. Government must show (1) a compelling public interest for laws restricting free exercise and (2) the lack of a less burdensome means of protecting the state's interests. In essence, the government needed a persuasive reason to restrict free exercise.

With *Smith*, however, the Court renounced this "strict scrutiny" concept, except in certain instances. Instead, it said that the free exercise clause never relieves an individual of the obligation to comply with a "valid and neutral law of general applicability" simply because that law interferes with his or her religious practice. As long as a law is religiously neutral and equitably applied, it is constitutional, regardless of any incidental burden on religion.

Voices from the bench question whether the Hialeah ordinances were directed at the Santeria religion itself or were merely a neutral ban. Even *Smith* said that though incidental restrictions on free exercise were constitutional, laws "specifically directed at religious practice" were not, unless the state could show a compelling state interest in upholding them.

Another justice queries whether the ordinances were intended to suppress not the religion but only certain acts thereof. If so, the ordinances were uniform, neutral laws that simply prohibit animal sacrifice by anyone. Why would they be considered unconstitutional?

Laycock argues: In order for the ban to be constitutional, it would have to include all animals killed in the city. He says that the bans were "underinclusive with a vengeance" against Santeria and therefore should be struck down.

I remember reading earlier the story from the Santeros' perspective. They complained that one can boil lobsters alive, feed rats to snakes, butcher animals in a slaughterhouse, hunt them with a bow and arrow, and kill unwanted pets publically— as long as none of this is done for religious reasons. As an amicus brief filed on behalf of the Santeros said: "One may get Chicken McNuggets in Hialeah, but one may not partake of chicken roasted at a religious service of the Santeria faith."

Smith also said that the state would be violating the free exercise clause "if it sought to ban such acts or force abstention, when they are engaged in for religious reasons, or only because of the religious belief that they display. It would doubtless be unconstitutional, for example, to ban the casting of 'statutes that are used for worship purposes' or to prohibit the bowing down [to] a golden calf."

Hialeah city officials, however, believe the city does have compelling reasons to prohibit the practice. A new voice I identify as belonging to defense council Richard Garrett argues for the city of Hialeah. I lean over as far as I can, hoping to see what he looks like, but he's well-hidden behind the pillar. The reporter to my left sneezes, and I get a momentary glimpse of David Souter sitting quietly, listening to Garrett.

Garrett asserts: The city is concerned about the thousands of animals being sacrificed within its limits, the carcasses left to rot in public places, animals being tortured, and the health hazards caused by dozens of animals killed daily in private homes.

In an earlier defense of the ordinances, I read that Garrett claimed that the city had no interest in suppressing the Santeria faith; rather, it wanted to avoid the "specter of thousands, indeed tens of thousands, of animals being killed in homes and in the streets throughout south Florida, with the attendant problems of keeping and feeding animals and later disposing of the remains." He said that the flies and rats attracted to the remains of animals found at intersections, [in] backyards, [along] railroad tracks, [in] homes, rivers, and by the sides of roads" constituted enough of a health hazard to warrant a compelling interest in banning the sacrifices. Garrett mentioned cruelty to animals as another sufficient reason to ban the rituals. He said that the city's legitimate concern about animal sacrifices encompassed everything about the act, from the beginning of the process to the disposal of the remains.

O'Connor interrupts Garret, asking why the city couldn't adopt ordinances regulating the manner in which animals are killed as well as disposed of.

Garrett answers that such ordinances would be too difficult to regulate because the killing happens in private homes. The city would be forced, for example, to tell the priests how to hold the knife when slaughtering the animals, and this could lead to entanglement problems. The Santeros could say that the city regulations are not in conformity with how their gods tell them to do it, and they would be back in court with another free exercise appeal.

More voices from the bench ask why the killing of animals in the city for reasons other than sacrifice is not covered in the ordinances.

Garrett replies that the ban was limited only to animal sacrifices because the other types of killing, such as hunting and slaughterhouse carnage, were not causing problems.

The questions then revolve around cruelty to animals. In the lower court hearing, the Humane Society testified that the Santeria method of slaughter—jabbing a knife through the animal's throat—causes more suffering to the animals than either the Jewish or Muslim method, which cuts cleanly through the carotid arteries. Therefore, the city had a reason to ban sacrifices. (I wonder whether Hialeah's wish to spare chickens a few extra seconds of pain warrants restricting a fundamental constitutional right). A voice from the bench asks if it would be lawful in Hialeah to kill one's cat in order to "put it out of its misery."

Garrett answers Yes.

The voice then asks whether it would be lawful to drown the cat in the bathtub.

No, Garrett answers. It would be cruelty to the animal, and Hialeah has laws against that.

O'Connor asks about boiling lobsters alive or killing mice and rats. Another voice incredulously asks: "You can't eat lobster in Hialeah?" Another helps Garrett along by saying that killing mice and rats does not constitute sacrifice and therefore is not included in the ordinances.

The justices then ask about slaughterhouses. If animal sacrifices were conducted in a properly zoned slaughterhouse with rules to ensure that the animals were not treated cruelly (though how can you slice an animal's throat in a manner that's not cruel?), the conditions were sanitary, and the disposal problem taken care of in an adequate manner, would Hialeah still prohibit sacrifices?

Yes, says Garrett, an answer that seems to weaken his first two major arguments.

First, his answer asserts that the ordinances prohibit any animal sacrifice, even in a regulated slaughterhouse, but not other animal killings (which include slaughterhouse killing for nonreligious reasons). This response enhances Laycock's position that the Hialeah ordinances were aimed specifically at a religious practice (the concept of animal sacrifice itself implies a religious dimension). Second, if the Court rules that the ordinances are not neutral and then applies the "strict scrutiny" test to them, Hialeah's compelling state interest strategy should be invalidated as well. If the city's concerns about health, cruelty to animals, and sanitation are relieved by relegating the sacrifices to slaughterhouses, its reasons to stop the sacrifices would be nullified. Citizens would sleep well, knowing that they wouldn't find decapitated goats under park benches and that chicken throats were being cut in a kind way.

Soon after this exchange, the oral arguments ended, and I exit with the other reporters. On the courthouse steps, crowds of journalists with microphones, tape recorders, and TV cameras gather around Laycock. This case has garnered publicity not only because of its gory circumstances but also because of the chance that it could mitigate or even reverse *Smith*. The great hope is that Hialeah will do to *Smith* what *Barnette* did to *Gobitis*.

In *Gobitis*, using some of the same jurisprudence that reappeared fifty years later in *Smith* (indeed, Scalia quoted *Gobitis* in *Smith*), the Supreme Court upheld a neutral and generally applicable law that pressured Jehovah's Witnesses' children to salute the flag despite religious objections. It resulted in a severe wave of persecution against the Jehovah's Witnesses. Three years later, in *Barnette*, the Court reversed. Could Hialeah do the same to *Smith*? It's not likely. More likely, a majority of justices will strike down the four ordinances as being neither neutral nor generally applicable, thus leaving *Smith* not only in place but affirmed.

Of course, it is difficult to predict how a Court that could go from *Smith* (which decimated religious freedom) to *Wiseman* (which upheld it) within two years will rule on any religious liberty appeal. What we can hope for, however, is that the justices will see their way in adjudicating *Church of the Lukumi Babalu Aye v. City of Hialeah* much better than I, lodged behind my pillar, could see in reporting the case.

This article orginally appeared in *Liberty*, March/April 1993.

CHAPTER THIRTY-FOUR

My Creationist-Separationist Dilemma

I believe in a literal creation accomplished in six twenty-hour days, about six thousand years ago. I believe in the Garden of Eden, Adam and Eve, Noah's ark, the talking snake—the whole story just as Moses wrote it, literally.

I also believe in the First Amendment, literally. When it says "Congress shall make no law respecting an establishment of religion," I believe it means just that—the government has no business establishing, advancing, or subsidizing religious beliefs.

Now for the dilemma: How can I reconcile my belief in creationism and the court decisions that have declared the teaching of creation science in public schools unconstitutional? While I rejoice that the courts are keeping Jefferson's walls of separation high by forbidding religious indoctrination in public school, I cringe at the specter of evolution—with all its speculations, leaps of faith, and unproven premises—being pawned off as truth.

I haven't always been a Creationist—I used to be an evolutionist. My earliest recollection of evolutionary tendencies goes back to the fifth grade, in which, under the tutelage of Mrs. Catleet, I learned math, English, social studies, history, geography, and evolution. I still remember the different ages of the earth—Archeozoic, Proterozoic, Paleozoic, Mesozoic, Cenozoic—right off the top of my head.

In the eighth grade Mrs. Rubin taught me about Charles Darwin, the H.M.S. *Beagle*, and the Galapagos Islands. Her charts delineated how one species changed into another and then into another over billions of years. First, she would show a single-celled creature, followed by a protoplasmic blob, then a jellyfish, then a frog, followed by a dog, a monkey, a primate (either *Pithecanthropus erectus*, *Ramapithecus*, or good old Neanderthal man—usually hairy, needing a shave, and holding a spear), and then two *Homo sapiens*.

It all seemed so clear, so plain, so simple. No intelligent, educated, sensible person believed otherwise. And just as the class would laugh at the ancient myth that life spawned from inorganic matter—a pile of dry rags, for instance, could "spontaneously generate" mice and maggots—we laughed at those who didn't believe in evolution.

Mrs. Catleet and Mrs. Rubin didn't tell me, though, that the probability of even the least complex forms of life originating on the earth by natural processes is considered extremely remote, virtually a statistical impossibility.

They neglected to mention that Nobel laureate Francis Crick—of Watson and Crick fame and certainly not a creationist—said that the probabilities of life originating on the earth by chance are as remote as those of "a billion monkeys, on a billion typewriters, ever typing correctly even one sonnet of Shakespeare's during the present time of the universe."

They did not read to us these words: "To suppose that the eye, with all its inimitable contrivances for adjusting the focus to different distances, for admitting different distances, for admitting different amounts of light, and for the correction of spherical and chromatic aberration, could have been formed by natural selection seems, I freely confess, absurd in the highest degree." Nor did they tell us it was Charles Darwin who wrote them.

They never said that the key to the evolutionary theory—the life forms that link the species—has never been found. This problem is so important that evolutionist Stephen Jay Gould devised his "punctuated equilibrium" hypothesis—the belief that instead of occurring in a slow, gradual process, evolutionary change came in relatively quick jumps and spurts—to help explain why no transitional forms exist.

The point is that I reject evolution for a number of reasons. Primarily, I reject it because I'm a creationist. But I must admit I am a creationist *because of my religious views*—not because of creation science.

Rather than being a slow, gradual, Darwinian process, my transformation from evolutionist to creationist was more like Gould's "punctuated equilibrium." It happened quickly. I had an experience with the Lord and accepted the Bible as the Word of God. Unlike some, I found Genesis as compatible with *Origin of the Species* as Meir Kahane is with Muammar Kaddafi. Because I believed Genesis as it reads, I became a creationist. Later, as I read creation-science literature, I saw the scientific evidence for creation. But my belief in creation is based on faith, not science—though science has strengthened that faith.

So what do I do now that the Supreme Court, in a 7 to 1 decision, has thrown out the "Balanced Treatment for Creation-Science and Evolution-Science in Public School Instruction" that the Louisiana state legislature passed overwhelmingly?

Unlike our esteemed Supreme Court chief justice, who fantasizes that the framers of our Constitution wanted only to prevent the "designation of any church as a 'national one,'" I read the First Amendment as a bulwark against government attempts to promote and advance any specific religious belief. The framers knew that when government promotes religion, oppression follows. They wanted to keep the church out of the state and the state out of the church, because they knew that when the state promotes a religious belief, no matter how benign, that belief has behind it the coercive power of the government—and the framers didn't want our nation coercing anyone regarding religion.

Teaching Creation Science

But what about creation *science* in public schools? Does teaching that involve coercion? Can it be taught as science and not as creation?

Opponents claim that the term *creation science* is a misnomer—that it is not really science to begin with. Carl Sagan describes it as "a small bunch of people putting out thinly disguised biblical literalism . . . in a package disguised as science."

I know that pigeonholing creation science in this way is not really fair or accurate. I know that good scientific evidence exists for the abrupt appearance of life forms, a universal flood, and so forth. And yet creation science itself, no matter how scientific, necessitates the concept of a Creator, just as Christianity inherently implies a belief in Jesus, salvation, and the Cross. Postulating a Creator inevitably implies a religious belief, and no public school should be promoting a religious belief.

But though creation science implies a Creator, teaching it does not necessarily entail promoting faith in Him any more than claiming to be a Christian entails proselytizing. Could creation science be taught like a class in American religious history, which—though it involves the study of Christianity and many of its elements, such as Jesus, salvation, and the Cross—does not advance these beliefs as religious dogma?

For me, a literal creationist and a strict separationist, the real question is not Is creation science a science? Nor is it Can creation science be taught without promoting a religion? The real question is Would creation science be taught correctly, or would it be used to promote religious beliefs at government expense?

The creation science controversy has arisen at an inopportune time for creationists. The nation has been invaded with swarms of anti-First Amendment marines who want the government to subsidize religion, or even to promote it in public school, and they have been conjuring up various ways and means to storm the wall that has been checking their advance.

The Supreme Court saw the Louisiana bill as such an assault. Wendell Bird, the attorney for the state, argued that the law was secular in intent and was to ensure academic freedom. But Justice William J. Brennan, Jr., speaking for the majority, said that they found no evidence to support that claim. Calling the bill a sham, he said that it violated any pretense of fairness by tilting toward creationism.

It was, he said, a religiously motivated attempt to suppress evolution and replace it with the "viewpoint that a supernatural being created humankind." Asserting that as such, it was a thinly veiled effort to require religious instruction in public schools, Brennan said that the law "violates the establishment clause of the First Amendment because it seeks to employ the symbolic and financial support of government to achieve a religious purpose."

The Court's decision didn't prohibit anyone from teaching creation, provided the aim was to give comprehensive instruction about scientific theories and not to promote a sectarian position.

Considering the current militancy of many fundamentalists regarding the use of public schools to promote their beliefs, the Court was most likely correct in declaring the bill unconstitutional. The Louisiana law probably was used to promulgate a fundamentalist religious belief, even if that wasn't its original intent.

The problem, then, is balance. The chances of a pro-creationist teacher giving fair presentation of evolution (or vice versa) are not good. Can you imagine Jerry Falwell standing before a class of fifth graders, pointing to a picture of a protoplasmic critter and saying "Man was created in the image of a jellyfish"?

When it comes to teaching origins in our public schools, the problem is not creation science versus evolution. Rather, it is the extremists on both sides. My teachers did not present evolution as a theory but as a fact as well established as a law of thermodynamics. They didn't tell us all of the problems, the conflicting theories within evolutionary circles, or of the infighting among evolutionists themselves. Mrs. Catleet's and Mrs. Rubin's presentations were as dogmatic as a Jimmy Swaggart sermon on Sunday morning.

Currently, evolution is taught as an established fact when in reality it is only a theory. The alternative is teaching creation science in public schools, but doing so could violate the First Amendment. What we need is a balanced presentation of both, but who can provide that for us? A Norman Lear would be as unbalanced as a Pat Robertson. Of course, we could always try a theistic evolutionist, one who says he believes in both Genesis and Darwin, but the kids who take the class will need a class in logic when they're through.

We could avoid teaching them anything about origins, or maybe we could have special classes after school hours in which they could study either science they wanted—though if the creation science class were on school property, the ACLU would sue, unless they were in Alabama, where the evolutionists would be convicted of violating the establishment clause by promoting the religion of secular humanism, at least until it was overturned by the Supreme Court, but now with Scalia and Kennedy on the court . . .

As I said, I am in a dilemma!

This article originally appeared in *Ministry*, July 1989.

IMAGE OF THE MESSIANIC

The four articles in this small chapter deal with Sabbath. All but one appeared in *Shabbat Shalom*, and all—though teaching what we believe—were written for non-Adventists.

Church members might particularly enjoy "Image of the Messianic," where I show from Jewish sources how the Jews saw in the Sabbath an image of the redemption, even the rest, that the Messiah brings. I quote one ancient Jewish text in which someone—asking to see an example of heaven—is told that they can get a foretaste of the *olom haba* (the world to come) in the Sabbath. With this article I originally wanted to teach Jews some SDA theology through their own material; by placing it in this compilation, I hope to show Adventists our theology from those same Jewish sources.

Meanwhile, "The Origin of Sunday," which first appeared in *Liberty*, traces the roots of ancient pagan hatred of the Jews to the rise of Sunday, the false Sabbath, a topic of considerable interest to Adventists.

"A Sanctuary in Time" deals with the concept of the Sabbath as found in the writing of the great Jewish scholar Abraham Joshua Heschel. Many Adventists over the years have been blessed by Heschel's writing on the Sabbath, and this short article catches some of the flavor and highlights of this great writer's insights on something so sacred to us.

CHAPTER THIRTY-FIVE

Image of the Messianic

From the sun-bleached tents scattered along ancient deserts to high-rise condominiums on Miami Beach, Jews have kept the Sabbath holy. From the *Bene Yisrael* who danced under shifting shadows of the temple walls to the *Juden* confined inside electrified wire, Jews have kept the Sabbath holy. Whether in Jerusalem or Johannesburg, in joy or sorrow, in freedom or chains, in every age, Jews have kept the Sabbath holy.

Of course, any religious tradition so dominant, so enduring as the Sabbath would leave in its wake waves of explanation regarding its significance, purpose, and practice. *Shabbat* is no exception. From the prophet Ezekiel, who declared, "Keep holy my Sabbaths, and they will be a sign between me and between you to know that I am the Lord your God" (Ezek. 20:20),[1] to Rabbi Abraham Joshua Heschel, who called the Sabbaths "our great cathedrals,"[2] Jewish literature expounds on the *Shabbat* as a memorial of Creation, a sign of the true God, the Creator of heaven and earth.

Intertwined within those sacred twenty-four hours of the seventh day, however, is another concept, the one of redemption, of salvation, of the Messiah Himself, which is why Sabbath has been called the image of the Messianic. Sabbath points not only back to Creation but forward to redemption, because the Lord is not only Creator but Redeemer as well.

"While it [Sabbath Halachah] finds a variety of expressions in Talmudic literature," writes Theodore Friedman, "all of them, in the end give voice to the idea that the Sabbath is the anticipation, the foretaste, the paradigm of life in the world to come. The abundance of such statements is the surest evidence of how deep-rooted and widespread that notion was in early rabbinic literature."[3] This idea flashes through not only Scripture, Midrash, Gemara, and Kabbalist literature but through modern Jewish thought as well.

According to the rabbis, the Sabbath preambled eternity. One legend states that as the Lord gave the commandments to Israel, He promised that if obedient, they would receive the reward of the next world. Israel then asked, "Show us . . . an example of the world to come," and the Lord responded: "The Sabbath is an example of the world to come."[4] The Midrash talks of three incomplete phenomena: "the incomplete experience of death is sleep; an incomplete form of prophecy is the dream; the incomplete form of the next world is the Sabbath."[5] The Mishnah reads: "A Psalm, a song for the Sabbath day—a song for the time to come, for the day that is all Sabbath rest in the eternal life."[6]

In the apocalyptic *Books of Adam and Eve*, the archangel Michael admonishes Seth, saying, "Man of God, mourn not for thy bread more than six days, for the seventh day is a sign of the resurrection and the rest of the age to come."[7] According to Nachmanides, "the seventh day is an indication of the world to come that is all Sabbath."[8] A later Jewish source calls the Sabbath "a reminder of the two worlds— this world and the world to come; it is an example of both worlds. For the Sabbath is joy, holiness and rest; joy is part of this world; holiness and rest are something of the world to come."[9]

In the modern age, Franz Rosenzweig calls Sabbath an anticipation of redemption: "On the Sabbath," he wrote, "the congregation feels as if it were already redeemed."[10] For Abraham Joshua Heschel, when the Sabbath arrives, "man is touched by a moment of actual redemption; as if for a moment the spirit of Messiah moved over the face of the earth."[11]

The link is clear. By looking at Creation, the Sabbath also points to redemption, which is merely the restoration of Creation. After the intrusion of evil, the harmony, joy, and love that suffused man's initial presence was uprooted and replaced by an endless cycle of violence, anxiety, and hate, which is why human existence for thousands of years has been just barely that, existence. Messianic redemption promises to reestablish that original Edenic bliss. For centuries the rabbis have noted the parallels between Adam's life in Eden before the Fall and expulsion and the time of redemption brought by the Messiah. "Consciously or unconsciously," wrote Theodore Friedman, "these parallels—the latter time as the return of Edenic conditions—must have registered on the Rabbinic mind."[12]

They had. The rabbis saw in numerous texts promises of great material abundance in the world to come. "And it will come to pass on that day that the mountains will drip juice and the hills will flow with milk" (Joel 3:18). "And they will come and sing in the exalted places of Zion, and they will be singing the goodness of the Lord upon the corn, and upon the wine, and upon the oil, and upon the sons of Zion and flocks, and their souls will be as a watered garden" (Jer. 31:12). For the rabbis, these verses reflected the abundances with which the Lord had originally blessed man in Eden, having given him "every tree that was pleasant to see and good for food" (Gen. 2:9). The warning that Adam would acquire his bread only "by the sweat of his brow" indicated that backbreaking labor wasn't required before sin entered. Therefore, the rabbis noted, after the advent of the Messiah and the initiation of the new age, the *Olam Haba*, when oil and juice will flow from the mountains and hills, man's toil for his bread would no longer draw sweat from his brow.

The Bible prophets wrote, too, that in the world to come, the age of redemption, man's physical defects would be eradicated: "Then the eyes of the blind shall be opened, the ears of the deaf shall be opened, the lame shall skip like the ram, and the tongue of the dumb shall sing" (Isa. 35:5, 6). And though the Bible doesn't detail Adam's physical state, except that all which God had made at Creation was *tovmeod*, coming directly from the hand of God, Adam must have been without defect.

Yet the damage of sin wasn't merely physical. Adam had lived in intimate harmony and closeness with God. Because of sin, that relationship ruptured. Adam became fearful, defensive, and guilty, even to the point of hiding from the presence of God (Gen. 3:10). This condition reflects unregenerate man's state ever since. Perhaps the greatest promise of redemption is to heal the rift and to bring man and God back into the harmonious relationship they had once enjoyed and thus end the suffering that the rift had caused: "For behold, I will create heaven new and earth new, and the former things will not be remembered nor rise upon the heart. But rejoice and be glad in what I create. For behold, I create Jerusalem a rejoicing and her people a gladness. For I will rejoice in Jerusalem and be glad in my people; and the voice of weeping will not be heard in her, nor the voice of crying" (Isa. 65:17-19).

Because the Jews saw creation closely linked to redemption, they linked the Sabbath experience itself with redemption too. The joy, the peace, the rest of the Sabbath was a shadow, an image of the joy, the peace, and the rest of the *Olam Haba*. "Sabbath," says the Talmud, "is one-sixtieth part of the world to come."[13]

This theology has been translated into Sabbath *halachah*. Certain things were not done on *Shabbat* simply because they will not be done in the Messianic era. According to one Rabbinic school, a person may not search his garments on the Sabbath because he might find vermin and kill them,[14] the idea that killing will not occur on the *Olam Haba*. Other activities, such as mourning the dead, visiting the sick, carrying weapons, and making contributions to the poor were considered, by some rabbis, forbidden for the same reason: They would not be done in the world to come. Some rabbis thought it was impossible to tell a lie on the Sabbath, for lies will not be told in the Messianic age.

Scholars have found in Scripture numerous links between the Sabbath and redemption. For Theodore Friedman "It is no mere coincidence that Isaiah employs the 'delight' (*oneg*) and 'honor' (*kavod*) in his description of both the Sabbath and the end of days. . . . The implication is clear. The delight and joy that will mark the end of days is made available here and now by the Sabbath."[15] In this context, it's no wonder that the Sabbath, anticipated by the Messianic Age, was to be a day of delight and gladness.

For the Jews, who have spent centuries under foreign dominion, the world to come promised freedom from bondage and oppression. The Exodus from Egypt prototypes the freedom and liberation that they expect in the *Olam Haba*. The Deuteronomic version of the Ten Commandments explicitly links the Sabbath to the Exodus: "And you will remember that you were a servant in the land of Egypt, and the Lord your God brought you from there with a strong hand and an outstretched arm. Therefore, the Lord your God commanded you to keep the Sabbath day" (Deut. 5:15). In the Exodus version, Sabbath is stressed as a memorial of Creation. Thus, both versions together expand the meaning of the Sabbath, not only as a memorial of God's power to create but of His power to liberate His people Israel. The Messianic era will be the ultimate Sabbath, which is why the *Olam Haba* is called "the day that will be all Sabbath and rest for everlasting life."[16]

Tied to the weekly Sabbath were the sabbatical seasons (Lev. 25:4), which came every seven years, and the jubilee, which came every forty-nine. Both institutions rested on the cycle of seven, as did the weekly Sabbath, and both were "a Sabbath of solemn rest to the land, a Sabbath to the Lord" (Lev. 25:4). In the jubilee, servants were freed, debts released, and property restored to original owners—a foretaste of Messianic liberation. In the jubilee year the Jews were "to proclaim emancipation in all the land, to all its inhabitants; it will be your jubilee; a man will return his property, and a man will return to his family" (Lev. 25:10). The jubilee was to be a time of peace, rest, and liberation, when one man "should not oppress another" (Lev. 25:17). Thus, in a minor way, it reflected the liberation, the freedom, and peace of a long-expected Messianic era.

According to the Talmud, if Israel had kept two successive Sabbaths as they should have, redemption would immediately come. Actually, if they kept one correctly, the Messiah would appear.[17] Of course, anything so closely related as the Sabbath, or the jubilees, to redemption would naturally spawn Messianic calculations. Over the centuries, both the Sabbath and the jubilees have been used to predict the Messiah's advent.

Daniel 9, for instance, begins with Daniel's prayer for the deliverance of Jerusalem, which, according to Jeremiah 29:10, was to be in captivity for seventy years—a prolonged Sabbath of desolation because of disobedience: "To fulfill the word of the Lord by the mouth of Jeremiah: until the land enjoyed her Sabbaths. All the days of desolation she rested, to fulfill seventy years" (2 Chron. 36:21). In response, the angel Gabriel appears and gives Daniel a Messianic calculation that extends far beyond the Babylonian captivity. "Seventy weeks of years" he says, "are determined upon your people" (Dan. 9:24). Instead of dealing with a mere seventy years of the Babylonian captivity, which were the *ten sabbatical years* (10 x 7) the "seventy weeks of years" contain *ten jubilee years* (10 x 49). One week of years is seven years, so seventy weeks of years is 490. This 490-year period points to the "Messianic Prince" (verse 25). The starting point of that 10-year cycle, the 490 years, is "from the command to restore and rebuild Jerusalem unto the Messiah Prince." That specific command to restore and rebuild Jerusalem was issued in 457 B.C.E., which places the fulfillment of the prophecy early in the Common Era.

In light of this calculation, the Talmud states that "the world is to exist for six thousand years. In the first two thousand there was desolation [i.e., no Torah]; two thousand years the Torah flourished; and the next two thousand years is the Messianic era, but through our many iniquities all these have been lost."[18] Footnotes to that section regarding the Messianic era state: "Messiah will come within that period. He should have come at the beginning of the last two thousand years; the delay is due to our sins."[19] These Talmudic predictions fit perfectly with jubilee calculations of Daniel, which place the coming of the Messiah at "the beginning of the last two thousand years."

With redemption so closely linked with it, *Shabbat* has endured. As long as the Jews anticipate the final day of redemption, they will observe Sabbath. And though they have waited patiently over the millennia for the Messiah, each Sabbath they can relish a morsel of the *Olam Haba*. Thus, with a weekly taste of eternity so succulent in their mouths, is it any wonder that the Jews, in every age, under every circumstance, have kept the Sabbath holy?

---

[1]All Bible texts in this article are the author's translations.

[2]Abraham Joshua Heschel, *The Sabbath* (New York: Farrar Straus, Girous, 1951), 8.

[3]Theodore Friedman, "The Sabbath: Anticipation of Redemption," *Judaism* 16 (1967), 443.

[4]Alphabet of Rabbi Akiba, *Otzar Midrashim*, p. 407, quoted in Heschel, 73.

[5]Midrash Rabbah on Genesis 17, Section 5.

[6]Tamid 33b.

[7]Vita Adae et Evae 51:2.

[8]Quoted in Friedman.

[9]Al Nakawa, *Menorat ha-Maor*, vol. II, 182, quoted in Heschel, 19.

[10]Franz Rosenweig, *The Star of Redemption* (New York: Beacon Press, 1971), 310, 311.

[11]Heschel, 68.

[12]Friedman, 444.

[13]Berakoth, 57b.

[14]Shabbat 12a.

[15]Friedman, 445.

[16]Tamid 33b.

[17]Shabbat 118b.

[18]Sanhedrin 97a, 97b.

[19]*Ibid.*

This article originally appeared in *Shabbat Shalom*, January-March 1991.

CHAPTER THIRTY-SIX

A Sanctuary in Time

Besides space, time is the dimension in which we exist. It is the stuff life is made of. The quality of our time measures the quality of our life. What we do with our time, even more important than with our space, is what we do with our life.

Yet, unlike space, man has never conquered time. We clasp space in our hands, but time is beyond our grasp. We buy vast amounts of space but never recoup a moment of time. We can move left or right, up or down in space, but in time we are swept away by a ceaseless stream of movements moving in a direction that ultimately wears down all things to dust.

Amid this torrent, however, exists a respite. It's called Sabbath. Not that the Sabbath slows down time or even changes its course. The Sabbath simply puts it into perspective.

Few men in modern times have understood this concept better than Abraham Joshua Heschel, whose classic work *The Sabbath: Its Meaning for Modern Man* expresses the contemporary purpose for this ancient day. "The meaning of the Sabbath," he wrote, "is to celebrate time rather than space. Six days a week we live under the tyranny of the things of space; on the Sabbath we try to become attuned to holiness in time. It is a day on which we are called upon to share in what is eternal in time."

For Heschel, the Sabbath "is the armistice in man's cruel struggle for existence, a truce in all conflicts." It is, he wrote, "a sanctuary in time."

According to Heschel, the Bible is more interested in time than in space. It pays more attention to generations and events than to countries or things. The main themes of faith deal with the realm of time. By celebrating Passover, the Jew celebrates the *day* of exodus from Egypt. The Feast of Weeks commemorates the *day* of the giving of the law at Sinai. With the Feast of Booths, the Jew commemorates the *time* that Israel lived in booths during the Exodus. Even the Messianic hope is the expectation of a *time*: the end of days. "Judaism," he wrote, "is a religion of time aiming at the sanctification of time."

Time, or at least a section of it, is the first thing God declares holy in the creation account of Genesis. "And God blessed the seventh day and declared it *holy*" (Gen. 2:3, Tanakh).* Time, not space, was first declared *qadesh*, or set apart for a holy use, by God. "This is a radical departure from the accustomed religious thinking," wrote Heschel. "The mythical mind would expect that, after heaven and earth had been established, God would create a holy place—a holy mountain or a holy spring—whereupon a sanctuary is to be established. Yet it seems as if to the Bible it is *holiness in time*, the Sabbath, which comes first."

Of course, Heschel does not disparage space, for that would be to "disparage the works of creation, the works which God beheld and saw 'it was good.' " Instead, he pleaded against man's "unconditional surrender" to space and to his enslavement by things. "In spite of our triumphs, we have fallen victim to the work of our hands; it is as if the forces we have conquered have conquered us." For Heschel, the Sabbath sets men free not only from the tyranny of space but even from the covetousness that enslaves us to our own passions and greed.

"Nothing is as hard," he wrote, "to suppress as the will to be a slave to one's own pettiness. Gallantly, ceaselessly, quietly, man must fight for inner liberty. Inner liberty depends upon being exempt from the domination of things as well as from the domination of people. There are many who have acquired a high degree of political and social liberty, but only a very few are not enslaved to things."

For this reason, Heschel links the fourth commandment, the Sabbath, to the tenth, which forbids covetousness. In Deuteronomy 5:15 the Lord concludes the Sabbath commandment with these words: "And remember that thou wast a servant in the land of Egypt, and that the Lord thy God brought thee out thence through a mighty hand and by a stretched out arm: therefore the Lord thy God commanded thee to keep the Sabbath day." Thus the Sabbath reminds them of their liberty from the bondage of men, while the tenth commandment reminds them that they also must achieve inner liberty, freedom from greed. Thus, the Sabbath commandment, by forbidding men to seek the things of space at least once a week, helps protect man against covetousness and greed.

"We know that passion cannot be vanquished by decree. The tenth injunction would, therefore, be practically futile, were it not for the 'commandment' regarding the Sabbath day to which about a third of the text of the Decalogue is devoted and which is an epitome of all other commandments. We must seek to find a relation between the two 'commandments.' Do not covet anything belonging to thy neighbor; I have given thee something that belongs to Me. What is that something? A day." Thus, for Heschel, the Sabbath teaches men to covet not the things of space but the things of time, for the Sabbath is called a *Hemdat Yamin*, "a day to be coveted."

For most of humanity, however, time has been an unconquerable enemy. No matter one's greatness, prowess, or power, time ultimately consumes it all, leaving only dust behind.

"Men talk of killing time," said Dion Boucicault, "while time quietly kills them."

Yet, like space, time is a gift from God, as much a part of His creation as the moon and stars. Time is the dimension in which space exists, in which it is framed, in which it moves. God created time, not as an enemy but as an instrument in which man and God can coexist together. Hence, the importance of Sabbath. For through it we momentarily step back from the overwhelming dimension of space and get a new perspective on time, seeing it not as that which slowly, silently hurls us into oblivion but as a medium by which we relate with God, who is ever calling us to a relationship that can lead to eternal life. Rabbinic Judaism has called the Sabbath "a reminder of the world to come." Sabbath, therefore, shows that God is not only our Creator but our Redeemer, as well. Indeed, within the Sabbath flashes eternity.

"This, then," wrote Heschel, "is the answer to the problem of civilization: not to flee from the realm of space; to work with the things of space but to be in love with eternity. Things are our tools; eternity, the Sabbath, is our mate. Israel is engaged to eternity. Even if they dedicate six days of the week to worldly pursuits, their soul is claimed by the seventh day."

The Sabbath becomes a window that allows us a look beyond space into eternity itself. "On the Sabbath it is given us to share in the holiness that is in the heart of time. Even when the soul is seared, even when no prayer can come out of our tightened throats, the clean, silent rest of the Sabbath leads us to a realm of endless peace, or to the beginning of an awareness of what eternity means."

In modern life we live for the evanescent only, even though something inside us cries out for permanence. The Sabbath, nurturing within its essence the seeds of eternity, helps answer that cry. Sabbath assumes such importance because it moves us from the temporal to the eternal, from that which is transient to that which exists forever. Time, instead of mercilessly slipping away, becomes eternity in disguise.

"There are few ideas in the world of thought which contain so much spiritual power as the idea of the Sabbath," wrote Heschel. "Aeons hence, when of many of our cherished theories only shreds will remain, that cosmic tapestry will continue to shine."

"Eternity utters a day."

And Sabbath utters eternity.

---

*Text credited to NIV is from the *Holy Bible, New International Version.* Copyright © 1973, 1978, International Bible Society. Used by permission of Zondervan Bible Publishers. This article originally appeared in *Shabbat Shalom*, July-September 1990.

CHAPTER THIRTY-SEVEN

The Origin of Sunday

Under the cover of night vandals spray-paint hate across a synagogue wall. Swastikas, anti-Semitic slogans, curses—crude blemishes, like numbers tattooed on a prisoner's arm.

When the sun rises, the mayor utters a sympathetic shibboleth, the police ask questions, the reporter scribbles on his pad, and the rabbi grinds his teeth.

And Sunday morning, Christians on their way to church lament the deed; the pastor, who has seen the desecration, encourages the congregation to "love thy neighbor"; and the church that evening votes to send a letter of sympathy. Christian concern and irony mingle in the gesture. None know that, in their weekly ritual of Sunday keeping, they have celebrated a day rooted in hatred of the Jews.

The Roots

The pagan Romans hated the Jews because of Jewish rebellions throughout the empire. In A.D. 115 Jews revolted in Cyrene, Egypt, and Cyprus. More than two hundred and twenty thousand Greeks and Romans perished in Cyrene alone, according to Roman historian Dio Cassius. After ruthlessly suppressing a revolt, the Romans would tighten their yoke around the Jews: When General Martius Turbo squashed the insurrection in Cyprus, a new law forbade Jews, on the pain of death, to disembark on the island. If shipwrecked, they weren't even allowed to drift to the beach.[1]

Under the leadership of Bar Kochba, who declared, "I am the Messiah!"[2] the Jews revolted in Palestine in A.D. 132–135. The Jews had hoped that Emperor Hadrian would rebuild the temple. When they learned that he had planned to dedicate it to a Roman deity, Jupiter Capitolunus, not Jehovah, they attacked their Roman masters.

188

Within the first year, the Romans were driven out of more than fifty cities and villages. Bar Kochba proclaimed himself king and even struck his own coinage. In one of Hadrian's early reports to the Roman Senate, he omitted the customary opening: "I and the army are well." The Romans lost so much blood that Hadrian called for more troops and brought his top general, Julius Servus, the governor of Britain, to lead them. After three years, the revolt was crushed and Bar Kochba killed.

These rebellions inflamed Roman anti-Judaism. Alexandria, Antioch, and Caesarea exploded in riots against the Jews. In Rome, anti-Jewish fervor forced crown prince Titus to end his plans to marry Bernice, sister of Herod Agrippa the Younger, because of her family ties to the Jews, even though she was a fervent supporter of the dynasty. Vaspasian levied a special tax (*fiscus judaicus*) against the Jews, and Domitian and Hadrian expanded it. Originally, only adult Jewish males paid the *fiscus judaicus*; eventually, every Jew, male or female, from three to sixty-two, was forced to drop coins into the royal coffers.

After the Bar Kochba revolt, the Jews were forbidden, under threat of death, to enter Jerusalem. Hadrian outlawed Judaism, the study of the Torah, and Sabbath-keeping. The period became known to the Jews as "the era of religious persecution."[3]

While the imperial armies used swords against the Jews, the Greek and Roman intelligentsia used words. Cicero called Judaism a "barbaric superstition."[4] Seneca referred to Jews as an "accursed race."[5] Petronius claimed that they worshiped a pig-God. Plutarch thought that the Jews kept Sabbath as a day to get drunk. Pompeius Torgus claimed that the Jews were descendants of lepers expelled from Egypt and abstained from pork in remembrance of their leprosy. These attacks, and the diatribes of Juvenal, Horace, Persius, Quintilian, Dio Cassius, and others accelerated the rush of Roman anti-Judaism.

Cannons to the Right of Them

Caught in the crunch between Roman imperialism and Jewish nationalism were the Christians. Because Christianity originated in the land of the Jews and because its early leaders and apostles were Jewish, its holy writings Jewish, its God that of the Jews, and because its holy days, such as Sabbath and Easter (Passover), were celebrated at the same time as the Jewish festivals, Christians were mistaken for Jews. Especially in early Christianity, "the Roman police had not yet come to distinguish the Christians from the Jews."[6] Because of the severe anti-Jewish sentiments, "many Christians did take steps to appear, especially in the imperial city, different and clearly distinct from the Jews in the eyes of the Romans. Under the emperor Hadrian (A.D. 117–138) particularly, a clear differentiation from the Jews became a more urgent necessity, due to the punitive measure taken by the emperor against them."[7]

And what did some Christians do to appear different from the Jews? Among other changes, they eased away from the seventh-day Sabbath. Considering that the "Sabbath [was] not only outlawed by Hadrian's edict but also consistently attacked and ridiculed by Greek and Latin authors, it should not surprise one that many

Christians severed their ties with Judaism by substituting their distinctive religious observances, such as the Sabbath . . . , for new ones."[8]

Cannons to the Left of Them

The Jews encouraged the distinction between themselves and Christians, especially Jewish Christians, because the tension "became so great that complete separation had to be achieved."[9] The book of Acts records the hostility of the Jews toward their countrymen who believed in Jesus, such as Paul, whom they accused of undermining the law. To keep Jewish Christians out of the synagogue, Rabban Gamaliel II (c. A.D. 90) added a "prayer against the heretics" to the liturgy. Because no one was allowed to avoid reciting the prayer, which cursed Jewish Christians, the follower of Jesus, unwilling to recite it, was exposed and expelled. During Bar Kochba's rebellion, the Jewish Christians, already considered traitors for abandoning Jerusalem in A.D. 70, were persecuted by the rebelling forces.

Bar Kochba's rebellion caused a decisive break between Judaism and Christianity, and it gave Christians added cause to disassociate from the Jews. Until then, Christians had hoped that the Jews would collectively acknowledge Jesus as Messiah. But when, influenced by the famous Rabbi Akiba, multitudes of Jews proclaimed Bar Kochba Messiah, many Christians must have seen this act as the final rejection. The false Messiah's brutal persecution of Jewish Christians alienated Gentile Christians previously sympathetic to the Jews. Although Jews who kept their Hebrew traditions comprised the early church, in the following decades increasing numbers of Gentile converts lacked these traditions. Considering Hadrian's prohibitions, they would be severely disadvantaged by following them. As a result, the church began to disassociate from the Jews. Abandoning the Sabbath as a day of worship and rest is probably the most evident sign of this estrangement."[10]

"Volleyed and Thundered"

Besides the social and political impetus to change the Sabbath, the transition also had a theological thrust. Early Christians such as Justyn Martyr attacked the Sabbath as a custom that God imposed solely upon the Jews, terming it "a mark to single them out for punishment they so well deserved for their infidelities."[11] Though Ignatius, the bishop of Antioch, didn't attack the Sabbath, his warnings against keeping it in the manner of the Jews showed the tendency of the Christian community toward separation. The Epistle of Barnabas (c. A.D. 130) called the Jews wretched men, abandoned by God and deceived by an evil angel. The author emptied the Sabbath of significance, asserting that it was never to be literally kept and would be spiritually fulfilled at the coming of Christ. These writings, along with the social and political factors, helped transfer the Sabbath to Sunday.

The change didn't happen in a day. In Rome, where the transition was initiated, the Sabbath, along with Sunday, was kept until the fifth century, though not as a holy day. In contrast to the Jews, who regarded the seventh day as a time for feasting and joy, the church made Sabbath into a day of fasting and mourning. Marcion, in the second century, fasted on Sabbath to show his hatred of God and the Jews. According to Pope Sylvester (A.D. 314–355), the Sabbath should be spent fasting to mourn the death of Jesus, as well as to show "execration of the Jews." Victorinus, bishop of Pettau, urged Christians "to extend their Friday fast into Saturday, to make it appear that they did not observe the seventh day as the Jews did."[12]

Put on Your Easter Bonnet

Hatred for the Jews might not have been the only factor that initiated the Sabbath fast. Christians originally celebrated the death of Jesus with a yearly Easter commemoration held on the same day as the Passover, the fourteenth of Nisan, the date of the crucifixion. Wishing to avoid identification with the Jews, the Roman Church began celebrating the holy day on the first weekend following the weekday on which the fourteenth of Nisan fell. The celebration began on Friday, with a fast, and climaxed on Easter Sunday, with the partaking of the Lord's Supper. Eventually, "there developed a tendency to extend the Paschal fasting of Friday over into the Sabbath in order to end the fasting by partaking of the Lord's Supper early on Sunday morning."[13]

Early church writings from Origen, Eusebius, and Pope Innocent I show that the weekly Sunday and Easter Sunday often were regarded as the same feast celebrating the same event. Some scholars have concluded that the weekly Sabbath fast might have "originated as an extension of the annual Holy Saturday of the Easter season, when all Christians fasted."[14] The Sabbath fast, besides weaning Christians from Saturday as the biblical Sabbath, also enhanced Sunday as a day of rejoicing because the hungry adherents hadn't eaten since Friday.

Dawn of a New Day

Sunday was the logical substitute for Sabbath. Through the influence of Eastern sun cults, sun worship had become dominant in Rome by the early second century. Obelisks and altars dedicated to the sun proliferated throughout the city. Nero credited the sun when a plot against him was uncovered, and he erected the famous "Collossus Neronis" in honor of the sun and himself. Hadrian, also, after removing Nero's image from the monument, dedicated it to the sun. Sunday, the day of the sun, became the predominant day of the week, superseding Saturday, the day of Saturn, about the same time Roman Christians started favoring Sunday, the day of the resurrection, over the Sabbath. The early Church Fathers frequently chided certain of the faithful for venerating the sun, indicating the tendency to backslide among those converted from sun worship.

The backsliders, however, apparently allowed some of their "light" to shine into Christianity. In early Christian art the sun was often used as a symbol of Christ, "the Sun of Righteousness." In pagan art, a man with a disk at the back of his head was sometimes represented as the sun, with rays of light shining from the back of his head. The church at Rome began celebrating the birth of Jesus, the Son, the same day (December 25) that the pagans celebrated the birth of the Invincible Sun. Also, like sun worshipers, Christians started praying toward the east, the direction of the rising sun. As a result, church fathers—Tertullian, for one—had to refute charges that Christians were also sun worshipers.

Ergo: A New Theology

Just as the church fathers devised a theology for abandoning the seventh day, they devised a theology for keeping the first. Sunday was designated as "the eighth day," a day of mysterious import that enjoyed superiority over the seventh. This eighth day became symbolic of the old world passing away. For Justyn Martyr, Sunday commemorated the first day of Creation, particularly the creation of light. Christians, he said, assemble on the day called Sunday "because it is the first day on which God, transforming the darkness and [prime] matter, created the world."[15] Eusebius (c. A.D. 260–340) and Jerome (A.D. 340–420) also cited the creation of light as reason for the veneration of Sunday. "In this day of light," Eusebius wrote, "first day and true day of the sun, . . . we celebrate the holy and spiritual sabbaths. . . . It is on this day of the creation of the world that God said: 'Let there be light' (Gen. 1:3, R.S.V.)."[16] For the early church fathers, the resurrection of Jesus on the first day of the week served only a secondary reason for Sunday observance. As sun worship started to fade in the empire, the Resurrection became the primary motive, and still is today.

A Christian Institution

Indeed, Sunday has become a Christian institution, even an enforced one. In the early fourth century, Constantine the Great issued the first known secular Sunday blue law, ordering that "all judges, city people, and craftsmen shall rest on the venerable day of the sun." During the next few years, he issued other Sunday laws, including one that permitted Christian soldiers to attend church on Sunday. Pepin the Short, Charlemagne, and their successors enacted strict Sunday laws in the Middle Ages, and King Stephan of Hungary, trying to Christianize his realm, issued Sunday edicts in 1016, including one that gave priests the right to confiscate an ox from a man working with it on Sunday.[17] Early American Puritans adamantly kept Sunday holy; penalties for failure to keep Sunday ranged from loss of provisions to whipping and even death. In the 1800s in America, Seventh-day Adventists in several Southern states spent time on chain gangs for working on Sunday after observing the seventh-day Sabbath. Some thirty states still retain Sunday laws on their books—but with a civil rationale.

Though Christians throughout history have, with the Jews, adhered to the biblical Sabbath, for most Christians today, Sunday is the day of worship.

A Clean Wall?

Jews and Gentiles together repaint the synagogue wall. It's clean. Yet the wall is like Sunday keeping: If you get up close and look carefully, you can still see traces of anti-Judaism beneath the coating.

[1] Isaac Landman, ed., *The Universal Jewish Encyclopedia and Readers Guide* (New York: Ktav Publishing House Incorporated, 1969), 3:438.

[2] Babylonian Talmud, Sanhedrin 93b, Soncino edition, 627.

[3] Landman, 5:151.

[4] Quoted in Samuele Bacchiocchi, *From Sabbath to Sunday* (Rome: Pontifical Gregorian University Press, 1977), 173.

[5] *Ibid.,* 173, 174.

[6] Pierre Batiffol, *Primitive Catholicism* (New York: Longmans, Green and Co., 1911), 19.

[7] Samuele Bacchiocchi, *Anti-Judaism and the Origin of Sunday* (Rome: Pontifical Gregorian University Press, 1975), 58.

[8] Bacchiocchi, *From Sabbath to Sunday,* 185.

[9] Landman, 4:24.

[10] Bacchiocchi, *Anti-Judaism and the Origin of Sunday,* 52.

[11] Quoted in Bacchiocchi, *Anti-Judiasm and the Origin of Sunday,* 107.

[12] Robert Odom, *Sabbath and Sunday in Early Christianity* (Washington, D.C.: Review and Herald Pub. Assn., 1977), 225, 226.

[13] *Ibid.,* 107.

[14] Kenneth Strand, ed. *The Sabbath in Scripture and History* (Washington, D.C.: Review and Herald Pub. Assn., 1982), 138.

[15] Bacchiocchi, *From Sabbath to Sunday,* 272.

[16] Strand, 141. Scripture quotations marked R.S.V. are from the Revised Standard Version of the Bible, copyrighted 1946, 1952 © 1971, 1973.

[17] *Ibid.,* 202.

This article originally appeared in *Liberty,* January/February 1986.

CHAPTER THIRTY-EIGHT

Surprise! Shabbat Isn't Jewish

The Sabbath has been called one of the Jews' greatest contributions to the world. What a hoax! The Jews had nothing to do with it.

The seventh-day Sabbath, *Shabbat*, is not Jewish. Nothing about it is Jewish, nothing in its creation, purpose, or origin. The first Sabbath was created before any Jews existed, was first kept by non-Jews, and wasn't created specifically for Jews.

But from where did the Jews get it?

Most people assume at Sinai. Most people are wrong here too.

Notice how the Sabbath commandment given at Sinai reads:

"Remember the Sabbath day, to keep it holy. Six days shalt thou labor, and do all thy work; but the seventh is a Sabbath unto the Lord thy God, in it thou shalt not do any manner of work, thou, nor thy son, nor thy daughter, nor thy man-servant, nor thy maid-servant, nor thy cattle, nor thy stranger that is within thy gates; for in six days the Lord made the heaven and earth, the sea, and all that in them is, and rested on the seventh day; wherefore the Lord blessed the Sabbath day, and hallowed it" (Exod. 20:8-11).*

In Exodus 16, before the Jews reached Sinai, Moses said to Israel: " 'Eat [the manna] to-day; for to-day is a Sabbath unto the Lord; to-day ye shall not find it in the field. Six days ye shall gather it; but on the seventh day is the Sabbath.' . . . And the Lord said unto Moses: . . . 'See that the Lord hath given you the Sabbath; therefore He giveth you on the sixth day the bread of two days; abide ye every man in his place, let no man go out of his place on the seventh day.' So the people rested on the seventh day" (verses 25-30).

The Jews were keeping Sabbath before they reached Mount Sinai!

The commandment given at Sinai tells about the origin of the Sabbath: "For in six days the Lord made the heaven and earth, the sea, and all that in them is, and rested on the seventh day; wherefore the Lord blessed the Sabbath day, and hallowed it."

The Sinai commandment places the first Sabbath at the creation of the world, long before Abraham, Isaac, or Jacob, long before any Jews existed at all.

According to Genesis, God created the earth in six full days, "and on the seventh day God finished His work which He had made; and He rested on the seventh day from all His work which He had made. And God blessed the seventh day, and hallowed it; because that in it He rested from all His work which God in creating had made" (Gen. 2:2, 3).

The Holy Scriptures show that the Creator Himself instituted the seventh-day Sabbath—a memorial to the earth's birth—at the creation of the world, centuries before any Jews existed and millennia before Mount Sinai.

Neither the Babylonians nor the Egyptians nor the Hebrews nor any other people instituted the seven-day week or the observance of the seventh-day Sabbath. The Jews no more originated Shabbat than Jesus originated Easter bunnies, Santa Claus, and Rudolf the Red-Nosed Reindeer.

The Bible teaches that the seven-day week, like the seventh-day Sabbath, was instituted at Creation too. Unlike certain other time periods, the week, a period of seven days, has no reference to any celestial motions.

The day, for example, is measured by the time it takes for the earth to make one rotation on its axis. A synodic month—the time between one new moon and the next—is 29 days, 12 hours, 44 minutes, and 2.8 seconds, or 29.530588 days. The synodic month forms the basis of the alternating twenty-nine-day and thirty-day lunar-month calendars used in many lands. The mean length of the tropical year—the time between one vernal equinox and the next—is 365 days, 5 hours, 48 minutes, 46.2 seconds, or 365.242198 days.

So dependable are the movements of the earth, moon, and sun that astronomers can years in advance tell the exact hour and minute of the rising and setting of the sun and moon, the phases of the moon, the position of many stars and planets, the tides, and eclipses. Yet no known celestial motions occur on a weekly basis. The moon, sun, or stars don't complete any motion every seven days. In the Creation account, the Lord said that the lights in the sky were to be for "signs, and for seasons, and for days and years" (Gen. 1:14)—*but not weeks.*

Also the number seven cannot be integrated into either the monthly or yearly measure of time or into any combination of them without a fraction remaining. These figures show that the seven-day week is not an aliquot (or exact divisional) part of either the lunar month or the solar year. According to the Sacred Scriptures, the seven-day week and the seventh-day Sabbath were established by God at Creation.

Why, then, is the seventh day often referred to as the Jewish Sabbath, and why is the day usually associated with the Jews?

Because the Jews have been one of the few peoples to keep it holy.

God called out the Hebrews as a special people because He wanted them to give the world a revelation of the true God, the Creator. And one of the signs that they were worshiping the true God, the Creator, was their allegiance to the Sabbath, a memorial of Creation. "The children of Israel shall keep the Sabbath, to observe the Sabbath throughout their generations, for a perpetual covenant. It is a sign between Me and the children of Israel for ever; for in six days the Lord made heaven and earth, and on the seventh day He ceased from work and rested" (Exod. 31:6, 7).

Though the Jews did not originate Sabbath observance, they have so institutionalized the Sabbath that it has institutionalized them. "More than Israel has kept the Sabbath, the Sabbath has kept Israel." And it is because of Jewish faithfulness in adhering to the Sabbath that the true day of worship has been kept before the world.

Though the Jews have been one of the few peoples to partake of the Sabbath blessing, the day is for everyone, Jew and Gentile. It's a sacred day, commemorating the birthday of Creation and of the entire human race. Even in ancient Israel, Gentiles were also to keep the day holy: "Also the aliens, that join themselves to the Lord, to minister unto Him, and to love the name of the Lord, to be His servants, every one that keepeth the sabbath from profaning it, and holdeth fast by My covenant: even them will I bring to My holy mountain. . . . My house shall be called a house of prayer for all peoples" (Isa. 56:6, 7).

So this week, as the seventh day races through your town at a thousand miles per hour (the speed at which the earth rotates on its axis), don't miss the occasion. Jew, Gentile—celebrate this Sabbath as the birthday of the world.

---

* Bible texts in this article are from *The Holy Scriptures according to the Masoretic Text* (Philadelphia: Jewish Publication Society of America, 1917). This article originally appeared in *Shabbat Shalom*, April-June 1986.

FAITH THAT HURTS

Readers might find this section the most interesting and in some ways most informative of all, because these articles were almost all written to present our message to the Jews and thus take a perspective on things that could help Adventists as well.

"Marduk and the Lord," for instance, attempts to contrast the beauty and sublimity of the Hebrew creation account to the crudity of many of the creation myths in circulation at the time of ancient Israel. My goal, of course, was to help refute the notions, so common today, even among secular Jews, that the Genesis creation account is nothing but a Hebraized adaptation" of ancient Babylonian epic poetry.

In the same vein, "Israel Against Its Environment," contrasts the difference between the Jewish religion and the ancient pagan faiths that surrounded Israel in Bible times. Few things have done more to strengthen my faith in the inspiration and truthfulness of the Scripture than to see the radical difference between the teaching of the Bible and the other religions that were contemporary to ancient Israel. When so much of Ancient Near Eastern scholarship tries to prove that the religion of the Bible was borrowed from the surrounding cultures, this article shows just how ridiculous a notion that is and that the teachings of the Jews were given to them directly by God, who wanted them to spread these truths to the world.

"Freedom Feast" uses Jewish sources to teach SDA theology, in this case vicarious atonement. Dealing with the Jewish understanding of the Passover, this article shows how inherent in the Passover is a crucial topic for Adventist theology: how a substitute dies for our sins.

Along with these are numerous other articles on Jewish topics, many of them filled with aspects of truth taken directly from the Bible. My hope is that many SDA readers will benefit from the different perspectives on truth as revealed in these pieces.

CHAPTER THIRTY-NINE

Marduk and the Lord: A Contrast of Creations

In a world so different from today that it could have been another planet, Moses penned the Creation story. While the Babylonian, Persian, Greek, and Roman creation accounts have been trashed like rotted leaves, the thirty-one verses of the Bereshit persist, stubborn as roots. Despite attempts to destroy them with fire and sword or to dilute them with science and philosophy, these words still hover in the souls of millions with the same authenticity as they did when Moses, sheep at his feet, wrote them under the ancient sun. The Hebrew account still commands such authority that men have gone to the highest court in the most powerful nation in history in order to stop it (not the Greek, Babylonian, or Persian version, which nobody today believes) from being taught in public schools. After 3,500 years, this is tenacity!

Yet opposition still exists. Since the beginning of the twentieth century, one attempt to sever the biblical Creation from its divine origins, and thus neutralize its authority, has been to conclude that the Hebrew account has its genesis in Mesopotamian traditions, such as Enuma Elish, an ancient Babylonian epic that includes the creation of earth and man. By comparing similar aspects between Genesis and the Enuma Elish, some scholars have concluded that Genesis is simply a Hebraized adaptation of this Babylonian poem.

Indeed, both accounts refer to a watery chaos that existed from the beginning. Both refer to the existence of light before the creation of luminous bodies. Both have a similar order for the formation of the earth and sky, and the last act of creation in both is man. Few will call these parallels coincidence.

In the early 1900s Fredrich Delitzsch proclaimed the Bible's links to ancient Babylon in his famous *Babel and Bible.* In recent years E. A. Speiser, in the *Anchor Bible* commentary on Genesis, ties the Creation account to "Babylonian prototypes." Speiser writes that "derivation from Mesopotamia in this instance means no more

198

and no less than that on the subject of creation biblical tradition aligned itself with the traditional tenets of Babylonian 'science.' The reasons should not be far to seek. For one thing, Mesopotamia's achievements in that field were highly advanced, respected, and influential. And for another, the patriarchs constituted a direct link between early Hebrews and Mesopotamia, and the cultural effects of that start persisted long thereafter."[1]

Is, however, the biblical account of Creation nothing but warmed-over Babylonian myths? Did Moses creatively edit an earlier story in order to produce Genesis 1? A comparison between the Enuma Elish and Genesis helps answer the question.

"When Above"

The first fragments of the Enuma Elish were discovered in the mid-1800s among the ruins of Assyrian king Ashubanipal's (c. 668–626 B.C.E.) vast library at Nineveh, while other fragments were unearthed at different sites in the Near East. The story itself was incised on seven clay tablets, covering a little more than one thousand lines of cuneiform, the earliest surviving form of written language. Over the next century, translations, transliterations, and commentaries about the poem have been published. Though the date of its composition cannot be ascertained, scholars cite evidence to place it as far back as the First Babylonian Dynasty (1894–1595 B.C.E.), thus predating even the earliest dates given for Moses.

Though often called a creation account, the Enuma Elish is much more. Only a small part of the epic deals with the creation of the earth and man. As much space is devoted to the fifty names of the god Marduk as is the creation of the universe. If anything, the poem is a literary monument honoring Marduk as the champion of the gods and creator of heaven and earth. Marduk also happened to be the chief deity of Babylon, and thus making Marduk the greatest of the gods, the poem, composed by Babylonian priests, attempts to establish Babylon as the chief of the cities in its day. "Our epic is thus not only a religious treatise," wrote Assyriologist Alexander Heidel, "but also a political one."[2]

The poem commences with a reference to a time when nothing existed except the parent gods Apsu (the sweet-water ocean) and Tiamat (the saltwater ocean) and their son Mummu (possibly a mist rising above the two bodies). The name Enuma Elish comes from the first two words of the poem, translated as "When Above."

When above the earth had not (yet) been named,
(And) below the earth had not (yet) been called by a name;
(When) Apsu primeval, their begetter,
Mummu, (and) Tiamat, she who gave birth to them all,
(Still) mingled their waters together,
And no pasture land had been
(and) not (even) a reed marsh was to be seen;
(When) they had not (yet) been called by (their) name

(and their) destinies had not yet been fixed,

(At that time) were the gods created within them.[3]

Apsu and Tiamat, the epic says, begat other gods, who in turn begat more gods. These younger gods, however, made too much noise and disturbed the older ones. Apsu, after conferring with Tiamat, planned on destroying the noisemakers. When these younger gods heard of the impending attack, one of them, Ea, put Apsu to sleep and then killed him. Tiamat then encouraged by the other gods, led by Kingu, to revenge the death of her spouse, agrees: "They held a meeting and planned the conflict." Tiamat then gives birth to eleven kinds of monsters and serpents and dragons that will battle for her, including "the great lion, the mad dog, and the scorpion-man." Ea hears of Tiamat's plans and, terrified, seeks advice from his grandfather Anshar, who tells him to make peace with Tiamat. Unfortunately, the only way for Tiamat to be subdued is by force. Ea, fearful that he doesn't have the power to withstand Tiamat, returns to his grandfather and asks what can be done. Anshar then says that Marduk is the only god who can defeat Tiamat. Marduk is summoned before Anshar, and he agrees to fight Tiamat, but with a price: He must be made chief of all the gods.

If I am indeed to be your avenger

To vanquish Tiamat and keep you alive,

Convene the assembly and proclaim my lot supreme.

When ye are joyfully seated together in the Court of Assembly,

May I through the utterance of my mouth determine the destinies, instead of you.

Whatever I create shall remain unaltered.

The command of my lips shall not return (void), it shall not be changed.

The gods agree, and in a solemn ceremony they declare to Marduk: "To thee we have given kingship over the totality of the whole universe."

Their new ruler then prepares to battle. Armed with a bow, a club, lightning, "a blazing flame," a net, eleven winds (four from his grandfather, seven of his own creating), and a storm chariot drawn by four frightful creatures, "sharp of tooth, bearing poison," Marduk, clad in a coat of mail, approaches Tiamat. Though Kingu and the other gods fall into confusion at his appearance, Tiamat stays to fight. "Tiamat (and) Marduk, the wisest of gods, advanced against one another; they pressed on to single combat, they approached for battle."

When Tiamat opens her mouth to devour Marduk, he drives the wind into her until "the raging winds filled her belly." She becomes distended, and he shoots an arrow into her mouth that tears her apart, even splitting her heart. He then captures her followers, who tried to escape after Tiamat was killed. Marduk then splits Tiamat's body open with his club, and with one-half of her carcass he creates the heavens, and with the other half he creates the earth. Then he puts the heavenly bodies in the sky. Eventually Marduk lets all the captive gods go free, except for Kingu, who is brought before Ea. Ea cuts Kingu's arteries and then uses his blood, mixed with clay, to make man, who will do the menial work that the captured gods did while in captivity.

They bound him and led him before Ea;
Punishment they inflicted upon him by cutting (the arteries of) his blood.
With his blood they created mankind;
He imposed the service of the gods (upon them) and set the gods free.

Thus we have the Babylonian understanding of the creation not only of earth but of the universe and man.

"In the Beginning"

Obviously, despite whichever parallels might be found between the Enuma Elish and Genesis, their basic accounts of creation differ as vastly as do the sexual views of the Ayatollah Khomeini and Dr. Ruth.

First, the Enuma Elish is saturated with polytheism. Tiamat, Marduk, Apsu, Ea, and Nudimmud are a few of the deities in the vast pantheon of gods and goddesses of Babylonian creation stories. In contrast, Genesis teaches only one God, *Elohim*, who is the Creator, a theme that permeates the Hebrew Bible: "Hear O Israel, the Lord is our God, the Lord is one."[4] The Jews believed in, and Genesis teaches, only one God, who created the universe. Not a hint of the Enuma Elish's polytheism is found in the Bible.

Another basic discrepancy between the two ancient creation stories deals with the very nature of God and the universe. Apsu and Tiamat were not only the first gods but were part of the creation itself. Apsu was the primeval sweet-water ocean, and Tiamat was the primeval saltwater ocean. "They were matter and divine spirit united and coexistent, like body and soul," writes Heidel. "In them were contained all the elements of which the universe was later made on, and from them descended all the gods and goddesses of the vast Babylonian-Assyrian pantheon."[5] The Babylonian account teaches also that the earth and heaven were made directly out of the body of the goddess Tiamat, while man was made from the blood of Kingu. What the Enuma advocates, then, is a type of *polypantheism*, with the creation being a distinct part of divinity itself.

The Hebrews had no such conception of God, nor does Genesis teach anything similar to it. The Bible sees the Creator not as part of the universe but as separate and distinct from it. Nothing implies that God Himself was part of the creation, or that the universe was created from His own being. Genesis teaches that "God created the heavens and the earth," and it does so without a trace of the concept that the creation itself was part of God's own divine nature. God spoke the earth into existence, and by this act the earth was created separate and distinct from God Himself. Man, instead of being formed from the spilled blood of a god, came from the "dust of the earth." Here, too, the Genesis account differs greatly from the Enuma Elish, which depicts man as composed of the same elements that made up divinity, a concept alien to Genesis.

Also, in the Enuma Elish man was created for the benefit of the gods, to minister to their whims. He was to do the work that the captive gods, who had been forced into slave labor, didn't want to perform. Man, then, was an afterthought, a being that the gods concocted in order to take care of their needs after setting the prisoners free.

In Genesis, however, man was not a secondary consideration, made ad hoc in order to alleviate an unexpected situation. Instead, man was planned from the beginning, the crowning act of the earthly Creation. "In the beginning," God created the heaven (the sky) and the earth—for the benefit of man: "And God said, 'Behold, I have given to you [man] every herb bearing seed that is upon the face of all the earth, and every tree in which is in it the fruit of a tree bearing seed; to you it will be for food' " (Gen. 1:29). God gave to man the fruit trees and herbs bearing seed, which He created beforehand, all for man, who was to rule his little corner of the universe. "Thou madest him [man] to have dominion over the works of thy hands. Thou hast put all things under his feet" (Ps. 8:6). Man was made to have dominion over the earth, not to be a slave of the gods.

In Enuma Elish the deities have the characteristics of fallen man: violent, arrogant, hateful, vengeful, and power-hungry; these gods eat, drink, sleep, fear, procreate, conspire, and kill as well. In contrast, the Old Testament teaches a God who is holy, upright, righteous, and perfect. "In Genesis man is created in the image of God," wrote Heidel. "But the Babylonians created their gods in the image of man."[6]

Nowhere does the Enuma Elish talk about the fall of man. Because the gods who created man, and from whom man came (i.e., Kingu), had evil traits too. Man was created evil from the start; therefore no need exists to talk about a fall from perfection, because perfection never existed. Here, again, a vast contrast from Genesis, which says that "God saw all that He made and, behold, it was very good" (Gen. 1:30).

Perhaps the greatest difference comes from the essence of the stories themselves. The Enuma Elish describes a gigantic cosmic battle between violent gods who battle each other out of vengeance and arrogance, the results of their struggle bringing the creation of the universe and man. How does one get from victorious Marduk splitting Tiamat's body—using one part to form the universe, the other to form the earth—to Genesis, in which God purposely makes the earth and sky and then ultimately creates man out of the dust of the earth? Genesis depicts a carefully planned and calculated Creation, and the complexity of life attests to just how carefully that Creation was calculated. Indeed, the physical mechanisms of life are so complicated that biologist Francis Crick, famed for his DNA studies, believes that life must have originated from an extraterrestrial source, because DNA *alone* is too complicated to have formed unassisted in a mere 3.8 billion years (the age, he believes, of the earth).[7] Genesis teaches who that extraterrestrial source is, and it does so without the "Star Wars" nonsense found in the Enuma Elish.

Conclusion

In their basic understanding of man, Deity, creation—indeed, in their entire cosmology—the Enuma Elish and Genesis have almost nothing in common. In smaller details striking resemblances do exist, and it has been these details that have led some to conclude that the Genesis account had its roots in the Enuma. What is the answer? Though the parallels don't prove that Genesis borrowed from the Babylonians, the major differences don't prove that it didn't.

Perhaps another explanation might work. Whatever date one gives to Moses, either in the 1500s or the 1300s B.C.E., the Enuma Elish was composed earlier than the *written* Hebrew account. Therefore, the parallels can't be explained as the work of a Babylonian priest who got a copy of Bereshit and paganized it.

But what about a general understanding of Creation held by earlier generations, such as the patriarchs Abraham, Isaac, and Jacob, all of whom worshiped the same God as Moses? The Jews did not originate belief in *Elohim*; they were later adherents to a faith that, according to the Bible, goes back to the beginning of man. Though not written down until the time of Moses, the true Creation account could have been spread for generations by followers of the Lord. Meanwhile, as paganism and polytheism spread, the history became distorted, transmuted into various polytheistic myths, such as the Enuma Elish. The reason the Enuma has any similarities to Genesis is because it was taken from the same archetypal story, which was around from the event itself. Who knows how distorted the rendering was by the time it reached the Babylonians, who then customized it further in order to meet their specific cultural and political needs.

"A common stream of traditions existed in the ancient world that went back to the original event," says archaeologist and Near Eastern specialist Dr. William Shea of the Biblical Institute in Washington, D.C. "This stream of tradition divided into various forms among different people and cultures. The Hebrew rendering, however, under the influence of inspiration, preserved the most accurate version of the event. And from this account other versions have diverged, though they maintain some of the details of the original story. Thus we can account for any similarities between them."

Though archaeology has furnished no positive proof either way, it's possible that instead of the "Hebrew" Creation story being rooted in Babylonian myths, the Babylonian myths could be rooted in the "Hebrew" Creation story, which existed for generations but wasn't penned until the second millennium B.C.E. by the Jews, who were called to preserve a knowledge of the true God, and this knowledge certainly would include the true Creation story.

Whatever the answer is, one thing stands sure: While Marduk, Ea, and Tiamat have long been silenced, dying with the civilizations that created and worshiped them, the God of Genesis still speaks, His words loud and clear despite the cacophony that for millennia has been trying to drown them out.

[1]E. A. Speiser, *Genesis* (*Anchor Bible*) (New York: Doubleday, 1985), 11.

[2]Alexander Heidel, *The Babylonian Genesis* (Chicago: University of Chicago Press, 1969), 11.

[3]All cuneiform translations are from *The Babylonian Genesis*.

[4]All biblical translations in this article are the author's.

[5]Heidel, 88.

[6]*Ibid.*, 125.

[7]Greg Easterbrook, "Are We Alone?" *Atlantic Monthly*, August 1988, 34.

This article originally appeared in *Shabbat Shalom*, April-June 1986.

CHAPTER FORTY

Israel Against Its Environment

Vastly outnumbered by the religions in which we have been submerged—the Jews have nevertheless maintained a distinct faith, a piccolo solo amid an orchestra of drums, violins, and clarinets. No matter what was performed, we were never in harmony, either by choice or because we were not allowed in the band. Whatever the reasons, we have ever played our own songs.

And never did the music differ more than in the days of ancient Israel. A study of the contrasts between ancient Judiasm and paganism reveals not only how different were the songs the first Jews sang—but that God wrote the first score!

The Hebrews were a late arrival in the Near East. A dozen Egyptian dynasties had risen and fallen even before Israel sprang from Abraham's loins. By the time the Hebrew nation was born, Egypt's Great Pyramid—2 million blocks of about two and a half tons each—was nearly 1,000 years old! In Mesopotamia, the Sumerians, with their great city-states, gem-cutting, and metal works, reached heights of splendor, only to be overthrown by Sargon the Great, whose great Akkadian Empire was later picked apart by the barbarian Guti from the Zargos Mountains. The Sumerians then rose again, flourishing in a golden age that produced some of its greatest art, literature, and architecture, only to sputter out. All this and yet Israel had not yet crossed the Sea of Reeds! Clearly, the Jews emerged in a world already ancient.

And it was a world saturated in polytheism. From the Nile to the Euphrates, the ancient Near East worshiped a highly developed pantheon of gods and goddesses: Enlil, Anu, Horus, Sin, Nut, Ishtar, Dagan, Baal Hadad, Marduk, Chemosh, Adad, Shamash, Thoth, Anath, Milkom, Qosh, Ashur, Inanna, El, Yerach, Tiamat, and on and on, an endless symphony of divinity.

Ancient Near Eastern polytheism was rooted in nature, and in nature the Near Easterner confronted his gods. In a storm, for instance, he met the storm god; in the daily sunshine, he experienced a manifestation of the sun god. In Mesopotamia, the earth, sea, and the sky were the respective realms of the three great gods, Enlil, Enki, and An, who also divided the heavens.

Each city was devoted to a god and/or goddess. Ur had the moon god Nanna. Uruk was devoted to Anu, the god of heaven, and Ianna, the "lady of the heaven." Nippur, the ancient center of Sumerian religion, had Enlil, the chief of the Sumerian gods. Each god had his goddess, and they bred children, likewise part of the cosmic order.

Just as nature was not peaceful, neither were the divine families. The gods were often given the attributes of men, and they could be vengeful, fickle, violent. The moon, for example, was said to be the product of the rape of the goddess Ninlil by Enlil. The ancient Near Easterner, living (he believed) amid this throbbing, changing realm of the gods, had to learn how to adjust his life to these cosmic forces, over which he had no control.

Then, amid this endless parade of gods and goddesses, a small nation of ex-slaves, refugees without their own land, wanderers without a country, proclaimed one of the most radical ideas of antiquity: "*Shema Yisrael, Andonai Elohanu, Adonai Echad)*"—the belief that God is one. While Enlil, Tiamat, and Mot have long been consigned to museum displays, Hebrew monotheism—proclaimed by the Jews from the sands of the Sinai—has gripped humanity and never let go.

"When we read in Psalm 19 that 'the heavens declare the glory of God,'" writes an expert on ancient polytheism, Professor Henri Frankfort, "'and the firmament sheweth his handiwork,' we hear a voice which mocks the beliefs of the Egyptians and Babylonians. The heavens, which were to the psalmist but a witness of God's greatness, were to the Mesopotamians the very majesty of the godhead, the highest ruler, Anu. To the Egyptians the heavens signified the mystery of the divine mother through whom man was reborn. In Egypt and Mesopotamia the divine was comprehended as immanent: the gods were in nature. The Egyptians saw in the sun all that a man may know of the Creator; the Mesopotamians viewed the sun as the god Shamash, the guarantor of justice. But to the psalmist the sun was God's devoted servant who is as a bridegroom coming out of his chamber, and 'rejoiceth as a strong man to run a race.' The God of the psalmist and the prophets was not in nature. He transcended nature—and transcended, likewise, mythopoeic thought. It would seem that the Hebrews . . . broke with the mode of speculation which had prevailed up to their time."[1]

The Hebrews—instead of worshiping a pantheon of gods or goddesses (no word for *goddess* in Hebrew even exists)—worshiped only one God, the Creator, who was identified with no specific force. He created the sun, the moon, or a storm, but He was not the sun god, the moon god, or the storm god. He was linked no more closely to one part of nature than another. Not localized at any one point in heaven or earth, as the pagan gods had been since recorded history, He could be anywhere, anytime—not part of the events, but above them, controlling them, bringing all things into ultimate harmony with His divine will. This Jewish concept of divine purpose in history was lacking in the pagan beliefs.

Writing about the Hebrew religion, scholar John Bright claims that Israel's "conception of God was from the beginning so remarkable, and . . . without parallel in the ancient world."[2] It is as if after centuries of nothing but raucous sound, the Jews breathed Beethoven out their flutes.

Another sound in the pagan symphony was idolatry. Israel's neighbors had carved armies of idols, gods of wood and stone, to represent the deities whom they served—and they built lavish temples in which they worshiped them. The ancient Near Easterner might not necessarily have seen the idol as the god itself but as a representation of that deity in which its spirit would reside, enabling the god to be physically present in different places simultaneously. As a result, he would bow down, pray to, and offer sacrifices to statues of bulls, goats, frogs, either in temples, in the open air, or in his own home. Some of these idols were human (male or female) figures; others were half human, half animal.

In Egypt almost every type of animal or bird represented a god. Horus, symbolized by the hawk, was one of Egypt's chief gods, and the pharaoh was Horus in human form. Images of fish, snakes, cats, and bulls were worshiped all through the ancient Near East, and had been for centuries. Bastet, represented by a bronze cat with gold earrings, was an Egyptian goddess who symbolized the sun's warmth and joy. Hapi was the Nile River god. Baal images were often stick figures of a man with a pitchfork of lightning in his hand. Ashtoreth, the Canaanite goddess of fertility, love, and war, was often represented by a nude female statue. The bull of heaven was a symbol commonly used for El in Canaan and for Anu and Enlil in Mesopotamia.

In short, from years before the Jews entered their land to years after they were driven out from it—idolatry in the Near East was more widespread than Islam is in those same lands today.

Yet, while dirt from Egypt was still under their nails, the Jews were told: "You will not make for yourself an image or any likeness that is in heaven above or in the water beneath the earth. You will not bow yourself down to them, and you will not serve them" (Exod. 20:4)*—a command that came after 400 years of slavery in a nation that for more than a millennium had bowed down and worshiped images of everything from cats to women with cows' ears!

For the Jews, the God of Israel was, simply, not to be worshiped with images. Isaiah warned against those who used a tree for heat or cooking and then made a god out of what was left: "He cuts himself cedars and takes the cypress and the oak. . . . He burns half of it in fire; with half of it he will eat flesh; he will roast, and is satisfied, yea, he warms himself and says, Ah, I am warm, I have seen the fire. And with the residue of it he makes a god, his carved image, he bows down to it, he worships it, he prays to it, and says, Deliver me, for you are my god" (Isa. 44:14-17).

According to Jeremiah, no deliverance would come from idols: "Saying to a tree, You are my father; and to a stone, You have brought me forth, because they have turned their back on Me, and not their face. But in the time of their trouble they will say, Rise up and save us. But where are the gods that you made for yourself? Let them arise, if they can save you in the time of your trouble" (Jer. 2:27, 28).

The Bible writers warned the Jews against worshiping idols, which were just the work of men's hands.

Their idols are silver and gold,
The work of the hands of men.
They have mouths but speak not;
They have eyes but see not.
They have ears but hear not.
They have noses but smell not.
They have hands but they handle not.
They have feet but they walk not;
Neither speak they through their throat.
They who make them are like them;
So are all who trust in them.
Israel, trust in the Lord:
He is their help and their shield
(Ps. 115:4-9).

Israel's pagan neighbors were also into divination, astrology, and magic. These practices were used for religious, political, and military purposes. The largest single category of Akkadian literature known today dealt with divination. A staggering number of techniques, each with its own exhaustive handbooks, became a distinguishing mark of later Akkadian culture either in Mesopotamia or wherever that culture was exported. In the huge library of Assyrian king Ashurbanipal uncovered in Nineveh, vast numbers of tablets deal with divination, magic, and astrology. So carefully did they study the stars that some of their observations are said to be more accurate than were the estimates of Ptolemy, Kepler, or Copernicus thousands of years later.[3]

Despite their accuracy, however, the study of the stars was linked to astrology. "When Mars approaches the moon and stands," reads an astrologer's report to an Assyrian king, "the moon will cause evil to inhabit the land. When a planet stands at the left horn of the moon, the king will act mightily. When Virgo stands at its left horn, in that year the vegetables of Akkad will prosper. . . .When Mars approaches Scorpio, the prince will die by a scorpion's sting, and his son after will take the throne."[4]

In Mesopotamia, the commoner—who didn't have court astrologers—at least had the livers of sheep and other animals. By studying configurations of the liver, and other entrails, they sought to discern the future. Beginning in Babylonian times (c. 1800 B.C.E.), this method of divination was collected in systematic handbooks (on cuneiform tablets). *If the organ has the shape of an X, then the outcome of the campaign (business, war, health) will be Y.* If this method became too expensive, other means were used. Observing the configuration of smoke rising from a censer, observing the configuration of oil poured on water, observing deformed babies, even shooting arrows—all were seen as ways of divining the future.[5]

The ancient Near Easterner's view of reality greatly affected their magic. For him, the *idea* of a chair and the actual chair were the same thing. The person who appeared in a dream *was* that person. In ancient Egypt, the name of her Asiatic enemies were written on potsherds and then smashed—a way, they believed, to destroy these enemies.

Hieroglyphs didn't just spell out a word but could represent the actual object itself, which is why in some tombs hieroglyphs that represent evil animals were drawn without legs or heads or chopped in half or even nailed down so that the animals could not eat the food left in the tomb for the dead person.[6] An Egyptian believed that if his name were written down, he would live forever after death. A common painting on a tomb would be of a person hunting and fishing to ensure that he would continue these pursuits in the next life.[7]

At the same time, the way to make a dead person disappear was to chisel out their name. When Queen Hatshepsut died in 1470 B.C.E., her stepson, Thutmose III, who hated the queen, had her name chiseled off all her temples and anywhere it was written. Thus, to him and to everyone else, it was as if she never existed.[8] For the Egyptians, the nose was the "seat of life," so to destroy an enemy after he had died, one simply smashed the nose of a statue representing that person. Many statues of pharaohs in the British Museum today have their noses broken off.

Magic and incantation were used to cast spells upon people, as well as to cure disease. One cure for a fever involved placing the heart of a white kid in the hands of the sick man while appealing to the gods: "Invoke the great gods and the evil Spirit, the evil Demon, evil Ghost, Hag-Demon, Ghoul, Fever, or heavy sickness, which is in the body of the man, may be removed and go forth from the house! May a kindly Spirit, a kindly Genius be present! Oh evil Spirit! O evil Ghost! O Hag-Demon! O Ghoul! O sickness of the heart! O Heartache! O Headache! O Toothache! O Pestilence! O grievous Fever! By Heaven and Earth may be ye exorcized!"

The Bible has much to say about divination, astrology, and magic. Isaiah, in an oracle against Babylon, expressed it clearly:

Stand now in your incantations,
In the multitude of your sorceries
In which you have toiled from thy youth!
Perhaps you will succeed;
Perhaps you will prevail.
You are wearied in the multitude of thy counsels;
Let them stand now and save you,

Those who divide the heavens,
Who gaze at the stars,
Who make known by the new moons,
From what will come upon you.
Behold, they are like stubble;

Fire consumes them;
They cannot save their souls
From the power of the flame. . . .
Thus shall they be to you
Those for whom you have worked,
Your merchants from your youth.
They wander, each his own way;
There is none to save you!
(Isa. 47:12-15).

Again, despite its environment, Israel had radically broken away, at least in theory, from the prevailing norm. From the earliest days in the Sinai, even before entering the Land of Promise, they had been warned against the divination and magic that permeated the nations around them: "When you come into the land which the Lord your God gives you, you will not learn to imitate the abominations of those nations. There shall not be found among you one that causes his son or daughter to pass through fire, a diviner, a soothsayer, a magician, a sorcerer, a conjurer of spells, a spiritualist, an augur, or a necromancer. . . . For these nations, which you are to drive out, listen to soothsayers and diviners; but you, the Lord your God has not given you to do the same" (Deut. 18:9-14). The ban was serious. "A man or a woman that has a familiar spirit, or that is a wizard, shall surely be put to death" (Lev. 20:27).

All through the Bible, the prophets warn against the use of divination or magic. During the Assyrians peril Isaiah taunts those who seek out spiritualists and diviners that "chirp and that mutter" when they should be seeking the true God. Jeremiah warns Jerusalem against their diviners, dreamers, soothsayers, and magicians who say, "You shall not serve the king of Babylon. For they prophesy a lie unto you, to remove you from the land" (Jer. 27:9, 10). Ezekiel derided these practices: "For the king of Babylon stood at the parting of the way, at the head of two ways, to use divination: he made his arrows bright, he consulted with images, he looked in the liver" (Ezek. 21:21).

Despite the prevalence of magic and divination among the nations surrounding Israel, these practices were forbidden—sometimes on the pain of death—to the Jews.

Unfortunately, what the Israelites were forbidden to do is often what they did. No matter how advanced their faith was in theory, in practice the people very often retreated into the pagan forms of their neighbors. Much of the Bible, whether the narratives of Israel's history or the pleas of the prophets, dealt with Israel's battle against heathenism. Though the Israelites had been raised up to spread their faith and religious forms to the heathen, the heathen had, at times, better success in spreading their faith to the Jews.

No sooner had the dust settled from Sinai, where they were given the Ten Commandments, than the Israelites fell into idolatry, even polytheism. Standing before the golden calf, which they pressured Aaron to forge for them, they exclaimed, "These are your gods, O Israel, who brought you out of the land of Egypt!" (Exod. 32:4). Centuries later, King Jeroboam made two golden calves, recognized Canaanite symbols, and repeated the words of his forefathers: "Behold your gods, O Israel, who brought you out of Egypt" (1 Kings 12:28).

Under Ahab and Jezebel, Baal worship flourished in Israel. Manasseh permitted and practiced the occult art that had been forbidden in Deuteronomy. He even "put an idol, the idol which he had made, in the house of God, of which God has said to David and Solomon his son, in this house and in Jerusalem, which I have chosen from all the tribes of Israel, I will put my name forever" (2 Chron. 33:7). Ezekiel described what he saw in the temple at Jerusalem: "And he brought me into the inner court of the house of the Lord, and, behold, at the door of the temple of the Lord, between the porch and the altar, were about twenty-five men, their backs toward the temple of the Lord, and their faces eastward. And they worshiped the sun to the east" (Ezek. 8:16).

No wonder the Lord said of Israel: "Yet I planted you a noble vine, wholly a right seed: how is it then that you turned into the degenerate plant of a strange vine unto me?" (Jer. 2:21).

Israel's unfaithfulness, however, doesn't lessen the uniqueness of her beliefs. The remarkable thing is the religion itself, not the people's failure to adhere to it.

How, amid a world that from antiquity worshiped fish gods, hawk gods, and sun gods, did a wondering horde of ex-slaves proclaim the belief in just one God who was superior to all creation, a God who purposely and carefully created the earth? How in the midst of an endless procession of idols and images, which the heathen believed were their gods, did the Jews have a prohibition against making these gods of wood and stone, gods that they were told were just the work of men's hands? How in a world steeped in divination, magic, and astrology did the Jews have a prohibition against this hocus-pocus?

The answer is simple: The teachings came not from paganism but from God!

For years, scholars have been looking to Egypt for traces of doctrines from which the Jews could have borrowed these unique teachings. They still are looking. Israel's faith was as different from Egypt's as ancient Chinese is from COBOL. "In its essential structure," writes John Bright of the religion of Israel, "was as little like the Egyptian religions as possible."[9]

Some have looked to Canaan. Yet the Canaanite religion was an extraordinarily debasing form of paganism, complete with a bloodthirsty goddess of war, as well as sacred prostitution, homosexuality, and various orgiastic rites. "Nor can environment provide the answer," writes scholar G. Ernest Wright about Canaanite influence on Israel's faith. "Since the Old Testament bears eloquent witness to the fact that the Canaanite religion was the most dangerous and disintegrative factor which the faith of Israel had to face."[10]

To this day scholars have been unable to trace Hebrew monotheism, as well as its ban on idolatry and divination, to the surrounding nations. "It is impossible to see how this God of Israel could have slowly evolved from polytheism," explains Wright. For him, Israel's faith was too different from all contemporary faiths to have originated from them. "How can we explain it [Israelite religion]," he writes, "except that it is a new creation?"[11]

Clearly, the answers to the origins of this "new creation" are not in the dirt of Iraq or Syria but in God. Judaism didn't originate from an ecumenical compromise with sun worshipers—but from the Lord Himself, just as the Bible says!

Throughout the Scriptures, the words "Thus saith the Lord" are repeated. Here alone was the source of Judaism, the source of the beauty and genius of Israel's faith in contrast to the barbarity and nonsense of her pagan neighbors.

While the nations served fish gods and cat gods, the Jews served just one God, the Creator of the universe—because the Lord, not the Babylonians, had taught them true worship. While the world bowed down and prayed to idols, the Jews would bow down and pray to the living God, not to blocks of wood and stone—because they had received a "Thus saith the Lord." While the heathen world was steeped in divination and astrology, the Jews were to trust in the Lord, not in the configuration of sheep livers—because God Himself, not the Egyptians, warned them against those practices.

The Jews, awash in a world of paganism, knew just how nonsensical these practices were because God had told them! From where else, except God, could these wondering ex-slaves, desert nomads living 3,000 years ago have learned that it is fruitless to worship a block of wood, or to peer into a sheep liver in order to learn the future—when these false teachings had been the norm for centuries? Even today, Christianity and Islam, the world's great religions, acknowledge the divine origins of Judaism because many of their basic tenets came from the statutes and judgments of the Jews!

"And what great nation has statutes and judgments so righteous as all this law that I have set before you this day" (Deut. 4:8). Because of these statutes and judgments, the Jews were to give the world a distinct sound, a sound that has been played through the centuries. A sound that is still heard today.

Indeed, no matter how poorly they performed, the Jews still sang a unique song—but only because God Himself wrote the music!

> Sing to the Lord a new song:
> Sing to the Lord, all the earth.
> Sing to the Lord, bless His name;
> Proclaim His salvation from day to day.

Declare His glory among the heathen,
His wonders to all people.
For great is the Lord, and greatly to be praised.
He is to be feared above all gods.
For all the gods of the nations are idols,
But the Lord made the heavens
(Ps. 96:1-5).

---

[1] Quoted in G. Ernest Wright, *The Old Testament Against Its Environment* (London: SCM Press, 1949), 20.

[2] John Bright, *A History of Israel*, third ed. (Philadelphia: Westminster Press, 1981), 157.

[3] Wright, 80.

[4] R. C. Thompson, *The Reports of the Magicians and Astrologers of Nineveh and Babylon*, in Wright, 81.

[5] William W. Hallow and William K. Simpson, *The Ancient Near East: A History* (New York: Harcourt Brace Jovanovich, 1971), 159.

[6] Norma J. Katan, *Hieroglyphs: The Writing of Ancient Egypt* (London: British Museum Pub., Ltd., 1987), 9.

[7] *Ibid.*, 15.

[8] *Ibid.*, 11.

[9] Bright, 160.

[10] Wright, 13.

[11] *Ibid.*, 28, 29.

* All Bible translations in this article are the author's. This article originally appeared in *Shabbat Shalom*, April-June 1989.

CHAPTER FORTY-ONE

The Real Story of the Jews

Tevye, the dairyman of *Fiddler on the Roof,* was complaining to God about the plight of the Jews as the chosen people. "Lord," he bemoaned, "can't you choose someone else for a while?"

Jews can sympathize with this prayer. While the Torah does refer to the ancient Hebrews as God's chosen people, we might ask, Chosen for what? To be conquered, captured, enslaved, first by the Egyptians, then the Assyrians, the Babylonians, and the Romans, to be driven from our land and scattered with no home, no security, no peace, to be burned, gassed, cheated, maligned, robbed, tortured, raped, massacred, and driven from country to country only to regain a piece of Palestine yet have to arm every man, woman, child, and dog in order to keep it? Chosen indeed—but for this?

Yet there is another view of our history which we dare not miss lest we wallow in self-pity. True, to follow the path of the Jews, you simply track the thick trails of our blood shed across continents and centuries. But don't just look at the blood. Look up! or you will miss the miracle of the Jews always at the end of the trail. This is the real story of the Jews, and to miss this is to miss a miracle.

That I, a Jew, am here to write this article and you, perhaps, a Jew, are here to read it—this is a phenomenon that breaks the rules, baffles the historians, defies the books. According to all historical, cultural, social, and military theories, the Jews should have vanished thousands of years ago, nothing remaining but a few cracked tablets unearthed out of the desert sands. Like many of the nations that first appeared with the Jews, we should have become nothing more than a mere minor footnote amid the vast volumes of world history; instead, our history book is the world's Bible.

There are various methodologies for interpreting the history of cultures and nations. The Jews fit none and defy all. The geographic method contends that only through a study of climate, topography, and soil can a scientific understanding of culture be reached; yet since the Jews have lived in almost every type of climate, tilled every type of soil, and have survived with their basic culture and identity intact, the geographic method, while possibly applicable to Eskimos, does not explain us.

The Marxist ideal teaches that people are shaped by their economic system and the way they produce goods; yet since the Jews have been everything from slave laborers in Egypt to capitalists on Wall Street and have still survived as Jews, Marxian dialectics might explain Albania but not Israel.

"The Cult of Personality" is the belief that nations and people are shaped by the great men who lead them and that these charismatic supermen mold events which mold nations—yet the Jews have not had a leader in two thousand years.

Oswald Spengler wrote that civilizations go through cyclical phases. Like the seasons, they begin in the early growth, mature into the summer and autumn of great military power, and decline and die in their winter phase. But not the Jews. If Spengler was right, we should have fossilized thousands of winters and springs and summers ago.

While these systems might explain the rise and fall of other nations and people, they do not the Jews. We do not fit the molds—we smash them.

How can this be explained? The sociologists can't do it, the historians can't, neither can the Marxists or the geographers. And that is because they, along with us, have been seeking answers in the wrong direction.

Though we must lift our eyes off the trails of blood, we must not keep them on ourselves. Continue upward! Let the geographer peer into the dirt for answers: We must look heavenward, to the God of Abraham, Isaac, and Jacob—for He alone has preserved us.

Though the Jews have been "removed into all the kingdoms of the earth" (Deut. 28:25) and though "among these nations shall thou have no repose, and there shall be no rest for the sole of thy foot . . . And thy life shall hang in doubt before thee; thou shall fear day and night, and shall have no assurance of thy life" (Deut. 28:65, 66), we have not been destroyed. And we need to thank our God—for He has preserved a remnant.

Despite Hitlers and Hamans, pogroms and Romans, Iraqis and Inquisitors, Assyrians and Babylonians, Kadaffis and Nazis, here we are, you and I and sixteen million others—and it is a miracle that any of us are here at all. So next time, after we mourn the six million, let us wipe away the tears, lift up our heads, and praise and thank our God for the millions of us left, for this is the real story of the Jews, and to miss this is to miss a miracle.

This article originally appeared in *The New Israelite*, Summer 1984.

CHAPTER FORTY-TWO

Faith That Hurts

Imagine: Abraham, wrinkled deep from 120 years of trials, now seeking rest. Instead, in a vision, he's called to kill, then burn, his son. Like a Nazi.

Imagine: He had forsaken his kinsmen, his home, and wandered unwelcomed in a strange land. At the command of an angel, he had to banish his son Ishmael, whom he loved. And before that, waiting decade after decade for the promise "Sarah thy wife shall bear thee a son indeed" (Gen. 17:19), though nothing came from her womb.

Imagine: Sarah bears Isaac, and, when the child fringes on manhood, Abraham, who with his loins brought Isaac out from the ground, must with his hands place him back.

The night of the vision Abraham leaves the tent and eyes the stars. He remembers that half a century earlier the Lord pointed him upward and promised: " 'Look toward heaven, and number the stars, if you are able to number them. . . . So shall your descendants be'" (15:5, RSV).* He bows upon the earth in prayer, pleading for answers. Nothing comes, only the echo: "Take now thy son, thine only son Isaac, whom thou lovest, and get thee into the land of Moriah; and offer him there for a burnt offering upon one of the mountains which I will tell thee of" (22:2).

Abraham returns to the tent, to his son, and trembles. He approaches Sarah, also asleep, and longs to mingle his tears with hers. But he leaves his wife unburdened, awakes Isaac, and they depart for a distant mountain.

"So, Abraham rose early in the morning, saddled his ass, and took two of his young men with him, and his son Isaac; and he cut wood for the burnt offering, and arose and went to the place of which God had told him" (verse 3, RSV).

The boy, the servants, journey in peaceful ease, unaware of the quiet riot inside the old man, who thinks of the mother, of when he returns and she runs, her arms wide to embrace the boy, only nothing's left, except the ashes in Abraham's hair and the smell of smoke in his beard.

The first day's journey ends and, while his companions sleep, Abraham fills heaven with prayers, hoping that divine messengers, perhaps those who first gave him the promise of Isaac, will appear, saying that the boy may return unharmed to his mother. But heaven appears Godless, and the next night, after another painful day, Abraham's prayers again seem to crowd a vacant sky. On the morning of the third day, Abraham, looking northward, sees the promised sign: a cloud of glory hovering over Mount Moriah. Now, certain that God is leading, he knows his boy must die.

" 'Stay here with the ass,' " Abraham tells his servants. " 'I and the lad will go yonder and worship, and come again to you' " (verse 5, RSV).

Isaac carries the wood—Abraham, the fire and knife. As they ascend to the summit, Isaac says, " 'My father!' "

" 'Here I am, my son.' "

" 'Behold, the fire and the wood; but where is the lamb for a burnt offering?' "

" 'God will provide himself the lamb, . . . my son' " (verses 7, 8, RSV).

At the appointed place, they build: Isaac a sacrificial altar, Abraham a funeral pyre. Then, trembling, Abraham tells Isaac that God has called him to be the slain lamb. Amazed, terrified, he does not flee. Instead, Isaac, a sharer in Abraham's faith, tries to ease his father's tears and encourages him to bind his body on top of the wood on the altar.

Imagine: Abraham looks at Isaac bound. They cry, he bends and embraces his son. He swings the blade—

To obey God, despite the pain, despite every nerve rebelling—this is the faith that hurts.

Not the kamikaze, not the Palestinian guerrilla, not the human waves of Iranian suicide youths, not the Nazis who died for the honor of the Third Reich. The world reeks from the flesh of those who have shed their lives for lies. This is not the faith that hurts.

There's a Hebrew story: Abraham's father, Terah, was an idolmaker. One day when Abraham stood alone in his father's idol shop, he smashed the gods of wood and stone. When Terah returned he asked, "What happened?"

Abraham replied, "The idols attacked each other."

"But that's impossible," Terah retorted. "They are only wood and stone."

"Then why do you worship them?" Abraham asked.

Abraham smashed his father's idols, broke free from lies as inherited as his looks, and at the command of God he left the security of his home, only to encounter Canaanites, Egyptians, and famine. But Abraham determined to obey God, no matter what he suffered, no matter where it brought him, even to his son's throat. This is faith that hurts.

Who has courage to smash his father's idols, to admit he might have inherited lies, and to seek the truth of God even if, like Abraham, he is alienated from family and friends and becomes a stranger in a famished land? And who, once he's found the truth, will, like Abraham, follow it to Mount Moriah?

Faith that hurts. It makes angels sing and demons shudder.

Imagine. . . .

---

*Scripture quotations marked RSV are from the Revised Standard Version of the Bible, copyright ©1946, 1952, 1971, 1973. This article originally appeared in *The New Israelite*, October-December 1984.

CHAPTER FORTY-THREE

Baptism in Blood

During the Crusades, the Jews were given two choices: convert or die.

In 1492, the Jews are expelled from Spain. On one condition they can stay: baptism.

During the Dark Ages, Jews in Germany who refuse baptism are drowned in the Danube.

In Portugal in the 1400s, thousands of Jewish children are wrenched from their parents' arms and raised Christian.

In the fifteenth century, Inquisitor John of Capistrano, "The Scourge of the Jews," incites a mob to attack Jews who refuse baptism.

In 1555, Pope Paul IV bans Jews from all trades and occupations except manual labor, unless they become Christians.

For centuries Christians have tried to convert Jews. Out of professed love for Jewish souls, they have racked, hacked, beaten, and burned Jewish flesh. Wanting Jews in heaven, they have put them through hell; promising Jews eternal life, they have killed them instead. Despite all the attempts to have Jews justified, sanctified, and redeemed by Christ's covering blood, the only blood that ever covered most Jews was their own.

And those who persecuted, tortured, and killed Jews were usually God-fearing, cross-wearing, hymn-singing, almsgiving, Sunday-keeping churchgoers. But were they Christian?

What is a Christian?

A Christian is a follower of Christ. To be Christian is to be like Christ.

What was Christ like? How did He convert souls?

The Gospels show that Jesus' life, teaching, and methods of preaching were so alien to that of the life, teaching, and methods of many professed followers that *anti-*

219

Christian, rather than *Christian*, might appropriately modify *church*.

When Jesus sought to convert the Samaritan woman at the well (John 4), He didn't wave a sword over her head. He asked for a drink of water. When His trust awakened her trust, Jesus pointed out her spiritual needs and offered to fulfill them, an offer she accepted. The closest He came to the sword was when He pricked her conscience.

Even when rejected, Jesus never used violence. When the Nazarene preached in His home synagogue (Luke 4), the people rebelled. "Is not this the carpenter's son?" they hooted before they dragged Jesus from the synagogue, intending to throw Him over a cliff.

After escaping, Jesus didn't retaliate; instead, at a later time He returned to preach again.

When Jesus and the disciples were rebuffed in a Samaritan village (Luke 9), John and James said, "Lord, wilt thou that we command fire to come down from heaven, and consume them, even as Elias did?"

He turned and rebuked them, saying, "Ye know not what manner of spirit ye are of. For the Son of man is not come to destroy men's lives, but to save them."

Jesus reached the people of Israel, not by threats but by mingling among them as one who desired their good. He met them on their own ground, as one who was acquainted with their perplexities. He showed sympathy and ministered to their needs. By His sympathy and kindness He showed that He recognized the dignity of all humans, no matter what their beliefs, problems, sins, or social standing. He won souls not just by preaching a message of love but by living it too.

And His messages were Jewish. "Initially, I was surprised at how easy it was for me as a Jew to relate to the teachings of Jesus," writes Leonard C. Yaseen in his recently published book *The Jesus Connection*. "In retrospect, I see nothing unusual in this, for everything Jesus preached had its origins in Old Testament teachings, in particular the command to 'love thy neighbor as thyself,' which was singled out by the great Jewish scholar and sage Hillel as the epitome of the Law."

When Jesus preached, He was never rude, never needlessly severe in word, never insensitive to a sensitive soul. He never grabbed a child out of the arms of an unbelieving parent or amassed an army to kill those who rejected Him. He fearlessly denounced unbelief, hypocrisy, and iniquity, yet His discourses were often punctuated with tears as He spoke in love for those He sought to reach.

Jesus walked among men to do them good. He sought them in streets, in homes, on the boats, in synagogues, by the shores, at marriages, and during feasts. He met them in their daily vocations and manifested an interest in their affairs. He ministered to their needs, won their confidence, and then said "Follow Me."

Have our churches done likewise? Was Pope Paul IV following the biblical injunction to "let this mind be in you, which was also in Christ Jesus" when he burned synagogues, forced the Jews to wear yellow leper badges, and banned them from most occupations? Did Jesus threaten Jews with death for refusing baptism, or did He issue a decree forcing them to attend weekly sermons on Christianity, as the church did for centuries? What is Christlike about taking children from their parents or imposing economic and social sanctions on those who reject Christianity? These methods show that the church, despite its name, had no Christ to give the Jews.

Jesus said, "Love your enemies, bless them that curse you, do good to them that hate you, and pray for them which despitefully use you." The church forbade Jews on the street during Passion Week (Third Synod of Orleans, 538), forbade them to work on Sunday (Synod of Szabolcs, 1092), forbade Christians to use Jewish doctors (Trullanic Synod, 692), forced Jews into ghettos (Synod of Breslau, 1227), and burned Jewish religious books (Twelfth Synod of Toledo, 681).

Though Jesus said, "Blessed are the merciful," the Inquisition tortured, burned, and killed thousands of Jews and Christians, all in the name of God. Jesus said, "Judge not, and ye shall not be judged"; Church Father John Chrysotsom said, "Are [Jews] not inverate murderers, destroyers, men possessed by the devil? . . . They know only one thing, to satisfy their gullets, get drunk and maim one another."

Though Jesus preached forgiveness, "Christians" haven't been able to forgive the Jews for the role the New Testament gives to the few leaders involved with the death of Jesus.

Not until 1965 did the papacy finally "exonerate" Jews collectively for "killing Christ." Meanwhile, countless Jews suffered for a crime with which they had nothing to do.

In the city of Czernnowitz in Poland, a mob led by Peter the Lame avenged the killing of Jesus by a massacre of the Jews.

During the Crusades, clergy-led mobs seeking revenge for the death of Jesus massacred thousands of Jews, destroying their homes, and leveling their communities. In Rameru, France, Rabbi Jacob Tam was stabbed five times in the head by a mob as punishment for the "five injuries inflicted" upon Jesus. But Jesus preached, "For if ye forgive men their trespasses, your heavenly Father will also forgive you," and "But I say unto you, that ye resist not evil: whosoever shall smite thee on thy right cheek, turn to him the other also." When Peter asked Jesus whether seven would be enough times to forgive a person who has sinned against him, Jesus replied: "I say not unto thee, until seven times: but until seventy times seven."

On the way to Calvary, suffering from scourging and weighed down under the cross, Jesus noticed women weeping for Him. Did He hurl accusations at them? Did He, in a frenzy of pain, threaten retribution for what the nation was doing? Quite the contrary.

Foreseeing the destruction of Jerusalem, where many of these women and their children would perish, He said, "Daughters of Jerusalem, weep not for me, but weep for yourselves, and for your children."

And when His hands and feet were pierced and when He was hung on the cross and mocked, did He cry out for vengeance? Did He curse the mob? Did He call upon his followers to avenge His death? Did He say, Kill the Jews, drive them from their homes, denigrate them in sermons, burn their synagogues, issue decrees against them, force them into ghettos? Did He call upon God to punish those and the children of those directly responsible for His death?

He said, "Father, forgive them, for they know not what they do."

How ironic when a "Christian" says that suffering is the Jews' fate because they killed Christ—when most Jewish suffering has come from "Christians" who persecuted them because "they killed Christ." It's like saying to someone, "I'd hate to see you bleed," and then slicing his throat.

Michael Davitt, an Irish Nationalist leader, witnessed a Russian pogrom in 1903. "From their hiding places in cellars and garrets the Jews were dragged forth, tortured, and killed," he wrote. "Many who had been mortally wounded were denied the final stroke and left to die in their agony. In not a few cases nails were driven into the skull and eyes gouged out. Babies were thrown from high stories to the street pavement. The bodies of young women were mutilated after being dishonored. The local bishop drove in a carriage through the crowd, giving them his blessing as he passed."

And they call *that* fate?

So little Christ has been manifested in Christendom that instead of bringing Jesus to the Jews ("to the Jew first, and also the Greek"), "Christians" have been not only a stumbling stone but a roadblock.

The New Testament teaches that those who accept Jesus have a new life through Him. Said Paul: "I am crucified with Christ: nevertheless I live; yet not I, but Christ liveth in me" (Gal. 2:20). Through the indwelling Christ, believers are to become "partakers of the divine nature." Only thus can they reflect the attributes of Jesus— love, compassion, patience, peace, gentleness, forgiveness, mercy, meekness.

Despite its tarnished record, Christianity has produced Christians who have lived in the love of Jesus. Through the centuries laymen, priests, nuns, and even popes have, like their Master, served others, even Jews, even at risk to themselves.

Yet for the most part, the religion that should have produced a whole church of selfless saints produced Pope Paul IV, who forced Jews into ghettos; Peter of Cluny, who implored King Louis VII to kill Jews; Tomás de Torquemada, the grand inquisitor of Spain; and Radulph, a French monk who during the Second Crusade incited mobs against the Jews.

Were these and other persecutors really Christians? A Christian is a follower of Christ. A Christian is to be *like* Christ. The case rests.

This article originally appeared *Liberty*, March/April 1987.

CHAPTER FORTY-FOUR

The Protocols Bug: A Notorious Forgery and Fraud

Blonde as a Nordic God, Virgil lingers on the fringe of the Aryan right. Not that he beats on Ethiopian immigrants or has a swastika tattooed on his nose. But he does rattle on about the Illuminati, the Masons, the Tri-Lateral Commission, and other conspiratorial conclaves supposedly bent on world dominion. One day he asked about *The Protocols of the Learned Elders of Zion*, which he had just read, and when I explained that the book had been long discarded as a forgery concocted by the Tsarist secret police about the turn of the century, he listened with increasing skepticism. "Are you sure?" he asked.

Hard to believe, this man, in the late 1980s, believed that *The Protocols of the Learned Elders of Zion* was true!

He's not alone. Though *Protocols* has nowhere near the influence and circulation that it had before the Second World War when, as worldwide bestseller, it was promoted by such prominent anti-Semites as Henry Ford and Adolph Hitler, the book is still printed and promoted everywhere from Japan to Egypt. "In fact," writes Kenneth Jacobson of *B'nai B'rith*, "a substantial number of reports dealing with the *Protocols'* reappearance have cropped up in recent years. This has been particularly true of the Arab world and the Soviet Union, but Latin America, Europe and the U.S. have also witnessed a resurgence of the old anti-Semitic standby."[1]

Protocols tells of a secret cabal, composed of 300 international Jews, who—through moral, political, and economic schemes—are contriving to subvert "the *goyim* states" and establish a kingdom ruled by a Jewish king, whom they call "the supreme Lord of all the world of the holy seed of David." Alleged to be the secret minutes of the 1897 Basel Congress of the World Zionist Organization, in which this conspiracy was unfolded, the book reveals the Elder's strategy for world dominion.

First, they are to ruin the morals of the Gentiles: "The peoples of the *goyim* are bemused with alcoholic liquors; their youth have grown stupid on classicism and from early immorality, into which they have been inducted by our special agents—by our tutors, lackeys, governesses in the houses of the wealthy, by clerks and others, by our women in the places of dissipation frequented by the *goyim*" (*Protocol* No. 1).

Next, they get economic control of the world: "We shall create by all the secret subterranean methods open to us and with the aid of gold, which is in our hands, a universal economic crisis whereby we shall throw upon the streets whole mobs of workers simultaneously in all the countries of Europe" (No. 3).

Afterward, they will subvert the religious beliefs of the Gentiles: "It is indispensable for us to undermine all faith, to tear out of the mind of the *goyim* the very principle of Godhead and his spirit, and to put in its place arithmetical calculations and material needs" (No. 4).

They also have plans for controlling public opinion: "In order to put public opinion into our hands we must bring it into a state of bewilderment by giving expression from all sides to so many contradictory opinions and for such a length of time as will suffice to make the *goyim* lose their heads in the labyrinth and come to see that the best thing is to have no opinion of any kind in matters political . . ." (No. 5).

Meanwhile, "we shall destroy among the *goyim* the importance of the family and its educational value. . . . In this way we shall create a blind, mighty force which will never be in a position to move in any direction without the guidance of our agents set at its head by us as leaders of the mob" (No. 10).

According to the book, these Learned Elders were already responsible for some of the past century's more degrading philosophies: "Think carefully of the successes we arranged for Darwinism, Marxism, and Nietzscheism. To us Jews, at any rate, it should be plain to see what a disintegrating importance these directives have had on the minds of the *goyim*" (No. 5).

Fearful that a coalition of the *goyim* could counteract their diabolical schemes, the Learned Elders have for the past 2,000 years kept the *goyim* fighting each other instead of them: "We have set one against another the personal and national reckonings of the *goyim*, religious and race hatreds, which we have fostered into a huge growth in the course of the past twenty centuries" (No. 5).

Then, at the right time, they will take over all world governments at once: "When we at last definitely come into our kingdom by the aids of *coups d' etat* prepared everywhere for one and the same day . . ." (No. 15).

And when they do establish their reign, these Jews, surprisingly enough, explain that: "Our kingdom will be an apologia of the divinity Vishnu, in whom is found its personification" (No. 17).

The Arabs have it the worst. At least nine Arabic translations of *Protocols* exist, more than in any other language, including German. *Protocols* is the basic sourcebook not only on Zionism and Judaism in general but on all Jewish history for the past three thousand years. Unlike the West, where the book is now produced mostly by the lunatic fringe, in some Middle East countries it is printed by established, sometimes even government, publishing houses. Endorsed by major religious, political, and intellectual figures, including Muammar Kadaffi, *Protocols* is "quoted on national television and radio programs and in some of the most respected newspapers and magazines" and is "the basis of discussion of Jews and Judaism in many school, college, and teacher-seminary textbooks."[2]

A student at the American University in Cairo explained, "I bought the *Protocols* because I'm majoring in political science. . . . The book is a record of the Jews' decision at the Zionist Congress made by Herzel. That is what they believe in, their ideology."[3]

An article in one Middle East newspaper said that "*The Protocols of the Elders of Zion* reflect their [the Jews] plans to corrupt society."

Though some Moslems have warned that the book is "of questionable authenticity," Iran has distributed copies of it all over the world, notably in Africa and in Southeast Asia, countries where it had not previously been circulated. Recently a Portuguese translation, printed in Iran, was sold in Brazil, advertised in San Paulo publications for $2 a copy.

In Japan, a new edition of *Protocols* is being circulated, along with a book called *How To Read the Protocols of the Elders of Zion*.

In November of 1987, *Chiesa Viva* (*The Live Church*), a small Catholic magazine printed in the Italian city of Brescia, republished extracts from *Protocols*. "Obviously we don't want to engage in anti-Semitism," explained Father Luigi Villa in the introduction, "but we continue our struggle against the minority of ultrapowerful Jews who conspire to divide the church of Christ. We say that the Jews, although called the Chosen People in the Old Testament, have used their undeniable intellectual talents in the service of Evil, Perversion, and Mammon . . . in order to complete the Jews' ancient plan of universal domination."[4]

In earlier times, the basic themes of *Protocols* had been promoted by the Soviet government as part of its ongoing anti-Zionism. Today, in the atmosphere of *glasnost*, these themes have been gleefully embraced by the right-wing nationalist group Pamyat, a Russian version of the Ku Klux Klan. In one meeting, well-known Pamyat patriot and writer Dimitri Vasiliev told his audience: "Comrades, if you look up the full catalog of the personal library of the great Vladimir Ilyich Lenin, you will find that the leader of the international proletariat and the founder of our state had not fewer than three copies of a book called *The Protocols of the Elders of Zion*. . . . I shall tell you what this book reveals: a satanic conspiracy of Freemasons and Zionists is afoot to destroy our sacred country, its culture, all that is dear to us. . . .Unless we unite and smash these evil forces now—for there is very little time left—it will be the end of our people and our fatherland."[5]

In America, various far-right groups such as the KKK have promoted *Protocols*. My own copy was distributed by the Christian Nationalist Crusade out of Los Angles, whose introduction to the book warns that this Jewish conspiracy originated when

Israelite King "Solomon and Jewish learned men already, in 929 B.C., thought out a scheme in theory for a peaceful conquest of the whole universe by Zion." The Christian Nationalists were selling *Protocols* for $1 a copy, 100 for $50. Liberty Bell publications out of West Virginia sells it for $2.50, the American Nazis for $3.00 each.

Yet no matter its price, the real cost of *Protocols* can be calculated only in hatred, fear, even blood.

In early twentieth-century Russia, the Tsarists, in an attempt to discredit the Bolshevik revolution, claimed that the revolt was part of a Jewish plan to enslave the world and that *Protocols* was blueprint of this plan. Incited partially by the book, Tsarist sympathizers murdered thousands of Jews.

Though the exact origin of *Protocols* is not known, evidence links it to the early 1900s in Russia, possibly to the Russian Secret Police (some sources credit it to a Russian monk named Sergi Nilius). Whatever its origins, it appears to have been forged from a book *Dialogue in Hell Between Machiavelli and Montesque*, written by Paris lawyer Maurice Joly in 1865 to discredit the Second Empire of Napoleon III. Though Joly's book had nothing to do with Jews, whoever wrote *Protocols* took Joly's work and gave it a Jewish slant.

By the early 1920s *Protocols*, an international bestseller, was infecting the world with its racism and lies. Car magnate Henry Ford, severely afflicted with the *Protocols* bug, said that the book "fitted the world situation up to this time," and under a series of articles titled "The International Jew: the world's foremost problem," Ford printed an American edition of *Protocols* in his newspaper The Dearborn *Independent.* He then published that series in a book with a circulation of half a million in the United States alone. He also printed several foreign language versions. But when Jews suddenly started driving Chevrolets instead of Fords, Henry had a miraculous recovery, even apologizing in The Dearborn *Independent* to his former customers: "To my great regret I have learned that Jews generally, and particularly those of this country, not only resent these publications as promoting anti-Semitism, but regard me as their enemy. . . . I am deeply mortified."[6]

The *Protocols* was pandemic in post-World War I Germany, where in 1922 Minister of Foreign Affairs, Walter Rathenau, was assassinated because, according to the accused killer, "Rathenau had himself confessed, and boasted, that he was one of the 300 Elders of Zion, whose purpose and aim was to bring the whole world under Jewish influence, as the example of Bolshevist Russia has already shown." By 1933, about thirty-three editions had been printed, and the Nazis used the book to justify their "self-defensive" actions against the Jewish conspiracy to subjugate the world. "The central issue of this war," said the Nazi Ministry of Propaganda in 1944, "is the breaking of Jewish world-domination. If it were possible to checkmate the 300 secret Jewish kings who rule the world, the peoples of the earth would at last find their peace."

If, however, the Jews, as *Protocols* said, possessed massive power—"At the present day, we are, as an international force, invincible" (No. 3)—why were they almost eradicated in Europe by the Nazis? Why would the Jews boast that they controlled all the gold supplies (No. 3) and yet advocate abolition of the gold standard (No. 20)? Why would the Jews want to establish a kingdom devoted to the Hindu God Vishnu (strange enough in itself), all the while they were attempting "to undermine all faith, [and] to tear out of the mind of the *goyim* the very principle of God-head and the spirit"?

Nevertheless, despite obvious absurdities, a right-winger could find in the present world situation "evidence" that *Protocols* is true, just as Hitler and Ford found "evidence" from the world situation. *Protocols* (No. 7), for example, says that the Jews control the press, and because the publishers of the *New York Times* (Schulzburger), the Washington *Post* (Graham, nee Meyer), and *U.S. News and World Report* (Zimmerman), are Jews; and because Joseph Pulitzer, Ted Koppel, Mike Wallace, Barbara Walters, and Howard Cosell are all Jews, the anti-Semite could undoubtedly cite this as evidence that *Protocols* must be true.

The book also reveals that Jews plan to corrupt morals, and what has been more morally corrupting than movies and television? Therefore, because big names in the industry like Steven Speilberg, William Paley (president of CBS), Lew Wasserman (*The Last Temptation of Christ*), Paul Newman, Dustin Hoffman, William Shatner, Leonard Nimoy, Kirk Douglas, Goldie Hawn, Cary Grant, and Joan Collins are Jewish, the anti-Semite has more "proof" of the *Protocols* conspiracy.

Meanwhile, Wall Street shysters Ivan Boesky and Michael Milliken, both Jews, probably confirmed in Virgil and others like him the truth of *Protocols* Nos. 3 and 20, which deal with financial conspiracies (might as well throw in Leona *Rosenthal* Helmsly). Jonathan Pollard and Sidney Bloch (the Jewish diplomat implicated in spying) certainly didn't squelch poor Virgil's delusions about No. 15, the plot to overthrow all governments.

Of course, just because some Jews are involved in finance, journalism, or even spying doesn't prove the *Protocols* conspiracy true any more than Ollie North's membership in a tongues-speaking church proves that all charismatics sold TOW missiles to the Ayatollah Khomeini!

Nevertheless, the masses tend to swallow a big lie easier than little ones, and *Protocols* continues to be a big lie that some easily swallow. *Today in America*, warns Christian Patriot Crusader Jack Mohy, "non-Jews, and especially Christians, are being slowly and surely reduced to the status of slaves, just as predicted in the Jewish Talmud and the so-called 'fake *Protocols*.' " The book still attracts eager (if not necessarily bright) minds looking for international conspiracies to explain world events. Yet as asinine as *Protocols* might be, one cannot forget that Germany, one of the most "enlightened" nations in the world, dogmatized the book until it became public policy.

Today, with the exception of the Far Right, most Westerners seem immune to the *Protocols* bug; under the right economic and political conditions, however, the book could again spread like the plague. Thousands of otherwise healthy people could find themselves, like Virgil, afflicted. And while the symptoms are usually just hatred, racism, and paranoia—some strains, such as the one virulent in Nazi Germany, have proven fatal.

----

[1]Kenneth Jacobson, "The Protocols: Myth and History" (New York: Anti-Defamation League of B'nai B'rith, 1981), 4.

[2]Bernard Lewis, "The Arab World Discovers Anti-Semitism" *Commentary*, May 1986, 30.

[3]Elaine Ruth Fletcher, "The Uneasy Peace" The Jerusalem *Post International Edition*, November 21, 1987, 12.

[4]Alexander Stillie, "A Disturbing Echo" quoted in *The Atlantic*, February 1989, 24.

[5]Walter Laqueur, "Glastnost's Ghosts" quoted in *The New Republic*, August 3, 1987, 13.

[6]Edwin Black, "Henry Ford: Model Anti-Semite," Baltimore *Jewish Times*, April 11, 1986, 32.

This article originally appeared in *Liberty*, November/December 1990.

CHAPTER FORTY-FIVE

What the Jews Owe Martin Luther

"The Jews are veritable liars and vampires. . . . A more bloodthirsty and vindictive race has never seen the light of day. . . . I pray all our rulers, in whose territories there are also Jewish subjects, to practice severe justice in regard to this despicable people. . . . Burn their synagogues, prohibit all the practices I have described and compel them to work. . . . If all this is to no avail, they must be cast out like rabid dogs. . . ."[1]

These lines were published in a pamphlet edited by a Protestant bishop named Martin Sasse. The date of the publication, 1939—the place, National Socialist Germany. The words, however, did not seep from the pens of Nazis, fascists, and other National Socialist racists; rather, they were excerpts from the pages of one of history's greatest personages: Dr. Martin Luther.

Jews, though, do not consider Luther a great personage. For us, he's just another Jew-hater. Rarely is a history of the Jews published without space devoted to Luther's invective. In H. H. Ben-Sasson's *A History of the Jewish People*, the author states that the reformer's writings "almost place him in a class with the likes of Hitler."[2]

Though that comparison is extreme, it's true that Luther will never have his name honored on the Avenue of Righteous Gentiles in Israel. Yet is it possible that we owe him more than we might think? Has the good which has come to us because of Luther exceeded the evil? Have we been too hard on him?

To start, Dr. Luther wasn't always an enemy. Believing that the Jews rejected Christianity because the papacy had perverted the gospel, Luther championed them during the early years of the Reformation:

> For our fools—the popes, bishops, sophists, and monks—the coarse blockheads! have until this time so treated the Jews that to be a good Christian one would have to become a Jew. And if I had been a Jew and seen such idiots and blockheads ruling and teaching the Christian religion, I would have rather

been a hog than a Christian.

For they have dealt with the Jews as if they were dogs and not human beings. . . . Whenever they converted them, they did not teach them either Christian law or life but only subjected them to papistry and monkery. When these Jews saw that Judaism has such a strong scriptural basis and that Christianity [Catholicism] was pure nonsense without biblical support, how could they quiet their hearts and become real, good Christians. . . . I would advise them in the Scriptures . . . . we must deal with them not according to the law of the pope, but according to the law of Christian charity . . . and if some remain obstinate, what of it? Not every one of us is a good Christian.[3]

Nothing like this has been heard for a thousand years, and as Luther's words echoed through Europe, the Jews rejoiced. For centuries despised, degraded, and downtrodden—the Jews took interest in this monk who defied the power which persecuted them. Some Jews saw the Reformation "as the first indication of the advent of the messianic age,"[4] which would lead to the "extinction of Christianity and the triumph of Judaism."[5] Rumors that Luther was becoming Jewish spread to Jerusalem, and at Worms three rabbis offered to help him convert. Other, more level-headed Jews were content to see the papacy suffer a blow, especially in regard to worship of images and relics, and they all were thrilled to have such a figure defend them. In Martin Luther, the Jews found a friend.

The friendship, however, didn't last. Luther, who wrote that "the Jews are of the best blood on the earth"[6] and who advocated that they be allowed to compete with Gentiles in earning a living (a radical idea in medieval Germany), later urged that the Jews be forced to prove that "Christians do not worship one God, under the penalty of having their tongues torn out of the backs of their necks."[7] He advised that their homes and synagogues be destroyed, that they be deprived of their religious books, their rabbis forbidden to teach, and that they be forced in manual labor and eventually deported to Palestine.[8]

To understand Luther's attacks, we must understand Luther's times: the Middle Ages. Not since man began had so many for so long been so covered in darkness. And while more than any other man, Luther cut through that darkness, it shadowed him all his life. He correctly labeled the papal system as anti-Christian and rejected much of their nonbiblical doctrines, but he was such a product of his times that he didn't break away completely, adhering to such errors as infant baptism, the real presence of Christ in the Eucharist, and Sunday sacredness. He accused the Jews of sorcery, host desecration, poisoning wells, drinking the blood of Christian children, and ritual murder—the lies which had been circulating for centuries. His only progressive thinking toward the Jews was when he earlier championed them.

His nastiness wasn't only for the Jews; anyone—from peasants to kings—who irked him felt the ire of his ink, often worse than the Jews ever did. When the peasants revolted and Luther appealed to them personally, they scorned him—so he replied with the tract, *Against the Murderous and Thieving Hordes of Peasants*, in which he admonished rulers to "smite, slay, stab, secretly or openly, remembering that nothing can be more poisonous, hurtful, or devilish than a rebel."[9] He called King Henry VIII a jackass, advocated that Anabaptists be killed, witches burned, and even prayed for the death of his enemies (when Duke George of Saxony died, Luther took credit, claiming that his prayers had been answered).[10] He considered Ulrich Zwingli an enemy and wrote violently against him and other Protestant Reformers. None, though, got it more than the papacy, particularly the pope. In contrast to all that he wrote against his enemies, only three small tracts at the end of his life attacked the Jews.

While Luther was always troubled by a temper, there was a vast difference between the gallant young monk who gutted Rome and the ailing old man who bruised the Jews. In his last years, his personality was soured by gallstones, angina, bleeding ulcers, hemorrhoids, depression, gout, impaired vision, ear trouble, and kidney stones. Biographer E. G. Haile believes that Luther's kidney condition could have led to uremic psychosis, a possible cause of his cantankerousness.[11] Besides his ills, all was not well with the Reformation: the Counter-Reformation had commenced, with the papacy regaining losses; armies were amassing that could bring Imperial troops into Thuringia and flood the heartland of the Reformation—and the Turk was approaching. Fanatical splinter groups split the ranks, caused dissension, and weakened the movement. Disturbed about the levity of the student body at Wittenberg, Luther moved away in protest, leaving the town he labored to reform. As these pressures mounted—Luther unleashed, attacking anyone in his way, including the Jews.

Yet he was not anti-Semitic and his writing not racist. The enemy was not the Jew—but their religion. If they would accept Jesus, Luther would accept them; if they reject Jesus, Luther rejected them. In the last sermon he preached, he said that if the Jews would "receive Christ we will willingly receive them as our brethren;"[12] if not, they must be expelled.

This sentiment was not Aryan racism, just medieval religion—and it explains Luther's flip-flop. Though skeptical about a mass conversion of the Jews, he had hoped that they would be receptive to Christianity, now that it wasn't covered in papal tapestry. Despite his efforts, few Jews converted—so he retaliated, bitterly claiming: "It is as easy to convert a Jew as the Devil himself."[13]

But it was more than Jewish obstinacy that incited Luther. Blasphemy had been a crime since the earliest church days, and in 1530 "Luther advanced the view that two offenses should be penalized by death, namely sedition and blasphemy."[14] This explains his reaction against the peasant revolt, and since he considered "a rejection of an article of the Apostles' creed as blasphemy"[15]—it is not hard to imagine his anger with the Jews, whom he believed blasphemed Christianity.

Suspicion that Jews cursed Christianity was as old as the religion itself. Accusations came from "converted" Jews with the "inside scoop." Luther devoured their writings and repeated the charges that praying Jews called Mary a harlot and Jesus her illegitimate son. For Luther, this was a grim crime, and he had to act: "If a government does not choose to provoke God's wrath," he wrote, "it must take steps against this open blasphemy."[16] If he could advocate death for Anabaptists, who were Protestants—it's a wonder he wasn't harsher with the Jews, who rejected Christianity totally.

Not only did the Jews reject Christianity—but Christians were becoming like Jews. In previous tumultuous periods in Christianity, a tendency to follow Jewish customs arose. It also happened in the Reformation, when the Moravian Anabaptists and others kept Jewish laws. Luther "became alarmed to find among those sects which sprouted like mushrooms in the fertile soil of Protestant revolt a dangerous tendency to revert to Jewish type. . . ."[17] As Jewish influence penetrated, he feared infiltration of the ultimate heresy—salvation by works, the error that spawned his revolution. Remembering his experience when rabbis tried to convert him, he feared that this current could undermine his reform, so he "busied himself against the 'menace' of Jewish proselytism, and repeatedly warned Christians lest Judaism should triumph over Christianity."[18]

Still, despite his hemorrhoids, kidney stones, the Turk, and Jewish obstinacy—Luther's attacks seem inexcusable. And, by our standards, they are. But to apply First Amendment mentality to a medieval European is unfairly anachronistic. The concept of a free pluralistic society with a separate church and state, where individuals could worship, pray, even proselytize without political interference was unknown. Though living less than thirty years after he began the Reformation, Luther tried to move away from a thousand years of intolerance; and while he progressed far, he didn't progress that far, and shadows cast from that massive past tainted even his final steps.

But what Luther lacked in forward motion was made up for by the advancing Reformation which, despite Luther, forged an environment that eventually became better for the Jews.

As papal supremacy shattered, the pieces divided into a myriad of churches, sects, and movements unable to exert the authority that the medieval church had exercised. Since many of these groups were considered heretical, the Jews ceased to be the only nonconformists in Europe. "This sectarian divisiveness and the expression of individualist opinions would in due course undermine all tendencies to compulsion and religious intoleration."[19] The new toleration reluctantly embraced the Jews—and life improved.

As the Reformation grew, so did the Protestant desire to learn the Hebrew Bible. Since the papacy had suppressed its study, the Jews were about the only ones who knew the language, and the Protestants sought them out. As the demand for Hebrew literature, Bibles, and teachers became great, friendships formed between Jews and Gentiles, prejudices died, and acceptance of Jews increased.

Scripture study kindled interest in biblical values and laws. In search of an ideal Christian society, Protestants delved into the Hebrew Bible. All across Reformation Europe, Jews and Jewish ways became respectable, even exemplary. "Gradually this appreciation of the Jewish past developed into an appreciation of the Jews of the day, as abundantly shown by the paintings of Rembrandt and a great deal of literary and social evidence."[20] In the Bible-reading cultures of the Dutch Calvinists and the

English Puritans, the Jews "were first granted refuge and then full toleration to practice their religion."[21] By 1697, London had demanded that Jews be admitted to the London Stock Exchange, when for years they had been banished from the country. Generally, where the Reformation succeeded, the Jews were permitted to live their faith, not that Judaism and Christianity had become more similar.

Because some aspects of the Roman religion were pagan, there were some course differences between Catholics and Jews. Yet as the Protestants shed their papal shackles, a purer form of Christianity emerged. Priestly celibacy, monasticism, saint veneration, and idolatry—as these errors were erased, many distinctions between church and synagogue disappeared. Charges of host desecration didn't occur in Protestant areas because of their new understanding of the nature of the Lord's Supper, thus eliminating a major cause of anti-Jewish violence.

These benefits, though, were just short-term, and some argue that, in the short-term, the Reformation was not a blessing for the Jews. But the Jews derived most from the long-term effects—effects which we are still enjoying today.

While religious freedom, liberty of conscience, and separation of church and state did not originate in the Reformation—the Reformation produced the environment in which these ideas were created and applied. The United States was founded by Protestants fleeing the intolerance that had remained after a thousand years of religious persecution. Had there been no Reformation, there would not have been that religious dissension that helped result in the founding of the United States, and had there not been the progressive thinking that the Reformation fomented, the nation might have become another oppressor of the Jews. If not for Luther's Reformation, we might still be locked in the ghettos of Europe, instead of free in the United States, or in the nations modeled after it.

But what about the evil started by Luther's attacks? Despite their savagery, they may not have been that harmful. After their publication, his recommendations were ignored by most Protestant princes, and "the Lutheran Church quickly forgot about them."[22] They gathered dust for centuries, until grasped by the Nazis, but even then "they may have been less useful to Nazi propagandists than one might expect."[23] The Germans had to apply them out of context, because "his arguments tend more to undermine than support the racist policy of National Socialism."[24] According to Luther, if a Jew accepted Jesus he was a brother; but according to the Nazis, if your grandparents were Jewish, you were a Jew (and gassed, too) despite your beliefs. The Nazis used other sources to legitimize their anti-Semitism, and the Holocaust would have occurred without Luther's input. While his words did help convince certain German Lutherans of the validity of Hitler's policies, many of the Scandinavians who risked their lives to save Jews were Lutherans too.

The paradox is personified by Luther himself. Though he did more to reveal the religion of Jesus than any man since apostolic days (his legacy to the Scandinavians), he didn't follow it with the Jews (his legacy to the Germans). "Love your enemies, bless them that curse you, do good to them that despitefully use you, and persecute you"[25] was not always Luther's method. But he was not the only godly man with spiritual defects. David committed adultery then lied and murdered—though he was Israel's greatest king. Moses, the meekest man who ever lived, dishonored God by smiting the rock in a fit of passion. Aaron allowed the worship of a golden calf; the sons of Jacob threw their brother into a pit and then lied. Jonah, Eli, Jacob, and even Abraham had, like Luther, done mighty deeds for God, but who, like Luther, too, revealed defective characters, spiritual weakness, and lack of faith—yet they will rise to glory on judgment day.

And this judgment should give us peace. "For God will bring every work into the judgment, concerning every hidden thing, whether it be good or whether it be evil."[26] God will ultimately judge Luther's works—we don't have to. Instead, we can be thankful for the benefits we have derived from Luther, even if we are not thankful for the man himself.

[1]Martin Sasse, editor, *Martin Luther and the Jews*, (Bar & Bartosh, Frieburg/Br., 1939).

[2]H. H. Ben-Sasson, *A History of the Jewish People*. (Cambridge, Mass.: Harvard University Press, 1976), 659.

[3]Martin Luther, *That Jesus Christ Was Born a Jew*, (Wittenberg, 1523).

[4]L. I. Newman, *Jewish Influence on Christian Reform Movement*, 1925, 628.

[5]H. Graetz, *History of the Jews* (Philadelphia: Jewish Publication Society., 1897), 4:471.

[6]Martin Luther, *l.c. XXV*, quoted in "Luther, Martin." *The Jewish Encyclopedia*, (N.Y.: Funk and Wagnalls, 1904), 8:213.

[7]*Luther's Sammtliche Werke*, Erlangen and Franfort-on-the Main, 32:257. Quoted in op. cit., 6:214.

[8]Martin Luther, *Concerning Jews and Their Lies*, (Wittenberg, 1543).

[9]Martin Luther, *Against the Murderous and Thieving Hordes of Peasants*, (Wittenberg, 1543).

[10]E. G. Haile, *Luther, An Experiment in Biography*, (Princeton, N.J.: Princeton University Press, 1980), 151.

[11]Haile, 221.

[12]*Weimarare Ausgabe*, 51. 195, 196. Quoted by Gordon Rupp, "In the Context of His Times," *Face to Face, an Interreligious Bulletin*, Vol. X, Spring 1983, 10.

[13]Marwin Lowenthal, *The Jews of Germany, a Story of Sixteen Centuries*, 1936, 86.

[14]Roland H. Bainton, *Here I Stand—A Life of Martin Luther*, (Nashville, Tenn.: Abingdon Press, 1950), 295.

[15]*Ibid.*, 295.

[16]Bornkamm, *Luther's World of Thought*, 31. Quoted by Aarne Siirla in "A Theological Analysis," *Face to Face, an Interreligious Bulletin*, Vol. X, Spring 1983.

[17]Lowenthal, op, cit., 159.

[18]Newman, op. cit., 621.

[19]Ben Sasson, op. cit., 646.

[20]*Reformation, Encyclopedia Judaica*, (Israel: Macmillan Company, 1971), 20.

[21]Fredrick Schweitzer, *A History of the Jews Since the First Century A.D.*, (New York: Macmillan Company, 1971), 132.

[22]"Luther: Giant of His Time and Ours," TIME, October 31, 1983, 102.

[23]Mark Edwards, "Is There a Holocaust Connection?" *Face to Face, An Interreligious Bulletin*, Vol. X, Spring 1983, 24.
[24]Edwards, op. cit., 25.
[25]Matthew 5:44 (KJV)
[26]Ecclesiastes 12:14. The Jewish Publication Society.

This article originally appeared in *The New Israelite*, Spring 1984.

CHAPTER FORTY-SIX

Anti-Semites and the City of God

If the apostle Paul had lived during the reign of Pope Paul IV, he would not have been able to support his European travels as a tentmaker because in 1555 the pope ordered that "Jews may only engage in the work of street-sweepers and rag-pickers, and may not be producers, merchants, nor trade in things necessary for human use."

When German theologian Jakob Friedrich Fried (1773–1843) suggested that a simple solution to the "Jewish problem" was to drown all Jewish babies—would he have tossed the Jewish infant Jesus into the Danube too?

Peter of Cluny, a revered church figure during the Second Crusade, implored King Louis VII to first torture, then kill, Jews. Had Peter such power in first-century Palestine, it might have been he and his cohorts who crucified Christ.

Had Pope Innocent IV really been serious about his order to burn all Jewish books, he would have had to consign his Bible to the flames too. After all, it was written mostly by Jews, takes place in a Jewish land, is filled with Jewish characters, and is saturated with Jewish laws and customs.

If Pope Innocent had completed his task, the Bible would have been destroyed and Christians would have never had their description of heaven. "It shone with the glory of God, and its brilliance was like that of a very precious jewel, like a jasper, clear as crystal. It had a great, high wall with twelve gates, and twelve angels at the gates. On the gates were written the names of the twelve tribes of Israel. There were three gates on the east, three on the north, three on the south and three on the west" (Rev. 21:10-13, NIV).*

Now, imagine the image: the New Jerusalem coming down from heaven and touching the earth, while a vast multitude, too numerous to number, approaches. A mad mob, the march toward the city they claim as their own. There, amid the confusion of faces, are legions of anti-Semites—unconverted Protestants, popes, preachers, priests, monks, theologians, false prophets, proud kings and queens, Klansmen, racists, and Crusaders—

who, despite their open and often violent anti-Semitism, think that because they believed in Jesus, because they read the Bible, prayed in Christ's name, even professed Him to others, the heavenly city is their resurrection reward. They get closer and closer to the walls, when, suddenly, a hush rushes through them, and they stop. They stand outside the city, their eyes fastened to the names above the gates.

Surprised, they see, above a gate, the name ASHER. Quickly, they look to another gate, and it says JUDAH. The next gate says—oh no!—REUBEN. Desperately, they run around the corner to another wall. There, in big bold letters above another gate is—LEVI. The bigots moan. *Those are all Jewish names!*

Realizing now that this New Jerusalem is a Jewish city (though it is Christian too because Revelation 21:14 says that its foundations have the names of the twelve apostles), with Jewish names on the gates, with many Jewish people on the streets, with a leader who is a Jew—they ask themselves, *"Do we really want to go in?"*

How happy would Peter of Cluny be in New Jerusalem? Unless he had a change of heart sometime in his life, at his resurrection he will awaken as the same violent anti-Semite he was when he died. Unless Pope Paul IV eventually became converted, how could he be happy in a city whose leader, Jesus, is a Jew—when the pope himself would not allow Jews to be anything better than street-sweepers? Indeed, unless they were eventually converted, would any of the crusaders, Inquisitors, Klansmen, bigots, and racists who cursed, harassed, tortured, and killed Jews really be happy in the New Jerusalem, with its Jewish leader, Jewish symbols, and Jewish inhabitants?

And yet, despite the reproach and blood they have brought upon His name, Jesus—who could love His own killers enough to pray for them—loves those anti-Semites too. He loves them so much that He does not want them to be unhappy in the Holy City. He knows that the spirit of selfless love and compassion in those who live there would be hateful to the racist outside the city wall. They would be so out of place that heaven, for them, would be hell.

Imagine: Jesus stands on the heavenly wall and looks, with pity, on the poor deluded souls below. He can't let them inside the city, for they would be miserable amid all the love, compassion, and Jews. Yet they are miserable outside the heavenly kingdom too. What can be done for them? Finally, Jesus, out of love and pity even for them, His enemies, does the only compassionate thing He can: put them out of their misery, forever and ever.

"For behold, the day cometh, it burneth as a furnace; and all the proud, and all that work wickedness, shall be stubble; and the day that cometh shall set them ablaze, saith the Lord of hosts, that it shall leave them neither root or branch" (Mal. 3:19, Jewish Publication Society).

CHAPTER FORTY-SEVEN

Is the New Testament Anti-Semitic?

What book depicts Jews as hypocrites, apostates, liars, and sinners? What book denounces Jewish leaders and the Jewish nation? What book scolds its priests, claims its temple services are corrupt, and spews forth warnings that God's judgments will fall upon the Jews? What book—accusing the Jews of murder, corruption, greed, and robbery—declares that they have forsaken God?

Sounds like the New Testament, long indicted as the Perian Spring of Western anti-Semitism. Some believe the hands that signed the "final solution" simply finished the script begun by Matthew, Mark, Luke, and John. Hitler, others claim, was the logical, inevitable result of Paul. Christian historian James Parkes writes that "more than 6 million deliberate murders are the consequences of the teaching about Jews for which the Christian church is ultimately responsible, and our attitude to Judaism which is not only maintained by all Christian churches but has its ultimate resting place in the teaching of the New Testament itself."

"The New Testament," writes Harry Kimball, "is the primary source of anti-Semitism, [and] every generation of Christians has been brought up on it."

The Gospels are stigmatized as the primary source of New Testament anti-Semitism. "The authors of the Gospels," wrote Jewish historian Heinrich Graetz, "by putting these words of violent hatred against the preservers of Judaism into the mouth of Jesus Himself, stamped Him thereby as a relentless foe of the members of His own race who did not believe in Him but clung to their original faith."

Yet the book described in the opening paragraph is not the New Testament—it is the Old! Indeed, if the criteria for determining anti-Judaism in the New Testament were applied to the Old, it would be declared the more anti-Jewish of the two.

Incorrigible Villains

Scholars have long debated about anti-Judaism in the New Testament, but rarely, if at all, anti-Judiasm in the Old. It, after all, is a book written about Jews, by Jews who considered themselves loyal Jews. Yet except for Luke (not considered the most anti-Jewish of the Gospel writers), the New Testament was written about Jews, by Jews who considered themselves loyal Jews too.

The New Testament, though, has pages of anti-Jewish calumny. "The New Testament contains 102 references to the Jews of [the] most degrading and malevolent kind," wrote Dagobert Runes, "thereby creating in the minds and hearts of Christian children and adults ineradicable hatred toward the Jewish people."

In the Gospels, Jewish leaders, priests, scribes, and Pharisees play the role of incorrigible villains. Depicted as cold and heartless formalists, they appear pious outside but seethe with treachery inside. Jesus labels them hypocrites, deceivers, even murderers—words later used to help formulate a theology of anti-Semitism. "Nowhere is this theological anti-Judaism more apparent," writes Princeton religious historian John G. Gager, "than in the dialogue between Jesus and the Pharisees in [John] 8." Here, after telling Jewish leaders that they are not the true children of Abraham and accusing them of plotting His murder, Jesus says, "Ye are of your father the devil, and the lusts of your father ye will do. He was a murderer from the beginning" (verse 44).

Matthew 23 is nothing but a denunciation: "But woe unto you, scribes and Pharisees, hypocrites! . . . Ye blind guides . . . Ye fools and blind. . . . Fill ye up then the measure of your fathers. Ye serpents, ye gatherers of vipers, how can ye escape the damnation of hell?" (verses 13-33).

The Gospel writers depict Jewish leaders as planning Jesus' death: "And the scribes and chief priests . . . sought how they might destroy him" (Mark 11:8). Indeed, all the Gospels implicate the leaders in His death.

Jesus' denunciations not only of the leaders but also of the nation have fueled the anti-Semite's fire. In Luke 20 Jesus, symbolizing Israel as a vineyard, tells of a master who planted a vineyard and "let it forth to husbandmen" (verse 9). Later when the servants came to collect the fruit from the master's vineyard, the husbandmen beat them. He sends more servants, and they beat them too. Finally the master says, "I will send my beloved son: it may be they will reverence him when they see him" (verse 13). Instead, the husbandmen killed him! Said Jesus: "What therefore shall the Lord of the vineyard do unto them? He shall come and destroy these husbandmen, and shall give the vineyard to others" (verses 15, 16). Luke recorded the leaders' response: "And the chief priests and scribes the same hour sought to lay hands on him; and they feared the people; for they perceived that he had spoken this parable against them" (verse 19).

Matthew has Jesus blaming the Jews for the murder of the prophets—"O Jerusalem, Jerusalem, thou that killest the prophets, and stonest them which are sent to thee" (Matt. 23:37)—and leaving a judgment upon them: "Behold, your house is left unto you desolate" (verse 38).

The Gospels depict Jesus as critical also of national religious rites and of the nation, including the worship at the temple—criticisms gleefully seen as anti-Jewish polemics. At the start of His ministry Jesus cleansed the temple from merchants who had turned it into an unsanctified flea market. "And [He] said unto them, It is written, My house shall be called a house of prayer; but ye have made it a den of thieves" (Matt. 21:13). He warns that even the temple itself, the center of Jewish religion, will be destroyed: "And Jesus went out, and departed from the temple: and his disciples came to him for to shew him the buildings of the temple. And Jesus said unto them, See ye not all these things? verily I say unto you, there shall not be left here one stone upon another, that shall not be thrown down" (Matt. 24:1, 2).

The New Testament, obviously, portrays many Jews in ancient Israel as corrupt, iniquitous, and separated from God. Does this description, therefore, mean that the book is anti-Jewish? For many scholars, both Jew and Gentile, it does.

A Sinful Nation

A problem exists, though, with that conclusion: Line for line, verse for verse, chapter for chapter, the Old Testament has more denunciations than does the New. If criticizing the spiritual ills of ancient Israel is anti-Jewish, then the most anti-Jewish section of the Bible is not in Greek but Hebrew!

"Ah, sinful nation, a people laden with iniquity," says Isaiah about Judah. "A seed of evildoers, children that are corrupters: they have forsaken the Lord" (Isa. 1:4).

The prophet compares Judah to Sodom and Gomorrah: "Hear the word of the Lord, ye rulers of Sodom; give ear unto the law of our God, ye people of Gomorrah. . . . How is the faithful city become an harlot! It was full of judgment; righteousness lodged in it; but now murderers" (verses 10-21). The New Testament does speak harshly against corrupt leaders, but so does the Old: "O heads of Jacob," warns Micah, "and ye princes of the house of Israel; Is it not for you to know judgment? Who hate the good, and love the evil; who pluck off their skin from off them, and their flesh from off their bones; who also eat the flesh of my people, and flay their skin from off them" (Mic. 3:1-3).

Jesus' denunciation of the priests were no worse than Malachi's: "O priests, that despise my name. Ye offer polluted bread upon mine altar." "And now, O ye priests, this commandment is for you. If ye will not hear, . . . I will even send a curse upon you, and I will curse your blessings; yea, I have cursed them already, because you do not lay it to heart. Behold, I will corrupt your seed, and spread dung upon your faces" (Mal. 1:6, 7, 2:1-3).

The Old Testament has more stories of corrupt leaders than does the New Testament. Ahab, Jehoram, Ahaz, and Manasseh are just a few of the corrupt kings of Israel denounced in the Old Testament. As in the New, rulers and priests are depicted as plotting, scheming, and killing off enemies, including prophets who spoke against them.

Because Luke and Matthew recorded Jesus' warnings of doom upon Israel, they are labeled anti-Jewish. But what about Jeremiah, who recorded the Lord's warning to Israel: "I will bring evil from the north, and a great destruction. The lion is come up from his thicket . . . he is gone forth from his place to make thy land desolate; and thy cities shall be laid waste, without an inhabitant" (Jer. 4:6, 7).

What about Isaiah, who proclaimed: "O Assyrians, the rod of mine anger. . . . I will send him against an hypocritical nation, and against the people of my wrath will I give him a charge, to take the spoil, and to take the prey, and to tread them down like the mire of the streets" (Isa. 10:5).

Is Luke's parable of Israel as a vineyard worse than Isaiah's? "I will tell you what I will do to my vineyard: I will take away the hedge thereof, and it shall be eaten up; and break down the wall thereof, and it shall be trodden down" (Isa. 5:5).

The Gospels record Jesus speaking against corrupt practices in the temple, but Ezekiel decries the sin of the people who had brought idols into the temple area, where they prayed to other gods and even worshiped the sun. "Hast thou seen this . . . ? Is it a light thing to the house of Judah that they commit the abominations which they commit here? for they have filled the land with violence" (Ezek. 8:17). Jesus prophesied against the temple; so did Amos: "And the songs of the temple shall be howlings in that day, saith the Lord God: there shall be many dead bodies in every place" (Amos 8:3).

Bigots and Enemies

If these Hebrew texts had been written in the New Testament, they would be added to the long list of other "anti-Jewish" vituperation. But they are from the Old Testament, and yet no one claims that the Old Testament is anti-Jewish.

Why? Because a writer who depicts the spiritual ills of his people can't automatically be branded anti-Jewish. If so, then Ezekiel, Isaiah, Jeremiah, even Moses—almost every Hebrew prophet—would be labeled as anti-Jewish, an absurd claim. Why, however, do Jews such as Matthew and Mark become bigots and enemies when they chronicle the ills of Israel?

In the "Hebrew Bible," writes Jewish scholar Samuel Sandmel, "the prophets of the age before the Babylonian exile provide variations of a similar theme, that the Hebrew people had in their actions proved false to the religious-ethical standards expressed in a covenant with God and expected of a holy people. Accordingly, an Amos, an Isaiah, and a Jeremiah each speak with wondrous poetic eloquence about the shortcomings of the people, whether monarchs or priests are denunciation from within; surely no one would ascribe to Amos, Isaiah, or Jeremiah that form of hostility which we call anti-Semitism. . . . It was out of loyalty to them and identification with the people and their religion that the Hebrew prophets spoke their sharp criticisms. When in the Gospels the Jew Jesus speaks in criticism of Jews, is it not reasonable that He too speaks out of loyalty and identification?"

The claim that the New Testament is anti-Jewish because it points out Israel's spiritual ills is as absurd as claiming that the Old Testament is anti-Jewish because it is doing the same thing. Both Testaments portray human nature as inherently bad. The greatest biblical characters have their spiritual and moral faults on display before the world. Whether Abraham taking Hagar to produce a son, Moses losing his temper, David fornicating with Bathsheba, Peter denying Jesus, or the apostles Paul and Barnabas bickering over John Mark—the sins of humanity are openly displayed. The motif of the sinfulness of man permeates the Hebrew and Greek Scriptures. And because the Jews comprise the main biblical characters, because their lives occupy most of the pages, because Jewish history is the primary focus of the Bible—their dirty laundry has become the most prominent. Even if not as filthy as others, it is Jewish linen that hangs on the line for the world to see.

Blindness of Heart

And yet the Bible doesn't speak harshly of just Jews. Jesus told His followers not to pray "as the heathen do" and not to pray for the things "the Gentiles seek." Paul writes: "Ye know that ye were Gentiles, carried away unto these dumb idols" (1 Cor. 12:2). In Ephesians Paul warns followers that "ye henceforth walk not as other Gentiles walk, in the vanity of your mind, having the understanding darkened, being alienated from the life of God through the ignorance that is in them, because of the blindness of their heart: who being past feeling have given themselves over unto lasciviousness, to work all uncleanness with greediness" (Eph. 4:17-19). In Thessalonians he warns followers to act "not in the lust of concupiscence, even as the Gentiles which know not God" (1 Thess. 4:5). Is the New Testament, therefore, anti-Gentile too?

The Old Testament also denounces heathens. Israel's problem is that it followed the practices of the Gentile nations. The whole purpose of Israel was to be separate from the Gentiles so that the Jews would "learn not the way of the heathen" (Jer. 10:2). Their greatest sins occurred when they followed the sinful practices of the Gentiles. Obviously, sin was a bigger problem for the heathen than it was for the Jews.

Yet the New Testament shows the Jews as not only rejecting Jesus but killing him, too—a teaching not found in the Old Testament.

No question, the New Testament implicates some Jews in Jesus' death. But whom does Jesus Himself implicate? Talking about the chief priests and scribes, Jesus says that they "shall deliver him to the *Gentiles* to mock, and to scourge, and to crucify him" (Matt. 20:19). Jesus says that Gentiles—not Jews—will mock, scourge, and crucify Him. Though some scribes and chief priests were involved, the people who directly killed Jesus—according to Matthew, Mark, Luke, and John—were Gentile Romans. If the New Testament is anti-Jewish because it implicates Jews, then it must be anti-Roman or anti-Gentle as well, because Gentile Romans were also involved.

Heroes and Villains

While the New Testament shows that many Jews rejected Jesus, it also shows that many Jews accepted Him. Indeed, the heroes of the New Testament are Jews who accepted Jesus, while often the villains are Gentiles who rejected Him. Paul wrote epistles from prison, where he was jailed—by Gentiles. In Philippi, Paul and Silas were beaten by Gentiles. In Ephesus, because Paul's preaching hurt the religion of the goddess Diana, he and two companions were dragged into an amphitheater where for two hours the Gentiles—rejecting Paul's message—chanted, "Great is Diana of the Ephesians" (Acts 19:34). At Mars Hill in Athens, after Paul preached, he was mocked and rejected by Athenians—Gentiles. The early persecution of the church, mentioned in Revelation, was conducted by Gentiles. Paul was killed by Gentiles. John was exiled to Patmos by Gentiles. In Luke 21:17 Jesus told His followers that they "shall be hated of *all* men for my name's sake." "All men" includes Gentiles.

Is the New Testament, therefore, anti-Gentile because it depicts Gentiles as rejecting the gospel? Here, too, the claim of the New Testament anti-Judaism is built on a straw.

A Fertile Fount

Even if the New Testament is not a bubbling source of hatred against the Jews, few deny that it has served as a fertile fount of anti-Semitism. Yet throughout history the Bible has been used to justify everything from slavery to Star Wars. Cutting, pasting, and patching verses together, the faithful have made the Bible sanction war, apartheid, celibacy, aid to the contras, genocide, not eating meat on Friday, castration, pacifism, Marxism, cuts in food stamps, the MX missile, sexual promiscuity, burning people alive—and yes, even anti-Semitism.

Indeed, the problem is not with the New Testament or even the Old—but with those who, through reading them, have never learned the lesson of brotherly love taught within their pages.

The Problem with Paul's Theology

While the Gospels have traditionally been branded as the main source of New Testament anti-Judaism, Paul, too, is indicted as anti-Jewish. "Whatsoever the general effect of the Gospels," writes Lloyd Gaston, "it is Paul who has provided the theoretical structure for Christian anti-Judaism."

What about Paul's theology, which some claim teaches that the Jews as a nation have been forsaken by God—a teaching often regarded as another pillar in the theological foundation of New Testament anti-Semitism?

First of all, this interpretation is hotly contested within Christianity. "God has but one chosen people," write Jerry Combee and Cline Hall of Liberty Baptist College, "the Jews, to whom His promises remain as valid as ever." Other Christians believe that Paul teaches that corporate Israel, the Jews as a nation, no longer enjoy the special covenant status they once had. Hence, they are no longer the chosen people.

Even if one believes that the Jews as a nation have lost the special covenant relationship they once enjoyed with God—the more potentially dangerous of the two positions—that belief is not more anti-Jewish than it is anti-Hindu, anti-Islamic, or anti-Buddhist. It says only that the Jews are not just like everyone else—saved as Hindus, Buddhists, or Muslims are: through faith in Jesus. "There is neither Jew nor Greek," Paul wrote in Galatians 3:28, "there is neither bond nor free, there is neither male nor female: for ye are all one in Christ Jesus."

If anything, according to Paul, the Jew still has one up on everyone else. "What advantage hath the Jew?" Paul asks. Much every way: chiefly, because that unto them were committed the oracles of God" (Rom. 3:1, 2).

Even if Paul believed that Israel as a nation is no longer chosen, this position doesn't mean he believed that God has forsaken the Jews any more than He has forsaken other people individually. "I say then," he asks, "hath God cast away his people? God forbid. For I also am an Israelite, of the seed of Abraham, of the tribe of Benjamin. God hath not cast away his people which he foreknew" (Rom. 11:1, 2). Three times Paul, talking about the gospel, repeated: "To the Jew first, and also the Greek." Hardly sounds like a man who believed the Jews were forsaken by God.

If in the worst-case scenario Paul taught that the Jews are no longer the chosen nation, this belief still places the Jews above any other religion or nation, because the Gentile religions and nations never even once enjoyed the status of "chosen people." Is the New Testament anti-Gentile because it might teach that only the Jews as a nation once had special status with God, while the Gentile nations never had any?

This article originally appeared in *Liberty*, July/August 1989.

CHAPTER FORTY-EIGHT

No Jew Signed the Constitution

Study the history of early America, and few Jews appear. Stuyvesant, Mather, Edwards, Williams, Washington, Jefferson, Madison, Adams, Mason, Franklin Sherman—not exactly the names found in a synagogue directory. No Jew helped write the Declaration of Independence, no Jew signed the Constitution of the United States, no Jew fashioned the Bill of Rights. The closest thing a Jew had to do with the foundation of the republic was to write the words at the base of the Statue of Liberty, "Give me your tired, your poor, your huddled masses yearning to breathe free. . . ."

Nevertheless, Jews profoundly influenced the establishment of the American republic. Not Jews with the names Katz, Rabinowitz, or Cohen, but with the names Moses, Jeremiah, and Isaiah—and their influence was so great that one historian declared: "The Hebraic mortar cemented the foundations of American democracy."

The first Americans, purebred Puritans, accepted the Bible as the basis for morals, worship, and government. Though they worshiped, praised, and sang hymns to Jesus, they attempted to base their government upon the Old Testament model, the theocratic system detailed in the Hebrew Bible, particularly the five books of Moses. So serious was this intent that many of their leaders were skilled in the Hebrew language. "The Laws of Harvard College" in 1655, for example, required that "in the first year after admissions for four days of the week all students shall be exercised in the studies of Greek and Hebrew tongues."

For better or for worse, the Puritans wanted a theocratic commonwealth at Plymouth "like that of the children of Israel in the good old days before their forward hearts conceived the desire for a King." As early as 1636 Plymouth Colony renounced the authority of English laws and adopted the Pilgrim Code, which in its foreword stated: "It was the great privilege of Israel of old and so was acknowledged by them, Nehemiah the ninth and tenth, that God gave them right judgments and true laws.

They are for the many so exemplary, being grounded on principles of moral equity, as that all Christians especially ought to have an eye thereunto in the framing of their political constitutions."

In 1650 the colony of New Haven in Connecticut adopted this code: "It was ordered that the judicial laws of God, as they were delivered by Moses and as they are a fence to the moral law, being neither typical nor commercial, nor had any reference to Canaan, should be accounted of moral equity, and generally bind all offenders, till they be branched out into particular hereafter."

New Haven attempted to adhere so strictly to the Mosaic code that it didn't allow trial by jury because the practice was not mentioned in the Old Testament.

Roger Williams, however, argued that the Puritans had no right to establish a theocracy, that the theocracy was meant only for the Jews in ancient Palestine at a specific time, for a specific purpose. Williams, himself a staunch Puritan, rejected the identification of Old Testament Israel with any existing state, such as Massachusetts Bay Colony, Plymouth, or New Haven. Many early colonists, however, saw themselves as modern Israelites, the American continent as the new Canaan, and the nation they were to form as the new Israel. As late as 1783, Dr. Ezra Stiles, president of Yale, called this land "God's American Israel," a belief held by some even today.

For Williams, Israel was a one-time arrangement. No other nation in any age was under the same rule. People were saved as individuals, not as nations. The New Testament said nothing about a theocracy. Thus, no need for one existed.

History bore Williams out: the Colonies failed miserably in forming a theocracy. Instead, they created religious dictatorships. The despotism that they themselves fled from, they created for others.

Despite the Puritans' misinterpretation and misapplication of Israel, none can dispute the Hebrew Bible's beneficent influence on the emerging nation.

The Old Testament influenced the struggle for American independence from England. Here its principles gave the leaders of the American Revolution the philosophical inspiration to revolt against British tyranny. While Jean-Jacques Rousseau and the Jacobin political philosophers might have influenced Thomas Jefferson's arguments for the Declaration of Independence, the average agrarian American would need more than the atheistic musings of the French in order to rebel against the mother country. The people needed to be convinced not only that the British monarch had done them intolerable wrongs but that the whole concept of the divine right of kings and their demand for absolute submission was sinful in the eyes of God.

So where did they go? To the Old Testament, to Israel's request for a king and Samuel's answer that a king would become despotic, arbitrary, and that he would "take your fields, and your vineyards, and your oliveyards, even the best of them, and give them to his servants" (1 Sam. 8:14). They told of Gideon's refusal to become the king: "I will not rule over you, neither shall my son rule over you: the Lord shall rule over you" (Judg. 8:23). They used even the story from Exodus, when Moses' father-in-law, Jethro, told him to appoint various rulers over the people rather than take all the responsibility upon himself. "Moreover thou shalt provide out of all the people able men, such as fear God, men of truth, hating covetousness; and place such over them, to be rulers of thousands, and rulers of hundreds, rulers of fifties, and rulers of tens" (Exod. 18:21). In the days prior to and during the Revolution, in order to rouse the people against the Crown and break the hold that the monarchical system had upon their minds, the revolutionary leaders used the Hebrew Bible.

"The Jewish government," said Samuel Langdon, president of Harvard College, "according to the original constitution which was divinely established, if considered merely in a civil view, was a perfect republic." Simon Howard, pastor of the West Church of Boston, delivered a sermon before the Massachusetts House of Representatives in 1780. He said: "Indeed the Jews always exercised the right of choosing their own rulers: even Saul and David and all their successors on the throne were made king by the voice of the people."

Thomas Paine, while overtly hostile to religion, based his final argument against the monarchy on the Old Testament stories of Samuel and Gideon. In *Common Sense* he wrote: "Monarchy is ranked in Scripture as one of the sins of the Jews. . . . Gideon doth not decline the honor [of the kingship offered to him] but denieth the right to give it. . . . These portions of Scripture are direct and positive. They admit of no equivocal construction. That the Almighty hath here entered His protest against monarchial government is true, or the Scripture is false."

The inscription on the Liberty Bell—"*Proclaim Liberty throughout the land unto all the inhabitants thereof*"—came from the pen of a Jew: Moses (see Lev. 25:10).

On the day the Declaration of Independence was adopted, a committee composed of Thomas Jefferson, Benjamin Franklin, and John Adams was appointed to "prepare a proper device for a Seal for the United States of America." They proposed a seal with an image of Pharaoh seated in a chariot, a sword in his hand, and hot on the trail of the Jews. Safe on the opposite shore of the divided sea was Moses and Israel under rays of a pillar of fire, while Moses played his part in causing the water to engulf Pharaoh and his army. Around the edge of the seal were the words *"Rebellion to tyrants is obedience to God."* Though never adopted, this seal exemplifies the influence of the Hebrew Bible upon early American leaders.

The Declaration of Independence reads: "We hold these truths to be self-evident, that all Men are created equal, that they are endowed by their Creator with certain inalienable Rights, that among these are Life, Liberty, and the Pursuit of Happiness." While written in the rationalistic, deistic style of the eighteenth century, the doctrine is firmly rooted in ancient Judaism, which held to the individual worth and equality of man. "Have we not all one father? Hath not one God created us? why do we deal treacherously every man against his brother?" (Mal. 2:10). Or the words of Micah 6:8: "He hath shewed thee, O man, what is good; and what doth the Lord require of thee; but to do justly, and to love mercy, and to walk humbly with thy God."

John Adams, one of the nation's earliest presidents, in a letter written in 1809, said: "In spite of Bolingbroke and Voltaire, I will insist that the Hebrews have done more to civilize men than any other nation. If I were an atheist, and believed in blind eternal fate, I should still believe that fate had ordained the Jews to be the most essential instrument for civilizing the nations. If I were an atheist of the other sect, who believe and pretend that all is ordered by chance, I should believe that chance had ordained the Jews to preserve and propagate to all mankind the doctrine of a supreme, intelligent, wise, almighty Sovereign of the Universe, which I believe to be the most essential principle of all morality and consequently of all civilization."

Sure, no Jews signed the Declaration of Independence. We had already done our share.

This article originally appeared in *Liberty*, July/August 1989.

CHAPTER FORTY-NINE

The Plague

Sweeping over from Asia in the fourteenth century, the Black Death blitzed Europe and killed more people in three years than the Nazis did in six. An estimated one-fourth to three-fourths of Europe perished—from 25 to 60 million souls.[1] Entire towns, villages, and farms were wiped out. Half of London died, perhaps a third of England. The dead were piled in the streets, and wagons would carry them to burial. In Avignon, there were so many bodies that, instead of being buried, they were tossed in the Rhone River. In the Paris hospital, 500 bodies a day were interred. The Black Death was probably the greatest disaster in thousands of years. Everybody—noblemen, serfs, priests, landlords, and merchants—was equally devastated.

Except the Jews. While they were infected, proportionally fewer died than did the rest of the population.[2, 3, 4] The difference was so great that the masses believed that the Jews had started the plague by contaminating the water and air with a poison concocted from spiders, lizards, and the hearts of Christians mixed with the sacred host. The rumor spread as quick as the epidemic, and all across Europe frenzied mobs crying "Kill a Jew and save your soul" dragged thousands of Jews from their homes and burned them at the stake.

What was the secret of the Jews? How did they manage to avoid the plague better than the Gentiles? The answer is simple: lifestyle.

Most medieval cities and towns were unfit for habitation, yet here the masses huddled. The cities were often walled to keep out hordes of invaders, while inside hordes of germs massacred millions. During papal Christianity, the biblical conception of cleanliness was lost under reeking piles of garbage, refuse, and waste sometimes stacked so high the people could not walk the streets. Pigs, geese, and ducks wandered free—rodents too. Sewers and cesspools were open, brewing disease. Often, local lakes and streams served both for drinking water and sewage disposal.

As the pagan error of an immortal soul was adopted by the church, rational care for the human body died. The soul, not the body, was important. People stopped bathing for a thousand years. Cleanliness was considered worldliness, while the dirtier you were the more sanctified you became, and some people boasted that they had never bathed. When they stank, they used perfume.

Illness was considered punishment for sin, devil possession, witchcraft—or, in the case of the plague, from the Jews.[5] Cures supposedly came from magic oils, holy relics, and prayers to the saints. A trip to St. Martin's shrine was supposed to cure anything. Early in the medieval period, the sick who consulted a physician were considered heretics, which meant that the church might have cauterized their illness for them—at the stake! Centuries later, with the pronouncement, *Ecclesia abhorret a sanguine* (the church does not shed blood) Rome forbade the clergy to perform surgery, and since most physicians were clergymen, it was left to barbers, butchers, sowgelders, bathkeepers, and hangmen. This decree, as well as others forbidding the dissection of the human body, brought the study of medicine and physiology almost to a standstill.

But the Jews were not Catholics, and many of the church rules did not apply to them. While the Gentiles—relics in their hands, prayers to saints on their lips—were decimated in the plague, the Jews kept healthy by following the basic health laws found in the Bible. They were about the only ones who read the Scriptures, and the benefits were apparent.

The most basic biblical health principle is cleanliness, a tradition the Jews have been following for millennia. While contaminated by the degeneration and ignorance of the era, the Jews did keep their neighborhoods clean and in good repair. Across town, however, the Gentiles waded through piles of filth and garbage which brought rats, the reservoir of the plague bacillus. A flea would bite an infected rat, get infected itself, and then bite humans, infecting them too. Once infected, a human could spread one form of the plague merely by breathing.

The Jews, though, had less garbage, fewer rats, fewer fleas, and therefore—less plague. It was that simple.

In rabbinic tradition, there are 613 commandments in the Torah. Exactly 213 are medical, mostly preventive. Prevention of epidemics, suppression of venereal disease, care of skin, dietetic regulations, sanitary procedures, rules for sexuality, and other provisions, though written thousands of years ago, are some of the finest health principles in the world.

The ancient Hebrews knew that certain diseases were spread by contact with people, clothing, utensils, and other objects, even if they did not know why. To prevent epidemics, they were given in the Torah a series of sanitary regulations, including sterilization of infected garments and utensils, scrubbing of houses suspected of carrying infections, and scrupulous inspections of the diseased person after recovery. Anyone coming into contact with a corpse or suffering from an abnormal discharge also required a thorough cleansing of himself and his belongings before being allowed back into society.

These and other principles have been carried on by the Jews through various rabbinical customs and traditions for thousands of years. It was by following these principles that the Jews were able to keep so much cleaner and healthier than the rest of the population, and this is what enabled them to resist so many of the diseases that ravaged Europe, including the plague.

Because the church ran Europe, people cite the ignorance of the era as an example of a Bible-based society. Nothing could be further from the truth.

Except for a few pockets of resistance, the Jews were about the only ones who had any Bible truth, and the results were revealed by how much better they handled the plague than did their Gentile neighbors, who had almost no Bible truth at all. So, far from being an example of a Bible-based society, this era showed how low man can go without the uplifting truth of the Holy Scriptures.

---

[1] F. Matthews, "Black Death," *Collier's Encyclopedia* (Crowell Collier Macmillan, 1967), 234.

[2] I. K. Sulamith, *Everyman's History of the Jews,* (New York: Frederick Fell, Inc., 1958), 122.

[3] H. Graetz, *History of the Jews,* (Philadelphia: Publication Society of America, 1894), 4:101.

[4] C. Roth, *Collier's Encyclopedia,* (Crowell Collier &Macmillan, 1967), 579.

[5] E. Ackermack, M.D., *A Short History of Medicine,* (New York: Roland Press Co., 1955), 75.

This article originally appeared in *The New Israelite*, Spring 1984.

CHAPTER FIFTY

Freedom Feast

For more than three thousand years, with few interruptions, Jews have kept Passover. Whether on the gutted plains of Ethiopia, in a Manhattan penthouse, or along the frostbitten Volga, Jews have, in one form or another, celebrated this feast—first observed so long ago that the bones of its first celebrants no longer exist, not even as dust along a bedouin's brow. Passover, the oldest Jewish cultus (Shabbat began with Gentiles before Jews existed [see Genesis 2:3]), binds Jews today with those thirty centuries ago and allows us to experience the Exodus.

More than a worship service, more than a historical narrative, Pesach is a reenactment. We feel as if we were in Egypt, under the bondage of taskmasters who forced us to build bricks from stubble rather than straw. And yet we experience the joy of deliverance, the exhilaration of freedom, as if we were standing on the shore while Pharaoh's chariots were swallowed in the waves.

For centuries rabbis have noted that the Torah uses the first-person expression in describing how to recount the story: "And thou shalt tell to thy son on that day, saying, This is done because of [what] the Lord did *for me* when I went out from Egypt" (Exod. 13:8).* Says the Passover Haggadah: "In each generation a person must feel as if he himself just came out of Egypt."

No wonder, then, that Passover commemorates more than national liberation, more than release from chains. For the Jews, freedom is also spiritual, which is why Jews celebrate the Passover even during times of oppression. Passover teaches that no matter what man does to us physically, we can—by the power of God—be free.

Even today—through recounting the Exodus in morning and evening prayer, in grace after meals, and as he wears his prayer shawl—the Jew is reminded of the day he "went out from Egypt." The Exodus story is included even in the phylacteries. The deliverance from Egypt and the redemption it symbolizes are tied into the daily aspects of Jewish life, because redemption should be a daily experience.

God's commands to the Jews, even those that dealt with the mundane dailies, were often tied to the deliverance from Egypt. In Leviticus 11, after detailed instructions regarding diet, the Lord says, "For I am the Lord who bringeth you out of the land of Egypt, to be your God. And you will be holy, for I am holy" (verse 45).

Indeed, this month of redemption from Egypt became "the beginning of months" (Exod. 12:2), the first month of the Jewish religious calendar, known now as Nisan. After the second destruction of Jerusalem (70 C.E.), the themes of deliverance and redemption permeated the feast. The prayer books call this festival "the time of deliverance." Midrash Rabbah on Exodus 15:12 says: "Another explanation of *this month shall be unto you.* R. Meir said: The redemption will be Mine and yours; as if to say: 'I will be redeemed with you,' as it says: *Whom Thou didst redeem to Thee out of Egypt, the nations and their gods* (2 Sam. 7:23)."

Redemption is symbolized throughout the Passover service. Since the ancient times of the temple, the Jews have drunk four cups of raisin wine at each Passover. The poor were required to pawn goods, even their clothes if necessary, in order to secure the wine. "Whosoever has not got wine transgresses a command of the rabbis," says the Talmud, "for they have said that there is to be no diminution from the four cups. And it is necessary to sell what he has in order to keep the command of the wise men. . . . Therefore let him sell what he has, and furnish the expense, until he procure wine or raisins." If so poor that he couldn't sell anything, then, according to the Talmud, he must secure money from a poverty fund set up specifically to provide wine for the Passover poor.

According to the Mishnah, the four cups of wine symbolize trust in God's fourfold promise of redemption found in Exodus 6:6, 7: "And I the Lord will *bring you* forth from under the burdens of Egypt, and I will *deliver you* from their bondage, and I will *redeem you* with an outstretched arm and with great judgments, and I will *take you* to me as a people."

Linked to this redemption is the Messianic hope, which burns more passionately during Passover than at any other season. A fifth goblet of wine, called Elijah's cup, is poured but not drunk at Passover. Elijah is the forerunner of the Messiah, and the Jews pray: "May God send the Messiah, heralded by the prophet Elijah, to vanquish all our enemies and set up his kingdom of peace." According to Jewish tradition, Elijah, who was taken to heaven in a flaming chariot, will appear before the coming of the Messiah. "Behold, I will send you Elijah the prophet before the coming of the great and dreadful day of the Lord: and he shall turn the heart of the fathers to the children, and the heart of the children to their fathers" (Mal. 4:5, 6). Midrashic tradition teaches that when the archangel Michael blows his trumpet, Elijah will appear with the Messiah, whom Elijah will present to the Jews. Elijah will then perform numerous miracles, including the destruction of Samael (Satan), and thus bring an end to all evil.

At the modern Seder, this Messianic hope is acted out by the children, one of whom opens the door to see whether Elijah has come. Just as the door opens, everyone usually exclaims: "Blessed is he who cometh in the name of the Lord!"

Numerous transformations of the Passover feast have occurred since that first Egyptian night on the fourteenth of Abib, when the Jews slaughtered the Paschal lamb. Though that first Passover was celebrated at home, Deuteronomy 16:6 hinted that they would one day sacrifice the Passover at "the place that the Lord your God chooses to place His name"—that is, the temple. For centuries, Passover was celebrated in Jerusalem, at the temple, the blood of the lamb sprinkled by priests on the altar of burnt offering. Since the destruction of the temple in 70 C.E., the Jews have kept Passover at home, the way they first did 3,000 years ago, the way they have been for the past 1,900.

Though the Samaritans in Israel slay a lamb on Passover, the modern Jew sacrifices no Passover animal. At his Seder, the sacrifice is symbolized by the roasted shankbone of a lamb, though in the ancient service, whether in Egypt or Canaan, the lamb and its blood formed the central part of the feast. At the first Passover, the Lord said: "And I will see the blood and pass over you" (Exod. 12:13). Says the Midrash (on Exod. 15:12): "Fix ye, therefore, this month for Me and for you, because I will see therein the blood of the Passover and will make atonement for you. . . . *your lamb shall be without blemish, a male of the first year* (Exod. 12:5). *A lamb*, because *God will provide Himself the Lamb*, etc., (Gen. 22:8); *without blemish*, symbolic of the Holy One, blessed be He."

Here, too, in the lamb without blemish (which the Midrash says is a symbol of "the Holy One"), the theme of redemption is explicit, for the blood of the Passover saved the Hebrews preparatory to their deliverance from Egypt. For centuries, animals were slain in the temple sacrificial service, their blood used to make atonement for the people's sin and, thus, "save" them. At Passover we see not only physical redemption from Egypt but spiritual redemption as well—for as in the daily services, the Passover blood makes atonement.

Passover, then, is our "season of redemption." It celebrates the deliverance of the sons of Israel from the "iron furnace" of Pharaoh as well as deliverance, or atonement, from sin. Yet these deliverances symbolize the promise of future redemption when our children will, in a sense, open the Passover door and Elijah will appear heralding the Messiah, whom the Lord had promised even before he took our fathers out of Egypt.

This article originally appeared in *Shabbat Shalom*, April-June 1988.

DEAD MEAT

This final section is composed of a variety of articles that didn't quite fit in the previous categories. I could have just as easily titled it, "Miscellaneous."

"Mind Over Matter? Never Mind!" was the first article I ever published in a denominational magazine, and the oldest one to appear in this book. The year was 1983, and I was only twenty-eight years old. All things considered, though I would have changed a bit here and there, I still agree with what I wrote. I don't know whether that means I haven't done much growing or that I was basically on target to begin with. Read it and let me know.

"Dead Meat" attempts, from a philosophical perspective, to show the futility of life without the Lord. "If there is no God, who offers us eternal life?" I wrote; "we're ultimately nothing but—dead meat." Crude, but it does get the point across, especially in context.

"The Unlikely Odyssey of Clifford Goldstein," published in *Signs of the Times*® (1988), tells of one late afternoon back in 1979, when I walked into my room in Gainesville, Florida, a secular, agnostic Jew and how, by midnight that same evening, I had a dramatic confrontation with Christ and became a born-again believer in Jesus Christ.

"Between the First and Last Tear" deals with what has been and always will be a major problem regarding faith: If there's a loving God in heaven, why are His creatures such wretches here on earth? The article argues that the book of Job gives answers but only if the story is taken literally. In other words, I claim that all attempts to turn it into nothing but an allegory destroy the gist of the book, which is really a behind-the-scenes look at the great controversy. To study Job as an allegory is, I wrote, the same as trying to analyze "a Renoir by studying only a black-and-white print."

Also included in this section are three articles from a series in *Signs of the Times*®

255

on the prophetic parables of Jesus. There's also a short piece from the *Review* (1989) called "Bones," which tells how after I became a believer in Christ I returned home wondering if any of my friends had become believers, too, only to find that a kid I knew had become a Christian, a homosexual we called Bones who later died of AIDS.

"Love Beyond Reason" attempts to show that, while reason and rational thought have a role in faith, if we limit what we believe to reason and logic alone, we could never be authentic New Testament Christians, and no one proves this point better than Jesus Himself.

CHAPTER FIFTY-ONE

Mind Over Matter? Never Mind!

We're in an era where absolutes are out and ambiguities in. Truth is all in your head—and reality, a subjective extension of the brain. One man's faith is another man's fairy tale, one man's beauty is another's beast, one's sinner is another's saint. For one human, A equals B, for another A does not equal B because—due to differences in heredity, circumstances, environment, providence, even chance—the synaptic connections of their brains are wired so individually that the same A and B that one perceives as equal, another sees as different, perhaps even opposite. Yet, according to contemporary philosophy—they are both right!

Existentialism, as well as its brother phenomenology, are both rebellious offspring of the twentieth century—"The Age of Anxiety." By the time the mustard gas mists of Verdun and the Marne cleared, the death clouds over Auschwitz and Dachau rose, and while Auschwitz still stank—Hiroshima and Nagasaki sizzled. Out of the rubble crawled some morally wounded men, men who stopped trying to put the pieces of the puzzle together. Instead they created their own puzzle, a jigsaw that enabled every individual to shape his own pieces, to place them together in his own individual way, and to come out with an individual picture with its own personal, individual meaning. Man became a minigod, able to create his own truth according to personal choices. Jean-Paul Sartre, the patron rabbi of post-Auschwitz existentialism, wrote that man even has "freedom to create meaning for his own life."

In science, this philosophy is reflected in erroneous interpretations of Einstein's theory of relativity. In modern literature, a story is no longer merely told; instead, varied subjective viewpoints of the same incidents are depicted, showing how differently people can perceive common occurrences—and this was probably no better exemplified than in William Faulkner's *The Sound and the Fury*. Marcel Duchamp, the undisputed master of existentialist expression in art, reveals the subjectivity of human existence with art so ambiguous the individual viewer can decide for himself exactly what he thinks it means. Indeed, this is the century of mind over matter.

Never mind! Modern relativism is a cop-out. Of course, on the level of human perception, no two people, not even Siamese twins, can perceive precisely the same way. But truth, even reality, is not boxed in by man's senses. Truth extends beyond an individual's eyes, ears, and nose. We are just a small part of reality, not the defining boundary. Truth defines us, not we truth.

One fact is certain: We do exist (squeeze yourself), and because we are here we had to come from somewhere, and to know from where, from whom, how and why—this is tantamount to knowing the absolute truth. Somewhere *out there*—and not inside our heads—an absolute truth exists because we absolutely exist.

Can we know this absolute truth? If we are the result of impersonal powers or if there is a supernatural creator who chooses to remain anonymous, then—no, we will never understand the purpose of our existence; and the meaning of all our toils, joys, trials, and sufferings will continue to be guessed at, mused about, philosophized upon, and mostly missed. But if there does exist a loving creator, a personal God who knows the thoughts, the pains, the needs of all His creatures, a God who personally rejoices in their joys and suffers in their sorrows, who is constantly striving to reveal Himself, His love, His character to all His creation, then—yes, we can know absolute truth.

This is the God of the Bible, and He claims to be the absolute: "He is God; that formed the earth and made it, He established it, He created it not a waste, He formed it to be inhabited; I am the Lord, and there is none else" (Isa. 45:18). He is a God of love: "Yea, I have loved thee with an everlasting love," (Jer. 31:3); a God who rejoices with His creatures: "The Lord thy God is in the midst of thee, a Mighty One who will save; He will rejoice over thee with joy. . . . He will joy over thee with singing" (Zeph. 3:17). He knows His creatures: "Before I formed thee in the belly I knew thee" (Jer. 1:5). And not only does He know us, He wants us to know Him, and by knowing and understanding Him, we learn about ourselves—and that is real truth: "But let Him that glorieth glory in this, that He understandeth, and knoweth me, that I am the Lord who exercises mercy, justice, and righteousness, in the earth" (Jer. 9:23).

For those who are open, there are a number of ways to show that the Scriptures are a revelation of truth. Archaeology, once thought to be the weapon to nullify Scripture, has instead validated it by repeatedly proving its historical accuracy—and while historical veracity is not proof of divine inspiration, it does silence the critics. In the Bible there is a unity of thought which is remarkable, considering the incredibly wide and varying circumstances under which it was written. Whether in the writing of Daniel, a captive child in Babylon, Moses, leader of the Exodus, or Amos, a shepherd—there is a unity and coherency of thought regarding the nature of God, man, evil, and redemption that could have been only divinely inspired.

Today, we can read prophecies written thousands of years ago and look back at history and see how they were fulfilled hundreds, thousands of years after they were first written—some even fulfilled in the past few centuries, some fulfilling now, some fulfilled on the exact dates predicted thousands of years in advance of the event! No man, no matter how gifted or foresighted, could have written these prophecies without divine aid. It is impossible.

While these factors can help convince us of truth, the most important way is to experience it ourselves. We do not create truth in our minds; indeed, Truth created our minds—yet in our mind is where we experience it.

The question is: How badly do you want to know truth? If you are not a true seeker but are looking for an explanation of life that will conform to your own personal ideas of morality, mercy, and justice—then all the miracles, proofs, prophecies, and experiences will not convince you. If, however, somewhere inside you is an insatiate desire, an indefatigable longing to know and experience and follow absolute truth, no matter what it is, no matter what it costs, no matter what you must suffer—then you will have it. This is not my promise but God's. "And ye shall seek me, and find me, when ye shall search for me with all your heart" (Jer. 29:13). There are lots of beliefs, philosophies, and religions—yet just one absolute. The God of the Bible claims to be this Absolute. And He is also calling you to seek Him, but it must be with *all your heart*. Truth will cost you everything. Are you willing to spend it?

This article originally appeared in *The New Israelite*, Fall 1983.

CHAPTER FIFTY-TWO

Dead Meat

Sitting next to my karate teacher in his souped-up blue Camaro, I questioned him about the large wooden cross dangling from a silver chain on the rearview mirror. "If I didn't have hope that there was another world beyond this one," he answered, "why should I go on living?"

Fueled with the foolish optimism of youth, when I knew I could karate-chop my way through anything, I thought his answer was the stupidest ever. Now, fifteen years of broken bones later, I realize that he had summarized the essence of the human predicament: If our earthly existence *is* it, why bother? If we end at death, why ever have been born to begin with?

If nothing's beyond the grave, what's before it? If there is no God who offers us eternal life, then we are nothing but blobs of flawed tissue that inevitably disintegrate into fumes and putrefied dust. All our lessons, trials, joys, and triumphs ultimately mean nothing because they all end up as nothing. If nothing exists for us beyond what we have here, then we ultimately have nothing; we ultimately *are* nothing.

"In some remote corner of the universe," wrote Friedrich Nietzsche, "effused into innumerable solar systems there was a star upon which clever animals invented cognition. It was the haughtiest, most mendacious moment in the history of the world, but only a moment. After Nature had taken breath awhile, the star congealed and the clever animals had to die. Someone might write a fable about this, and yet he would not have sufficiently illustrated how wretched, shadowy, transitory, purposeless, and fanciful the human intellect appears in nature. There were endless eternities during which this intellect did not exist, and when it has once more passed away, there will be nothing to show that it has existed."

We are Nietzsche's "clever animals," and we have no say over our creation or (except for suicide) our dissolution, while existence between creation and dissolution is often swept along by a raging tide beyond our control. "For though I can neither fully grasp my situation nor see through its origin," wrote philosopher Karl Jaspers, "the sense of it oppresses me with a vague fear. I can see the situation only as a motion that keeps transforming me along with itself, a motion that carries me from a darkness in which I did not exist to a darkness in which I shall not exist."

In a Woody Allen movie a mother takes to the doctor her twelve-year-old boy named Billy who refuses to study, go to school, or clean his room because he has read that in a few million years the sun is going to burn out and all life on earth will cease. "It's none of your business!" the hysterical mother repeats, while Billy explains that he doesn't see any reason to do anything if one day the sun is going to fizzle out and all life on earth will die. "But, Billy," the doctor answers, "it doesn't matter, because we will all be dead by then anyway."

That's part of the point, Doc. Billy's argument is flawless. Grasping the big picture, he logically responds to the dilemma of existential transience. Why struggle through school, college, work, family, sickness, and mortgages if sooner (at death) or later (when the sun burns out) it all comes to nothing? If life means nothing, why hassle with it at all? The only logical conclusion, after the step Billy has just taken, is to kill yourself.

Albert Camus grasped the situation, asserting that one truly important philosophical question existed, "and that," he wrote, "is suicide." Camus bluntly framed what he considered the fundamental question of philosophy: whether life, essentially meaningless, was worth living. In *The Myth of Sisyphus,* Camus asked how a life that is meaningless could be lived, or even if it should be. Camus opted against suicide, but considering the philosophical framework from which he drew conclusions, he never gave a convincing reason why. In modern society, people who attempt suicide are labeled sick, insane, and in need of help, but if there is no God who ultimately offers us an eternity of bliss, what enduring reason can society give to a person choosing death to put it off temporarily? Why prolong the agony when life ultimately means nothing anyway?

Many people would nevertheless argue that life is worth living. Yet if nothing exists for them beyond what they have now, if they disappear into the blackness out of which they appeared, what reason can they give?

The joy of raising a family? Please! Why produce what will ultimately be, after a spasm of existence, more dead meat? Why hurl innocent little people into the maelstrom in which most of humanity find themselves painfully strewn? Father a thousand generations, and sooner or later they and whatever great things they accomplished will vanish. If nothing else, time alone will grind them to dust. If we have no promise of eternal life to offer our children, then the best thing we can do for our offspring is to never have them.

But the trials of life make us better people. So what? If I am a better person today than yesterday, and will be even better tomorrow, where does it lead? I won't be a better person a mere 100 years from now. I won't even be a person 100 years from now. I will be brittle bones in a box, and eventually whatever good I have left behind me will disappear too. Being a better person is fine, but it doesn't give life meaning. Multiply zero by any number, no matter how large, and we still get zero.

Most people enjoy some bliss, some happiness, some moments when life seems to exude with purpose, greatness, and majesty. Jean-Paul Sartre, criticized for his gloomy existentialism, was confronted by someone who argued something like "What about the smile of a baby?" What about it? The smile is wonderful, the baby is wonderful, but ultimately the smile, the baby, and the joy end in nothingness, so what can life really mean? If the only meaning of life is joy of the moment, then hedonism is the highest purpose of human existence. People should live to satiate their lusts, appetites, and passions, and nothing else. The Greek philosopher Epicurus would be right when he declared pleasure "to be the beginning and end of the blessed life" or Ayn Rand when she asserted that "my happiness needs no higher aim to vindicate itself. My happiness is not the means to any end. It is the end. It is its own goal. It is its own purpose."

Even if one spends his life, not going to brothels or bars, but starting rescue missions, adopting orphans, helping lepers, ministering to AIDS victims—in the end the poor, orphans, lepers, and AIDS patients are gone and every cup of cool water, every tear wiped away, every warm meal, every hug, and every remembrance of them is lost forever amid the endless expanse of time and space.

At seventeen, I parked cars for patrons of the Pub Restaurant in the Newport Hotel on the corner of 163rd Street and Collins Avenue in Miami Beach. A few hundred yards up the block, a tour helicopter took off and landed in a small field. One bright summer afternoon the helicopter, while landing, chopped off a man's head and hurled it 100 feet. I walked over a few hours later, and nothing was changed from any other day. Tourists in flowered shirts and sunglasses strolled by chatting, kids in the amusement park next door shrieked gleefully, and on the street convertibles whizzed by, music trailing like banners. I couldn't even find blood. If it had been me instead of him, the scene would have been the same. I touched my neck and, realizing how little I mattered, I left.

Of course, I was just a seventeen-year-old who hadn't yet had a chance to impact society. Please! Even if I had changed or will change the world, what does it matter? King Solomon, one of the wealthiest and wisest men of antiquity, one whose writings impact even today, wrote: "I built for myself houses and planted for myself vineyards. I made for myself gardens and orchards, and planted in them trees of every fruit. . . . I gathered for myself also silver and gold, and the treasures of kings and provinces. . . . So I became great and I increased more than all who were before me in Jerusalem, and my wisdom remained with me. And all that my eyes asked I did not restrain from them, and I did not withhold from my heart all the pleasures that pleased it from all my labor. . . . And I looked at all my work that my hands had done and in all the toil that I toiled in and did, and behold, it was all vanity and painful of spirit and there is no profit under the sun" (Eccl. 2:4-11).*

The Hebrew word translated "vanity" here is *hebel,* which means literally "vapor" or "breath." Despite his orchards, vineyards, and all his accomplishments, Solomon regarded it all as vapor. To accomplish all that he did and then realize its meaninglessness would be "painful of spirit." No wonder he cried that "there is no profit under the sun."

Though Solomon believed in a reigning God who held man accountable for his deeds, even in a final judgment and in an afterlife, his works were *in and of themselves* of no lasting value, even though they have endured. I'm using them now. They have impacted unlike few writings ever have. But unless there is a God who offers us the hope of eternal life, these words and their readers face oblivion. No matter how many millions read them for how many generations, no matter how much good they do, in contrast to the infinity and eternity in which they fleetingly exist, they, like us, are vapor—even less.

How did we get in such a predicament?

It's easy. We are beings who in every cell cry for meaning, permanence, and purpose, and yet the only way to attain these is from God, who alone can give us eternal life because He alone possesses it. Yet modern man has consigned God to the ideological junk heap, lodged somewhere between spontaneous generation and Communism. In evolving beyond the "superstitions" of our fathers, we have abandoned the meaning, permanence, and purpose that our natures require, leaving ourselves vulnerable to the traumatic realization of our own transience amid eternity.

Friedrich Nietzsche wrote about a madman "who on a bright morning lighted a lantern and ran to the marketplace calling out unceasingly: 'I seek God!' " Atheists standing around mocked him. "Is He lost? Has He strayed away like a child?" Others said, "Has He taken a sea voyage? Has He emigrated?"

The insane man then jumped into their midst and cried, "I mean to tell you! *We have killed Him*— you and I! We are all His murderers! But how have we done it? How were we able to drink up the sea? Who gave us the sponge to wipe away the whole horizon? What did we do when we loosened this earth from its sun? Whither does it now move? Whither do we move? Away from all suns? Do we not dash unceasingly? Backwards, sideways, forwards, in all directions? Is there still an above and below? Do we not stray, as through infinite nothingness? Does not empty space breathe upon us? Has it not become colder? Does not night come on continually, darker and darker? Do we not hear the noise of the gravediggers who are burying God? . . . God is dead! God remains dead! And we have killed Him! How shall we console ourselves?"

Nietzsche's famous "God is dead" dictum expressed his belief that because the basis of faith was gone, modern man needed to replace it with something else, and those who could create new values to substitute for the transcendent ones who died with God were the *Ubermensch,* a new humanity that could fill the vacuum left by God's demise. Without God, as the madman shouted, "Do we not dash unceasingly?" Man was left with nothing transcendent to fall back on, nothing out of himself to rely on, and therefore he must take upon himself the task of self-realization and self-affirmation. He must, out of sheer desperation if nothing else, become his own god.

In the Genesis account, when the serpent promised Eve that if she ate from the forbidden fruit she would be like God (Gen. 3:5), she gobbled it up. Jean-Paul Sartre, millennia later, wrote that man's prime desire was to be God. Now, through the chimerical delusions of modern philosophy, humanity hopes to fulfill its archetypal Edenic dream.

We laugh at the ignorant ancients who, under the Ptolemaic system, believed that the sun, moon, planets, and stars revolved around the earth, the apex of the universe. Yet modern man has gone a step farther. In a deviant solipsism, man has made himself the center of the universe, with all truth, absolutes, and values centering on himself. The starting point of all things, the absolute from which all values are determined, is not a Creator, but man himself. Humans believe that they have evicted God from His throne, having traded Omnipotent omniscience for transient fearful, and vacillating animals instead. We have become heaven's squatters.

Sartre's famous "Existentialism Is Humanism" essay summarized this thought in three words: "Existence precedes essence." Using the analogy of the manufacture of a book or a paper knife, Sartre explained that prior to the existence of this object, the artisan already had a conception of it. Its essence existed prior to its production. "Let us say, then, of the paper knife that its essence—that is to say, the sum of the formulae and the qualities which made its production and its definition possible—precedes its existence." Before one makes an object, the essence of that object previously exists in one's head. Hence, its essence has preceded its existence.

But man, Sartre wrote, is a being "whose existence comes before its essence, a being which exists before it can be defined by any conception of it."

Sartre asked: "What do we mean when we say that existence precedes essence? We mean that man first of all exists, encounters himself, surges up in the world—and defines himself afterwards. If man as the existentialist sees him is not definable, it is because, to begin with, he is nothing. He will not be anything until later, and then he will be what he makes of himself. Thus, there is no human nature, because there is no God to have a conception of it. Man simply is."

Though not all modern thought can be defined as strictly existentialism, the existentialist premise about man as the starting point had been previously expounded on by Marx, Heidegger, and Nietzsche. This whole train of philosophy has, especially in the case of Marxism, been translated into political and social reality. In more popular terms, this philosophy can be labeled secular humanism, a laymen's phrase for a philosophy that, having no transcendent God, had to find something else to believe in. Man, apparently, needs something to put his faith in, something to give him a perspective on existence, and with God out of the picture, where else can he turn but to himself and his own potential?

Buried deep in the loins of those who worshiped the hills, trees, and fish, we began surfacing in those who worshiped a transcendent God, but by the time we burst out we rejected both, worshiping ourselves instead of what was either around us in nature or beyond us in heaven. Considering that we are basically composed of what hills, trees, and fish are too, we're not much better than the nature worshipers from whom we sprang. Indeed, with each man as his own god, we're not only idolaters but polytheists as well.

"My faith," wrote Julian Huxley, "is in the possibilities of man." Ayn Rand said, "And now I see the face of god, and I raise this god over the earth, this god whom men have sought since men came into being, this god who will grant them joy and peace and pride. This god, this one word: I." For Francis Ponge, "Man is the future of man." Unlike modern nihilists, Sartre believed absolute truth did exist: "There must be an absolute truth, and there is such a truth, which is simple, easily attainable, and within the reach of everybody; it consists in one's immediate sense of one's self."

This extreme subjectivism has consequences. Sartre wrote that the existentialist finds it "extremely embarrassing" that God does not exist, because "there disappears with Him all possibility of finding values in an intelligent universe." Thus he says that man is condemned to be free, condemned because he is thrown into a world he did not create and is thus burdened with the responsibility of making his own choices.

True, as the secular humanist or existentialist claims, we have the freedom to make choices, and those choices involve a responsibility that ultimately rests upon ourselves, no one else. We do become, as Sartre said, what we make of ourselves, but only to a degree. Because we originally didn't make ourselves, we are limited to what we can become, and we can never in and of ourselves become eternal—and that's the rub.

Clay can become a pot, an earring, even a house, but never a word processor, an African violet, or a waterfall. Whatever grand designs modern philosophy promises about the possibilities of man, we can in and of ourselves no more become eternal than clay can become a waterfall. Whatever we make of ourselves, we have no hope of being freed from what Freud called "a sense of man's insignificance and impotence in the face of the universe," because we ultimately perish. Though we fancy ourselves as gods, we can never be God, because God is eternal and we are transient, and so are all our dreams, projects, and accomplishments. Our evanescence is the ultimate catch, the one irrevocable clause in a contract that voids us and everything we do, a clause not written in fine print but embossed across every page of our existence.

"Man," Sartre wrote, "is nothing else but that which he makes of himself." Yet, ultimately, whatever he makes of himself comes to nothing, which is why he in and of himself is meaningless; and for a being who cries out for meaning, that realization is unbearable. No wonder the language of modern philosophy is despair, angst, nausea, nothingness, dread, meaninglessness, fear, anxiety, absurdity, even suicide.

Three words of Sartre's, "Existence precedes essence," summarize modern existentialism; three other of his words, "Man simply is," reveals its idiocy. Man simply *isn't* anything. There's nothing simple about man. Sartre admits that a paper knife or a book must have had an essence before it existed, yet a human being (in which a simple epidermal cell—no, in which a single membrane in an epidermal cell—is infinitely more complex, more designed, and more functional than a paper knife or a book) just simply is, without any previous essence that defined him? Man no more just simply is than Brahms's "The Alsto Rhapsody" just simply is. Sartre took man as the starting point, an axiom, when in reality he's the conclusion, more complex, thought out, and planned than the most profound geometric formula.

Determining man's purpose by starting with his existence and then moving forward, rather than first looking backward to man's origin and then determining his purpose, is like handing a computer to a native from Borneo who has never left the jungle. He might use the screen as a mirror, and he might even turn the computer on and warm himself by it at night, but one thing for sure, the machine will never fulfill the purpose for which it was intended, anymore than without knowing our origin can we fulfill ours. We are not the starting point; we are the sentient, cognitive product of a complex process in which we had no part, and until we understand how that process began, and why, we can no more understand our purpose as that product than the native can the computer. No wonder modern philosophy is so empty, futile, ridiculous. It doesn't fit reality. It's like giving that native, along with the computer, instructions—not on how to use the computer, but on how to tune an Edsel.

The answer, then, has to be found outside ourselves, because we didn't create ourselves, any more than Cezanne's *Still Life With Cupid* created itself. Aspects of its meaning can be gleaned from the painting, but the real motive, purpose, and origin behind it were within Cezanne alone, its creator. To a degree we can measure ourselves by ourselves, but until we understand the purpose of our creation, we shall never fulfill our potential, in the same way that our native Bornean who, not knowing the painting's real purpose, would use *Still Life With Cupid* for kindling. The painting wouldn't fulfill its potential. It would end up as ashes, we as fumes and putrefied dust.

Today those who laugh at the ignorant ancients' belief that life spawned from inorganic matter— that a pile of dirty rags, for instance, could spontaneously generate maggots or mice—are the same ones who accept evolution. Time, they say, is the crucial factor. Yet time will no more turn a mass of molten rock into Euripides or Joe Montana than it will a pile of rags into maggots. Francis Crick (of Crick and Watson fame), rejecting evolution as a statistical impossibility, wrote that the chances of life having formed by accident are the same as the chance of a "billion monkeys, on a billion typewriters, ever typing correctly even one sonnet of Shakespeare during the present lifetime of the universe." A more appropriate analogy would be the impossibility of a billion monkeys on a billion typewriters ever producing a ham and Swiss on rye, with lettuce, tomato, and Dijon—to go.

Human life is too complex, grand, and well designed to be merely accidental, in the same way that *Still Life With Cupid is* too complex, grand, and designed to be accidental. "The clock," as Voltaire admitted, "had to have a clockmaker." By our existence alone, we point to the existence of a Power who preceded us, who conceived our essence before us, and who created us. And until we understand who that Power is and why He created us, we will never know or fulfill the purpose of our lives. We will simply be like that native Bornean playing with his mirror and heater.

No wonder modern philosophy has written us off as absurd. Our savants, with or without the evolutionary premise but certainly without God, promise us nothing but fumes and putrefied dust, which is why it's the philosophy, not life, that is absurd. Too much has gone into us, too much that is not absurd, and we are too wonderfully made to dismiss ourselves as the products of some sort of cosmic lottery that has left us stranded here on a molten mass amid a cold, dead universe. The incredible complexity of life implies that we were meant to be more than just the spasm we are. Our essence had to have been conceived in the mind of a Creator, and as long as we ignore Him, premising our meaning and purpose upon ourselves only, we'll face nothing but the dark prospect of our own dissolution.

Man is not the starting point; the God who created him is. Thus God is man's only hope, and far from being a faint one, He is the only logical, sensible one, the only one with any possibility of giving life meaning, because God is the only one who can make us eternal. The statement "I just don't have faith" is nonsense. Atheists have faith that we are here only by chance, a long shot at best. The atheist is the true believer, reaching out and accepting by blind faith the statistical impossibility of his existence being by chance alone, while the one who at least acknowledges a Creator is exercising as much common rationality as he is faith.

And until we seek that Creator and the eternal life He offers, we will either subsist with no hope or plod along numbed by the empty promises that false faiths dangle before those so desperate that they cling to anything that might free them from their own mortality.

Imagine being diagnosed as having a disease that unless treated will inevitably kill you. You're not going to just press on as if nothing were wrong but will expend every energy to find a solution. As you search, people will place various prospects before you, each one claiming his or her cure is the only true one. Some will give you advice opposed, even opposite, to another; some will say the disease won't kill you, that you really are fine and should just go on living; others will advise you merely to do the best you can, that nothing can be done, that there is no hope.

That's our situation. Birth is the first step toward death. Thus, it becomes the prime imperative of every person to seek out with all possible energy eternal life. Everything else becomes secondary, essentially meaningless in the face of oblivion. If there is a God who will teach you your origin, who will give you the assurance of eternal life and the knowledge that you have it—how can any rational, sane person do anything other than, with the same fervency a dying person would a cure, seek that God and the eternal life He offers?

If God doesn't offer us eternal life, if this existence is it—then we're better off getting old, achy, shriveling up, and popping pipes before sputtering out into nothingness, because what kind of God would ingrain such a fervent desire for eternity within us and then deny it to us? The sooner we dissolve, the better. However, perhaps we so fervently desire eternity, perhaps it is so much a part of our basic nature, because we were originally created to have it, in the same way that we crave water because it was part of our original nature to drink it, and thus by seeking eternity we are reaching back to our primal roots, to the essence of our being.

If this existence, wretched and miserable, is all life offers, then Camus is right: The fundamental question of philosophy is suicide. But if God offers us eternal life, and He must—because otherwise our lives are meaningless and there's too much proving that they can't be—then the fundamental question of philosophy is really theological: Who is this God, and what must I do to obtain the eternal life He gives?

Everything else isn't commentary. Everything else, as my karate teacher knew but didn't express it, is *hebel.*

---

*Author's translation. This article originally appeared in *Shabbat Shalom*, April-June 1992.

CHAPTER FIFTY-THREE

The Unlikely Odyssey of Clifford Goldstein

If you shook my family tree—pens, pencils, typewriters, and books would clatter to the ground, followed by reams of fluttering manuscripts, magazines, and newspapers. I have generations of writers in my blood, and whatever inspired them pulses through me too.

By the time I learned to read I wanted to write, and while still a teenager I had been published. In cafes in Iceland, on beaches in Portugal, in the hills of Galilee, I wrote—frantically, incessantly, seriously.

As a senior in college, I started a novel that took me across the Atlantic, to two continents, and then to the States again. The book became an obsession; I was driven by an inexplicable passion, a personal version of whatever madness drives men to sell their souls carving statues out of stone or brushing colors across canvas.

So while my friends were becoming doctors or making big money on Wall Street or selling IBM computers, I was peddling blue and red and purple snow cones to schoolchildren who would storm my white truck and plop their dimes and quarters before me three days a week. Not exactly Wall Street, but it kept food in my stomach. All I needed was food and a place to write—at that time an $80-per-month hovel in a Gainesville, Florida, ghetto.

Subsisting on cherry snow cones that turned my teeth red, I kept writing, furiously writing, pouring all my soul into every sentence, paragraph, and page. The novel was the center of my life. Everything else was peripheral.

Yet one night, after working on the book for two years, I sat down to write, and before I typed the first letter, the Holy Spirit came to me and said: *Cliff, you have been playing with Me long enough. If you want Me tonight, burn the book!*

I jumped up from my seat. "Please, God," I answered, "let me finish the book, and then I will give my life to You."

If you want Me tonight, burn the book.
"Please, I will write it all to Your glory, but let me keep it."
If you want Me, burn the book.
"Please, let me just put it away for a while."
Burn the book!

I fled outside. It was almost dusk, a bluish light had settled over the street, and somewhere a distant dog's lonely bark chopped into the stillness. I walked fast.

This sudden confrontation with the Holy Spirit wasn't as unexpected as it might seem. For the past months, I had been a believer in Jesus—which, considering my background, was a miracle itself. Raised in a non-religious Jewish home, I grew up on Miami Beach and went to a high school where everyone was either Jewish or stoned, or both, and where I learned nothing about religion, either my own or anyone else's. Indeed, the only time I ever spoke the name of Jesus was as a curse.

I hadn't, however, been neutral toward Christianity. I burned with bitterness because of persecution done to the Jews in the name of Christ. From the Crusades to the Inquisition to pogroms in Russia, even to the restricted housing in America (I lived two blocks from a country club that didn't allow the "Hebrew" race privileges), anti-Semitism seemed an integral part of the "good news."

At college I vented my anger at a hellfire-and-brimstone preacher who stood on the campus lawn and endlessly screamed about a loving God who was going to burn us all in a lake of fire for eternity. Crowds would form around us as I stood at his heels and cursed him, God, and the Bible. At times I would spit on him as he damned my soul to hell. These theological debates were repeated year after year until eventually my friends nicknamed me *Heckle.*

Our public "discussions" ended in 1978, when I graduated from college and went overseas. I planned to live in Europe and write there, but I wound up on a kibbutz in Israel. "At least here," I thought, "there will be no Christians to harass me." Yet at the close of my first week there, a group of devout Christians from America came to live on the kibbutz.

I started in on them immediately (I had my whole repertoire of jokes and insults which I had used on the preacher), and yet no matter what abuse and blasphemy came out of my loud, dirty mouth, these people showed me continual kindness and love. I had arguments against all doctrines and beliefs, but I had no argument against kindness and love.

Indeed, as I saw the love of God reflected in their characters, my prejudices crumbled. I knew that I couldn't judge all Christianity because of what some people had done in its name, not when there were Christians in the world like these. Not only did my animosity cease but I began to believe that what they said about God might really be true. Later, after some intense experiences, I came to believe that Jesus Christ died for my sins. Two days before I returned to America, these Christians baptized me in the Jordan River.

Yet little had changed. Sure, I now had a Bible; I even read it on occasion. I muttered a prayer here and there and drew some comfort from the little faith I had. Yet I was no more born again than a corpse nor had I a semblance of a relationship with Jesus.

The problem, I knew, was the book I was writing.

Not the book itself but my attitude toward it. The novel wasn't inherently evil or even anti-Christian. But it was my god, and the same Lord who 3,000 years ago told the Jews at Mount Sinai, "Ye shall have no other gods before me," was now telling me the same thing. For months the Holy Spirit had been quietly convicting me that my commitment to Christ must be total, absolute, and that my fervent, unwavering devotion toward the book needed to be directed toward God alone. At last, that night in Florida, the Spirit wasn't so quiet.

"Whoever is not willing to give up mother, father, sister, or brother for me," Jesus had said, "is not worthy of me." I was willing to give up mother and father and sister and brother for Jesus—but not the book. I had staked everything, my whole future, on this novel. If I burned it, I would have nothing but ashes on the floor of a ramshackle room which was all I could afford because I didn't want a normal job; I wanted to write instead.

Writing fiction was all that I had been trained for, all that I knew, all that I really cared about. What would my family say? What would my friends, the doctors, the Wall Street brokers—say? I was going to set the world on fire with that book, and now God was asking me to set the book on fire instead?

It was dark now, the dusk pushed aside by the shadows of night, and in the distance a police siren scratched the sky. No matter how far I walked, the conviction that had overwhelmed me in the room followed: If I was going to get serious with God, the book had to go.

I had always been a seeker. I had traveled the world, seeking. I had read philosophy, Eastern religions, Karl Marx, and at times my heart raged with the desire to know where we came from and what it all meant. If God existed, I wanted to know. "Show Your face," I once challenged God in a poem, "if You have one, if You dare."

He did, and that night He did so again, and though I could have rejected Him and gone back to my room and pounded keys as if nothing happened, I didn't. Instead, I walked the streets.

"What shall a man give in exchange for his soul?" Jesus had asked 1,900 years ago. He now asked the question that night to me. And what was I to answer? A manuscript that I might never publish? Or if I did, a book that might sell only a few thousand copies? Or even if it sold a few million, was it worth my own soul? All my life, every moment, I wanted to know truth, and now the moment of truth had come. Was I going to let it slip away?

"OK, God." I said, stopping underneath the cold, dull light of a streetlamp. "I want You; I want truth, more than I want the book. If You want it burned, You'll have to do it yourself."

Suddenly, the pressure lifted. The moment I made that decision, it was as if a pair of giant, invisible hands released me. The turmoil ceased, instantly. The fears, the qualms, the worries about what would happen if I burned the book stopped. I teetered on the edge of a new realm of existence; a surge of excitement rushed through me.

I disappeared into the darkness. When I had asked God to burn the book, I somehow expected a bolt of lightning to crash through my window and vaporize it. But I knew at once to expect no fire from the sky. Five minutes before, if someone had threatened to tear a page of the manuscript, it would have cost him blood. Now I was going to burn it myself, and without a qualm!

I put the key in the door and flipped the switch. The room exploded with light. There, on my desk, a blank sheet curled over the top. I tore it out, crumbled it, and threw it away. Piled by the typewriter was the manuscript, inches thick. I picked it up, turned my chair around, and sat. At my feet sat an electric hot plate, its burners black and cold, like a pair of coiled snakes. I hesitated, ran my fingers along the edges of the pages, then set them on the left burner and turned the switch.

For two minutes nothing happened. Then a thin stream of smoke rolled around the side of the manuscript. I never saw flames. The book just smouldered, each sheet crumbling into ashes onto the floor while smoke surged into my face. As the ashes dropped, I swept them out the door.

In an hour all that remained of two years' work lay scattered on my front porch—smouldering, like war ruins. The battle was over. I had surrendered, unconditionally. And though aware that my life had taken its most radical, dramatic turn and realizing that nothing would ever again be the same for me and that I might never write, I went to bed and lay there quietly, the smoke lingering like a divine presence.

This article originally appeared in the *Signs of the Times,*® September 1988.

CHAPTER FIFTY-FOUR

Our Genesis Roots

From reed huts baking in the mud of Mesopotamia to skyscrapers scraping the sky over Manhattan—mankind has pondered its roots.

The Babylonians believed that the god Marduk split the goddess Tiamat in two like a shellfish, using one part of her body to form the earth and the other part heaven. Then man came about when another god, Ea, mingled the blood of a severed sea monster with dust.

The Egyptians believed that the universe resulted when a giant cosmic egg exploded. A Norse myth taught that the cosmos came from the dismembered body of the great Ymir.

Modern man, of course, rejects myths about eggs, gods, and severed sea monsters. For him, humanity is rooted in chance, like a throw of dice. Modern man believes that billions of years ago a huge explosion created the stars and planets and that over endless eons primitive life happened to form, eventually evolving into mankind.

Seventh-day Adventists reject the evolutionists' cosmic dice, as well as myths about exploding eggs and severed sea monsters. For them, ten simple words recount the creation: "In the beginning God created the heaven and the earth" (Gen. 1:1).

The doctrine of divine creation is the warp and woof of Adventist theology. Creation tells us who we are, how we got here (and why), and where we are ultimately going. It reveals who God is and why—even how—we should worship Him. And, most important, understanding Creation helps us understand Jesus Christ and the Cross at Calvary.

Indeed, for Seventh-day Adventists, Creation is more than a matter of roots: it is *the* root, the basis of our faith—just as it was for ancient Israel. The nations alongside Israel, such as Assyria, Babylon, and Egypt, worshiped manmade images that they praised as gods. The Hebrews, however, had been forbidden to make or worship idols. The reason? Because only the Lord, the God of Creation, the One who made everything, deserved their worship. As their prophets put it: "Great is the Lord, and greatly to be praised: he also is to be feared above all gods. For all the gods of the people are idols: but the Lord made the heavens" (l Chron. 16:25, 26). "Know ye that the Lord he is God: it is he that hath made us, and not we ourselves" (Ps. 100:3).

Adventists, like ancient Israel, worship this same Lord—and for the same reasons: because He is the Creator, the One who put breath into our lungs, rhythm into our hearts, and light into our eyes. The concept of God as Creator permeates Scripture. The first verse of the Bible is about Creation, and the first chapter is devoted to it alone. Repeatedly Israel's prophets called the people to worship God because He is the Creator: "The Lord is a great God. . . . The sea is his, and he made it: and his hands formed the dry land. O come, let us worship and bow down: let us kneel before the Lord our maker. For he is our God" (Ps. 95:3-7). And at the end time, just before the second coming of Jesus, an angel calls mankind (as men have been called from the beginning) to worship the Creator: "Fear God, and give glory to him; for the hour of his judgment is come: and worship him that made heaven, and earth, and the sea, and the fountains of waters" (Rev. 14:7).

So crucial is the theme of God as Creator that we have been given a weekly reminder—a twenty-four-hour block of time pointing us back to our origins. To find our roots we just need to "Remember the sabbath day, to keep it holy. Six days shalt thou labour, and do all thy work: but the seventh day is the sabbath of the Lord. . . : for in six days the Lord made heaven and earth, the sea, and all that in them is, and rested the seventh day: wherefore the Lord blessed the sabbath day, and hallowed it" (Exod. 20:8-11).

By teaching us where we have come from, Creation also teaches us who we are. Rather than tracing our roots to a primeval pit of ooze from which our first parent(s) crawled in the image of a crude cell, Creation traces our roots directly to God Himself, who made us in His own image. We are the offspring of God Himself, the Bible tells us, the sons and daughters of Adam, who was himself "a son of God."

God spoke the earth into existence, but He created man differently; He formed man out of "the dust of the ground." And then, in an act of unique intimacy, God "breathed into his nostrils the breath of life; and man became a living soul" (Gen. 2:7). We are the children of a miracle. We stand at the center of a deliberate act of creation. Our existence, our being, comes not from chance, not from some cosmic sweepstakes that fortunately (or unfortunately) we happened to win. If created by chance, our lives have no meaning because then any meaning we might conceive for ourselves would simply be the result of chance as well. But the truth is that we were planned and created for a purpose.

And what is this purpose? According to Isaiah 43:7, God created us to bring glory to the Creator. In many respects, the attributes with which God originally endowed us were similar to those He Himself possessed. His plan was that as these attributes matured more and more into the image of the Creator, He would be glorified. Man stood as the crowning act of an already perfect creation. "God saw every thing that he had made, and, behold, it was very good" (Gen. 1:31).

Unfortunately, sin entered. The serpent told Eve that if she ate of the forbidden tree, she would be like God Himself (see Gen. 3:5) when in reality she was already created in God's image! After she and Adam ate from the tree, they became *less* like God, not more. The image of their Maker became defaced—which was why Jesus Christ came, to restore His own image, the image of the Creator, in us.

For the Scriptures are clear: Jesus Christ, the One who redeemed us is also the One who created us. Referring to the Genesis Creation account, John wrote: "In the beginning was the Word, and the Word was with God, and the Word was God. . . . All things were made by him; and without him was not any thing made." "The Word was made flesh, and dwelt among us" (John 1:1-3, 14). Paul explicitly names Jesus as Creator: "By him were all things created, that are in heaven, and that are in earth, visible and invisible, whether they be thrones, or dominions, or principalities, or powers: all things were created by him, and for him" (Col. 1:16).

Although the Bible says that Jesus created the universe, it teaches also that He became a helpless infant in the world He had made! Jesus created the fruit, the vegetables, the grains, the legumes—all that we savor and consume—yet He "fasted forty days and forty nights" (Matt. 4:2). He made the wood and the stone with which we build our homes, yet He had "no where to lay his head" (Luke 9:58). He sustained innumerable galaxies, yet He carried upon His bloody back the cross on which He was to die (see John 19:17). And finally, though He gave man life, He gave up His own life for man. Indeed, only by seeing Jesus as God, as the Creator, can we appreciate the sacrifice He made in becoming "flesh," and then dying in that flesh.

Yet never, even in the flesh, did Christ cease His creative power. Nothing, either in earth or heaven, operates without Him. Christ sustains it all, "upholding all things by the word of his power" (Heb. 1:3). Every breath, every heartbeat, every blink of our eyes comes from Jesus. "In him we live, and move, and have our being" (Acts 17:28).

While upon earth, Jesus used the same creative power that had brought life to Adam to heal and minister to those suffering from sin. Today, He employs that same creative power to restore and re-create us in His image.

The gospel of Jesus, though founded on forgiveness, includes more than forgiveness. Jesus wants not only to forgive our sins; He also wants to re-create us, to restore us in His image, so that we don't have to continue in our sins. Because Jesus is God, He has the right to forgive our sins. But because He is the Creator, He has the power to turn us from them. "Create in me a clean heart, O God," says Psalm 5 1:10. Literally, it reads, "Create *for* me a clean heart, O God." Through His creative power, God can create clean hearts for us. He can change us, remold our thinking, and create in us new wants, desires, and goals that are in harmony with His own desires and goals for us. God, who created galaxies that He hurled spinning across the cosmos in pinwheels of fire and light, uses that same creative power to re-create even the most degraded sinner into His own image. We belong to Christ—first by creation, then by redemption.

And God's creative power will not end with what He does in us now. With the same creative power He used to ignite the stars, Jesus will at the second coming give us new bodies that will never wrinkle, die, or rot. "Behold, I shew you a mystery; . . . we shall all be changed, in a moment in the twinkling of an eye. . . . This corruptible must put on incorruption, and this mortal must put on immortality" (1 Cor. 15:51-53).

Creation, clearly, serves as a fundamental Christian doctrine. It digs up our roots, explains how we can grow spiritually, and reveals what the ultimate harvest will be.

The Babylonians had their Marduk, the Egyptians their cosmic eggs, the Assyrians their gods of wood and stone. Modern men and women have their evolutionary theories. Christians have Jesus, whom they worship not only as Saviour of the world but as its Creator too. "To whom then will ye liken me, or shall I be equal? saith the Holy One. Lift up your eyes on high, and behold who hath created these things" (Isa. 40:25, 26).

This article originally appeared in *Signs of the Times,*® August 1988.

CHAPTER FIFTY-FIVE

The Fruit Stand

I love a fruit stand. The shapes, the colors splatter across my eyes, the smells curl up my nose, and my mouth secretes imaginary tastes.

Next time you eat an apple, red, yellow, or green, think about the shape, the color, the smell, and the taste oozing with nutrients and minerals—the stuff men are made of. To eat calcium, potassium, chlorine, iron, copper, and zinc, we don't chew, lick, or suck them raw and grainy out of the ground; instead we crunch into an apple, burst a grape in our mouth, or mash a banana with our teeth.

We learn about creators by their creations. Bosch's painting *The Garden of Earthly Delights* crawls with grotesque fantasies, degrading sensuality, monsters, demons, and violence, which reveals the evil in his heart. William Faulkner paraded so many murderers, bigots, perverts, thieves, adulterers, rapists, necrophiliacs, and arsonists across the pages of his novels, they must have been permanent residents of his mind. Goya's *Black Paintings*, mythological scenes of savagery and violence, show his gloomy, twisted soul. Albert Camus's books display the despair, pessimism, and hopelessness that tormented him. Sylvia Plath's poetry cried out with the pain that pushed her head into the oven where she gassed herself. Be glad that the mind that imagined and made the strawberry, not the *Black Paintings*, is the mind that imagined and made man too.

Yet man has the violence, suffering, hate, tragedy, perversions, hunger, and anger that these artists have depicted.

But these aberrations are not God's. He made marriage and sex, and men become adulterers and pornographers. He stocked the earth with material blessings, and men become selfish. He created races and weaved fire, and men burn crosses. He gave us words, and we lie and curse; He gave us intelligence, and we are proud; He breathed into us life, and we kill. He gave us freedom, and we have stitched the

277

planet in barbed wire. He gave us music, and men are punk rockers. He gave us grapes, and men become drunks.

And these are the reasons why war, disease, violence, hatred, suffering, alienation, death, and poverty scar the world. This is not God's doing; instead, the vines that wrap the earth with grapes and watermelons, and the trees that cover the earth with tangerines, lemons, cherries, and bananas, are God's doing—His thoughts, ideas, and words made real, tangibles that we can sink our teeth into. And if there is a blotch on the banana, remember that God made the banana first—the blotch came after.

There's more than fruit in the fruit stand. There's hope. When I look at peaches, pears, plums, I know that God must exist. Cranberries, cherries, and pineapples are unmistakable evidence that God cares. Mangoes, bananas, and strawberries show that, despite despair, we can trust God. The Bible says that God loves us, and raspberries, blackberries, avocados make it easier to believe. In the fruit stand I can feel God smiling down upon me and hear Him from heaven, saying, "See, I really do love you. Just trust Me."

That's why I love a fruit stand. An apricot might not be the answer to my problems, but it shows me that God is.

I don't have the faith to believe that chance put a peach tree in the pit, put the pit in the peach, and put the peach on a tree, any more than I believe that evolution made watermelon melt in my mouth. There's a story about a man who mocked God because acorns sat atop tall trees while watermelon crushed thin vines into the ground. If God was so smart, why didn't He place the acorn on the vine and the watermelon atop the tree? he chided—until one day an acorn fell on his head. A rabbi once wrote that the heathen, who have never known about the true God or the Holy Scriptures, can learn enough about God through nature that on judgment day they will be without excuse.

Next time you enter a fruit stand, pick up an orange. No earthly parents could have imagined anything so perfect for their children, and they grow on trees, millions upon millions, juicy, tasty, saturated with the elements of life. Imagine if, instead of squashing an orange in your mouth, the only way to get your vitamin C was to eat tablets or get an injection. Grab a pomegranate, a melon, a pear—and open your eyes! Forget your own ideas, your preconceived opinions, prejudices, and worldly philosophies and get back to basics. Whoever made the melon had to be good!

Raspberries, boysenberries, guava, pomegranates (how could anyone look at these and not see the love of God?), passion fruit, papaya, grapes, limes, cantaloupe, nectarines (it's like the Garden of Eden, almost), pineapple, cranberries, blueberries . . .

And we haven't even got to the veggies!

This article originally appeared in *Liberty*, January/February 1985.

CHAPTER FIFTY-SIX

Between the First and Last Tear

When God created man, He gave him tears, for He knew what was coming. Man is wired for suffering. Nerves through his body signal pain. And as long as man has hurt, he has asked why. And for thousands of years he has studied the book of Job for answers—usually without finding them.

Why? Because Job has been psychoanalyzed, criticized, assayed, diagnosed, analogized, and explicated. He has been labeled paranoid, neurotic, psychotic, melancholic, even syphilitic. Prosodists have metered the book's rhythm, linguists have studied its verbs, Jungians have researched its symbols, poets have admired its images, philosophers have studied its meanings, and theologians have debated its authorship. Some interpret Job as an allegory, a parable, a poeticized fantasy or fiction, an interpretation akin to analyzing a Renoir by studying only a black-and-white print. Others scrutinize every letter, image, syllable, which is like studying the Renoir through a microscope. In short, man has done everything but take the book literally—the only way it works!

Job must be taken literally or not at all. Job, literally, goes behind things seen to things unseen, to the root of all sorrow; interpreted any other way, the book barely scratches the surface. Only a literal interpretation gives a complete picture. All others show just shades of gray or meaningless streaks of color.

To accept Job literally means to accept the existence of God, and of the supernatural. It means to accept that we are not alone in the creation but that certain more powerful intelligences also exist, and it means accepting that it is these intelligences, not God, who have caused the earth to cringe with pain. To accept Job is to accept that man, no matter how fervently and eloquently he proclaims independence, is not the sole master of his life. It means accepting that our lives and words have universal and eternal consequences and that our existence, our sufferings, our joys have more meaning, more pertinence, and more importance than imaginable. And finally, to accept Job is to accept that God will ultimately make good for all that we have suffered and that He will replace all tears and pain with laughter and joy forever.

And what is hard to accept? From the billions of galaxies to the single atom, and from all things in between, the existence of the Creator is revealed. The book of Job doesn't even bother to prove it. And with these galaxies, each shimmering like an infinity of flaming crystal, it's the epitome of ethnocentricity to believe that we, on this little planet, a faint glimmer amid blazes of celestial glory, are alone. The book of Job teaches about other intelligent life, life not bound by the restraints of time and space that lock man in his limited dimensions. And these beings, operating outside our restrictive dimensions, constitute the supernatural.

Imagine sitting in a silent room. You then turn on a radio and run the dial across the channels. Music, laughter, news, advertisements, and static blur across your ears. The sounds were always in the room, yet until you turned on the radio you were aware of none of them. Why? Because you weren't tuned in! This is how the supernatural operates. Like radio waves, the supernatural exists all around us but outside our senses. Job tunes us in. A person may be exposed to intense radiation for days. He hears, smells, feels, tastes, sees none of it—until the results: sickness, maybe even death. With the supernatural, men see, feel, and suffer the results, but the causes are concealed, unseen, hidden behind a veil. The book of Job lifts the veil.

The story of Job is the story of humanity. All, like Job, have rejoiced in moments of triumph and cheer, and all, like Job, have languished in misery and despair. Like Job, many have misunderstood the reasons for their suffering, and, like Job, many have blamed their trials on God. Job's experiences were just more intense than ours.

Indeed, Job's prosperity was so great that even God proclaimed, "There is none like him in the earth" (Job 1:8). An Ediniclike aura enveloped him; he enjoyed an abundance of material blessings; he loved humanity and loved God; and with ten children, he had been faithful to the command to "be fruitful, and multiply." Job was eyes to the blind, feet to the lame, food for the hungry, shelter for the homeless, and clothing for the naked. Exceedingly rich, he didn't rejoice because his wealth was great, he didn't make gold his hope, and therefore he could enjoy material prosperity as well as a relationship with God. No wonder "this man was the greatest of all the men of the east" (Job 1:3).

Then the Sabeans stole his oxen and asses. Fire consumed his sheep. The Chaldeans stole his camels. A wind blew down his house. His children were killed. His servants were killed. Suppurating boils erupted all over his body. He was abandoned and derided. All that Job had and loved he lost. Reduced to groveling on a pile of ashes, he cried, "Why died I not from the womb?" (Job 3:11).

What happened? The first chapter removes the barrier between the seen and unseen, between the natural and supernatural. The scene shifts, away not only from Job but from the earth, into another dimension into the realm of other worlds—into where the answer lies: "Now there was a day when the sons of God came to present themselves before the Lord, and Satan came also among them. And the Lord said unto Satan, Whence comest thou? Then Satan answered the Lord, and said, From going to and fro in the earth, and from walking up and down it. And the Lord said unto Satan, hast thou considered my servant Job, that there is none like him in the earth, a perfect and upright man, one that feareth God, and escheweth evil? Then Satan answered the Lord, and said, Doth Job fear God for nought? Hast thou not made an hedge about him, and about his house, and about all that he hath on every side? thou hast blessed the work of his hands, and his substance is increased in the land. But put forth thine hand now, and touch all that he hath, and he will curse thee to thy face. And the Lord said unto Satan, Behold, all that he hath is in thy power. . . . So Satan went forth from the presence of the Lord" (verses 6-12).

These verses reveal an extraterrestrial life that is powerful, vengeful, evil, able to travel to, even dwell upon, the earth—life overtly hostile to God and man. These verses give glimpses of a battle, a great controversy, between God and part of His creation, a creature known by the Hebrews as the Adversary. To believe in the Adversary and in demons is simply to believe that God created other creatures, creatures able to transcend barriers of time and space, creatures who have rebelled against God and who, unable to hurt Him directly, have instead attacked that which God loves: His creation, particularly man. It's the ultimate in star wars, a cosmic conflict started elsewhere in the universe but waged in the souls of men.

The book of Job also reveals that God has not authored the evil that incites men to steal, to murder, to plunder and pillage, and that God has not initiated the suffering, disease, and violence that batter the earth black and blue. To attribute evil to God is to attribute it to a supernatural source—but the wrong one! Forces unseen, hidden, powerful, like radio waves, operate all around us. How else can all the evil be accounted for, other than to supernatural sources?

God created a little Austrian boy; the Adversary turned him into Hitler. God created a cuddly Black baby; the Adversary turned him into Idi Amin. A halcyon sea breeze, groves glowing with bright oranges, a mother breast-feeding her baby all testify to the love and character of the Creator. But a typhoon flooding a city, a blight that extinguishes the orange glow, a mother strangling her infant all testify to an intruder, an unwanted invader defacing the creation and eradicating the image of God from man. Evil and good are not philosophy, semantics, or poetry but literal realities embodied in supernatural powers contending for the souls of men.

But if God is so powerful that He can create and uphold billions of galaxies, if He is so full of compassion that "his mercy endureth for ever," why has He allowed the Adversary to afflict men with disease and inspire them to steal, murder, and lie? If the Adversary can bring famine to Ethiopia, why didn't the Lord, who "made heaven and earth, the sea, and all that in them is" bring rain before the first baby dried up and died? Why didn't God wipe out Treblinka before it wiped out Jews? And what kind of God, who has the power to end evil but doesn't, asks man to love

Him "with all thine heart, and with all thy soul, and with all thy might"?

Here, too, the book of Job has answers. First, it shows that other intelligent life besides the Adversary exists in the universe. "Now there was a day when the sons of God came to present themselves before the Lord, and Satan came also among them" (Job 1:6). These "sons of God" have not rebelled against God, and it was before them, these loyal intelligences, that the Adversary accused the Lord. The Adversary's accusations gives insight into the nature of his rebellion: He questioned the creation's reason for serving God. "Doth Job fear God for nought?" he asked (verse 9). He insinuated that Job served God not out of love or reverence but because it was in Job's own selfish interest. Inherent in the Adversary's accusation was the charge that God's creatures don't serve Him for the right reason. If God is so good, His government so just, would His creatures be loyal no matter what? The Adversary said No. "But put forth thine hand now, and touch all that he [Job] hath," he challenged, "and he will curse thee to thy face" (verse 11).

Of course, God could have blotted out the Adversary in front of these "sons of God." The rebellion would have been ended and Job spared. But had the Lord eradicated the enemy, then the original accusations would not have been answered; if anything, destroying the Adversary without answering the accusations would have made the accusations about God's government appear more legitimate. Had He destroyed the Adversary at the first instant of rebellion—just blotted him out of existence!—without proving him wrong, the unfallen universe, before whom God was accused, might have also started harboring doubts about God's government. Indeed, they might have truly started serving Him out of their own selfish interest— such as fear of being blotted out themselves!

It's easy from man's limited perspective to ask, "Why doesn't God just end the evil?" without understanding that the issues go beyond the earth, beyond man. Though evil is focused here, the conflict is, literally, universal. God will end the rebellion. He will prove the accusations of the Adversary wrong, but in a manner that will satisfy all the universe, not just man. God is not a fascist who instantly wipes out all opposition; instead, He's a benevolent king who runs the universe by moral laws, and without violating His own moral laws He will end the problem of sin and suffering. For the good of man, of the universe, He will let evil run its course so all creation will see the fruits of rebellion contrasted with the goodness of God's government. When a parent puts medicine that stings on a child's wound, the child doesn't understand why the parent is hurting him even more. If we don't understand all the issues involved in the struggle with sin, we can't see why God allows it to continue, any more than the child understands why the parent hurt him with the medicine, any more than Job himself understood the bigger issues that revolved around him and his trials.

And it was around Job that these issues—which concerned the justness and righteousness of God's government—were contested. Though the conflict began in another part of the universe, it was brought to the earth—and more specifically, to man. And here on earth, with man in the middle, it will be resolved.

Job is a microcosm, one man's example of all men. Though expressed under different circumstances, in different cultures, in different terms, and manifested in as many different ways as there are human beings, the issue is the same: Will our lives prove God or the Adversary right? Whether we consciously choose sides, whether we even know which side we are on, or even if we aren't aware of the conflict—every human is intimately involved. The battle for Job is the same that is raging for the souls of all humanity. And by remaining faithful, by not sinning, by not cursing God, Job proved the Adversary's accusations wrong before the whole watching universe. This same opportunity is given to all men. How we react to trials, temptations, sin, good, and evil—indeed, every action of our whole lives!—all determine whom we will prove right and with whom we have sided.

We are not alone. The universe is watching. Our lives, like Job's, can help resolve the conflict; and therefore our joys, our sorrows, our actions, deeds, words, and every other aspect of our existence have a pertinence and importance and meaning extending way beyond the limited sphere of our earthly ties. Who we are and what we do has consequences that echo throughout the universe!

Yet would not have Job preferred, as he sat amid the ashes, open sores dripping, that God not have used him to prove His point? Had he the choice, would he have not cried, "God, find someone else! The pain is too great! Give me back my children, my home, my health!" Wouldn't most people choose not to be involved in resolving a controversy that began in a far corner of the universe, rather than suffer the terrible things humans do?

Yet our only choice is with whom we will side, not whether we will. And God is not unmindful of our sorrows and of the pain our choices bring. No tear, no heartache, no indignity suffered by anyone, anywhere, anytime, is not known, felt, and sympathized with by our Creator. God is closer than our own soul. And He has His angels—creatures who have not fallen, extraterrestrials who are infinitely more powerful than the Adversary and his host. And these angels are constantly ministering to man's needs, constantly working to uplift, protect, and comfort all involved in the struggle with evil.

God gave man choice in serving Him, even if this choice pursued the option of disobedience, and disobedience meant death. The Lord believed that man's right to choose allegiance was such a sacred prerogative that if man chose wrong, God would pay the death penalty Himself. This is the work of the Messiah, to pay for man's right to choose wrong. God didn't cause sin and suffering, but because He left the option for sin open, He would suffer for it Himself. Job understood something of the Messiah's work and the promise of eternal life it would bring. "For I know that my redeemer liveth," he said, "and that he shall stand at the latter day upon the earth: and though after my skin worms destroy this body, yet in my fresh shall I see God" (Job 19:25, 26).

No doubt this hope helped Job remain faithful, despite the catastrophes. And eventually his trials were over and he regained his health, received twice as many possessions as before, had 10 more children, and lived 140 more years! "So the Lord blessed the latter end of Job more than his beginning" (Job 42:12).

Obviously, not everyone's "latter end" is as prosperous as Job's. But if the Bible teaches anything, it teaches that sin and suffering will not last forever: "What do ye imagine against the Lord? he will make an utter end: affliction shall not rise up the second time" (Nah. 1:9). "For, behold, I create new heavens and a new earth: and the former shall not be remembered, nor come into mind" (Isa. 65:17).

The Bible promises that God will make up for all that His faithful have suffered, only better than He did for Job! Heaven is real, as real as God, and worth every tear and heartache here. In the light of eternity, when the redeemed stand robed in flesh that will never wrinkle, rot, or die, the veil between the seen and unseen will be lifted, and what now appears to be only turmoil, confusion, and broken plans will instead be seen as God's marvelous providence working to eradicate evil from the universe. When all the hidden things of darkness are brought to light, when all the secrets of men's hearts are shouted across the cosmos, not only the faithful but all the creation, even unredeemed humanity—even the Adversary himself!—will admit that God was just and fair in His dealing with sin and suffering, and all, the Adversary included, will exclaim as Job had centuries earlier: "Blessed be the name of the Lord!"

This article originally appeared in *Shabbat Shalom*, July-September 1986.

CHAPTER FIFTY-SEVEN

The Tenth Commandment

In his fictional nightmare *1984*, George Orwell created a society that punished illegal thoughts. Winston Smith, Orwell's main character, knew that even if he never breathed a word of what he was thinking, he had already committed the unforgivable crime: wrong thoughts.

"The Thought Police would get him just the same. He had committed—would still have committed, even if he never set pen to paper—the essential crime that contained all others in itself. Thoughtcrime, they called it. Thoughtcrime was not a thing that could be concealed forever. You might dodge successfully for a while, even for years, but sooner or later they were bound to get you."

Fortunately, Orwell's predictions about 1984 proved ultrapessimistic. Such totalitarian control of even thought processes themselves has never come to pass.

God, on the other hand, *can* read our minds, and He is interested in our thoughts. But unlike the leaders of Orwell's fascist fantasy land, who destroyed those who harbored "wrong" thought, God doesn't want to punish us for the evil that trespasses through our minds. Instead, He wants to change our thoughts, to bring them to harmony with His own thoughts of compassion, mercy, and self-sacrificing love. He wants to make these changes because He knows that if our hearts were pure, the rest of us would be too. "Keep thy heart with all diligence," says Proverbs 4:23, "for out of it are the issues of life."

For this reason, the tenth commandment towers over the rest. The first nine deal with actions, words, and physical manifestations of the thoughts that stir within. People don't steal, commit adultery, or kill unless first the thought originates in the mind, where it sprouts, grows, and finally ripens into the act itself. The same is true of using the Lord's name in vain, bearing false witness, or dishonoring parents. The first nine commandments deal with outward actions and words, but the tenth makes the transition from this physical world into the realm of the imagination, into the mysterious dimension of the soul. The tenth commandment deals with our thoughts alone, apart from our actions.

Of course, thoughts and deeds are linked. The thought is to the act as the egg is to the chick. You can't have the act without first the thought, any more than you can have a chick without first the egg. The tenth commandment is God's attempt to crush the egg before the chick ever hatches. "You shall not covet your neighbor's house. You shall not covet your neighbor's wife, or his manservant or maidservant, his ox or donkey, or anything that belongs to your neighbor" (Exod. 20:17, NIV).

But God is not like Orwell's Thought Police. He wants us to think to use our minds. He prohibits only certain thoughts. And His prohibition is not arbitrary; it deals only with covetousness. And not even every type of covetousness because not all covetousness is evil. The psalmist exclaims, "My soul longeth, yea, even fainteth for the courts of the Lord: my heart and my flesh crieth out for the living God" (Ps. 84:2). Like him, we may safely covet a relationship with God. The tenth commandment forbids coveting only that which does not, and should not, belong to us. We have no right to our neighbor's wife; therefore, we have no right even to desire her. Both the deed and the desire are sin.

Greed, covetousness, desire are not just ancient passions. If anything, greed has become almost an art form today, a philosophy, a way of life. "Greed is all right," announced former Wall Street arbitrageur Ivan Boesky during his commencement address at the University of California School of Business Administration in 1985. "Greed is healthy. You can be greedy and still feel good about yourself." Boesky should know. The year before his arrest for inside stock trading, he made $100 million on Wall Street.

What we think—not just what we say or do—has consequences, because what we think often translates into action. Just ask Ivan Boesky. The tenth commandment, therefore, serves as a hedge against trampling upon the rest. A person who obeys the tenth commandment will be better prepared to obey the first nine; a person who breaks the tenth is ripe to break any of them.

The tenth commandment is actually the legal formula for the basic biblical truth that God is concerned with our innermost being. "The Lord seeth not as man seeth," says the Bible, "for man looketh on the outward appearance, but the Lord looketh on the heart" (1 Sam. 16:7). David wrote, "O Lord, thou hast searched me, and known me. Thou knowest my downsitting and mine uprising, thou understandest my thoughts afar off" (Ps. 139:1, 2).

God's Ten-Commandment law towers over manmade legal codes because it deals with our thoughts, our motives, our innermost intents. No law in America can do that. God alone can discern the secrets of the soul. "For thou, even thou only, knowest the hearts of all the children of men" (1 Kings 8:39). Human laws legislate actions and sometimes words—lying in court, for example, is illegal. But God is calling us to a law that transcends the action—a legal code for the mind itself.

This principle bears on the very essence of Christianity. When asked what is the greatest commandment, Jesus replied, "Thou shalt love the Lord thy God with all thy heart, and with all thy soul, and with all thy mind. This is the first and great commandment. And the second is like unto it, Thou shalt love thy neighbour as thyself. On these two commandments hang all the law and the prophets" (Matt. 22:37-40).

Both deal with love—an emotion, a thought, a stirring of the heart. Like the tenth commandment, these two principles—love to God and love to man—are concerned with what goes on inside where God alone can see. Jesus hangs all the law and prophets on not just our actions but on our thoughts themselves. No wonder God is concerned with the heart!

For many of us, the idea that we can be condemned for our thoughts is terrifying. If apart from committing the act man is guilty simply by lusting in the heart, who is innocent? If God knows the evil that lurks within and judges us guilty of that evil even if it never comes out, who can stand in the day of judgment?

If, then, wrong thoughts alone are sin, all humanity stands condemned before God. We all, like Winston Smith, are guilty of Thoughtcrime. "Do not imagine that you will save yourself, Winston, however completely you surrender to us," said O'Brien, Winston's captor. "No one who has once gone astray is ever spared. . . . We shall crush you down to the point where there is no coming back."

Though we, too, have gone astray, God deals differently with us. All of us who have committed Thoughtcrime (or any other crime) can be spared, can be saved, thanks to Jesus Christ who has died in our behalf. "God commended his love toward us, in that, while we were yet sinners, Christ died for us" (Rom. 5:8).

Because Jesus became a human being with us, lived with us, and shared our temptations, He can sympathize with our struggles. "In that he himself hath suffered being tempted, he is able to succour them that are tempted" (Heb. 2:18). God "knoweth our frame; he remembereth that we are dust" (Ps. 103:14).

Jesus not only faced the same temptations we face, He overcame those temptations. "We do not have a high priest who is unable to sympathize with our weaknesses, but we have one who has been tempted in every way just as we are—yet was without sin," (Heb. 4:15, NIV). And through Jesus we can overcome temptation as well. The good news of the gospel is that besides forgiving our sins, Jesus gives us power to overcome them—all of them, even Thoughtcrime.

God will cleanse us from the filth and debris that have accumulated in the cracks and crevices of our brains. He wants to sweep away the trash that poisons our lives. He wants to purge the stains on our souls. He wants not just to heal our broken hearts but to create new hearts within us. And upon these new hearts—not upon tablets of stone—He wants to write His law. "I will put my law in their inward parts, and write it in their hearts; and I will be their God, and they shall be my people" (Jer. 31:33).

Many have longed for this change in their lives. "Create in me a clean heart, O

God; and renew a right spirit within me" (Ps. 51:10). "Search me, O God, and know my heart: try me, and know my thoughts: and see if there be any wicked way in me, and lead me in the way everlasting" (Ps. 139:23, 24).

And these longed-for changes can take place. "Let the wicked forsake his way, and the unrighteous man his thoughts: and let him return unto the Lord, and he will have mercy upon him; and to our God, for he will abundantly pardon" (Isa. 55:7).

But *how* can a person control his or her thoughts? That is the question. How can an unrighteous person forsake his or her unrighteous thoughts?

Without doubt, God's supernatural power can provide victory for us in Christ. But we must cooperate with that power. A fat man who continues to gorge himself on chocolate cakes and fudge bars while he prays for victory over appetite will not find his prayers answered. Neither will a lustful man who refuses to quit ogling dirty magazines and X-rated videos while he asks God to cleanse his mind.

By beholding we become changed. One key, then, to controlling covetousness and other sinful thoughts is to fill our minds with those things that do not incite such desires. "Finally, brethren, whatsoever things are true, whatsoever things are honest, whatsoever things are just, whatsoever things are pure, whatsoever things are lovely, whatsoever things are *of* good report; if there be any virtue, and if there be any praise, think on these things (Phil. 4:8). God will give us victory over covetousness, anger, lust, pride—all the silent inner sins of the soul that only we (and God) know about. But we must cooperate.

No question, you are guilty of Thoughtcrime. Had you lived in Orwell's 1984, your destiny would be certain. "People simply disappeared, always during the night. Your name was removed from the registrars, every record of everything you had done was wiped out, your one-time existence was denied and then forgotten. You were abolished, annihilated."

Fortunately, Orwell's nightmare fantasy was only that—a fantasy. In reality, we have a loving Creator, an all-powerful God who has no desire to destroy us for our sins. Instead, through Jesus Christ, God offers cleansing and victory and eternal life—to everyone, everywhere, for every sin.

Even for Thoughtcrime.

This article originally appeared in *Signs of the Times,*® December 1988.

CHAPTER FIFTY-EIGHT

Astral Travel and Near-Death Experiences

Joe* had been everywhere from Lapland to the Sea of Japan, but his strangest trip was down the block. Not that anything particularly exciting existed there. Nothing did. But then again, it was not *where* he went that was bizarre but *how*.

A few weeks earlier, when he had been lying on his bed, a strange tingling had begun in his toes. The sensation crawled up his body like a band of bugs until it centered in his head, encapsulating him in a loud, uncomfortable buzz. He felt himself falling through a gray, misty tunnel.

He sat up, mystified. The sensation occurred again and again, and each time, he became less fearful and more curious. Next time, instead of fighting it, he would go with the flow.

One afternoon Joe stretched out, closed his eyes, and relaxed when the tingling began. When the buzzing reached his head, he told himself not to be afraid.

Instantly he rocketed through the ceiling and found himself floating in a gray, crackling mistlike static on an empty TV channel. Too scared to even scream, he suddenly snapped out of it and sat up in his room, bug-eyed.

Astral Travel

When Joe asked his friend Fred about the experience, Fred believed he had the answer.

"Astral travel," Fred said. I've been doing it for years. I've been to Jupiter. I've even talked with my dead grandfather in the astral plane."

The experience enthralled Joe. All his life he'd believed that if something couldn't be put in a test tube, it didn't exist. After those few seconds in the "astral plane," however, he wasn't so sure.

The Austro-German poet Rilke once wrote, "Whoever you are: some evening take a step outside of your house, which you know so well. Enormous space is near." Joe had taken that step. Enormous space was, indeed, near. He wanted to step out farther.

A few days later, however, Joe became a Christian. And, once he'd made that total commitment to Jesus, those experiences in the twilight zone never returned.

He soon learned why. As he studied the Bible, Joe discovered that his "astral travel" wasn't travel at all. He had never left his body but was duped into thinking he had. Not only did Jesus save him from that deception, however, but through His Word He gave Joe a better understanding of what had happened and why so many people are being deceived.

Near-Death Experiences

One of the most interesting facets of astral travel is how closely it replicates near-death experiences (NDEs), the stories of those whose vital functions (heartbeat, breathing) stop, yet who, after being revived, give fantastic accounts of what they saw while "dead."

The phenomena that they describe—a buzzing, the sensation of going through a tunnel, the apparent release from the body—are what Joe and others have experienced during astral travel.

"There is a buzz or a ring at death," writes Dr. Raymond Moody, Jr., who has been documenting NDEs since the 1970s, "followed by a rapid progression through an enclosure or tunnel toward light. There is surprise at being outside the body."

Joe knew the feeling, yet he was nowhere near dead!

Apparently, those experiencing astral travel and NDEs experience identical phenomena. And no wonder, for they both spring from the same lies: that we possess immortal souls and that the dead live on.

Immortal Souls

Despite popular theology, the Word of God never teaches that within us is an immortal "soul"—one that can be coughed up at death (NDEs) or in an altered state (astral travel).

Genesis 2:7, for instance, teaches that God breathed into Adam the breath of life and he "became a living soul," that is, a living creature. The breath of life, together with a fleshly body (made from "the dust of the earth"), created a living soul.

In Genesis 2:19, the word for animals or "creatures" is the same word translated "soul" in scriptures that refer specifically to people (see Gen. 2:7).

The book of Revelation uses the word *soul* even for the creatures in the sea: "And it [the sea] became as the blood of a dead man, and every living soul died in the sea" (Rev. 16:3). Souls are what living beings *are*, in other words, not what they *possess*.

"Hundreds of outstanding Bible students of all faiths, spread over the centuries," writes church historian Leroy Froom, "attest that there is not a single passage in the Bible in which man, in his earthly life, is spoken of as immortal, either as a whole, or in any part of his being."

Life After Death

Linked to the lie of the immortal soul is the lie of "life after life." According to Scripture, the dead are not floating in some diaphanous mist but instead are resting in an unconscious sleep until the resurrection.

"For the living know that they shall die," says the Bible (Ecc. 9:5) "but the dead know not anything." Psalm 115:17 says, "The dead praise not the Lord, neither any that go down into silence."

When Lazarus died, Jesus said, "Our friend Lazarus sleepeth; but I go, that I may wake him out of sleep" (John 11:11). A few verses later, He said clearly, "Lazarus is dead" (verse 14).

Peter placed righteous King David not in heaven but in the grave. "Let me freely speak unto you of the patriarch David, that he is both dead and buried, and his sepulchre is with us unto this day . . . *for David is not ascended into the heavens" (Acts* 2:29, 34).

Though the Bible never teaches an immortal soul, however, it does warn about demonic powers that can deceive mankind with all types of lies.

"That great dragon was cast out, that old serpent, called the Devil, and Satan, which deceiveth the whole world: he was cast out into the earth and his angels were cast out with him" (Rev. 12:9).

And one of the ways they deceive "the whole world" is with the lie that though the body dies, we live on. That lie was first told to Eve in Eden—"Thou shall not surely die"—and it has been promoted, in one form or another, ever since.

Widespread Beliefs

That lie is believed by many people. A poll by the University of Chicago's National Opinion Research Council indicates that 42 percent of Americans say that they have contacted the dead. What's more, belief in an immortal soul and its logical corollary, an immediate afterlife, are the cornerstone of almost all Eastern religions and the New Age movement.

And though Christians scoff at New Age mysticism, those who believe in an immortal soul are open to similar deceptions. Talking about those who have experienced NDEs, for instance, televangelist Pat Robertson writes, in his book *Answers to 200 of Life's Most Probing Questions,* "Many of them have seen heaven and some have been allowed to see hell. . . . For all of them the experience has been a life-changing one, and this is a uniform testimony to the existence of life after death."

An article in *Christianity Today* (October 7, 1988) is more cautious. NDEs, it says, "fundamentally 'prove' nothing about life after death." "At best they are partial, ambiguous, fragmented and distorted glimpses of [another world]. . . ."

Supernatural Frauds

Are they?

A fundamental teaching of Scripture is that "all have sinned, and come short of the glory of God" (Rom. 3:23) and that Jesus Christ is our only hope of eternal life (see Acts 4:12). Yet few (if any) of those who've astral traveled or experienced NDEs come back convicted of their need for Christ.

"Instead," says *Christianity Today,* "they tend to become suspicious of religious 'sectarianism.' ... The modern visionary's conversion is not to an austere spirituality, but to one that affirms joy and laughter."

Christianity Today comes closest to the truth when it says, "Demonic (or New Age) elements cannot be ruled out." They certainly can't, for they are the only explanation in light of the Bible truth about the nature of man, the state of the dead, and salvation through Jesus Christ.

Though certain physiological factors could be involved in astral travel or NDEs, they are fundamentally frauds—supernaturally inspired frauds. They could be hallucinations, or demonic powers could be doing impersonations as well, for the Bible says that "Satan himself is transformed into an angel of light" (2 Cor. 11:14).

Clearly, when the Bible talks about the supernatural, it's not using poetic figures but warning us of literal powers whose deceptions are so vivid, so convincing and real that, without a proper understanding of the Bible, men are almost powerless against them.

After Joe's first time in the astral plane, some Christians warned him that he was dabbling with the devil. So convinced that his experiences were what he thought they were, he laughed in their faces. "Do you believe in Santa Claus as well?"

After his conversion to Christianity, however, and after he understood what had happened, he tried to convince Fred.

"You can't possibly be talking with your grandfather," he said, "because he is asleep."

When Joe explained that supernatural powers were behind these experiences, however, Fred wouldn't listen.

"No," Fred responded, "I know my grandfather."

He's not the only one.

---

*The name has been changed, of course. This article originally appeared in *Signs of the Times,*® January 1991.

CHAPTER FIFTY-NINE

The Great Controversy: Soldiers in a Great Campaign

"We are all soldiers," wrote Oliver Wendell Holmes, "in a great campaign, the details of which are veiled from us. But it is enough for us to know there is a campaign."

The justice had it partly right. We are all indeed "soldiers in a great campaign," but the details have not been veiled. Rather, God has revealed where the campaign began, what issues started it, who the commanders are, our role as "soldiers," how and where the conflict is being fought, and—most important—which side ultimately wins. The campaign even has a name. It is called the great controversy, and though the decisive victory was won 2,000 years ago at Calvary, the battle continues today.

Unfortunately, most people aren't even aware that there's a conflict, much less one that affects their lives and eternal destiny. Millions know about *Star Wars, ET,* the *Starship Enterprise* and Captain Kirk, but few understand anything about the great controversy—a battle that began eons ago in heaven but is being fought here on earth.

"And there was war in heaven: Michael and his angels fought against the dragon; and the dragon fought and his angels, and prevailed not; neither was their place found any more in heaven. And the great dragon was cast out . . . into the earth" (Rev. 12:7-9).

Though Revelation 12, along with Ezekiel 28 and Isaiah 14, vignette Lucifer's fall, Ellen White details it: "Satan was envious and jealous of Jesus Christ. . . . It was the highest crime to rebel against the government of God. All Heaven seemed in commotion. The angels were marshaled in companies, each division with a higher commanding angel at their head. Satan was warring against the law of God, because [he was] ambitious to exalt himself. . . . The Son of God and true, loyal angels prevailed; and Satan and his sympathizers were expelled from heaven."[1]

As both the Bible and the Spirit of Prophecy attest, the battle didn't end with

Satan's eviction from the heavenly courts. On the contrary, the controversy simply moved to the earth, where it has raged furiously ever since. "Woe to the inhabitors of the earth and of the sea! for the devil is come down unto you, having great wrath, because he knoweth that he hath but a short time" (verse 12).

Battle for the Mind

Unlike most wars, however, this battle isn't over land, political ideology, or natural resources; it is, instead, a supernatural struggle between good and evil, right and wrong. "We do not wrestle against flesh and blood, but against principalities, against powers, against the rulers of the darkness of this age, against spiritual hosts of wickedness in the heavenly places" (Eph. 6:12, NKJV). The battle is being waged, not on battlegrounds with missiles, tanks, and helicopters, but in our hearts and minds: "Be sober, be vigilant; because your adversary the devil, as a roaring lion, walketh about, seeking whom he may devour: whom resist stedfast in the faith" (1 Peter 5:8, 9).

The book of Job is a microcosm of this macrocosmic conflict. The story begins with the patriarch enjoying great material prosperity, including a large loving family, reflective of what Eden should have been; above them, however, the struggle between the Lord and Satan raged in heaven, with Satan making accusations against Job. "Doth Job fear God for nought? . . . Put forth thine hand now, and touch all that he hath, and he will curse thee to thy face" (Job 1:9-11).

At first glance Job seems to be the one on trial, but God really is. By impugning Job's motives for being faithful, Satan attacked God Himself. If God was so good, His law so wonderful, would Job serve Him no matter what? Satan implied that Job worshiped God not because the Lord was worthy but because it was in Job's best interest to do so. By claiming that Job would turn against Him once things went wrong, Satan, however subtly, insinuated that even Job himself had questions about the character of God. Maybe God wasn't so good after all?

The same basic conflict depicted in Job is fought over every individual. Though expressed under different circumstances, terms, and cultures—and manifested in as many different ways as there are people—we are all, like Job, entangled in this great controversy between Christ and Satan. Though it's a contest for our souls, how often, as with Job, our flesh gets caught in the middle.

Of course, we have not been left to struggle alone. We can no more ourselves defend against the devil than we could with spitballs defend against stealth bombers. All we can do is daily, consciously place ourselves under the care and protection of Jesus Christ, who not only won the key victory at Calvary but promises to share the fruits *of* that victory with us. His triumph embraces both earth—"Now thanks be unto God, which always causeth us to triumph in Christ" (2 Cor. 2:14)—and heaven: "And the city had no need of the sun, neither of the moon, to shine in it: for the glory of God did lighten it, and the Lamb is the light thereof. And the nations of them which are saved shall walk in the light of it" (Rev. 21:23, 24).

Calvary—Decisive Battle

Christ's great victory for us was not won when Jesus and His angels ousted Satan and his, nor will it be at the end of the millennium when Satan goes "out to deceive the nations which are in the four quarters of the earth, Gog and Magog, to gather them together to battle: the number of whom is as the sand of the sea" (Rev. 20:8) and is ultimately destroyed. Rather, the victory was won in a Galilean carpenter shop, in a fierce forty-day struggle in the wilderness, in assault after assault among the cities and towns of Judea, in a fearful contest in the Garden of Gethsemane, and finally at the decisive battle at Calvary, when Jesus cried: "It is finished" (John 19:30).

In these engagements, Jesus battled not from the safety, majesty, and comfort of heaven but in frontline trenches where He faced the full assault of the enemy. Having taken on humanity ("the seed of Abraham" [Heb. 2:16]), Jesus met the devil on the devil's turf: Indeed, in heaven Satan caused the fall of a third of the inhabitants; on earth he brought down them all!

Except one. For thirty-three years Jesus, in human flesh, withstood every barrage of Satan and his legions. Despite endless attempts by Satan to overcome Him, Jesus, at the end of His earthly sojourn, could proclaim: "For the prince of the world cometh, and hath nothing in me" (John 14:30).

The Gospels reveal the intensity of the assaults He faced. In the wilderness Jesus had "fasted forty days and forty nights" (Matt. 4:2). How amazed must Satan have been to see the Lord, with all His power and glory, transformed into a starving, weakened, emaciated human being. God had become part of humanity; Satan had controlled humanity for thousands of years. Jesus, half-dead already, should have been easy prey.

"And when the tempter came to him, he said, If thou be the Son of God, command that these stones be made bread. . . . If thou be the Son of God, cast thyself down. . . . Again, the devil taketh him up into an exceeding high mountain, and sheweth him all the kingdoms of the world, and the glory of them; and saith unto him, All these things will I give unto thee, if thou wilt fall down and worship me" (Matt. 4:3-9).

Here Christ was tempted when He languished in a barren wilderness—a sharp contrast to Adam and Eve, who thrived in a luxurious garden when enticed. Our genetic parents, their bellies filled in a garden shade, succumbed to temptation; our adopted Father, Jesus, His belly hollow in the heat of a desert, didn't.

Yet for Jesus the battle didn't end with the wilderness fast; on the contrary, that experience merely prepared Him for the sorrowful and painful struggle that climaxed at Calvary, where Satan threw his entire force at Jesus because he knew that this was his last chance to win. If he could get Jesus to abandon the plan of salvation, then Christ would have been defeated, the world would have been Satan's, and his accusations against God's government, His mercy, and His justice would have remained forever unanswered. In short, Satan would have won the great controversy!

Meanwhile, as the guilt of every sinner pressed upon His heart, as the malignity of evil separated Him from the Father, as those for whom He was dying taunted "If thou be the Son of God, come down from the cross" (Matt. 27:40)—Jesus knew that if He did come down from the cross, all would be lost. Only by His own death could Christ forever refute Satan's accusations that God could be either merciful or just, but not both. On the cross the Lord proved His justice, because by taking the punishment of sin upon Himself, He would pay the full legal penalty that transgression demanded—and His mercy, because only by paying that penalty Himself could the Lord save sinners from having to pay it themselves.

But with Christ's death, justice and mercy met and triumphed. The destruction of sin and Satan became certain, the redemption of humanity was assured, and the universe was eternally secured. The decisive battle was finished, and there was no question about who ultimately won the great controversy.

War Goes On

Nevertheless, even after Calvary the struggle wasn't over. "Yet Satan was not then destroyed," Ellen White wrote. "The angels did not even then understand all that was involved in the great controversy. The principles at stake were to be more fully revealed."[2]

Even after this display of God's love contrasted to Satan's evil, the Lord wanted to give more understanding to the angels, and He intends to use His people to help provide it: "His intent was that now, *through the church,* the manifold wisdom of God should be made known to the rulers and authorities in the heavenly realms" (Eph. 3:10, NIV).

This verse doesn't diminish work at the cross but simply shows that as far as "the rulers and authorities in the heavenly realms" were concerned, all their questions about the "manifold wisdom of God" were not fully answered, even after the death of Jesus, and that the Lord wanted to help answer them "through the church."

Ellen White expresses the same idea: "It becomes every child of God to vindicate His [God's] character."[3] Jesus said it as well: "Herein is my Father glorified, that ye bear much fruit" (John 15:8).

The concept of God being glorified, even vindicated, by His people forms a crucial aspect of present truth. The Seventh-day Adventist Church has been blessed with precious light about Jesus, theology, salvation, education, lifestyle, health, law, grace, and everything pertinent to Christianity—all to prepare a remnant to stand in the great day of God, when the battle between Christ and Satan reaches a crescendo at the end of the ages.

At this time, just before the Second Coming, the Lord will have prepared a people, for "the harvest of the earth is ripe" (Rev. 14:15); in contrast, Satan's "grapes are fully ripe" too (verse 18). Thus, there will be a faithful, obedient people who "keep the commandments of God, and the faith of Jesus" (verse 12), in direct and open contrast to the rest of the word, which is wholly under Satan's power. As the angels view the stunning differences between these two groups, as both righteousness and unrighteousness ripen in the climactic battle of Armageddon, more issues in the great controversy regarding good and evil, Christ and Satan, will be revealed and understood in what Ellen White calls "the final and full display of the love of God."[4]

Each of us, then, has a role in the great controversy. Paul expressed it best when he wrote: "And the God of peace will bruise Satan under your feet shortly" (Rom. 16:20). How is Satan bruised under our soles? Do we literally throw the devil to the ground and kick him? Of course not. Rather, we "bruise Satan" only by a complete surrender to Christ, which allows Him to work in us "both to will and to do of his good pleasure" (Phil. 2:13). A knowledge of the great controversy should bang us to our knees so we, through the power of Christ, can take up "the whole armour of God, that [we] may be able to withstand in the evil day" (Eph. 6:13). Without a daily, conscious walk with Jesus, we can't win the personal battles against sin that can glorify God; indeed, unless we put ourselves on Christ's side, we are on Satan's instead.

As Justice Holmes wrote, we are soldiers in a "great campaign." Our weapons, however, are not guns, tanks, or cruise missiles but the sword of the Spirit, the breastplate of righteousness, the helmet of salvation, and the shield of faith, all of which come through Jesus, the "captain of [our] salvation" (Heb. 2: 10), who has promised to make us "more than conquerors" (Rom. 8:37) through His triumph for us 2,000 years ago on the cross.

---

[1] *The Spirit of Prophecy,* 1:18-23.
[2] *The Desire of Ages,* 761.
[3] *Testimonies for the Church,* 5:317.
[4] *The Acts of the Apostles,* 9.

This article originally appeared in the *Adventist Review,* June 18, 1992.

CHAPTER SIXTY

A Faded Message, A Brilliant Promise

The wreck, eroded with rust, rotted in an empty, unkept field, its tailfins testifying to the glory of another era. Stripped by hoodlums who, if caught, would have been out of jail by then even if they had committed murder when they stole the car and pulled off its doors and hubcaps, the vehicle was so old that even the birds had abandoned it. The only signs of life near it were a prickly bush that had grown up through a rusty hole in the bottom of the trunk and a few scattered weeds that circled the wreck like a macabre garden.

The car's front bumper carried a sticker that had once trumpeted its message loudly but whose faded letters now barely whispered it: "Jesus is coming soon!"

Jesus is coming soon?

For almost two thousand years, Christians have been speaking those words. And the New Testament is replete, not only with promises of Jesus' return, but with lists of the signs that were to precede it—signs that the passing years have seen fulfilled.

That old wreck, with its faded bumper sticker, throws out a challenge to Christians today: How should Christians live in view of the apparent delay in Jesus' second coming? What should they beware of? What, on the other hand, *should* they do as they hover between the reality of this world and the promise of the next?

The Parable

Fortunately, in the parable of the faithful and wicked servants, Jesus gave clear, powerful answers to these important questions:

Who then is the faithful and wise servant, whom the master has put in charge of the servants in his household to give them their food at the proper time? It will be good for that servant whose master finds him doing so when he returns. I tell you the truth, he will put him in charge of all his possessions. But suppose that servant is wicked and says to himself, "My master is staying away a long time," and he then begins to beat his fellow servants and to eat and drink with drunkards. The master of that servant will come on a day when he does not expect him and at an hour he is not aware of. He will cut him to pieces and assign him a place with the hypocrites, where there will be weeping and gnashing of teeth (Matt. 24:45-51).

Jesus' parables were earthly illustrations of spiritual truths. Like many of His other parables, this one—in stark, almost harsh language, depicts those who profess to believe in God. Christ's wicked servant doesn't represent unbelievers, secularists, Marxists, New Agers, or skeptics. In today's vernacular, both the wise and the wicked servants would be churchgoing, Bible-believing Christians awaiting Jesus' return. The parable, then, contrasts not so much what they believed—because both believed basically the same thing (that their master would return)— but different manifestations of that belief. Just as neither the faithful nor the wicked servant knew when the master would come back, so Christians awaiting the Second Advent today don't know when it will happen. Over the years, some have projected dates, one of the most recent being September 1994. But these projections have always been speculation—often based on foolish, even reckless, misuse of Bible prophecy. So far, every date set for the Second Advent has been wrong. And it's no wonder, since Jesus Himself warned His followers that they would not know the time of His return: "No one knows about that day or hour, not even the angels in heaven, nor the Son, but only the Father" (Matt. 24:36). The basic message of the parable is impossible to miss. The wise and faithful servant, though not knowing when the master would come back, faithfully did his duties. In contrast, the wicked servant abused his trust. And the parable makes clear that the difference between the two included not only their deeds but also how those deeds would be recompensed. Through this simple story, Jesus sent to those living in the last days an unmistakable prophetic warning that belief in Him and His return isn't enough. In it He revealed that He expects His followers to be faithful to that belief, with a faithfulness that shows up in their deeds.

Every Christian Called

For the faithful and wise servant, the master's absence didn't matter. The delay, however keenly felt, didn't interfere with his responsibilities. He had his job, and he was going to do it the best he could. Like this servant, every Christian, whatever his or her situation, has been called to minister. All, in a sense, have a "household" entrusted to them.

And the world is filled with Christians exemplified by the faithful servant. From the larger-than-life Mother Teresa, toiling in the dankest slums of India, to Chuck Colson ministering in America's prisons, there are those who are carrying out their divine trusts. Whether missionaries living in huts among African pygmies or stay-at-home moms seeking to raise their young in godly families where Jesus has priority, Christ's faithful stewards are going about their appointed tasks, occupying until He comes.

On the other hand, the parable specifically depicts the wicked servant as thinking his master is delayed. He doesn't openly deny the return, but he thinks it so far in the future that he can live as if it will never happen. Unlike the faithful and wise servant, the wicked one focuses on the delay.

There's a story of three apprentice devils who, before coming to the earth to finish their apprenticeship, spoke with their master, Satan. The first devil said that he would tell Christians "There is no God"—to which Satan replied, "That won't delude many, for they know that there is a God." The second said that he would tell them "There is no divine judgment." To this suggestion, Satan responded, "That won't delude many either; they know there is a final judgment." Then the third devil said, "I'll tell Christians that there is no hurry." And at this proposal, Satan exulted. "Yes!" he exclaimed. "That will destroy them by the millions."

The wicked servant fell for this third delusion. As a result, even though he was a servant of the master, he began to act like those who make no profession at all of serving the master. He began "to eat and drink with drunkards."

Unfortunately, many Christians who claim to believe in the nearness of Christ's coming—when He will "give to everyone according to what he has done" (Rev. 22:12)—have begun to indulge themselves in the things of the world as well, in a sense eating and drinking with the drunken. Rather than living in anticipation of the Second Advent and the judgment that comes with it, they have put these events so far off that they no longer hold any meaning, no longer have any impact on their lives. They allow themselves to get trapped by the same vices as those who don't expect to answer for their deeds.

Abuse of Responsibilities

Yet even worse than the wicked servant's "eating and drinking with drunkards" was his abuse of the responsibilities given him as a servant of the master. While the faithful and wise servant fed the household at the proper time, the wicked one beat them. Once he started to doubt, he actually turned against his master.

In this story Jesus illustrated His words: "He who is not with me is against me, and he who does not gather with me scatters" (Matt. 12:30). With it Jesus shows that there's no such thing as a neutral Christian or a half-converted one. Whatever a person might call himself or herself, no matter how grand the profession, Christians are either serving Jesus or working against Him. They're either on one side or the other. Though Christians are not perfect, though at times they do bad things, in the end, their works will show whether they were gathering or scattering.

Unfortunately, the world is filled with those exemplified by the wicked servant, those who have become unfaithful to their trusts. From priests who molest children through televangelists who scam their flocks to Christians who merely backbite, gossip, and criticize, unfaithful servants continue to give the Master a bad name. How many people have been turned off to Christianity through the centuries—not because of what it teaches but because of the actions of those who call themselves

Christians—one can only wonder. Indian leader Gandhi once told a Christian missionary, "If you call me a Christian, you insult me, but if you call me Christlike, you pay me the highest tribute."

Apparently, according to the parable, "wicked servants" will continue to plague Christianity until Jesus Himself returns. The book of Revelation also warns about them. It says a great religious and political power will persecute God's people in the last days (chapters 13, 14). Many believe that this end-time persecution will be initiated by a so-called Christian power that, in reality, will no more be serving Christ than did the wicked servant.

When the Master Returns

Perhaps the parable's strongest message concerns what happens when the master returns. The contrast between the judgments that both faced was just as great as the contrast between their actions. Of God's faithful servants, the book of Revelation says that after Christ's return "they will reign for ever and ever" (Rev. 22:5). This parallels Jesus' story, in which after the master's return, the faithful and wise servant was "put in charge of all his [the master's] possessions." Whatever that means exactly, Christians can be sure it's a promise of future reward and glory.

The wicked servant, however, caught up in the world, was taken completely by surprise at the master's return (something not said about the wise servant, whose faithfulness left him ready and prepared). Besides being unpleasantly surprised, the wicked servant was ultimately cut to pieces and assigned a place with the hypocrites, where there was "weeping and gnashing of teeth"—phrases that depict the final punishment of the unrighteous at the end of time. Though a professed servant of the master, the wicked servant was, in reality, serving someone else. And, as Jesus said, "No one can serve two masters" (Matt. 6:24).

Jesus' parable of the wise and the wicked servants reveals that He foresaw—with clear prophetic insight—the ostensible delay in His second advent and the two major ways His servants would react to that apparent delay. Nineteen hundred years ago, He described the state of the Christian church today, and through His parable He warned those in His church to be faithful to their appointed trusts, whatever they might be.

Jesus' parable warns us against being fooled into complacency—or even worse, hypocrisy—by the rust on the wreck. It encourages us, instead, to concentrate on the promise on the bumper sticker—and to live as if we believe it.

This article originally appeared in *Signs of the Times,*® April 1996.

CHAPTER SIXTY-ONE

Maximize Your Talents

Meet Roy Carey, dumpster diver. Carey never really dives into a dumpster himself. Instead, he finds the trash he wants through the *Business Materials Exchange* newsletter, which—on the premise that one person's trash will be another's treasure—lists the garbage that member businesses accumulate. More than 2,000 businesses get the newsletter, which enables them to exchange everything from computer discs, gravel, old magazines, and baby-food jars to three-ring binders.

A newsletter that lists garbage?

Welcome to the age of waste management. As we careen into the twenty-first century, people are increasingly aware of the limits on earth's resources, so they're cutting back on the debris they leave in their wake. And if they can't cut down, they try to put their trash to some good use so they won't have to dump it in a landfill to do nothing but rot and eat space. Glass, tires, plastic, tin, leaves, grass, compact discs, and even old sneakers are turned into something useful. Last year, 1,200 tons of paper were recycled—enough to, if baled and stacked, reach three times higher than the world's tallest building.

No doubt, natural resources are a terrible thing to waste. The Bible, however, talks about another kind of waste, one worse than squandering paper, rubber, or glass. In the parable of the talents, Jesus warned God's people not to squander the "gifts" He has bestowed upon them individually. He shows that God expects those gifts to be multiplied for His glory.

On a Journey

The kingdom of heaven, Jesus said, is "like a man going on a journey, who called his servants and entrusted his property to them" (Matt. 25:14). As in all His other parables, here Jesus was using symbols to teach truths. In this case, the man "going on a journey" represented Himself, who would soon depart for heaven. After His death and resurrection, Jesus spent forty days with His disciples and then ascended to heaven, where, ever since, He has been ministering as our High Priest in the heavenly sanctuary.

The point of what we are saying is this: We do have such a high priest, who sat down at the right hand of the throne of the Majesty in heaven, and who serves in the sanctuary, the true tabernacle set up by the Lord, not by man. . . . When Christ came as high priest of the good things that are already here, he went through the greater and more perfect tabernacle that is not man-made, that is to say, not a part of this creation (Heb. 8:1, 2; 9:11).

Though Jesus is in heaven now, as the High Priest who "always lives to intercede" for His people (Heb. 7:25), Scripture teaches that one day He'll complete that work and return to the earth in judgment and in power. The parable we're considering focuses on what happens to His "servants" when that day comes. The servants, no doubt, represent His professed followers. Because Jesus is the Creator—the One in whom "we live and move and have our being" (Acts 17:28), the One through whom God "made the universe" (Heb. 1:2)—all people are, in a sense, His servants. Christ died for everyone; all have been bought with His blood. At the cross, Jesus paid the ransom for the sins of the whole world: "There is one God and one mediator between God and men, the man Christ Jesus, who gave himself as a ransom for all men" (1 Tim. 2:5, 6). Unfortunately, not all recognize or accept Christ. This parable is for those who do. The master, before leaving on his journey, called his servants in and asked them to manage his capital while he was gone. "To one he gave five talents [an amount] of money, to another two talents, and to another one talent, each according to his ability. Then he went on his journey" (Matt. 25:15). The master didn't ask each to handle the same amount. Instead, knowing the differences between his servants, he distributed the money according to the potential he saw in each of them. Nevertheless, each was given something—each had a responsibility, each had something for which he would have to answer.

Gifts of the Spirit

The talents represent personal gifts given by God, most basically (though not solely) the gifts of the Holy Spirit. Jesus promised His church that He would send the Holy Spirit, who would equip them for the work of preaching the gospel to the world. Not until He ascended to heaven was the Spirit poured out in full. " 'When he ascended on high, he led captives in his train and gave gifts to men' " (Eph. 4:8). What are the gifts of the Spirit? The apostle Paul lists some:

To one there is given through the Spirit the message of wisdom, to another the message of knowledge by means of the same Spirit, to another faith by the same Spirit, to another gifts of healing by that one Spirit, to another miraculous powers. . . . . All these are the work of one and the same Spirit, and he gives them to each one, just as he determines (1 Cor. 12:8-11).

Yet not all gifts from God are directly from the Holy Spirit. Many people, whether or not they're followers of Christ, have talents. We frequently say things like "he is a gifted writer," "she is a gifted actress," "he is a gifted speaker," or "the child is a gifted singer." A gift implies a giver, and that Giver, in these cases, is God alone—whether or not He is ever acknowledged as the source.

Whatever gifts He bestows, God never forces people to use them for His glory. Many of the world's most talented people employ their gifts in every conceivable way *but* for God. What a blessing had the voices of Paul McCartney, Sting, and Frank Sinatra been used for the Lord! How much good the pens of William Faulkner, Ernest Hemingway, and Virginia Woolf could have done for the advancement of the gospel! Imagine if Voltaire, Einstein, or Freud had been committed Christians dedicating their rare talents to the glory of God. But in this parable, neither these people nor their gifts are the issue. Those who profess Christ, and the gifts *they* have received from God, are.

After the master left, "the man who had received the five talents went at once and put his money to work and gained five more. So also, the one with the two talents gained two more. But the man who had received the one talent went off, dug a hole in the ground and hid his master's money" (Matt. 25:16-18).

Though it took time and work, two of the servants multiplied what they had received. Realizing that the money wasn't their own, that they had been given a trust—not for themselves, not to hold in limbo, but to invest for the master—they improved what had been entrusted to them. In contrast, the third servant simply dug a hole and buried his talent. Though he didn't squander it on himself, he didn't multiply the talent either.

The Master Returns

"After a long time the master of those servants returned and settled accounts with them" (verse 19). This part of the parable depicts the day when the Lord judges His people—a common theme in the Bible (see Dan. 7:26; Matt. 5:21; Acts 24:25; Rom. 14:10; 2 Cor. 5:10; Rev. 14:7). The two servants who multiplied the funds they held in trust were commended highly by the master, who promised to give them even more responsibilities: "Well done, good and faithful servant! You have been faithful with a few things; I will put you in charge of many things. Come and share your master's happiness!" (Matt. 25:23).

But the other servant, the one who merely hid his talent in the ground, received a rebuke and was ultimately condemned to hell—depicted here (and in other parts of Scripture) as "darkness," where "there will be weeping and gnashing of teeth" (verse 30). Obviously, the master expected that the trust wouldn't merely be preserved but that it would be improved. However laudable it might seem that this servant kept the money safe by burying it in the ground (a common method back then), the master berated him as "a wicked, lazy servant," saying that he should have "put my money on deposit with the bankers, so that when I returned I would have received it back with interest" (verses 26, 27).

Notice that Jesus had the master call the funds "my money," implying that the gifts they represent belong to God, not to those to whom He entrusts them. They're like funds given a stockbroker to invest. Though they're in the broker's control, they belong to the investor, not the broker.

Notice, also, that the real issue wasn't the *amount* the talents were increased— after all, the master gave the same commendation to the servant who returned four talents as he did to the one who returned ten. What concerned him was the talent that wasn't used at all but that instead was left stagnant.

Indeed, what gifts, continually applied, don't automatically increase? And on the other hand, what gifts, unused, don't degenerate?

Not only was the lazy servant rebuked but he lost the capital he had received. "Take the talent from him," the master said, "and give it to the one who has the ten talents" (verse 28). Apparently, the one who refuses to use what he has been given will soon find that he has nothing at all to give others.

By Faith Alone

It would be easy at this point to interpret this parable, isolated from the rest of Scripture, as teaching that we're saved by our diligent use of the gifts God has given us. That would be a tragic misinterpretation. The essential truth of all Scripture— from Genesis to Revelation—is that we obtain salvation only through faith in Jesus Christ. As Paul wrote, "We maintain that a man is justified by faith apart from observing the law" (Rom. 3:28).

This parable is concerned with a different aspect of salvation—not how people are saved but what effect salvation has on those who are saved. The bottom-line distinction between the servants who used their funds and the one who didn't was simply that the lazy servant wasn't converted, while the other two were.

People who have been "born again" have given themselves completely to Jesus Christ and are leaning wholly upon His merits as the only means of their salvation. They won't use their talents in an attempt to earn God's acceptance; instead, they'll use them for Him as a natural response to having been accepted.

Whether singers, writers, or speakers; whether in the ministry of counseling or healing or ministering to the basic needs of humankind; whether they have the gifts of love, faith, or encouragement; whether they are builders or painters or have the gift of making money—whatever talents the Master has bestowed upon those who have given their lives to Him, those talents will be used, in one capacity or another, for the glory of God. No one can be a Christian and bury his or her talents. "Let your light shine before men," Jesus said, "that they may see your good deeds and praise your Father in heaven" (Matt. 5:16).

So this parable tells us, who are living in the last days, to make sure that our hearts are surrendered to the Lord, that we have committed ourselves totally and completely to Him, and that our lives are "hidden with Christ in God" (Colossians

3:3). If so, we will multiply for Him the special gifts He has given us. And then, when the Master returns at the end of time, we'll hear the words "Well done, good and faithful servant."

To do anything else, especially considering the weighty consequences, would be a terrible waste.

Unless otherwise noted, all Scripture quotations are from the New International Version. This article originally appeared in *Signs of the Times,*® July 1996.

CHAPTER SIXTY-TWO

Street Jesus

Sometimes, particularly at summer sundowns when its mammoth stone buildings are basted in a light orange glow and its monuments rise firm and silent against the sky, downtown Washington, D.C., possesses a majestic, awesome beauty unlike any other city in the world.

Yet cowering within the shadows of these grand edifices, huddling on the steam grates outside their impenetrable walls, are the homeless. We can step to the other edge of the sidewalk or look away as we pass by, but there's no escaping their empty eyes, their effusive smells, or their outstretched hands grasping the dirty plastic cups with which they prick our consciences.

Who are these people who scavenge to survive in the streets much as animals do in the woods?

Finding the answer is easy. Jesus gave it Himself. He called these people "brothers of mine" (Matt. 25:40). And, note this, He said how we treat them will make a big difference as to how we'll be treated in the final judgment.

In the parable of the sheep and the goats, Jesus presented a principle regarding salvation by faith: Those who say they believe in Him but who don't act on that belief will, on the day of judgment, face God's condemnation. Merely to say that you are a Christian no more makes you one than saying you're a bird gives you wings. A mere claim to be following Christ is not evidence of saving faith. It is good works that show the presence of true saving faith—and among those works, according to this parable, will be benevolence to the downtrodden and needy.

The Parable

"When the Son of Man," Jesus said (speaking of Himself), "comes in his glory, and all the angels with him, he will sit on his throne in heavenly glory. All the nations will be gathered before him, and he will separate the people one from another as a shepherd separates the sheep from the goats. He will put the sheep on his right and the goats on his left" (Matthew 25:31-33). This parable of the sheep and the goats is also often called "the story of the great judgment." Jesus set it in the context of the last days, when He will return to earth. In His first advent, Jesus came as a poor Galilean peasant subject to death at the hands of the political and religious leaders of His land. In the last days, though, He won't come in the guise of a humble servant. Instead, He'll return as a King and Judge, with more power, authority, and glory than the most ambitious human leader could ever imagine.

See, the Lord is coming with thousands upon thousands of his holy ones [angels] to judge everyone, and to convict all the ungodly of all the ungodly acts they have done in the ungodly way, and of all the harsh words ungodly sinners have spoken against him (Jude 14, 15).

At that time the sign of the Son of Man will appear in the sky, and all the nations of the earth will mourn. They will see the Son of Man coming on the clouds of the sky, with power and great glory (Matthew 24:30).

Christians disagree on the manner of Jesus' coming. But with this parable, Jesus showed that His return won't be a secret event, as many who believe in the "rapture" teach. He, rather, will return with "all the angels," and "all the nations will be gathered before him" when He separates the "sheep" and the "goats." However and whenever this event takes place, one thing's for sure—it won't be a secret.

Next, the parable says that Jesus will tell the "sheep," whom He placed to His right,

"Come, you who are blessed by My Father; take your inheritance, the kingdom prepared for you since the creation of the world. For I was hungry and you gave me something to eat, I was thirsty and you gave me something to drink, I was a stranger and you invited me in, I needed clothes and you clothed me, I was sick and you looked after me, I was in prison and you came to visit me" (Matt. 25:34-36).

According to Jesus, this commendation will surprise the "sheep"; they won't recall doing these things for Him—and it's not likely that a person who ministered to the needs of Jesus Christ would ever forget it. "Lord," the "sheep" will ask, "when did we see you hungry and feed you, or thirsty and give you something to drink?" "I tell you the truth," Jesus will respond, "whatever you did for one of the least of these brothers of mine, you did for me" (verses 37, 40). Next, Jesus will turn to those on His left—the "goats"—and say, "Depart from me, you who are cursed, into the eternal fire prepared for the devil and his angels" (verse 41). Then He'll repeat what He said to the "sheep"—stressing, however, that the "goats" *didn't* feed, clothe, or help Him. Just like the "sheep"—almost word for word, actually—the "goats" will ask Him when they neglected to help Him, for certainly they wouldn't have done that to Jesus Christ! "I tell you the truth," Jesus said He'll reply, "whatever you did not do for one of the least of these, you did not do for me" (verse 45).

A Crucial Principle

Through this parable of the sheep and the goats, Jesus presented a crucial principle of the gospel, of the Christian faith itself. With the incarnation of Jesus Christ, the Creator Himself became part of the creation. In the book of Colossians, the apostle Paul wrote of Jesus Christ: "For by him all things were created: things in heaven and on earth, visible and invisible, whether thrones or powers or rulers or authorities; all things were created by him and for him. He is before all things, and in him all things hold together" (Col. 1:16, 17). Scripture, then, clearly depicts Jesus Christ as the active agent in the creation, not only of the earth, but of "all things." Yet Scripture also pictures Christ as human. He was born of human flesh: "Jacob [was] the father of Joseph, the husband of Mary, *of whom was born Jesus,* who is called Christ" (Matt. 1:16, emphasis supplied).

"Since the children have flesh and blood, he too shared in their humanity. . . . For surely it is not angels he helps, but Abraham's descendants. For this reason he had to be made like his brothers in every way (Heb. 2:14,16, 17).

Paul wrote of Jesus Christ that He, "being in very nature God, did not consider equality with God something to be grasped, but made himself nothing, taking the very nature of a servant, being made in human likeness" (Phil. 2:6, 7).

When we juxtapose the texts that say Jesus was the Creator with those about His birth, we learn the incredible truth that the Creator Himself became a human being. In the Bible, this is called a "mystery" (see, e.g., 1 Tim. 3:16). It's something that we could never have ferreted out ourselves; something we can only know because God has revealed it to us. All we can do is to believe this incredibly good news.

Perhaps Jesus called Himself "the Son of Man" rather than the "Son of God" at the beginning of this parable because He wanted to stress His indelible link to the human race. Whatever the case, what makes His tie to humanity even more incredible is the role that Jesus chose for Himself as a human. He didn't come as a great earthly ruler, surrounded by wealth, majesty, and pomp. Instead, He entered the world amid the smell of animal dung; He was born the child of impoverished peasants who lived in the hill country of a small, relatively insignificant nation.

Jesus could relate to the homeless and downtrodden because, in many ways, He was like them. Isaiah portrayed Him as cast out from society: "Despised and rejected by men," He had "no beauty or majesty to attract us to him" (53:2, 3). And Jesus Himself talked about His homelessness: "Foxes have holes and birds of the air have nests, but the Son of Man has no place to lay his head" (Luke 9:58).

Should we wonder, then, that Jesus called the hungry, the homeless, the outcasts, His "brothers"? Through His incarnation, Jesus bound Himself to humanity with ties that can never be broken, and He sealed those ties by associating Himself with the "lowest" rung of the human race. So whatever your place in life—whether you're drowning in a bottle of Seagram's in some alley or whether you own the company that makes Seagram's—you have, in Jesus Christ, Someone who can relate to your sorrows.

Salvation by Social Work?

Does this parable teach that our salvation is determined by how well we treat the homeless or how many of the hungry we feed or how often we visit those in prison? If so, Christianity would be no different from the many religions that teach salvation by works. The ancient Egyptian faith, at one point, taught that good deeds such as helping the poor would win one a special place in the afterlife. Modern Judaism, as well, places a great emphasis on caring for the poor as a means of redemption. Was Jesus, in this parable, likewise preaching salvation by social work?

Of course not. You won't understand this parable if you isolate it from the rest of the Bible. And from the statement in Genesis that Abraham "believed the LORD, and he credited it to him as righteousness" (15:6) to Revelation's "Then I saw another angel flying in midair, and he had the eternal gospel to proclaim to those who live on the earth" (14:6), the Bible stresses that we are sinners in need of a Saviour whose righteousness alone can make us acceptable to God. Nowhere does the Bible teach that we are saved by good works—even works as good as caring for the homeless.

But while Jesus' parable of the sheep and the goats doesn't teach that we must earn our right to heaven, it does show how much He cares about the suffering and needy souls among us. During His whole earthly ministry, He ministered to the needs of these kinds of people, and He made it clear that He expects those who follow Him to do the same. So however easy it is for us to forget the homeless, Jesus hasn't forgotten them—and He tells us that those who follow Him better not forget them either, because how we treat the downtrodden reveals how real our faith is.

The need is great. Twenty-five percent of the families in the United States have a net worth less than $10,000, and 20 percent don't even have a bank account. Millions of Americans live below the poverty level, and many wander the streets, without a job, a home, or even assurance of "daily bread." No doubt, Jesus has lots of "brothers" even in the United States, wealthy as it is.

We must be willing to do our part, not because we feel like it but because faith demands it. If we profess to be Christians, we must be like Christ, and He ministered to the poor, the needy, the hurting. True, there's only so much anyone can do, and we're not all called to be Mother Teresas. Nevertheless, Jesus made it clear that we are expected to do our share. How can those who profess to emulate Him do any less? According to this parable, they can't.

So the next time you see a homeless person whose dirty plastic cup is uttering a silent plea for help, don't turn your eyes away. If you profess to be a servant of Christ, take a second look at the one you're tempted to ignore. Remember that whatever you do for that person, you're doing for Christ.

Then, in the judgment, if you've trusted Him for righteousness and your works show your faith is real, you'll hear the words, "Come, you who are blessed by my

Father; take your inheritance, the kingdom prepared for you since the creation of the world" (Matt. 25:34)!

Unless otherwise noted all scripture quotations are taken from the New International Version. This article originally appeared in *Signs of the Times*,® August 1996.

CHAPTER SIXTY-THREE

Bones

Bones lived a few blocks away from the house I grew up in, in Miami Beach. Tall and brittle-skinny from a childhood disease, he was the first homosexual I ever knew. Even as a kid of twelve or thirteen, I realized that Bones was different. I called him "queer," to his face. More than once.

Bones lived with his mother and sister. Then his mother died, his sister moved away and married, and Bones lived alone. Well, not really alone. A constant flux of men, even small boys, inhabited his house. Though friends with Bones, all the kids knew that we didn't have to treat him as an equal. We rarely did.

By the time I was nineteen, I moved away from Miami Beach, and four years later I became a believer in Jesus. The many times I visited Miami Beach, I wondered whether any of my friends had found the Lord. The answer, year after year, was always No.

One of the last times I visited, I saw Bones. Blonde, freckled, tall, and skinny as ever, Bones said something about "the Lord" as we talked in front of his house. Though he was the last person I would have expected, Bones had become a Christian. He worshiped at a Pentecostal church. I was practically in tears as we talked, even prayed together. I saw such incredible changes in Bones that I didn't feel impressed to warn him about the mark of the beast and other important truths, at least not yet. I gave him *Steps to Christ*. The rest, I hoped, would come.

Occasionally when I would call my mother or my sister, I would ask about Bones. They said that he was selling his house and that he was going to travel with members of his church in order to preach the gospel. That was all I heard, until my mother said over the phone last week, "Bones died of AIDS."

She said that he had been walking with a cane, that he was not allowed in a restaurant because he would wet his pants, and that when he was confined to bed, no one would take care of him. Finally, she said, a woman nursed him in his last days.

Where was his church? Was he still going to church? Had he contracted the disease as a result of backsliding? Or did he have it before he became a believer?

I didn't know. All I knew was that I wished I could have prayed with Bones, could have comforted him. As he lay dying, questions probably racked his soul with the same intensity that the disease racked his body.

World of Sin

"No, Bones," I would have said, "this does not mean that God has forsaken you. This means only that we live in a world of sin, and though Jesus has paid the legal penalty for our sins, we are often left to suffer the earthly consequences of them."

I would have told him about John the Baptist, whom Jesus said was the greatest prophet of all and yet who rotted away in a dungeon and who, on the whim of a woman, had his head chopped off.

"No, Bones," I would have said, "AIDS no more means God has forsaken you than imprisonment and death meant that God had forsaken John."

I would have told him, too, that no matter how or when he contracted the disease, he could still ask forgiveness and that the Father would look down upon him and instead of seeing a sinner deserving the second death, He would see the perfect righteousness of Jesus. I would have told him that he, even dying of AIDS, could be accepted by God as if he had never sinned the sin that brought this horrible disease upon him. I would have told him all these things, and more. I wonder whether anyone did.

Not Too Late

It's too late to pray for Bones. But as I write these words, tears pushing out of my eyes, I realize that it's not too late to pray for ourselves. As a church, with the light poured out upon us as no people ever had since Jesus walked in the flesh, we are better suited than anyone to have comforted Bones, to have answered the questions that must have tormented his soul.

In Bones I saw a dying world. Millions, even billions, of Boneses are suffering from disease, physical and spiritual—often both—while we are fighting among ourselves for the highest seat or over what happened in 1888 or over the meaning of the "daily." We don't need more books or sermons on the nature of Christ. We need more of the love, the self-denying, self-sacrificing character of Jesus. We don't need more homilies on righteousness by faith; we need more of the total humiliation and selflessness that Jesus exuded while on earth.

It's too late to pray for Bones. We need to pray for ourselves, instead.

This article originally appeared in *Adventist Review*, May 4, 1989.

CHAPTER SIXTY-FOUR

Love Beyond Reason

After drafting the Declaration of Independence and the Virginia Statute for Religious Liberty, as well as establishing the University of Virginia (not to mention serving two terms as president of the United States), Thomas Jefferson did what he deemed a simple task: He separated the "gold from the dross" in the Gospels. Saying that "your own *reason* is the only oracle given you from heaven," he expunged from Matthew, Mark, Luke, and John whatever he believed contradicted reason, common sense, and rational thought.

The result was the Jefferson Bible, a highly abridged version of the Gospels in which the Annunciation, the virgin birth, the miraculous healings, the raising of the dead, Christ's claims to divinity, the Resurrection, and the Ascension were all— among other portions—edited out. Excised, too, was the heart of New Testament theology: the atonement of Jesus Christ as "the Lamb of God, which taketh away the sin of the world" (John 1:29).

All of this infers at least one conclusion: Authentic Christian faith, though sound rationally, must transcend logic, reason, and analytical thought, because if we submit what we believe merely to logic, reason, and rational thought, we will never be authentic Christians by New Testament definition. And nothing proves this point better than Jesus Himself.

Whether feeding 5,000 with food for one (Matt.14:15-21) or declaring that "before Abraham was, I am" (John 8:58) or telling Peter, "Go thou to the sea, and cast an hook, and take up the fish that first cometh up; and when thou hast opened his mouth, thou shalt find a piece of money: and that take, and give unto them for me" (Matt. 17:27), Jesus showed that aspects of reality transcend what our minds— processing knowledge and experience through logic and reason alone—can ever grasp. From His birth to His ascension, Christ's entire ministry functioned on a plane that crossed the boundary of logic and reason—and those who refuse even to look (much less to step) across that boundary, will, like Jefferson, remain landlocked in theological ignorance, unenlightened by the ultimate realities of universal eternal truth.

Limits of Logical Thought

Jesus, of course, wasn't the only one who showed the limits of logical thought. From Plato (who warned about the contingencies of reason) to Kant (who exposed its confines, particularly in the area of religion) up through the prophets of postmodernism (who deny its utility), humanity, in its quest for natural and spiritual truth, has always sensed that the "natural light of reason" is not that natural or that full of light.

"The deepest reason," wrote Huston Smith, "for the current crisis in philosophy is its realization that autonomous reason—reason without infusions that both power and vector it—is helpless. Reason can deliver nothing apodictic. Working (as it necessarily must) with variables—variables are all that it can come up with."

Centuries ago Epimenides illustrated the limits of logic when he said, "This statement is false." Is the statement true or false? If true, then the statement declares itself false; if false, the statement must be true. But doesn't logic teach that something can't be both true and false at the same time? In this context, obviously, logic by itself doesn't work.

Also, how reasonable is Einstein's special theory of relativity, in which he proved that the faster one moves, the slower time does, until, at the speed of light, time itself stops? Quantum physics, meanwhile, teaches that under certain conditions, if two subatomic particles are created in a collision, the mere act of observing the spin of one member of the pair will immediately cause the spin of the other member to move in the opposite direction—even if they are separated by a million light-years!

"The structure of nature," said Harvard physicist P. W. Bridgman, "may eventually be such that our processes of thought do not correspond to it sufficiently to permit us to think about it at all."

Relationship Between Faith and Reason

Of course, reason and rational thought, whatever their limitations, are gifts from God, which is why neither should be ignored. To reject or even to suspect reason itself outright is to risk the mindless mysticism that can degenerate into everything from Waco to snake-handling. On the other hand, to make reason one's sole epistemological judge risks reducing faith to nothing but a generic morality reflective of the messages left to earthlings by "UFOs." By far, in a contemporary Western society reared on scientific rationalism, the danger comes from the latter, which is why evangelical scholar Donald Bloesch warned that the relationship between faith and reason is "probably the single most important issue in the theological prolegomena."

The key, then, is balance, and Jesus helps establish that balance. When John, in prison, asked if Christ was the Messiah, Jesus answered by saying: "Go your way, and tell John what things ye have seen and heard; how that the blind see, the lame walk, the lepers are cleansed, the deaf hear, the dead are raised, to the poor the gospel is preached" (Luke 7:22). In other words, Jesus said to John, Use your reason and logical thought: How could I be doing these things if I weren't the Messiah?

To look at Christ's life, which defied reason and logic, and to conclude that truth exists transcendently beyond reason and logic, is to draw a logical and reasonable conclusion. Although Jesus was always logically sound and rationally cogent, He proved that it is logical to believe in things that aren't necessarily logical or reasonable. In Christ we find that perfect balance.

Prophecy, Reason and Logic

In fact, prophecy itself (often based on something as "irrational" as dreams and visions) is really premised on reason and logic. "Now I tell you before it comes," Jesus said, "that, when it is come to pass, ye may believe that I am he" (John 13:19). With these words Jesus was appealing to the rationality that He Himself had implanted in humanity. Jesus would predict things before they happened, so that when they did, people would have reasons for believing in Him. To conclude that Jesus was the Messiah—especially after hearing what He said about Himself and then seeing it come to pass—was to perform a rational act. Prophecy can't impact humans to any significant extent until processed with rational thought.

Daniel 2 illustrates this point. Daniel first recounts and then interprets a dream that the king himself can't even remember. The whole concept is unreasonable. Yet in many ways Daniel 2 is one of the most rational parts of the Bible. Six centuries before Christ the chapter lays out the bold strokes of the history of the world up through and beyond modern Europe, which (as the former Yugoslavia shows) might "mingle themselves with the seed of men" but shall not "cleave one to another." The entire chapter is such an appeal to logic and reason that it's hard to see how anyone studying Daniel 2 could conclude anything except that it was inspired by God.

Rational and Transrational

In Christ's life, as in Daniel 2, Scripture presents a mixture of the rational and the transrational, which is the essential Christian metaphysic. God presents the mind with reasonable and logical grounds for believing in things that are illogical and unreasonable. In fact, the central event of all Scripture, the Cross, was not only illogical and unreasonable but foolish, as the Bible refers to it. "For the preaching of the cross," wrote Paul, "is to them that perish foolishness" (1Cor. 1:18). The Cross takes this mixture of the rational and transrational to its apogee.

In *The Passion of the Western Mind*, Richard Tarnas wrote about the unreasonableness of the gospel: "In an era so unprecedently illuminated by science and reason, the 'good news' of Christianity became less and less convincing a metaphysical structure, less secure a foundation upon which to build one's life, and less psychologically necessary. The sheer improbability of the whole nexus of events was becoming painfully obvious—that an infinite eternal God would have suddenly become a particular human being in a specific historical time and place two millennia earlier in an obscure primitive nation, on a planet now known to be a relatively insignificant piece of matter revolving about one star among billions in an inconceivably vast and impersonal universe—that such an undistinguished event should have any overwhelming cosmic or eternal meaning could no longer be a compelling belief for *reasonable* men."

Reason and Love

Of course, to pure reason alone the gospel would be irreducibly untenable, because pure reason alone can't grasp that type of love. If human love—which at its purest barely reflects God's love—often causes humans to act unreasonable and irrationally, how much more would God's love impel Him to act in ways that transcend human concepts of rationality and reasonableness? This is exactly what happened at the Cross: God's love impelled Him to act in a manner that totally defied reason. To believe that the Creator stepped out of eternity and was incarnated into humanity, only to be crucified as a propitiation for our sins—and that He did it out of self-sacrificing love—is to accept a concept existing in a realm where reason itself simply cannot reach.

The sacrificial atonement of Christ, who suffered the second death in our stead, is not the kind of truth that one can find from pure reason alone. Logic in and of itself can take you far in the quest for truth but never to Golgotha. No equation proves "There is therefore now no condemnation to them which are in Christ Jesus, who walk not after the flesh, but after the Spirit" (Rom. 8:1). Systematic logic itself might point to the existence of a God but never to the truth that Jesus, "being in the form of God, thought it not robbery to be equal with God: but made himself of no reputation, and took upon him the form of a servant, and was made in the likeness of men: and being found in fashion as a man, he humbled himself, and became obedient unto death, even the death of the cross" (Phil. 2:6-8). No wonder Paul wrote, "As God in his wisdom ordained, the world failed to find him by its wisdom" (1 Cor. 1:21, NEB).

At the same time, however, Scripture provides rational evidence for something as transrational as the gospel. From the entire Hebrew cultus, which prefigured the cross centuries before it happened, up through the Messianic prophecies of Psalms, Isaiah, and Daniel to the forceful testimony of the New Testament, God has left the world with powerful, logical, and rational reasons to believe in the "foolishness" of Christ's substitutionary atonement. In fact, with all the light given through the prophetic Word, for someone to accept something as transrational as the gospel is, one could argue, the only rational thing to do.

Of course, logical and reasonable evidence for the Cross doesn't deny the work of the Holy Spirit in salvation; instead, it simply shows that the Holy Spirit can use logic and reason in helping people accept what isn't especially logical or reasonable.

Jefferson, unfortunately, took the unreasonable position that only that which is rational is real. Jesus, in contrast, by His life and teachings, has shown that the real transcends the rational. Jefferson's abridged Bible, in which the core of Christianity is lost, proves not only just how limited the rational really is but that Pascal was right when he wrote, "The heart has its reasons which reason cannot know."

This article originally appeared in *Ministery*, February 1997.